Lionel Atwill

The
Exquisite
Villain

Lionel Atwill, Hollywood's maddest doctor, in *The Mad Doctor of Market Street*

Lionel Atwill

The Exquisite Villain

by Neil Pettigrew

Midnight Marquee Press, Inc.
Baltimore, Maryland, USA, London, UK

ISBN 978-1-936168-48-4
Library of Congress Catalog Card Number 2014956456
Manufactured in the United States of America

First Printing by Midnight Marquee Press, Inc., November 2014

Dedication

Dedicated to all the staff at public institutions,
such as local history libraries and cinema and theater archives.
They are a hugely under-valued resource and,
despite almost invariably being under-paid,
are always happy to share their knowledge and
to offer assistance when needed.
Without their expertise, a work such as this one
could never be assembled.

Table of Contents

Preface
by Neil Pettigrew

I first encountered Lionel Atwill in 1967 when I was 11 years old. In those exciting times, I would lurk around the magazine racks of my local newsstands, drooling over all the wonderful magazine covers and spending most of my pocket money buying issues of *Famous Monsters of Filmland*. Back home, I would pore over every page, committing to memory all the facts and faces in the articles.

The pages were full of photographs of actors like Boris Karloff, Bela Lugosi, Lon Chaney … and occasionally someone called Lionel Atwill. I convinced my parents that letting me stay up to watch the late-night horror films on television would not harm my attendance at school the next day, and I got my first taste of seeing *Son of Frankenstein, House of Frankenstein* and many more. Over the years, I regularly scanned the television listings for films in which Atwill might make an appearance. It was always a treat if one of his non-horror films turned up, and I remember, as a teenager, enjoying watching him as the brutal Colonel Bishop in *Captain Blood*.

I have always loved the performances of Karloff, Lugosi and the other horror film actors, but I seem to have been drawn especially to Atwill. There were unique pleasures to be derived from watching him—that theatrically trained voice, the precise diction, the authoritative bearing … and the glint of evil in those steely, blue-gray eyes. He was a charismatic, highly skilled actor who could steal every scene he was in.

The cover of this 1934 Spanish magazine *Films Selectos* showcased Atwill subjecting Kathleen Burke to his depraved desires in *Murders in the Zoo.*

My research uncovered other possible reasons why I have always felt a special fascination for him. I was thrilled to find out that he was born in a house in South Norwood that is only two and a half miles from where I live now … a happy coincidence. I then discovered that when Lionel was around five, the Atwill family moved to a house in Lennard Road, Beckenham, which is less than a mile from my home. It is a house I knew well and which I passed at least 1,000 times while out walking or jogging, without giving it a second glance. Presumably … is this not just another happy coincidence?

I delved further and what I found next made me begin to wonder if there wasn't more to this than just mere coincidence. Old birth certificates showed that Lionel's father and grandfather had originally come from a small town called East Stonehouse, just outside Plymouth in Devon. Amazingly, I knew from my own family history that my great-grandparents had also come from East Stonehouse, and had been living there at the same time as the Atwills. In the mid-19ᵗʰ century, it would have been a small place with a close-knit community, most of whom probably knew one another. So it's entirely possible that Lionel's father Alfred, or his grandfather William, knew my great-grandfather Alfred Henry Pettigrew or one of his many brothers and sisters!

The exquisite villain in his most debonair attire

For me, researching Lionel Atwill's career for this book has been an exciting journey of discovery. I have viewed many of his non-horror films for the first time (his Baron von Merzbach in *The Song of Songs* was a revelation) and learned about his thrilling stage performances (especially in *Deburau* and *The Outsider*). Along the way, I have also had the huge pleasure of watching all his old horror films again, many of which I had not viewed for over three decades. I hope my readers will enjoy being taken on this journey as much as I have enjoyed writing about it.

Foreword
by Lionel A. Atwill

My father died when I was six months old. I never knew him as a man—the sound of his voice, his scent, the cadence of his footsteps on the hallway leading to my room. And I knew little of him as an actor, until I became an adult.

What few tidbits I did know about him came from my mother, who viewed their brief marriage through rose-colored lenses. She was in her late 20s, my father in his early 60s, when he died. He was a movie star, albeit an aging, fading one; she was something of an ingénue. She had had a first marriage that was measured in months; he had been married four times and had a son, killed in World War II before my parents were married, who, had he lived, would have been older than my mom.

Need I say more? Theirs was a classic May-December romance, and when my mother spoke about it—and she did so all her life, up until the day she died—her comments were of wispy, romanticized visions, abstract recollections of the most wonderful time in her life. In truth, I don't think she knew that much about my father (few 27-year-olds can grill details out of a worldly, 60-year-old man). I do believe, however, their time together was a happy one.

What I learned of him as an actor was, for many years, limited by the fact that his films spent so many years incarcerated in the dark vaults of Hollywood history before being liberated, starting in the mid-'80s, by the electron soldiers of the digital revolution. I remember seeing him on late-night television in the '50s from time to time. I watched those films more out of obligation than fascination, for I was a pre-teen, more interested in *The Mickey Mouse Club* (especially the budding Annette Funicello!) and, later, *American Bandstand*, than horror films nearly two decades old.

Moreover, when I was six, my mother remarried a patrician East Coaster, and we moved to New York City, a world apart from the glitter of Hollywood. The circle in which my stepfather moved viewed the West Coast with disdain (I once heard a harpyish step-aunt refer to my mother as, "That California woman ... married to an actor!" in a tone one might use in reference to an axe murderer or pedophile). I was young and I did not want to be an outsider, so I morphed into someone who never thought about the father he never knew.

Occasionally, however, something would remind me of my famous dad. Once in the mid-'60s in Grand Central Station, I bought a ticket to somewhere and paid the ticket salesman with what must have been my first credit card. He was a gruff man close to retirement, but when he saw the name Lionel Atwill on the card, a beatific smile came over his face, and he launched into a 30-second quiz: Was my mother simply a huge fan? No. Was I related? Yes. His son, oh my God, his son! This stolid New Yorker was an extreme movie buff of the right age. He shook my hand. He asked for my autograph (first and last time ever). I swear a tear came into his eye.

Times like that helped rekindle my interest in my father. In the mid-'80s I befriended a musician from Massachusetts who was a rabid horror film fan. Over the course of several years he sent me VHS tapes of my father's films, probably 30 in all.

Lionel A. Atwill poses with a photograph of his father.

I watched them religiously, first out of a sense of duty and then out of curiosity, not so much about the film but about the man. My father.

About that same time Kenneth Anger's *Hollywood Babylon II* came out, a titillating piece of trash recounting all the foibies of Hollywood. In a chapter called *The Two Faces of Tinseltown*, Anger described in salacious prose the famous alleged orgy and the subsequent trial that ultimately ruined my father's career. Wow, I thought, if only half of it is true, Pop was a pretty cool guy.

In the late '90s, Greg Mank's *Hollywood's Maddest Doctors* was published (by Midnight Marquee Press), and shortly after its debut, Greg got in touch with me (I was a magazine writer and not all that hard to find). He sent me a copy of the book, which I enjoyed immensely, and we made a date to get together. He visited me at my home in Vermont and wrote a retrospective of my father's film work for the aptly titled magazine, *Monsters from the Vault*. In that piece, Greg incorporated an interview he did with me, and for the first time I saw a picture of myself on the same spread as a picture of my father.

Greg and I have become friends. He is a serious scholar of film and a good man, and we have exchanged Christmas greetings and chitchat since we first met. Through him Neil Pettigrew, the author of this wonderful book, got in touch with me. Over the course of a few months, we have struck up a lively correspondence, and I have tried to help him by supplying pictures and recollections from those Hollywood days, now mostly faded from memory.

What truly excites me about this work is the fact that it covers my father's younger years, his early life in England and his time on the English stage in an age when film was still a dream. That is the period of a man's life when his character is formed, so through this book I am learning not only something of my father the actor, but also something of my father the man.

Neil also has stimulated my interest in my English heritage. He put me in touch with my only living relative, save for my daughter: my father's brother's granddaughter, Leslie Dale, with whom I have exchanged family pictures. And he has helped me locate my half-brother's grave and research the events of his death in the War. I plan to make a trip to England this fall to visit all these players and to reconnect with the country that gave me my dad.

The desire to make that connection started with this book. For me, it is a moving, important part of who I am. For you, I hope it is an enjoyable, well-researched look at the life and career of a man who was an important player in the transition of entertainment from stage to film. For Neil, I know it is a labor of love. For that I am grateful.

Lionel A. Atwill
Hotchkiss, Colorado, USA
April 29, 2014

Introduction
by Neil Pettigrew

Atwill will always be remembered as one of the screen's finest villains. There were many other actors who specialized in villainous roles, but Atwill took wickedness to a whole new level. Anyone who has seen him in *Murders in the Zoo*, for example, cannot fail to have been alarmed by the extent to which the actor actually seems to *enjoy* being evil. In his most extreme roles, his villainy was tinged with elements of insanity and sadism, which other screen villains lacked. Basil Rathbone was dashing, Bela Lugosi was exotic, George Zucco was sophisticated—but Lionel Atwill's villainy was so intense that it could be genuinely disturbing.

In many ways, he was an unlikely choice for villainous roles. His physical appearance was unremarkable. He wasn't tall (just over 5 feet 10 inches). By the time he started making films in Hollywood, he had put on a few extra pounds. Although he was handsome as a young man, by middle age—when he arrived in Hollywood—he wasn't strikingly attractive, nor did he have the face of a typical *heavy*. He certainly

The brutal Eric Gorman (Lionel Atwill) stands behind unsuspecting Jerry Evans (Gail Patrick)—and only he knows the secret of the *Murders in the Zoo*.

Atwill at the height of his Broadway fame in 1924

didn't have the kind of face—like Boris Karloff—which singled him out as a villain. In fact, facially he looked fairly ordinary. And his name was quite ordinary too. It didn't have the exoticism of the names of other horror legends such as Bela Lugosi, nor the menace of a name like Karloff.

And yet, through his sheer presence and his acting prowess, he managed to create one of the most exciting screen personae of all time. No one who has seen and enjoyed Atwill in one of his better performances can ever forget it. When Lionel Atwill let rip, his villainy and mania had no match in Hollywood. The thing about Atwill—when one of his mad villains was in full raving mode—was that here was this essentially ordinary-looking man being believably, sadistically and terrifyingly *evil*. To pick but one example, think of that climactic scene in *Sherlock Holmes and the Secret Weapon* where Professor Moriarty has Holmes strapped to an operating table and slowly drains the blood out of him. Moriarty relishes every second, grinning evilly, checking on the state of his victim with almost loving care and generally enjoying the ghastliness of the moment to an extent that is completely deranged.

But villainy was only one aspect of Atwill's acting repertoire. Onscreen he also created a colorful gallery of other types. He was always impressive as stern, uniformed military men and policemen—his Inspector Krogh in *Son of Frankenstein* is one of the legendary characters of 1930s horror films. He was superb at playing husbands and lovers who have been humiliated and broken by deceitful women. In a variety of films, he has been effective as a harsh prosecuting lawyer, as a womanizing scoundrel, as an avuncular private investigator, as an ostentatious dandy, as a stressed, over-worked businessman … the list goes on. He was certainly versatile. Throughout the 1930s he was very highly regarded by the major studios, which unusually did not pigeon-hole him as just a horror actor, but gave him steady employment in a stream of prestigious films acting alongside mainstream luminaries that included Marlene Dietrich, Myrna Loy, Irene Dunne, Spencer Tracy and Clark Gable.

Atwill's remarkable film career is what he will always be remembered for today, and yet the truth is that his most outstanding performances, and the period in which he

Lionel Atwill

received the most critical and public acclaim, came years before he ever set foot in Hollywood. For the first 26 years of his professional career, Atwill was primarily a theater actor. His Hollywood career, by comparison, lasted a mere 15 years. In Broadway plays like *Deburau* (1920-21) and *The Outsider* (1924), he was a sensation. Critics raved about him, calling him one of the greatest stage actors of the age. Audiences applauded him rapturously, giving him standing ovations. He was Guest of Honor at a number of sparkling social events. The newspapers were full of stories about him and his plays. He really was the toast of the town.

This book will cover Atwill's theater work in more detail than it has ever been looked at before. His films, especially his horror films, have been discussed again and again, but accounts of his stage appearances are usually rushed and brief. Atwill's prolific stage career was full of grand successes and crushing disappointments, and this in-depth examination will visit them all.

Many of these stage appearances hold extra interest for fans of his horror films because they contain large hints of his later screen persona. Throughout his career, Atwill was always attracted to the offbeat, the macabre and the risqué, and this applies to many of his stage roles. For example, how many fans of his films knew that in 1910 he produced and starred in a supernatural horror play called *The Fourth Kiss*, about a deadly Egyptian curse? Or that he appeared in a 1913 adaptation of H.G. Wells' *The Invisible Man?* Or that he was a Jack the Ripper suspect in a 1917 version of *The Lodger?* In *Deburau* (1920-21), probably his greatest triumph, he appeared in a chilling clown costume, brandishing an enormous knife. In *The Outsider* (1924), he played a character that was a prototype for all the mad doctor roles that would characterize his film work, and in that play he delivered his first-ever mad doctor speech. How many fans of Atwill's horror films knew that in 1930 he directed a Broadway play starring Basil Rathbone?

Another reason for giving such in-depth discussion to Atwill's 26-year stage career is its sheer longevity. Since it was so much longer than his film career, it would be inappropriate for this book not to give his theater work a proportionate amount of coverage.

Onstage Atwill played some exciting characters in highly dramatic scenes, and I have tried to recreate a small sample of some of his key scenes in the pages that follow. If the reader uses his or her imagination a little, it is possible to imagine Atwill in full flow on the stage, to get a flavor of what his performance must have been like, to get a hint of that thrilling Atwill charisma and, in one's mind, to hear that wonderfully precise diction.

Today we cannot experience the old plays in the same way that we can watch DVDs of an actor's films whenever we like. Almost without exception, Atwill's plays have never been revived since the time when he appeared in them. Only a very few of them were ever made into movies. In other words, today they are forgotten. But many of them deserve to be rediscovered and I have done my best to do just that in this book. Readers, those that might normally be tempted to skip over these chapters and hurry on to the film sections, will be rewarded if they take the time to read about Atwill's stage career.

One very important aspect of Atwill's career is largely forgotten today: He was not just an actor, but also a producer, director and writer. For the theater, he was the driving force behind the staging of a number of plays, and he was also heavily involved in the writing or re-writing of some of them. For example, he directed the formerly mentioned *The Lodger*, several 1920s Broadway plays, and, in 1930, he directed Basil Rathbone onstage in *A Kiss of Importance*. In 1931, he contributed to the writing of additional passages to the play *The Silent Witness*, one of his great successes, in order to make it a more dramatic and commercial venture.

For his film work, Atwill is remembered solely as an actor. In fact, this does him a disservice because he was never the kind of actor who would simply walk onto the set, say his lines and then depart. He was always far more involved. Numerous moments in his films leave no doubt that he had a quiet word with the director and suggested adding a little bit of business to spice up a scene. British writer O. Bristol, in a December 1936 issue of *Picture Show* magazine, furnished specific evidence that Atwill worked as a kind of uncredited assistant director on many of his films. He interviewed Atwill, who had returned to England in 1936 to film *High Command*, and watched him at work on the set at Ealing Studios. The reporter witnessed Atwill insisting on a number of re-takes, and also making various suggestions regarding costumes and sound effects.

Greg Mank's *Hollywood's Maddest Doctors* makes a reference to these contributions with this quote taken from an article about Atwill in a 1934 fan magazine:

> Lionel Atwill … thinks up his own bits of gruesome business (like
> putting out a cigarette on Marlene Dietrich's shoulder) …

Or how about that spellbinding moment in *Murders in the Zoo* when Atwill has the unwilling Kathleen Burke in his clutches and makes one of his hands walk up her arm as if it were a nasty, predatory spider? Likewise, in *Son of Frankenstein*, it may well be that some of the "gags" involving Inspector Krogh's prosthetic arm— such as using it to hold a monocle which Krogh then polishes with his good hand—were dreamed up by Atwill himself. No hard proof exists for this, but the rest of his career provides so much circumstantial evidence of similar creative flourishes that it would be surprising if it were not the case.

Another forgotten side of Atwill's multi-faceted talent is his mastery of comedy. He demonstrated a lightness of touch and an aptitude for comic delivery many, many times onstage, such as in *The Grand Duke* (1921). Unfortunately, this side of Atwill is rarely seen in his films. Only occasionally do we get a glimpse of his comic skills in films such as *The Great Garrick* (playing a foppish playwright) or *Mr. Moto Takes a Vacation* (as a blustering museum curator). It's a shame he didn't get more such roles in films.

Atwill was always keen to try new things and to be at the forefront of technology. For example, in April 1931 he took part in a remarkably early television broadcast, performing a scene from his great stage success, *The Silent Witness*. His distinctive voice could be heard broadcast on radio as early as 1925, when he took part in a show on a New York radio station. Throughout the rest of the 1920s he turned up regularly (although not frequently) on the radio, sometimes being interviewed, sometimes acting in a variety of plays including Ibsen's *Peer Gynt*, adaptations of his own plays (*Deburau* and *The Outsider*) and even a version of *Show Boat*. In the 1930s and early 1940s, he continued to grace the airwaves at infrequent intervals, acting in short one-hour plays that were often adaptations of recent screen successes.

Something else that has scarcely been reported at all is Atwill's benevolent support for worthy causes. Throughout his career he frequently gave his services for free to support various funds and charities. Sometimes he would stage shows himself, other times he would take part in a charity theater performance and sometimes he would speak at rallies to raise funds. The causes he supported between 1910-1919 included organizations helping relatives of the Titanic disaster, the WWI relief effort, an orphanage and more. During the 1920s he was no less generous, acting in shows to support charities which included the Near East Relief Fund, the New York League of Girls' Clubs, the Actors Equity Fund, the National Vaudeville Artists' Benefit Fund, the Marshall Stillman Movement and the Children's Village. He even took part in an event to raise money to complete the building of the Cathedral of St. John the Divine in New York. Throughout the 1930s, he was heavily involved with the Academy of Motion Picture Arts and Sciences, serving as a member of the Actors' Committee

The gruesome cover of the British pressbook for *Mystery of the Wax Museum*

and often being the spokesman in negotiations where some unfortunate actor needed assistance.

Atwill had a voracious appetite for life. He seemed determined to squeeze every drop of pleasure he could from it. He was driven by an ambition and a *wanderlust* that his three brothers lacked—they all stayed in England and had careers in insurance. But Lionel had a taste for the good life, and enjoyed living in big houses, driving expensive cars (including two Rolls Royce cars), taking long and exotic holidays and sailing yachts. He had homes on both the East and West Coast in the U.S.A., as well as more than one Malibu beach house. Entourages of servants, gardeners, cooks, maids, and so on served his needs in both primary houses. He had an appreciation of fine art, and after picking up his paycheck for each Hollywood film, he acquired a valuable painting to adorn his homes. No wonder that one reporter, after meeting the well-dressed actor at the height of his Broadway fame, was inclined to call him *The Exquisite Villain* (Barbara Beach in a 1919 issue of *Motion Picture Classic* magazine after seeing Atwill in the play *Tiger! Tiger!*). The phrase is particularly apt: There was not only something exquisite about Atwill's taste for the finer things in life, there was also something exquisite about the intensity of his villainy in his Hollywood films.

When Atwill wasn't acting, he was grabbing life by the throat, socializing and keeping in the public eye. The society pages in the newspapers are full of details of social events that Atwill attended. The phrase hadn't been invented back then, but Atwill was

Would you trust this doctor? Atwill as Dr. Bohmer from *Ghost of Frankenstein*

without doubt a party animal. In fact, he liked to party just a little bit *too much* ... as will be recounted later in this book.

Atwill has earned a special place in the hearts of horror film fans, not just because of the films themselves, but also because of his attitude toward them. He never belittled the horror roles he played. A number of actors who have been typecast in films of this genre have tried to play down this aspect of their careers. They do this out of insecurity and fear that they won't be treated seriously if they are regarded as a *horror* actor. But Atwill had no such insecurities. By the time he arrived in Hollywood, he had already proved to the public and the critics that he was a serious and talented actor. He lapped up the horror roles and enjoyed every villainous moment.

When it came to playing the horror parts, Atwill had a special gift for getting into the minds of the villains he played. Above all, it showed in his eyes. No other actor could *stare* quite like Lionel Atwill. It was a stare that could kill at 20 paces. He had eyes that possessed a cold intensity that few other actors have ever matched. Faith Service (in *Motion Picture* magazine in 1933) called them "the coldest and most merciless eyes ever set in a man's skull." As soon as a victim became the target of a stare from those eyes, he or she knew that they wouldn't last beyond the next reel. His repertoire of stares included the sinister stare that could freeze your blood. Or the insane stare of a man who cannot be reasoned with. Or the tormented stare of a man who has just realized that his wife has been cheating on him. Or the desperate gaze of a man who feels that a sudden turn of events has humiliated him. Whatever the cause, Atwill had a stare that suited the moment. He was a master at donning an expression that suggested hidden layers of thought and emotion. This wonderful liveliness of his eyes is one of the characteristics that make him such a watchable actor, even today, over a half-century after his death.

Atwill's life reads like something out of a Greek tragedy, scaling heights of success, fame and wealth, only to have Fate deal him a series of harsh blows which brought him low and robbed him of all that acclaim and status. First was a decade of success on the British stage. Then, 15 years of even greater acclaim on the stage in America. Then, a decade of still wider popularity as a highly regarded Hollywood character actor, earning substantial amounts of money, living a film star's lifestyle in big houses and sailing yachts. A succession of glamorous wives accompanied him through these different stages of his career. It must have seemed to him at times as if he were living a charmed life.

But in the early 1940s, it all started to go wrong. First was the heart-breaking loss of a family member during WWII. Then he found himself dragged into someone else's court case, which eventually led to him being put on trial, accused of lying under oath. The public humiliation that followed was further exacerbated by his newfound status as a felon, which meant that no Hollywood studio would hire him. To Lionel Atwill, it looked like he had reached the end of the road, both in his career and personal life.

The full story of Atwill's golden years and all his later ordeals will be told in the pages that follow. All of his theater productions and radio appearances are discussed. Also discussed in detail are his 65 sound feature films, his three short sound films, his five silent films and his four multi-chapter serials.

Although today we can enjoy his stage roles only in our imaginations, we are very fortunate that all of his sound feature films and serials have survived, providing us with a feast of fine performances to savor—performances which will be preserved for the appreciation of many future generations.

Chapter 1
The First 20 Years

Many articles have been written about Lionel Atwill and most state that he was born into a wealthy, privileged family. Atwill himself was happy to promote the public image that he came from a vaguely aristocratic background. His wonderful voice and his imposing manner seemed to bear out this version of events, which has been generally accepted. My research, however, suggests otherwise.

His grandfather, William Atwill, was a postmaster and pawnbroker (as shown by old government census documents) in the town of East Stonehouse, just outside Plymouth in Devon, a county in the southwest of England. One of William Atwill's three children was Alfred Atwill, who moved from Devon to London in the early 1880s to work as a clerk at the Board of Education. He met and married Ada Emily Dace, a Londoner born in Lambeth, in 1884. They were age 36 and 25 respectively when they married.

Every biographical account of Lionel Atwill's life has stated, rather vaguely, that he was born in Croydon, without specifying whether their research meant the town or the borough of that name. Croydon is a large borough approximately 13 miles due south of central London. Alfred and Ada Atwill moved, soon after marrying, to South Norwood, a suburb within the borough of Croydon. Theirs was a modest house at 2, Upton Villas, one of a row of houses in Albert Road. Lionel Alfred William Atwill was born here a year later on Sunday, March 1, 1885.

An indication of the kind of neighborhood in which Lionel was born is suggested by the occupations of other people living on the same street, as shown in the government census forms. At Number 1, Mrs. Buckton was a dressmaker and an undertaker lived a few doors away. This was hardly the aristocracy. The area should more accurately be described as a place where hard-working families of modest means were living in unremarkable two-bedroom houses. Might it be that Atwill himself deliberately promoted the misconception that he was born in the town of Croydon, to draw a smokescreen over his true origins?

The house where Hollywood's maddest doctor was born still stands. A while ago I knocked on the door to find out if the current occupants were aware that a former Broadway and Hollywood legend was born here well over a century ago. They weren't, and in fact they had never heard of Lionel Atwill.

Lionel was the first of four children born to Alfred and Ada, all boys. The others, each born two years apart, were Stanley, Clarence and Herbert. Lionel, Stanley and Clarence were all born at Upton Villas, but the family had moved by the time Herbert was born. Around 1890, when Lionel was five, the Atwills moved to 54 Lennard Road, a slightly larger property in a slightly leafier location, in Penge, in the borough of Bromley, about four miles closer to London.

Living with them was Charlotte Dace, Ada's mother. The family, although by no means wealthy, earned enough to be able to have a servant girl living in the house. Again, the house is still there, and it is highly unlikely that the current occupants are aware that a celebrity once lived there.

Lionel Atwill

Lionel Atwill's humble origins; he was born in the white-painted house in the middle of the photograph, 2, Upton Villas, South Norwood, in London.

No photographs of Lionel as a young boy seem to have survived, and not much is known about his very early years. A retrospective article that appeared in a New York newspaper called *The Fulton Register* (dated May 17, 1924) gives us some clues. "He declares that even as a child, he wanted to go on the stage. He began acting in his nursery days and at 14 years of age was doing plays in drawing rooms." Atwill's great-niece, Leslie Dale, told me how her grandfather Clarence remembered appearing on the school stage, then 8 years old, with his 10-year-old brother Lionel as part of a black-face minstrel troupe. What a sight it must have been.

Around this time the young Lionel got his first exposure to things macabre. He recalled it years later in a 1933 interview in the *Los Angeles Evening Herald Express*. "When I was a child my mother took me to see *Faust*. I wanted ever after to be Mephistopheles ..." For the rest of his life Atwill would be drawn to the macabre, both in his choice of stage and film roles, and in his personal life.

The *Fulton Register* article also relates that when Atwill was 18, "in his leisure hours, he formed a dramatic society, which still exists and with which he often played." But where did he acquire this interest in acting? Certainly not from his father: "On the paternal side he is descended from a long line of seafaring men, all of who were in the British Navy." More likely, he inherited his artistic leanings from his mother, because the article claims that, "his relatives on his mother's side leaned to painting and music." His three younger brothers, Clarence, Stanley and Herbert, could not have been more different, and all ended up having careers in insurance.

Lionel attended Mercers' School, a prestigious establishment with a lot of history: It had been in existence since the 16th century. Located in Barnard's Inn, High Holborn in central London, Mercers' was a fee-paying school and had around 300 pupils. One of

Lionel's family: His parents are on the extreme left.

the school's old registration books from that period has survived, and it features a page on Lionel that records that he was admitted to the school on January 24, 1898, age 12 years and 10 months. He was placed in form IIIB, and a teacher noted why Lionel was selected for this class: "Latin poor." Lionel's three brothers also attended the school and it is not hard to imagine them having a grand time together and getting in all manner of escapades.

Annual entries in the Mercers' schoolbook show that Lionel worked his way through various classes. He would have received a very good all-round education from Mercers', as well as being taught, naturally, such essentially British skills as how to play cricket. There is a final entry in the school record book: "Midsummer 1901: Withdrawn to go to architect" (sic).

For the next three years, Lionel studied architecture and surveying. He was *articled* to a firm of architects; in other words, he worked in some lowly position for a company who would have sent him off from time to time for periods of formal study at an architecture college. Where he worked and where he studied is unknown, despite enquiries having been made at all of the prominent architecture schools that had existed at the time. When interviewed years later, Atwill was guilty of some blatant self-aggrandizement when recalling his education. For example, in a 1919 interview for *Motion Picture Classic* magazine, he claimed falsely that he was a graduate of Oxford University. And a playbill for a 1929 theater production, *Stripped*, contained a condensed biography of the play's leading actor. It claimed that Lionel had not merely studied architecture, but had actually achieved an honors degree in the subject. This may be true, but since Lionel directed the play and very probably wrote his own publicity for the playbill, it is open to question. Let's give him the benefit of the doubt.

At this stage in his life, he had not considered a career in acting. But when he was 19 or 20, a story (as reported by Forrest J Ackerman in *Monster World* magazine, issue #1, 1964) related that, "a friend persuaded him to take a role in a Shakespeare play at college, just for kicks. He couldn't have spoken more than 9 or 10 lines … but he caught the spell of the stage." The friend was presumably someone who attended the same architectural school. We know (from a 1915 edition of *Who's Who in the Theatre*) that in early 1905 he took part in several Shakespearian costume recitals in and around London. These, however, were not professional appearances on a theater stage; they were probably more like amateur performances staged at social functions. They would have been something that Atwill indulged in during his spare time when he wasn't studying architecture.

Working in the musty offices of a firm of architects must have been a pretty dull and uneventful life and it's not hard to see why Atwill would have preferred the theater. Apart from anything else, the profession was in those days an all-male preserve, whereas in the theater the young Atwill would have been surrounded by young women … and hence Lionel decided that from now on he would follow a career that would combine two of his greatest interests—acting and the opposite sex!

He would have learned early on that in order to be successful on the British stage, it was vital to have the right sort of voice. Today, we take Atwill's inimitable voice for granted, but it almost certainly was not the voice with which he started out in life. He is remembered today for having the rare ability to deliver a line with a grand theatrical resonance and with impeccable diction. And yet, growing up where he did, the young Atwill may have started out with a south London accent, which, for those unfamiliar with the area, is not very dissimilar to a Cockney accent.

The explanation as to where his famous voice came from is contained in an old *Who's Who in the Theatre,* which informs us that very early in Atwill's career, he attended elocution classes given by S. L. Hasluck, a gentleman who around 1900 produced a series of books with titles like *Hasluck's Recitations for Boys and Girls, Recitations from Dickens* and *Recitations for Ladies.* The teenaged Atwill would have traveled up to Hasluck's school on Regent Street in London's West End on a regular basis. He may well have attended classes there after spending all day at the architecture firm. At Hasluck's school, he would have practiced his diction and vocal projection until finally developing that marvelous voice which served him so well throughout his career.

And we can be glad that he did, because his fine voice is one of his most appealing qualities, and today we remember him for all those horror films in which he spoke his lines in a way that uniquely combined the refined and clipped diction of an English gentleman with all the malevolence of a sadistic villain.

Chapter 2
Onstage in Britain

Atwill made his first professional appearance onstage in September 1905 and, satisfyingly, it is still possible today to visit the theater at which he made his debut. The grand old Garrick Theatre, a prestigious venue built in 1896, stills stands proudly in London's West End theater district, on Charing Cross Road. Should anyone wish, he or she could pay it a visit and, from a seat in the old-fashioned auditorium, imagine 21-year-old Lionel getting his first experience of performing in front of an appreciative paying audience.

The role he took was a very minor one, as one of two footmen in a production of *The Walls of Jericho*, a successful society comedy written by Alfred Sutro. It was a non-speaking part, requiring him to do very little, apart from walk onstage occasionally and serve tea to the lords and ladies who were the play's chief characters. On other nights, he was only engaged as an understudy for the footman role, so there were probably many evenings when Atwill merely sat in the wings, having nothing to do other than to enjoy soaking up the theater atmosphere. Alongside him in the cast was, among others, O.B. Clarence, who many years later provided the benevolent voice of Dr. Dearborn—alter ego of evil maniac Bela Lugosi—in *The Dark Eyes of London* (1939).

Some sources have suggested that Atwill's stage debut was in late 1904, but a 1915 edition of *Who's Who in the Theatre*, which contains a very accurate record of Atwill's theater appearances up to 1915, confirms the later date. Confusion may have been caused by the fact that *The Walls of Jericho* was indeed staged in late 1904, but theater programs from that earlier period list other actors in the roles of the two foot-men; Atwill only joined the cast much later on.

Having made his professional debut, Atwill now threw himself into acting. He spent a number of years touring around Britain's provincial theaters. Information about these very early stage performances is sometimes sketchy, and it is not possible today to construct a complete list of the names of every theater and town that he visited. All that remain are a few tantalizing photographs and some theatrical reviews that make reference to him. For many of Atwill's stage plays, not even a photograph survives. But enough is known to fire our imaginations and make us realize what a loss it is that no filmic record of Atwill onstage exists. Not only that, but very probably there is no one alive today who can claim to have seen him onstage. Even so, it is fascinating to look at some of these roles in detail, because in several of them we can see premonitions of his horror typecasting of many years later.

During 1906, he joined an acting company run by Harold V. Neilson. The group, whose leading actor was Courtenay Thorpe, staged a series of three plays by Ibsen, the Norwegian dramatist, at the Gaiety Theatre in Manchester, and they also toured around Britain. Atwill was in all three plays. As far as can be ascertained, the first was *A Doll's House*, giving Atwill his first professional speaking part. The *Stage* magazine of January 25, 1906 gave him his first ever mention in the press, reviewing the play when it was staged for three days at the Devonshire Park Theatre in Eastbourne on England's

South Coast. "Dr. Rank was fairly well undertaken by Mr. Lionel Atwill," wrote the reviewer. This was hardly the most exciting of reviews to launch a career.

In March, Atwill was in a second Ibsen play, *An Enemy of the People*, taking the lesser role of Horster, a ship's captain. The reviews make no mention of Atwill.

In April, he was back in *A Doll's House* again, this time at the Manchester Gaiety, and his appearance prompted a more substantial mention in the press.

The Garrick Theatre in London's West End, where Atwill made his professional acting debut.

A 1906 reviewer wrote in *The Manchester Courier*, "Mr. Atwill played Dr. Rank with distinction, toning down the gruesomeness of the part most acceptably." An ironic comment, to say the least, given that Atwill spent most of his later career doing all he could to *emphasize* "the gruesomeness." In *A Doll's House*, the gruesome angle is that Atwill's character professes his love for a married woman while, at the same time, admitting that he is in the terminal stages of syphilis.

Also in April 1906, and again at the Manchester Gaiety, he was in Shakespeare's *Measure for Measure*, starring Courtenay Thorpe, with Atwill in the minor but significant role of the Provost, a jail keeper. The play ran for six nights and *The Stage* thought that, "Mr. Lionel Atwill ably accounts for the Provost."

In May and June of 1906, he appeared in his third Ibsen play, *The Pillars of Society*. This time he had a larger role, playing Johan Tonnesen. When it played at the Grand in Leeds, the *Stage* thought that Atwill was "worthy of mention." In June, at the Royal Theatre in Bradford, *The Stage* reported that, "Mr. Atwill proves very successful in the part of Johan Tonneson."

Following the "gruesomeness" of *A Doll's House*, Atwill now found himself drawn to a role with even stronger macabre overtones. Sometime around late 1906 or early 1907, he was in *A Fool's Paradise*, a play by Sidney Grundy. Atwill played a major role as Philip Selwyn, a husband whose wife Beatrice is slowly poisoning him with arsenic. Philip, in love with his wife, is oblivious to the real state of affairs, as shown by this dramatic exchange:

> Beatrice: Dearest, don't talk of death. (*Withdraws hand*)
> Philip: (*Takes his arm from her, and leans forward*) I am more ill than I seem—more ill than anybody knows. I can't help thinking of death, for every day it seems to draw nearer and nearer. I can feel it coming—slowly, mysteriously, weirdly—gathering about me— wrapping me round and round. (*Almost to himself*)
> Beatrice: (*Rises*) Hush, Philip, hush! You are tired. (*Goes away two*

steps to center) Shall I leave you for a while?

Philip: No, no! Don't go away. (*Holding out his hands as she moves up to back of sofa, right of him*) You are all I have left, mousey. I am not tired; but oh, I feel so drowsy! I seem to get worse every day.

Beatrice: And why, my dear? Because you won't take your medicine! Come. Let me bring it to you now.

Philip: That beastly medicine!

On December 17, 1906 Atwill opened at the Osborne Theatre, Manchester, in a play that would keep him busy until May the next year. The *Tyrant* was a romantic melodrama set in Venice, and the *Stage* wrote that, "Mr. Atwill was the ardent lover, Rudolph, manly and forcible throughout." *The Tyrant* toured successfully around England, playing at Salford, Preston, Liverpool and Castleford. In its review of the play at the Prince of Wales Theatre in Grimsby, the *Stage* reported, "Mr. Lionel Atwill could not easily be improved upon as Prince Rudolph."

Atwill's next role gave him a real taste of theatrical success; he toured in *The Bondman* for 18 months, from mid-1907 until November 1908. The play was based on a successful novel by Hall Daine and had already proved very popular on the West End stage (with a different cast). *The Bondman*'s lengthy provincial tour visited most of the cities and bigger towns in England, playing for about a week in each. The tour included several visits to London theaters, including the Lyric (in Hammersmith) and the Shakespeare in southwest London.

Atwill starred as Michael Sunlocks, a *bondman*, or prisoner-slave, in a Sicilian penal colony, where work in the sulphur mines causes him to go blind. The Derby *Daily Telegraph* wrote a review of the play in December 1907 when it was at the Lyric: "The company is a capital one with Mr. Cecil A Collins and Mr. Lionel Atwill as the two brothers." About its run at the Crystal Palace Theatre, the *Stage* wrote:

> The sulphur mine scene is particularly admired, not only for the very capable acting of Cecil A. Collins and Lionel Atwill, but also for its spectacular effect.

Occasionally Atwill took a break from *The Bondman* to appear in other plays. In June 1907 he was in *Measure for Measure* again, this time at the Fulham Theatre, and with Lionel Belmore starring. From August to September 1907, he was kept intermittently busy in *The Prodigal Daughter*, with Millie Ford in the title role. The play toured theaters in Wigan, Preston and Oldham, and the *Stage* thought that, "Mr. Lionel Atwill scores as Julian Belford." In January 1908, he was in a romantic drama, *The City of Mystery*, at the Grand, Luton. It was set in Paris in 1718 and featured a cast largely borrowed from *The Bondman*.

From June to July 1908 he toured in *The Sheriff and the Rosebud*. Surviving records show that it was produced in at least two theaters, the Hippodrome, Manchester, and the Shepherd's Bush Empire, London. It was a one-act play (from a story by Horace Vachell) about a California sheriff, Jefferson Wells (Atwill), who is on the trail of a bank thief but falls in love with the thief's daughter (Ida Morgan). The *Stage* was impressed:

Mr. Lionel Atwill played cleverly as the sheriff, bringing out effectively the better feelings of the man's nature ... His portrayal of the sheriff's conflicting emotions is admirable, and goes a long way towards the success of the piece.

In May 1908, he was back playing Dr. Rank again in *A Doll's House* at Manchester's Athenaeum Theatre. The *Manchester Courier* thought:

Dr. Rank and Mrs. Linden (Rosemary Rees) were also well played, and with such a talented company to do Ibsen the service he demands, it is not too much to expect that the remaining performances this week will be well attended.

During the summer of 1908, Atwill also found time for some relaxing activities. The *Stage* reported that he took part in two cricket matches, as part of a team made up of the cast and crew of *The Bondman*. In one match, he played against a team from the Royal Naval Hospital in Great Yarmouth, and in the other he was up against the Eastbourne Hippodrome Cricket Club. Despite having learned the sport at the Mercers' School, Lionel proved himself to be singularly unskilled, being bowled out for no runs in one match and caught for no runs in the other!

From 1908 to 1909 he toured successfully in *The Flag Lieutenant*, playing the leading role, and the play helped to bring him to the notice of the British public. It was well received wherever it played. For example, in March 1909, it was at the Grand Theatre in Hull and that city's *Daily Mail* noted:

One of the two oldest surviving photos of Atwill, showing him in costume for *The Flag Lieutenant* in 1908 or 1909.

Mr. Lionel Atwill plays the part of Lascelles with frankness and breeziness—you can't help liking him.

When it played in April 1909 at the Theatre Royal in Exeter, a reviewer in the *Western Times* wrote, "Mr. Lionel Atwill, who takes the title role, has acted with success in many prominent and well-known plays, and nothing could excel his fine treatment of the part of *The Flag Lieutenant*." Also in April, the *Devon and Exeter Gazette* commented:

At the close of each act, the curtain had to be rung up again and again to enable the principals to bow their acknowledgements ... Mr. Lionel

Atwill was a breezy and manly Richard Lascelles, quickly establishing himself a favorite.

Fortunately, two stills of Atwill in this part have survived. They show him in military costume, a dashing foretaste of all the uniformed roles he would play later in his career,

as military men and police inspectors, such as one-armed Inspector Krogh in *Son of Frankenstein*. What a shame, though, that no photos seem to have survived of one scene in particular from this production, because Atwill's character, in order to sneak across enemy lines, dresses up as a bashi-bazouk, an elaborately costumed and turbaned Turkish soldier.

The plot of *The Flag Lieutenant* contains an uncanny foreshadowing of the court case that was to have such an impact on Atwill's life in the 1940s. The title character, Richard Lascelles, lies to protect the reputation of a friend on a battlefield. As a result, Lascelles is accused of cowardice in action. Only at the last minute does the truth come out, and Lascelles is saved from a court martial and his honor is upheld. Many years later, when Atwill was in court charged with perjury, he would convey via his lawyer, "I lied like a gentleman to protect friends."

A youthful Atwill in *The Flag Lieutenant*

This coincidental premonition of things to come might be dismissed as just that—a coincidence. However, similar parallels between fictional events and the misfortunes of Atwill's later real life occur with extraordinary frequency throughout his career. It sounds crazy, but it's almost as if some higher power were giving Atwill regular warnings of what was to befall him in later life. There are so many such coincidences that a list of them has been compiled and can be found among the appendices at the back of this book.

If only a time machine could be invented so that we could go back over a century to watch Atwill in *The Prisoner of the Bastille*, in which he toured in 1909. A review in the Hull *Daily Mail* suggests the grisly tone of the play:

> The Bastille may always be relied upon for giving us a thrill of horror. As the symbol of everything that is terrible and cruel, it is always effective.

This is the famous *Man in the Iron Mask* story, and it would have been a treat for Atwill fans because he played the dual roles of King Louis XIV and his twin brother Philippe.

The *Daily Mail* continued:

> Mr. Lionel Atwill plays with intelligence and force, and at times with distinction. A full house watched the play with unabated interest.

In those scenes in which Atwill's face was concealed by the iron mask, how wonderful it must have been to hear that distinctive voice booming forcefully into the auditorium. And no doubt there was a climactic scene in which Atwill as the imprisoned king screams and batters within the walls of his cell, slowly losing his mind. In November 1909, the *Manchester Guardian* praised Atwill:

> It was acted with a suitable vigor, and Mr. Atwill [was] good as both kings ... His quick changes were capital and would certainly please any student of technique, and he bore himself gallantly.

The *Manchester Courier* also praised Atwill's performance in *The Prisoner of the Bastille* and observed:

> Mr. Lionel Atwill plays the dual roles ... with nice discretion, differentiating skillfully between the two widely different characters and has, in a play that is obviously melodramatic, a keen sense of the value of reserve force.

This astute last comment tells us that, even this early in his career, Atwill had developed some of the stylistic nuances that would characterize his later acting in horror films.

Acting alongside Atwill in *The Prisoner of the Bastille* was Phyllis Relph, a young lady who would soon become very significant in Lionel's life.

In July 1909, Atwill took to wearing his cricket whites again in a match between the London Actors and the Provincial Actors. It was an annual event held at the prestigious Kennington Oval cricket ground, in south London. Atwill gave a slightly better account of himself than before, managing to achieve 13 runs before being stumped.

In February 1910, Atwill played the Chevalier de Mauprat in *Richelieu* at London's Strand Theatre. The *Times* didn't think much of the play but thought that, "Mr. Atwill is an agreeable Mauprat." Some years later, the *New York Tribune* (in 1917), looking back over Atwill's career,

Atwill's striking profile as seen on a British postcard from 1909

Atwill from *The Prisoner of the Bastille* (1909)—photo from The Billy Rose Theatre Division, The New York Public Library for the Performing Arts, Aston, Lenox and Tilden Foundations

highlighted his role in this play, "In the part of de Mauprat, he established himself over night as a leading man." It's just as well that he did it "overnight" since, according to the *Stage*, the play closed after just four days when the producer, Robert Hilton, failed to pay any salaries to cast, stagehands and orchestra, and Atwill did not receive a penny.

Atwill was far more than just an actor: He also wrote, directed and produced several plays and always seemed to have plans to produce others, even though many of them never came to fruition. A 1910 issue of the *Daily Express* provides the earliest record of this, informing us that,

> *The Fourth Kiss* is the name of a tragic little play by Mr. W. Douglas Newton—the short-story writer—which Mr. Lionel Atwill produces on Friday at the Peckham Hippodrome.

The Fourth Kiss is also significant in Atwill's career for another reason. The fact that he chose to produce this play gives us the strongest evidence so far of his career-long fascination with the macabre. The play is a full-blown drama of the supernatural, with Atwill playing a character who has just returned to London from Egypt, only to be pursued by a deadly curse, placed upon him when he drunkenly entered a sacred tomb and recklessly kissed the stone idol inside. The curse had stated that three people close to him would die, each kissed by the idol, and sure enough three of his relatives have recently suffered that grim fate. A door opens silently in his London room and he feels touched by the deadly fourth kiss, and he falls down dead. The *Stage* enjoyed the production:

> Mr. Atwill scored a success in the character of Hughes, his descriptive powers being excellent, while the intensity of his death scene was good.

It was the first of many dramatic, gruesome death scenes that the actor would perform in his long stage and film career.

Atwill enjoyed the macabre elements of *The Fourth Kiss* so much that he revived the play two months later at the Empress Theatre, Brixton, in July. But he made an important change to the cast. Originally, his character had recounted the Egyptian experience to a male friend, but Atwill decided that it would give the play extra punch if that character were female and his fiancée. Phyllis Relph played the part, she being the attractive young actress Atwill had met while working on *The Prisoner of the Bastille* and with whom he was developing a romantic relationship.

The *Daily Express* reviewed *The Fourth Kiss*, writing that Atwill "... has a picturesque, romantic manner in his acting." The review went on to say that Atwill "... gave evidence of great tragic power." We would be able to see exactly what the writer meant years later in many of Atwill's non-horror films, because in scene after scene, as a tortured lover or humiliated husband, he emoted real tragic force with just a gaze.

In June of 1910, Atwill starred in *Smiler's Watch* at the Camden Hippodrome. He played a seaman who gets mad-drunk on rum, murders the master-at-arms and then throws himself overboard. It was further evidence of Atwill's leaning toward the macabre, as suggested by a review in the *Stage*:

> Gruesome ... its horrors may be thought by some to cross the borderline into the domain of the grotesque.

In the spring of 1910, Atwill was engaged by the J.C. Williamson theatrical company with the intention of traveling with them to Australia where they would tour in several plays. The first was to be *The Whip* (with Atwill playing the Earl of Brancaster)*,* and the company rehearsed in early July before sailing on board the Orvieto on July 8. *The Whip* opened in Melbourne on September 3, and was followed by *Henry of Navarre* (with Atwill playing Henry) and *Via Wireless* (playing Lieutenant Sommers).

In an age when long-distance travel was not common, it must have been a real adventure for the 25-year-old actor, who had never left Britain before. Not much is known about this episode in Atwill's life and it is hoped that one day an Australian researcher will do a little delving and turn up some newspaper articles, theater reviews or old photographs. One piece of publicity for a later production in America (*Stripped* in 1929) stated that his 1910/11 Southern Hemisphere tour had also included theater engagements in New Zealand.

Old passenger lists show that the young Atwill certainly made the most of the return journey. After leaving Sydney, Australia in October 1911, he spent two months getting back to Britain, stopping off for a week's vacation in Honolulu, and from there heading for Vancouver, Canada, before eventually arriving back in Liverpool in December 1911.

The *Daily Express* reported on Atwill's return to England:

> Mr. Atwill has returned to London, via America, and has brought some romantic plays with him. One is *The Circle* and another is *The Prince in the Garret*, both adaptations of works by A.C. Gunter, the author of *Mr. Barnes of New York*. Mr. Atwill has also a scheme in hand for the presentation of these plays in the West End under somewhat novel conditions.

It all sounded very promising, with Atwill not merely acting but also serving as producer. However, there is no evidence that either of these plays ever reached the stage.

Instead he landed a part in *Milestones*, a three-act play written by Arnold Bennett and Edward Knoblock, and it was indeed a milestone in Atwill's career. He played a romantic role as a young engineer in the second act, returning in the third act as the same character, but now much older and a prominent political figure in the Labour Party. Highly popular at London's Royalty Theatre in the West End over a period of 18 months, the play had an impressive run of 609 performances (with Atwill in 603 of them). *The Times* considered, "There is some clever acting from ... Mr. Lionel Atwill."

Since *Milestones* was so crucial in Atwill's career, it is worth looking at it in some detail. We can imagine the handsome 27-year-old Atwill in the part to get an idea of why this role made him so popular. When his character first appears on the stage, the text of the play gives a telling description of him.

> Arthur Preece enters. His age is 25; he is a man of the clerk class, whose talent and energy have made him what he is. He is full of enthusiasm, earnest, but with a rough sense of humor. Rather short and stocky in figure, but important. His clothes are neat and useful—but very simple.

His first scene is an amusing, romantic dialogue with Emily (played by Evelyn Weeden). Preece, being an engineer, has rather different ideas than Emily of what constitutes being romantic.

"If I can make 19 tons of steel do the work of 20, well, I reckon, I've accomplished something in the world," he beams, full of enthusiasm for his latest invention.

"I'm sure auntie and I hadn't an idea it was anything half so romantic," replies Emily, playfully teasing him.

"It *is* romantic, isn't it?" he says, not realizing he is being teased.

"No wonder you're so excited."

"Am I? Well I don't care! It's all right. That's all I care about. Here's a bit of the steel now."

He offers her a small sample.

"Is it for me? May I keep it?" says Emily, even more playfully.

"I want you to."

"I'd part with all my jewelry before I parted with this."

Although she teases him, she is also impressed by his passion for his work, and a page or so later, the couple moves closer together.

Lionel Atwill plays a romantic young man in *Milestones* (1912), and he is about to plant a kiss on Evelyn Weeden.

"I'm very ambitious," Preece says. "I want a whole lot of things. But if I thought I could find someone—find a woman, who—who feels as I feel; who'd like before everything to make the world decent—I'd … "

Emily can only utter a brief, "I—," which is followed by the stage direction, "Profoundly stirred, she falls into his arms."

"Emily!" says Preece, and "he kisses her long, holding her close."

What a shame that no one thought to film a performance of *Milestones*. What a delight it would be to see Atwill in this light comic scene, so different from his later mad doctor roles. But perhaps it isn't so different. In the young engineer's obsession for his invention, one can't help but detect the early stirrings of a mad scientist who would one day love to rule the world. At one point another character says of him, "Why, the boy's invention mad. He thinks of nothing else."

In Act 3 of the play, it is now 27 years later. Preece makes another appearance. "His hair and moustache have grown gray. His expression and manner are slightly disillusioned and cynical. In figure he is the same." Her family forces Emily into an unhappy marriage to someone else, because they considered a mere engineer to be an unsuitable match. There is a brief, touching moment when "they kiss again."

Atwill's character delivers an enjoyable line when John, Emily's father, expresses his confusion on hearing of his granddaughter's choice for a husband.

"Are all you women gone mad tonight?" he asks. "Preece, do you reckon you understand women?"

"Now and then one gets a glimpse, sir," Preece replies.

I like to imagine myself to be back in 1912, sitting in the stalls of the Royalty Theatre in London, and laughing along with the rest of the audience.

On April 14 of that year, the Titanic, the largest ship afloat, sank on her maiden voyage to New York. Atwill was one of many actors who helped raise money for those affected by the tragedy. On May 10, he gave his acting services for free in a special matinee performance of a new play called *Kynaston's Wife*, which was performed at London's St James's Theatre to support "sufferers from the Titanic disaster." The story, according to a contemporary review, dealt with "wicked financiers, good-hearted millionaires and more-or-less ill-behaved ladies." All proceeds went to the Titanic fund, as they did five days later, on May 15, when an extra matinee of *Milestones* took place. A special program for the event was printed "with autographs and portraits of all concerned in the play." Have any of these survived, I wonder?

The extremely successful 18-month run of *Milestones* kept Atwill busy until August of 1913, but he did find time, in March, to act in a one-off matinee performance of *The Cradle* at London's Court Theatre. It was one of three different one-act plays performed. *The Cradle*, written by A. Rochester, according to the *Times*:

> Showed the anguish of a childless wife … who discovers that the cradle of the title formerly belonged to her husband's mistress. The husband's one ambition was to be a father. There is a thrilling scene between husband and wife, played with great intensity by Mr. Lionel Atwill and Miss Esme Beringer, and the tension is only relieved when the husband learns that after all his greatest wish may be realized.

The following month Atwill found time for something rather more significant. *The Observer* reported an important event in Lionel's life.

> A large number of actors and actresses attended the wedding at St George's Parish Church, Bloomsbury, yesterday, of Miss Phyllis Relph to Mr. Lionel A. W. Atwill, who is well known to theatergoers as the impersonator of the engineer in Mr. Arnold Bennett's play *Milestones*. Miss Relph is equally known by her performance in the part of Margaret Knox in *Fanny's First Play*.

Phyllis Relph, the British actress that Atwill married in 1913, is here seen in a nurse's costume for an unidentified stage play.

What a shame that no filmed record of *Years of Discretion* exists, staged at London's Globe Theatre (on Shaftesbury Avenue) from September 1913. We would have been treated to hearing Atwill adopt an Irish accent. He played Michael Doyle and, according to the *Times*, was "pleasingly stage Irish as the stage Irishman." Playing alongside him was C. Aubrey Smith, another Englishman who would uproot and move to Hollywood. Smith went on to become one of the most familiar supporting actors in Hollywood, and in fact he and Atwill appeared together in four films during the 1930s.

Also late in 1913, Atwill's interest in the macabre revealed itself again. He had the bright idea of producing a play inspired by H.G. Wells' *The Invisible Man*. It was described in newspaper ads as "a Farce suggested by the Story by H. G. Wells," so it probably bore very little relation to the original story. It was a *sketch,* and probably lasted no more than half an hour. It contained "illusions by Leslie Lambert." It opened at London's Coliseum Theatre in Charing Cross in November, and the *Observer* found it "of exceptional interest" and "notable." *The Manchester Courier* was impressed:

> Some of the effects are very cleverly contrived, and it is indeed a weird sight to see a suit of clothes walk about with apparently no one inside it.

Atwill appeared in *The Invisible Man* "twice daily" at the Coliseum. (Advertisements for the play show that also on the bill was a young comedian named W. C. Fields.) Later in the year it moved to two other London theaters, the Pavilion and the Stoll. In January of 1914, Atwill took the sketch to the Hippodrome in Manchester, and he continued to appear in it "twice nightly." Twenty years later, the distinctive voice of Claude Rains made him a superb choice for James Whale's 1933 film version of the story, but one cannot help but think that Atwill would also have been outstanding in the role.

In December 1913, Atwill was in *The Poor Little Rich Girl* at London's New Theatre, starring Helen Hayes. Atwill played a money-obsessed father who ignores his daughter. The play was later filmed twice by Hollywood, once starring Mary Pickford (in 1917) and another starring Shirley Temple (in 1936) ... and both times without Atwill.

The year 1914 was a busy one for Atwill, and he appeared in a number of plays in both London and the provinces.

In February he was at London's Palace Theatre, acting in *Rivals for Rosamund* (by Arnold Bennett), playing a character called Gerald O'Mara. *The Manchester Guardian* thought that:

Mr. LIONEL ATWILL

Lionel Atwill in 1913

> The players did their part high-spiritedly and gave the piece the right rapidity, Mr. Atwill doing wonders with an Irish accent.

This short playlet was one of several acts on the nightly bill.

April 1914 found Atwill at the Prince's Theatre in London, playing Paul Romaine in *The Story of the Rosary*, a new romantic melodrama written by Walter Howard.

In June and July 1914, Atwill was in *Getting Out Of It*, a one-act sketch in which he acted opposite Constance Collier. He was certainly putting in the hours. This was staged twice nightly at the Hippodrome in Manchester, with an additional three matinees during the week, and later in the month Atwill stayed with it when it moved to the Manchester Gaiety Theatre. In July the play traveled north of the border and was staged at the Alhambra Theatre in Glasgow.

In *Monna Vanna*, at the London's Queen's Theatre from July to August 1914, Atwill co-starred with Constance Collier in a controversial play that contained some early hints of the more depraved elements that would characterize his best non-horror parts in 1930s films. In fact, the play was so controversial that it had been banned in England for 12 years. Atwill plays Prinzivalle, the commander of an army that is about to destroy Pisa. But he gives an ultimatum: He will spare the city only if Monna Vanna, the beautiful wife of the commander of Pisa, will come to him and spend the night with him in his

In this rare photo from *Monna Vanna* **(1914), Atwill, in bandana, hopes to have his wicked way with Constance Collier.**

tent. And moreover, she must come wearing only a cloak! The thought of all that near-nudity had been too much for the delicate British censor, who feared that the audiences' morals would be permanently corrupted. Atwill must have lapped up all the notoriety.

For the play's opening night in London, Atwill had the honor of performing in front of Queen Alexandra and her sister, the Dowager Empress of Russia, who sat in the royal box.

The *Manchester Courier* thought that, "Mr. Lionel Atwill, if I mistake not, is no stranger to the part of the general Prinzivalle." Am I reading too much into this remark by inferring that the reviewer is suggesting that in real life Atwill was also no slouch when it came to demanding sexual services? It is almost certain that the writer was referring to a newspaper report that had appeared in the *Times* just six days earlier (on July 6, 1914) in which Atwill's name had been mentioned in a high-profile divorce case.

Her aggrieved husband charged actress Elsie Hissey with adultery and accused her of frequenting London nightclubs, such as the Cave of the Golden Calf and the Cabaret Club. The husband reeled off a list of actors known by his wife, including Sir George Robey and several in the theater company of which his wife was a member. It was implied that she "knew another actor in the company, a Mr. Lionel Atwill."

"You seem to suggest," the husband says, "that I accused her of misconduct with every actor we knew."

The lawyer replies, "That is precisely what we do suggest you did." Of course, no evidence that anything happened between Elsie Hissey and Atwill exists, but the suggestion is most definitely there.

Despite this, the reviewer from The *Manchester Courier* was full of praise for his performance in *Monna Vanna*.

> He made a picturesque figure and endued his lines with an appealing forcefulness that commanded attention.

This apposite phrase could just as well be applied to every one of Atwill's later film roles.

In September 1914, Atwill started a three-month run of a play by *Peter Pan* playwright J.M. Barrie. It was called *The Little Minister* and ran successfully until mid-December at London's Duke of York Theatre. The *Times* found an "ugly vindictiveness" in Atwill's character, Captain Halliwell, while the *Stage* wrote that, "Lionel Atwill acts with spirit." Playing alongside Atwill was Donald Calthrop, who was so memorable 22 years later when he co-starred with Boris Karloff in *The Man Who Changed His Mind*.

Some time in 1914—the exact month is not known—Atwill sailed across the English Channel with a company of actors and performed in *The School for Scandal*, Sheridan's popular 18th-century comedy. The play was staged at the Vieux Colombier Theatre in Paris and Atwill played Charles Surface, gambler, drinker and general ne'er-do-well. This episode must have been an adventure for Atwill and we only know about it today thanks to an article that appeared in the *New York Times* many years later, in April 1928, when Philip Carr, who had been the manager of the acting company, reminisced about it briefly.

On October 5, 1914 at the Gaiety in Manchester, Atwill played Leonard Scribner in *The New Shylock*, "a comedy of New York ghetto life." Sufficiently well received, the play was performed at the Lyric Theatre in London in November. *The Observer* thought that, "Mr. Lionel Atwill as the young Gentile did good work." The *Stage* reported that Atwill, "Played with much buoyancy and frankness."

In December of 1914, *The Poor Little Rich Girl* was taken to Manchester's Gaiety Theatre. This time Atwill starred alongside his wife Phyllis. *The Manchester Courier* described this work by Eleanor Gates as, "A play of fact and fantasy ... from the synopsis it would appear the play is full of delightfully whimsical and beautiful conceptions" and called it "a Christmas play for children." The review continued, "The cast is a strong one and includes ... Phyllis Relph and Lionel Atwill."

By the end of 1914, life was good for the 29-year-old Lionel Atwill. He was happily married to Phyllis. On June 30 that year he had become the proud father of a baby boy, John Atwill. Now that he was a well-regarded actor on the Londonstage, the money was rolling in. He could afford to rent a swanky riverside apartment in Hammersmith. Digby Mansions was a prestigious Victorian apartment block and the Atwills had a balcony that overlooked the River Thames. This eye-catching building is still there. Each apartment contains a small room whose original purpose was probably designed to be the sleeping quarters for a valet. So even this early in his career, Atwill may have been living a luxurious life, with a valet making sure he was always impeccably dressed, preparing his meals and giving him a morning shave. Throughout Atwill's career, news items and interviews make frequent references to valets, butlers and chauffeurs—the *exquisite villain* certainly enjoyed being pampered and living like royalty.

As well as an expensive apartment, Atwill could afford to buy a car. In 1914, few people owned cars. What a sight it must have been to see West End stage star Atwill and his wife driving around the streets of London, which in those days were still full of horse-drawn cabs and carriages.

Atwill recalled one such occasion (in an interview in a 1938 issue of the British film magazine *Picturegoer*):

> The film actor recalled the days when he lived in Kensington. "Motor-cars were then just coming into fashion," he declared. "I remember I bought a car for £200 and felt a terrific dog. I was so proud of it that the first Sunday morning I had it I decided to drive over to Bromley, where my parents lived, and give them a treat. Naturally I could not

drive very well, but undaunted I sailed along merrily till I turned into the road in which my parents lived. But then disaster came. I tried to swoop into the kerb and to pull up in style outside the old folks' home. But I had become too confident. I collided with the trunk of a chestnut tree and ripped the mudguards off!" He laughed heartily at the recollection.

On other days, an even more remarkable sight could be seen on London's roads—Lionel Atwill sitting in the sidecar of a Royal Enfield motorcycle ridden by his wife Phyllis. Both husband and wife were keen motorbike riders and they were even featured in a 1915 edition of *Royal* magazine. Said Phyllis:

> My six horsepower Royal Enfield is simply delightful. Together with my husband, Mr. Lionel Atwill, I have made many long trips, and I always take my turn in driving. I am sure that I have found great plea-sure in motor cycling, and the Side-car Combination is ideal—so easy to drive and so very dependable. We could not want anything better.

For Atwill, 1915 was just as busy as the previous year. Much of his time was spent in Manchester where, in January, he joined Annie Horniman's theater company at the Gaiety Theatre. Usually, a different play would be staged each week, and for a season Atwill and his wife acted in a great many plays at the Gaiety, becoming great favorites of the regular theatergoers of the region. Atwill also often served as associate director on many of these productions. It is important to remember Atwill was often involved

in the production and direction of the plays he was in, because throughout his film career, we can spot moments when it is apparent that he must have spoken to the director and suggested adding some little acting flourish with a view to giving a scene added dramatic punch. In January he was acting alongside his wife again, playing Young Marlow in *She Stoops To Conquer.* The *Manchester Evening News* thought he acted "with much spirit." In February he played Cli-tandre in *Blue Stockings* (an adaptation of Moliere's *Les Femmes Savantes*), and the *Manchester Evening News* reported that for "Mr. Lionel Atwill, nothing but praise is due."

In the same month he played Hylton Leverson in *The One Thing Needful* at the Gaiety, acting alongside Phyllis once again. *The Manchester Courier* wrote,

Digby Mansions was the prestigious riverside apartment block where Lionel and Phyllis lived from around 1913 to 1915.

"Mr. Charles Groves and Mr. Lionel Atwill gave charming character studies as the two fathers." When the play was taken to Blackpool's Grand Theatre in April, the *Stage* reported that, "Mr. Lionel Atwill has a part that fits him like a glove in Hylton Leverson."

Across the English Channel war was raging. Atwill was quick to do his bit to support the war effort. In February, he and Phyllis arranged a special matinee of *She Stoops To Conquer*, and £130 was raised for the Arts Fund, which was created "to relieve distress due to the war" in those working in the arts.

In March Atwill was at the Manchester Gaiety again in *Whimsies*, a "fantasy-burlesque," and again co-starring with his wife. *The Manchester Evening News* considered that Atwill and Phyllis were "worthy of special mention." The *Manchester Courier* was also impressed:

> Mr. Lionel Atwill takes the part of the playwright and subsequently a leading part in the play. His performance secured for him another of the successes, which have been his since he came to the Gaiety about Christmas time.

Still at the Gaiety, he received more good reviews for his part in *The Walls of Jericho*—now taking the leading role in the play in which he had made his debut back in 1905. The *Manchester Evening News* thought that, "In particular there is a display of very capable acting by Miss Edyth Goodall (Lady Alethea) and Lionel Atwill (Jack Frobisher)." Phyllis was also in the cast.

Also at the Gaiety in early 1915, he played George Dedmond in *The Fugitive*, with Atwill starring for 10 nights opposite his wife Phyllis.

In June, the Atwills were back in London and once again showing their charitable side. At the Playhouse Theatre the couple produced and starred in *Mater* (written by Percy Mackaye), all proceeds going to the Actors' Orphanage Fund. It was a comedy in which "a mother is mistaken for a daughter by an eager suitor" (Atwill being the eager suitor). The *Stage* reviewed it: "Mr. Lionel Atwill acted discreetly and well as the singularly obtuse Arthur Cullen."

Around the same time, it is said (in a career article that appeared in the *New York Tribune* in 1917) that he also produced a play called *The Tyranny of Tears* (by Charles Haddon Chambers), although the details of exactly when and where this was performed have proved elusive.

During this period, happily married Lionel and Phyllis were having the time of their lives. Back at the Manchester Gaiety, Atwill starred in a series of plays (often acting opposite his wife) and they include *Beauty and the Barge* (written by W.W. Jacobs, famous for the horror story *The Monkey's Paw)* and *Dark Horses* and *Amazons* (the latter a farcical romance by Sir Arthur Pinero).

Lionel and Phyllis acted together again in *One Summer's Day* at the Manchester Gaiety in August 1915. *The Manchester Guardian* wrote:

> Mr. Lionel Atwill is as complete and elegant a sentimentalist when it is his will as any on the stage. Miss Phyllis Relph can be as fascinating as flashing eyes and shrugs can make anyone.

Theatre legend Lily Langtry, Atwill's co-star in 1915, is seen here wearing the boots and short skirt that shocked her public. The *Boston Sunday Post*, Dec. 12, 1915, reported that the "Jersey Lily" was returning to the stage because she needed the money. Langtry passed away in 1929. The *NY Times* reported her death in the Feb. 13, 1929 issue.

Still at the Gaiety in September, the couple starred in *The Two Virtues*, a comedy by Alfred Sutro. *The Manchester Evening News* was impressed:

> No greater praise could be given to Mr. Lionel Atwill, who carries the new Sutro comedy *The Two Virtues* on his shoulders … It was a wonderful study of a lovable man—always pleasant to play, but often

difficult to deal with because of the complexities … The outstanding
success belonged to Mr. Atwill.

The *Manchester Courier* had mixed praise for him in *The Two Virtues*:

> Mr. Lionel Atwill is a fine comedy actor, but he rather overworks his
> genius for facial contortions.

It is often forgotten by admirers of his horror films of the 1930s and 1940s that
Atwill was an accomplished comedian. What a shame we can no longer enjoy his "facial
contortions" in this play.

The One Thing Needful and *The Walls of Jericho* were both revived for second
successful runs at the Gaiety in September and October. In early October, Atwill was
again supporting the war effort. As part of a recruitment drive, a large rally was held in
Manchester followed by an evening of entertainment at the Hippodrome Theatre. Atwill
was one of the performers donating his services, with Eva Moore joining him, and she
later turned up 17 years later in James Whale's *The Old Dark House*.

In July of 1915, Lionel acted alongside Lily Langtry (infamously a former mistress
of the Prince of Wales) in a play called *Mrs. Thompson*, at the Gaiety in Hastings. The
Stage wrote:

> Mr. Lionel Atwill has an arduous task in the role of Carpets, but he
> easily surmounts the difficulties, and repeatedly draws forth the ap-
> plause of his hearers.

Despite the applause, the play was not a success and never reached London. However,
Langtry liked the play and thought it had a better chance of success in America. She
suggested to Atwill that he travel with her to the States. After giving the idea much
thought, he decided to seize the opportunity, taking Phyllis and baby John with him.
Such a move would be a radical change to their lives.

First, though, he had to conclude his commitments at the Gaiety Theatre. *The
Manchester Evening News* wrote:

> The Gaiety will rely on *The Walls of Jericho* for another week—a
> safe card to play with such fine acting as that given by Lionel Atwill
> and Miss Phyllis Relph in the leading parts. These two players, by
> the way, are unfortunately nearing the end of their Gaiety engage-
> ment. *The Two Virtues* will be put on again on Monday week for their
> special benefit, after which they leave for America to appear there
> with Mrs. Langtry.

So great was the popularity of the couple that the local paper ran an advertisement
every night for a week announcing the "farewell performances" of Lionel and Phyllis.

When Atwill, Phyllis and their son John sailed for New York on October 16, 1915,
they could afford to do it in style: They traveled first class. For Lionel it was the end
of a decade of success on the British stage, and, he hoped, the beginning of an even
brighter career in America.

Chapter 3
Arriving in America

On October 16, 1915 the transatlantic liner St Paul sailed from Liverpool, bound for New York. Among its first-class passengers was actress Lily Langtry, and sailing with her was her entire theatrical company of 12 people, including Lionel Atwill and his wife Phyllis Relph. With Mr. and Mrs. Atwill was their 16-month-old son John.

All on board were leaving behind a Europe that was being ripped apart by The Great War. Sitting in the luxury of the ship's first-class saloon lounge, much of the talk among the theater people concerned a horrific incident that had happened just three days earlier in London, and Lily Langtry had been caught right in the heart of it. That night, a German zeppelin airship had dropped bombs on London and one had exploded outside the Savoy Hotel where Langtry was dining. She had witnessed the carnage and seen some of the injured civilians.

The conversation was considerably lighter when the ship reached New York on October 24. This was Langtry's first appearance in the United States since 1904, and she was determined to make an impressive entrance. She made sure her attire grabbed the interest of newspaper reporters waiting at the dockside.

"Lily Langtry Arrives in Boots" wrote the shocked *New York Tribune*, following it up with the sub-heading, "Talk on St. Paul Turns About Her Polish Footwear and High Skirts." Her scandalously short skirts revealed several inches of ankle. The Atwills must have found it all highly amusing and realized, no doubt, that if *Mrs. Thompson*, the play which the group planned to stage in America, was to be a success, then any publicity was good publicity.

The plan was to take *Mrs. Thompson* on a tour of some provincial cities, including a complete tour of the South, before showcasing it in New York. It all looked promising, and Atwill must have had high hopes, especially as Langtry, although now in her early sixties, was an acting legend. The play, written by Sydney Grundy, was "a modern comedy in four acts and in it Mrs. Langtry appears as a smart, up-to-date business woman" (according to the *Honolulu Star Bulletin*). They rehearsed the play first at the Eltinge Theatre on Broadway, then took it on the road. One venue where it played was the art nouveau Brandeis Theatre in Omaha, described as the most beautiful theater in the world. But the tour did not work out as planned. Audience reaction was poor. *The Washington Herald* reported that after a few final performances of *Mrs. Thompson* in Richmond, Virginia, Langtry was suspending the tour "for want of patronage." The play had now failed on both sides of the Atlantic.

Atwill must have been dismayed. After uprooting from England with his wife and baby son, it was all starting to go badly wrong. Would they have to return to England, or could Langtry find some way of rescuing her theatrical company from disaster? Atwill and Phyllis must have been thankful that they had decided to keep paying the rent on their Digby Mansions apartment in London—at least they had somewhere to go back to if necessary.

The experienced Langtry came up with an ingenious solution. She and her company would drop *Mrs. Thompson* and instead undertake a tour of New York's vaudeville theaters, performing a half-hour sketch.

"The *Jersey Lily* will be seen in a one-act play called *Ashes*," reported the *Omaha Daily Bee* in November, "written for her by Percy Fendell." This gave Atwill a good part as "a worthless social climber" and "caddish admirer" of Langtry, who tries to blackmail her by using a compromising letter she wrote to him years earlier. The play opened at the Orpheum Theatre in Brooklyn on November 22. Audience and critical reaction was good: The *New York Tribune* called it "an ingenious sketch."

Over the next few weeks, *Ashes* did the rounds of the New York vaudeville theaters, usually playing for around a week at each one: the Colonial Theatre on Broadway, the Bushwick Theatre in Brooklyn, B.F. Keith's Palace Theatre back on Broadway, then (in mid-December) the Alhambra Theatre, also on Broadway. It returned to B.F. Keith's Palace Theatre for a long run that saw it all the way through to February 1916. It was still on the road in mid-March, when it played at the Majestic Theatre in Chicago.

Each evening these vaudeville theaters put on a variety of acts and sketches. *Ashes* was the headlining act, and others on the same bill included a young Clifton Webb (fondly remembered for the film classic *Laura* many years later) doing a dance act.

At B.F. Keith's on February 10, Atwill found himself performing *Ashes* in front of VIP members of the audience—President Woodrow Wilson and his wife. The *Washington Herald* reported:

> The audience, which packed the playhouse, rose and stood, while the Keith orchestra played the National Anthem during the incoming of the distinguished party. Hearty handclapping concluded the public tribute.

Of course, the luminaries were there to see the legendary Lily Langtry, not Atwill, but even so, he must have enjoyed being part of such a celebrity occasion.

Ashes had provided Atwill with a regular income for several months, but appearing in vaudeville theaters was hardly the kind of fame he was seeking in America; he

Oakland Tribune, September 15, 1916

Lily Langtry Coming Is Vaudeville Star

MRS. LANGTRY.

Famous Beauty to Appear in 'Ashes'; New Sketch

England's perennial beauty, Mrs. Langtry—world famous as Lady de Bathe—comes to the Orpheum next Sunday in a one-act playlet of euonymous authorship called "Ashes." The celebrated English dramatic actress, assisted by Lionel Atwill and Leopold Stark, will be seen to splendid advantage in this sketch which is peculiarly well fitted to her capabilities. The story has to do with a woman whose happy married life is interrupted by the appearance upon the scene of a man to whom she once in a moment of pique wrote an indiscreet and compromising letter. In great need of money, he undertakes to blackmail her by the use of this letter. How a woman's wit proves too much wanted to be a success on the legitimate stage. But at least New York audiences now knew his name.

His next play, *The Double Cure*, found him, during the first week of June 1916, performing at the Apollo Theatre in Atlantic City, on the coast of New Jersey. Written by Edgar Selwyn, the plot revolved around the eternal triangle of a married couple (Lewis Stone and Christine Norman) and the wife's lover (Atwill). The dastardly Atwill manipulates Stone's stock market investments so that he loses his fortune. *The Evening Public Ledger* wasn't impressed and thought the play "smacks strongly of failure." The play closed shortly afterwards.

Also in June Atwill's generosity could be observed when it came to donating his acting services for free to support a charitable cause. A *Grand Bazaar* was staged over several weeks at the Grand Central Palace in New York. Its purpose was to raise money for the war effort, as well as other charities including American Ambulance Hospital Day and the BFB Blind Fund.

Large advertisements in the *New York Tribune* announced that the event would include two hundred booths selling all kinds of goods, an art gallery, films of fighting in Verdun, a dancing room and several tearooms, one of which staged "a cabaret given by some of the best-known names of Broadway." For the last three days of the Bazaar, one of these names attending was Atwill.

It was a stellar line-up, and others appearing included Mary Pickford, Constance Collier, Marie Tempest, Phyllis Neilson-Terry, Marie Dressler, Ethel Barrymore and Helen Terry. The cabaret acts took place over the afternoons and evenings, and, on the two closing nights of the bazaar, "the entire Ziegfeld Follies Company will attend as guests." They were billed as the "30 most beautiful girls in the world" and performed *Ziegfeld's Midnight Frolic.* On the last day, a grand ball occurred which went on until 3 a.m. Was Atwill a dutiful husband who went home early to his wife and young son, or did he party until the small hours, enjoying the company of the Ziegfeld girls?

For the next four months, Lionel and Phyllis seem to disappear from the records. Perhaps they took an extended vacation somewhere. But they were back at work in the theater again in November.

Three years earlier in England in 1913, Marie Belloc Lowndes had written *The Lodger*, a popular novel about Jack the Ripper. Soon afterwards, English playwright Horace Annesley Vachell had the unusual idea of making a comic adaptation of it for the stage, and it became a success in London. It's very likely that Atwill had seen the stage play in London; he was certainly familiar with it, because he now decided it could be a success in America. It's an early example of how Atwill was drawn to macabre subjects in his career. In later years he was always fond of telling interviewers that one of his hobbies was attending murder trials, so it was only natural that he should be fascinated by the mystery of the Ripper slayings.

In England, he had demonstrated on a number of occasions that his involvement in theater productions extended beyond merely acting. Now he would do the same in America. He had the bright idea of buying the American rights to *The Lodger,* and decided that he would not only produce and direct a version of the Vachell play, but star in it as well. His wife Phyllis would star alongside him. A far cry from the chilling film versions of *The Lodger* made years later, this version was billed as "an irresponsible comedy."

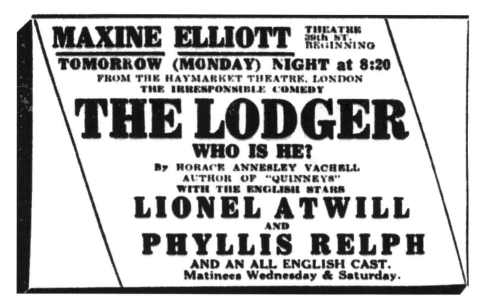

MAXINE ELLIOTT THEATRE
39th ST.
BEGINNING

TOMORROW (MONDAY) NIGHT at 8:20
FROM THE HAYMARKET THEATRE, LONDON
THE IRRESPONSIBLE COMEDY

THE LODGER
WHO IS HE?
By HORACE ANNESLEY VACHELL
AUTHOR OF "QUINNEYS"
WITH THE ENGLISH STARS
LIONEL ATWILL
AND
PHYLLIS RELPH
AND AN ALL ENGLISH CAST.
Matinees Wednesday & Saturday.

Atwill first tried out the play at a theater outside New York in November 1916, and then took it north over the border into Canada, where it played at a theater in Montreal for five weeks.

The play eventually opened in Broadway on January 8, 1917 at the Maxine Elliott Theatre. Daily ads for the play in New York newspapers (possibly designed by Atwill himself) boldly announced that it was staged "with the English stars Lionel Atwill and Phyllis Relph and an All English Cast."

The play was set at the time when all of London was hysterical with fear about the Jack the Ripper murders. Atwill played the character listed as *The Lodger*. It's a shame that no photographs of him in this role survive, since he must have looked most striking. It seems that the young actor dyed his full head of hair blond for the role, as described by a review in *Variety*:

> Mr. Atwell (sic), the star, is a good-looking blond type of man with
> a pleasant personality. He seemed more Austrian than English. Miss
> Relph is deliciously English.

The Lodger is a young man who rents a room in a house because he seeks solitude after being jilted by a lover. The fact that he takes long walks at night convinces his meddlesome landlady that he must be the Ripper. Various other incidents occur which seem to confirm in both the landlady's mind, and the audience's, that he is indeed the elusive murderer. She is horrified when he starts to make romantic advances toward her other lodger, a young lady (played by Phyllis). Naturally, all turns out for the good in the end, and Atwill's character is revealed not to be the Ripper after all. Lionel and Phyllis must have had a lot of fun playing the numerous romantic scenes that they shared.

It was a hit with most critics and certainly most audiences. "Instantaneous hit," wrote *The American*. "Unusually amusing," wrote the *Evening Post*. "Everybody was

The *New York Times*, January 22, 1917

laughing," reported The *Evening Herald*. "Miss Relph was charming," enthused the *Evening World*. The latter paper was flippant about Atwill's performance:

> Lionel Atwill played the strange adventurer so strenuously that he mixed a salad and his emotions without the slightest variety of acting.

Likewise, the reviewer for the *New York Times* had reservations. He thought it was:

> Well enough played, except by one Lionel Atwill and one Phyllis Relph, who for reasons not yet apparent, are presented in the programs as stars ... Mr. Atwill is pleasant in person and possesses a fine dynamic vitality, but he drives his every point as if he were bound that no defective in the last row of the gallery should miss one of them. It is acting of the hammer-and-tongs school, which raises havoc with a play of such light stuff as *The Lodger*.

On January 15 *The Lodger* moved to the Bandbox Theatre on 57th Street, and proved to be just as successful there. The *Evening World* wrote:

> Encouraged by the increasing popularity of *The Lodger* at the Bandbox Theatre, Lionel Atwill will give a series of special matinees, for which he will stage two new English plays. One will be *The Shadow*, by Eden Phillpotts.

It is not clear, however, whether or not these plays were ever produced.

On January 29, Atwill organized a one-off event at the Bandbox, sounding like a precursor of the wild parties that got him into so much trouble years later. Onstage, he held a party in honor of 20 English dancing girls who were collectively known as The Century Girls (the Century was a New York theater where they regularly performed). At least onstage, everything was certainly very civilized, with Lionel and Phyllis presiding over the event, serving tea and cake to all the girls and singing old English songs. The *Sun* newspaper couldn't resist lampooning the Britishness of the occasion:

Stage Britons Have a Rippin' Tea—Wot? Lionel Atwill of *The Lodger* is Host to 20 Century Dancing Girls.

Even when he wasn't onstage, Atwill was fully immersed in the theatrical world of New York. For example, the following Sunday, January 31, a special *drama day* luncheon was held at the Waldorf Hotel and Atwill (along with three other actors) was invited to give a lecture. Unfortunately no record survives of what he said. Perhaps he managed to sneak in a joke or two about his experiences with the Century dancing girls.

The Lodger ran successfully for over a month at the Bandbox Theatre and then transferred to the Randolph Theatre (also on Broadway) in the last week of February. Perhaps Atwill had read the disparaging remarks in *The New York Times* and learned from them, because by the time he was performing at the Randolph, a different reviewer (in *The El Paso Herald*) declared that:

> Lionel Atwill and Phyllis Relph ... give one of the most finished performances I have ever seen.

The Lodger was still going strong in May 1917 when Atwill and his wife took it to the Majestic Theatre in Brooklyn for a week.

Also in May 1917, Atwill appeared (probably for about a week) in a vaudeville sketch entitled *The Miss Market*, which played at the Colonial Theatre on Broadway. Nothing is known about this production; it sounds like another light comedy.

At the end of May, Atwill was busy rehearsing for *Eve's Daughter*, a play by Alicia Ramsey, which had its opening night in Washington at the Belasco Theatre on June 4. Here, at last, is a part that allowed Atwill to sink his teeth into a role that required him to be a dastardly villain. For one thing, he wore a monocle—a sure sign of villainy. It may well have been the first time Atwill wore a monocle, and he certainly seems to

STAGE BRITONS 'AVE A RIPPIN' TEA—WOT?

Lionel Atwill of "The Lodger" Is Host to 20 Century Dancing Girls.

One means to say—wot?—everything was perfectly rippin'—wot?—the jolly old toasted muffins and the marmalade and the tea and kykes and the silly old cucumber sandwiches and all that sort of thing—wot-wot-wot?—one means to say—when the real old fashioned English tea in honor of the twenty English dancing girls of the "Century Girl" company was given in their honor yesterday by Lionel Atwill, the *Lord Twyford* of Horace Vachell's "The Lodger" company, on the stage of the Bandbox Theatre, where "The Lodger" now is holding forth nightly.

Miss Phyllis Relph—Miss Relph is Mrs. Lionel Atwill when not acting up on top of the stage—presided over the tea things. And it should be remembered that to the immediate north, south, east and west of the Bandbox Theatre, in East Fifty-seventh street, the United States language is spoken almost exclusively in the German tongue. Up the street and down and across and around the corner from the spot where the theatrical Britishers yesterday made merry among their tea and kykes and old English songs on the Bandbox stage the belief is almost general among the delicatessen shops that the Kaiser lined in Paris last Christmas, but that a British controlled American press is withholding the truth.

From The *Sun*, January 29, 1917.

have taken a shine to it because dozens of his later villains also sported a monocle, and he even took to wearing one in his private life.

He played the Honorable Courtenay Urqhart, who turns out to be anything but honorable. Christine Norman played the young lady who finds herself on the receiving end of Urqhart's attentions. Urqhart is a roguish cad who wishes to take advantage of her, and is not concerned with the consequences. He even bribes the servants to facilitate his conquest. He encourages the young lady to indulge in a champagne supper, takes her to a hotel, intending to have his wicked way with her, and scandalously admits that he has no time for the institution of marriage.

For its day, *Eve's Daughter,* described as "a ripping peppery story," seems to have been rather audacious. The *Washington Herald* wrote:

> The conversation is full of swearing and daring, and the situations would, in a more timid generation, have been considered past the point of being risqué.

The same paper singled Atwill out for praise, reporting that he gave:

> A wonderfully natural and convincing rendering of the familiar type of the cynical aristocrat whose blackguardism is not untinged with sentiments of honor … Lionel Atwill's powerful portrayal of the bigot in the first act must not go without special mention.

Fortunately, a manly hero saves the day just in the nick of time and the young lady's reputation is preserved.

What is particularly fascinating is that Atwill made Urqhart into a very early anti-hero. The *New York Tribune* commented:

Lionel Atwill

He does the most villainous things in an entirely open-and-above-board manner; in his very perfidy he is the soul of honor, and many staid and estimable ladies in the audience have secretly, but none-the-less ardently, expressed considerable sympathy with Courtenay Urqhart and his villainous career.

Try to imagine yourself in a packed theater, surrounded by female members of the audience, their hearts aflutter at being spellbound by Atwill's good looks, his impeccable diction and—most of all—his brazen intention to seduce.

Also in the cast was Lionel Belmore, who would cross paths with Atwill several times during his film career, in *The Vampire Bat, Son of Frankenstein, The Sun Never Sets* and *Ghost of Frankenstein.*

Back in England, Atwill's three brothers, Clarence, Herbert and Stanley, had all signed up to fight in the Great War. Not wishing to be the black sheep of the family, Lionel decided that he too would join up. In June of 1917, there was a major drive to recruit British nationals who were living abroad in America. Atwill was one of 125 British subjects who signed up on June 12 to join the Royal Flying Corps, and one newspaper reported that the enthusiastic Atwill was one of the very first in the queue to join. But he was never asked to serve. The upper age limit was 25, making Atwill, who was now 32, ineligible. Let us give him the benefit of the doubt and say that he genuinely was willing to fight for his country. It would be churlish to suggest that he knew all along that he would be excused on account of his age.

Atwill enjoyed much of the summer of 1917 on the edge of Lake Michigan. With fellow actors Cathleen Nesbitt and Cecil Yapp, he joined a theatrical company in Milwaukee run by George Foster Platt. Atwill acted in a series of plays including (according to the *New York Times*) Masefield's *Nan*, four plays of Dunsany's, Shaw's *You Never Can Tell*, Wedekind's *Such Is Life* and others. The *Times* felt that Atwill's greatest success in Milwaukee was playing the title role in Arthur Schnitzler's *Anatol*, creating a bourgeois playboy indulging in a series of shallow relationships with women.

A report in the August 1917 *Stage* gives evidence that Atwill was more than just an actor and provides gossip about how he was perceived in his newly adopted country.

> *The Eye of Youth*, a comedy by Charles Huernon and Max Marcin, will be produced August 15 at the Maxine Elliott. Lionel Atwill, husband of Phyllis Relph, has supplied the idea and, with Mr. Marcin's help, has, I hear, a pretty sound play in hand, and one in which his charming wife will have a delightful part. Mr. Atwill's pushfulness and determination will probably bring him a well-deserved reward in this country, for American managers already recognize him as a hustler, and admire him for it. It was only the middle of last season when he landed here.

Also in August he acted in *Mrs. Prudence* for one week at the Paramount Theatre in Asbury Park, New Jersey, with Grace George as his co-star. He followed this by signing up to play alongside her for a season at the Playhouse Theatre for the New York run of *Eve's Daughter* (which lasted for 36 performances, from October to November 1917).

The New York reviewers of *Eve's Daughter* were as impressed by Atwill's performance as had been those in Washington. Ralph Block in the *New York Tribune* wrote:

> The young nobleman is the best-drawn figure in the play. He is full of desires but shrewd in realizing them, and inhibited by several of the more gentle instincts of his class. All this is ably set forth by Lionel Atwill.

The *Herald* was equally fervent, reporting that Atwill:

> Smashed the conventions of the theater so brilliantly that his suave performance seemed almost a perfect cameo.

The play was sufficiently successful that Paramount Studios decide to film it, and the film's producers liked Atwill's performance onstage so much that they wanted him for the screen version. It was his first experience with moving pictures. (See the separate section of this book for details of the film, which was released in February 1918.) To Atwill's disappointment, it seems that his stage role did not transfer well to the screen and he made little impression. As a result, he was less than enthusiastic about the relatively new medium of the cinema and returned to the stage.

In November and December of 1917 he starred opposite Grace George in *L'Elevation*, written by Henri Bernstein. It was a WWI drama and the final act ended with a dramatic scene with just the two of them onstage. Atwill played a patient in a hospital bed, and George a nurse. They profess their love for each other but he has been so badly wounded that he knows he will never recover, and so he encourages her to go back to her husband. No doubt there was not a dry eye in the house. "The acting ... of Lionel Atwill as the lover, is of a very high degree of excellence," reported the *Stage*.

In late November and early December 1917, Atwill once again gave his services for free, helping the war effort one more time. The Stage Women's War Relief put on a show called *Hero Land*, which lasted for 19 days, at the Grand Central Palace and it played almost continually during the days and evenings. Numerous leading actors, actresses, producers, dramatists and others donated their time at no charge. One of the acts was a playlet called *Little Theatre* and it starred Tyrone Power, Sr., Atwill and H.B. Warner. Both John and Lionel Barrymore also lent their talents to the event (though they probably did not appear in the same play that featured Atwill).

January 1, 1918 saw the opening night of a new play starring Atwill called *The Indestructible Wife*, at the Playhouse Theatre in Wilmington, Delaware. According to the *Sun*, it "seems to be written for laughing purposes only." Grace George played the title character, a woman so energetic that she exhausts anyone who comes into contact with her. At the end of January, Atwill stayed with the play when it moved to the Hudson Theatre, New York, with Minna Gombel taking the title role. John Cromwell directed the New York run, and he went on to become a significant Hollywood film director.

For months Atwill appeared in three Ibsen plays. He appeared in several Ibsen plays in England, so he was familiar with the parts. The first was *The Wild Duck*, where he played Hjalmar Ekdal, co-starring with flamboyant Russian star Alla Nazimova. Opening March 11 at the Plymouth Theatre, New York, it played for several weeks.

THE RISE OF LIONEL ATWILL

IF the present season has resulted in bringing any particular performer further into prominence than his fellow players—and it has not been conspicuous for new personalities brought forward—it is probable that Lionel Atwill is entitled to be regarded as the actor thus elevated. At the beginning of the season New York knew little about him; his sole appearance here, exclusive of a brief dip into vaudeville, had been made in a Horace Annesley Vachell comedy called "The Lodger,"

As Hjalmar Ekdal in "The Wild Duck."

which had only a brief life. This season, however, he has played leading rôles in no less than five New York productions—with Grace George in "Eve's Daughter" and "L'Elevation," in "The Indestructible Wife," and now with Mme. Nazimova in "The Wild Duck" and "Hedda Gabler," and with "A Doll's House" yet to come. In nearly all of these productions the honors of the performance have been Atwill's—a fact eloquently testified to by the zeal with which New York's managerial ranks are now seeking his services.

Atwill is English. Like a number of Englishmen who afterward took up the stage as a profession, he began his working career in the office of an architect and surveyor. Having no great flair for the commercial life, however, he began to take up Shakespearean recitations on the side, and built up something of a reputation in and about London as a reciter. That accomplished, he cast an architectural career definitely to the winds, and made his first stage appearance in the rôle of a footman in "The Walls of Jericho," in the Autumn of 1905.

From that he plunged to Ibsen. The company, headed by H. V. Neilson, toured the English provinces, and Atwill played, among other parts, Captain Horster in "An Enemy of the People" and Johann Tönnesen in "Pillars of Society." His next engagement was also in an Ibsen rôle—Dr. Rank, in Courtenay Thorpe's production of "A Doll's House." There followed a long Australian tour, and he returned to London just in time for a part in "Milestones," the first conspicuous success with which he was identified. The London "Milestones" ran for two years, and Atwill stayed with it during that time in the rôle of Arthur Preece.

Next he played Michael Doyle, the Herbert Kelsey part, in the London production of the Hattons' "Years of Discretion," but that piece failed to find in London the favor which it enjoyed in New York, and accordingly he went soon afterward to "The Poor Little Rich Girl," in which he played the father. Like "Years of Discretion," Miss Gates's play was not popular in London, but its unusual qualities attracted the attention of Miss Horniman, and the engagement was accordingly the means of introducing Atwill to the Horniman players. Accordingly he went to Manchester for a season with them, returned to London briefly to play Prinzevalle in Maeterlinck's "Monna Vanna," and then went back to Miss Horniman as her associate director. Here, playing many rôles and staging many plays, he laid the foundation for his future stage work.

There followed another interlude in July of 1915, when Lily Langtry decoyed him from Manchester to play the leading rôle in her production of a piece called "Mrs. Thompson." The play proved a sad failure, and Atwill returned to Manchester, but soon afterward Mrs. Langtry became obsessed with the idea that the failure of "Mrs. Thompson" in London made it the ideal play for America. Atwill accordingly left Manchester again, and this time he did not return. His first appearance in America was made under circumstances as inauspicious as can well be imagined, for "Mrs. Thompson," played for a few weeks somewhere to the north of us, scored a failure even more dismal than that in London. Thereupon Mrs. Langtry entered vaudeville, taking along Atwill and Leo Stark, another member of the "Mrs. Thompson" company. The three played a piece called "Ashes" for the balance of the season.

The appearance in "The Lodger" was made early last season—Atwill co-starring with Julia Ralph, who is Mrs. Atwill. This starring venture, although somewhat ill-advised, had the effect of compelling audiences to think deeply in

an effort to recall where and in what they had previously seen Lionel Atwill and Julia Ralph, and accordingly was beneficial in that it did something to fix their names in the public mind. The play was seen for a week at the Maxine Elliott Theatre, and force of circumstances then compelled its removal to the Bandbox, where it suffered the fate of all other pieces which ever dared defy the inaccessibility of East Fifty-seventh Street.

For the remainder of the season

As George Tesman in "Hedda Gabler."

Atwill was little heard of, but last Summer he played an important part in the interesting répertoire experiment which George Foster Platt made in Milwaukee. Here, with Cathleen Nesbit, Cecil Yapp, and other well-known players, Atwill played in Maeterlinck's "Nan," four plays of Dunsany's, Shaw's "You Never Can Tell," Wedekind's "Such Is Life," and other plays. Probably his greatest Milwaukee success was made as Anatol in the Schnitzler episodes.

News of his work in Milwaukee may have reached Broadway, or—more likely —it may have been just a twist of the wheel of fate which gave him his chance with Grace George early in the season. At all events, he achieved two distinct triumphs in Miss George's productions of "Eve's Daughter" and "L'Elevation," and when Miss George abandoned her répertoire season Atwill was firmly established. At present, in the Hopkins Ibsen productions, Atwill is riveting his position as one of the most valuable stage importations from England in several seasons.

"The Rise of Lionel Atwill" appeared in The *New York Times*, April 14, 1918. The article contains two rare photos of Atwill performing in plays written by Ibsen.

The Wild Duck is another reminder of an aspect of Atwill's repertoire that is often forgotten but was a fundamental part of his stage career—his talent for comedy. In his films, we get occasional flashes of his comic skills, but they are few and far between. The *New York Tribune* thought that,

> Nazimova appeared to advantage, although this is not quite her play. It belongs rather to Lionel Atwill [who gets] … all the funny speeches … Lionel Atwill was exceedingly clever in the part. He played it with fine strokes and broad.

This was followed by *Hedda Gabler,* which opened on April 8 at the Plymouth Theatre and ran for two weeks. Atwill played George Tesman and Alla Nazimova was his wife. The *New York Tribune* was impressed:

> For the second production in the Ibsen series, Arthur Hopkins has again gathered an admirable cast but this time, in spite of the fine playing of Lionel Atwill, Mme. Nazimova took the chief honors … There were 15 curtain calls at the end of the second act … Lionel Atwill succeeded in making Tesman a fool, but no bore, and he commanded sympathy for the character, too, in a splendidly conceived performance.

The *Sun* was equally impressed:

> Mr. Atwill is at present winning honors as the absent-minded professorial George Tesman in *Hedda Gabler*.

The third and last of the Ibsen plays was *A Doll's House.* It opened April 29 at the Plymouth and it too was met with a rapturous response from audiences. The *New York Tribune* reported that:

> The warmth of the applause for *A Doll's House* last night probably indicates that Ibsen will go far on Broadway.

Like the preceding two productions, it played at the Plymouth and co-starred the legendary Nazimova. Atwill played Torvald Helmer, "the average husband" whom she leaves. Co-starring was a young Roland Young, later familiar to fantasy fans for the *Topper* film series. The *Tribune* also reported that Nazimova's performance got better as the play progressed but "curiously enough, Lionel Atwill played on a descending scale …"

A retrospective article two years later in the *Washington Times* stated that Atwill's next production was a fourth Ibsen play, *The Pillars of Society*, but research indicates that, although planned, it was never staged.

By this stage in his American theatrical career, Atwill was established and well known, even though he had only been in the country for a little over two years. The theater critics recognized this. *The Washington Herald* (on June 16, 1918) observed:

His rise to stellar honors after but two seasons in this country has made theatrical history.

A week later the same paper remarked:

Lionel Atwill ... has probably achieved a larger measure of success during the past season in New York than any other actor in the public eye today.

This was quite a claim.

Even this early in his career, Atwill's earnings from the stage were considerable, allowing the *exquisite villain* to enjoy a grand lifestyle. He and Phyllis were able to live in a substantial property in Beechhurst on Long Island, New York, an area that attracted the rich and famous. In June 1918, the *Washington Post* described their home as one of the show places of that delightful countryside and mentioned that Atwill owned a motorboat, while his string of polo ponies was the envy of all the locals. Adding further details about the Atwills' lavish lifestyle, the article went on to inform readers that dog-loving Lionel owned a pack of beagles which he had shipped over from England, and that he was a keen golf player, having won several cups in Long Island tournaments.

A newspaper photo of Atwill in *Another Man's Shoes* (1918)

The next four months—from June to September 1918—saw Atwill getting good reviews again for his role in a "new American comedy" called *Another Man's Shoes,* in which the actor again demonstrated his considerable comic talents. The play was also significant because he was acting alongside a pretty 24-year-old actress named Elsie Mackay. Very soon she would be the cause of much upheaval in the Atwill household. While Atwill's wife Phyllis was busy at home looking after their four-year-old son John, Lionel meanwhile was becoming increasingly interested in his new co-star, Elsie.

In *Another Man's Shoes*, written by Laura Hinkley and Mabel Ferris, Atwill plays a man suffering from a complex case of amnesia. A knock on the head incurred in a train crash has left him thinking that he isn't himself, but instead he believes he is a resident of a small Nebraskan town. After this, complication follows complication. After the play's opening night at the Belasco Theatre in Washington on June 24, the *New York Tribune* wrote:

With Lionel Atwill, an English actor, as Dick, the hero whose muddled brain led to comical complications, the plot unwound itself delightfully.

Atwill's impeccable diction impressed the reviewer of the *Sun*:

There was not a syllable in his role to which he did not give expressive emphasis. It was a pleasure to watch such easy and polished acting.

The same could be said of just about every role he ever took on.

Elsie Mackay played Dick's wife Dora, and Atwill must have been impressed not only by her good looks, but also by her acting skills; she also got glowing reviews. In the romantic scenes where he took her in his arms, Atwill probably enjoyed himself just a little too enthusiastically.

On September 12 *Another Man's Shoes* moved to the 39th Street Theatre in New York. President Woodrow Wilson must have been impressed back in 1916 when he saw Atwill in *Ashes*, because he came along to see Atwill a second time in *Another Man's Shoes*, and later adverts for the play quoted the President as describing it as: "A most unusual and delightful comedy." And the *New York Herald* thought: "Cleverest comedy in a long time. Fits Lionel Atwill perfectly." In the supporting cast was a young William Powell, who Atwill would meet again years later in one of his Hollywood films.

His next play *Tiger! Tiger!* cemented his growing reputation as a handsome but dishonorable womanizer—and his female fans found him irresistible. Barbara Beach in

Motion Picture Classic dubbed him "the breath-taking lover" after seeing the play. It would prove to be his most successful play so far, and it kept him occupied on the stage for well over a year from November 1918 until February 1920.

Tiger! Tiger! told the story of Clive Cooper, a restrained, upper-class Englishman (Atwill) who, when his eyes meet a girl passing him in the street, suddenly finds that his passions rise like a springing tiger. Soon he is in love with the girl, and they have weekly Tuesday evening encounters. But he discovers she is a lowly cook, and from then on things start to go horribly wrong. The girl gives up her beloved in order to save his political career from harm. For his part, he misinterprets her sacrifice as being a rejection, abandons his career and goes off to fight in the war, where he is killed. Corny? Of course, it is deliciously so.

The *Washington Herald* was clearly impressed by Atwill's acting, feeling that the play's hero:

> ... superbly portrayed by Lionel Atwill, is a cold, self-contained Englishman of the ruling caste, with the carefully cultivated tastes of his breed, in whose heart the hidden spark of passion suddenly flames at a glance from the eyes of an illiterate woman passing on the street.

A newspaper photo of Atwill and Frances Starr in *Tiger! Tiger!* (1918)

Playing the girl was Frances Starr, and the *Herald* continued by predicting:

> Her acting and that of Mr. Atwill make the production one that will be long remembered.

The *New York Tribune* enjoyed the fact that Atwill:

> ... was called upon to be a most fearful cad and at the same time expected to win a certain amount of sympathy from the audience.

The Exquisite Villain

Also in the cast was O.P. Heggie, fondly remembered as the blind hermit in *Bride of Frankenstein* (1935).

The play, which opened at New York's Belasco Theatre on the November 11, 1918, achieved some notoriety because certain factions considered its implications of a weekly physical liaison to be sinful. John Daly, Chief Inspector of the New York police, found the play offensive and instructed that charges should be brought against the play's producer, David Belasco, as well as its two stars, Atwill and Starr. All three were charged with "participating in and producing an obscene, indecent and impure drama or play, to wit *Tiger! Tiger!*" Nothing came of the charges, and Atwill, no doubt, thoroughly enjoyed all the publicity, which probably only served to make the play even more popular.

The indecency accusations make one wonder if this isn't another example of some mysterious higher power giving Atwill a warning to watch out. He now had a taste of what it was like to be indicted in an obscenity case. This time, he got off without any damage being done to his career. But unfortunately, 20 years later, he would find out the full consequences of choosing not to heed the warning signs.

As well as acting in *Tiger! Tiger!* Atwill somehow found time for other projects.

He directed a play called *Penny Wise*, an English farce written by Mary Stafford Smith about working-class folk in Lancashire. *Variety* thought it:

> ... a clever piece of theatrical construction, humorous in conception,
> and teaching a little moral.

However, the reviewer found the play far too slow, and concluded, "*Penny Wise* will probably misfire in New York." Atwill arranged an advertising stunt for the play by having an airplane flying over New York dropping pennies. Despite this, the play was not a success and was not around for long.

Belasco offered Atwill the chance to tour all over the States with *Tiger! Tiger!*, but the star had his reservations, as reported in *Variety* in May 1919.

> Mr. Atwill ... fears he is sacrificing his reputation as a popular matinee
> idol by playing what some women consider a "bounder"—one who
> seduces an innocent girl. To friends he has stated that he has been
> in receipt of most astounding letters protesting against his portray-
> ing the leading male part and for this reason he would rather not
> undertake the tour.

After 183 performances at the Belasco theatre, *Tiger! Tiger!* toured around a number of New York theaters, usually staying at each for around two weeks. They included the Standard Theatre in April, then, in May, the Montauk Theatre and the Bronx Opera House. In the summer of 1919, the stars took a break from the play, and Atwill used the time productively by appearing in his fourth motion picture. With summer over, Atwill was back in *Tiger! Tiger!*, this time in September at the Montauk Theatre. In the second half of October, the play could be seen for a month at the Belasco Theatre in Washington. In November it was back at the Standard, and then may have toured for while. Certainly by February 1920, it was being staged in Chicago.

Atwill's theatrical career was going from strength to strength, but his personal life was far more turbulent. His marriage to Phyllis, which since 1913 had been such a happy one, was destined to come to end. "Atwill Divorce Suit" declared an article in *Variety* on October 24, 1919.

> Lionel Atwill has been sued for divorce by his wife, Phyllis Relph, of Amityville, Long Island, who asks $50 a week alimony and the custody of their five-year-old child. She has been receiving that allowance from her husband regularly and now alleges he was guilty of an indiscretion with an unnamed woman on July 1, 1919, at the Murray Hill Hotel.

A shipping passenger list tells us that in November 1919 Phyllis sailed back to England, taking young John with her. In Britain in 1919 a lot of stigma was attached to divorce so, even though Phyllis had done no wrong, it cannot have been easy for her to make the drastic decision of taking her son away from his father and returning to face possible disapproval and embarrassment back home. Clearly, she could not forgive Lionel for his *indiscretion* and had decided to walk out on him.

That "unnamed woman" was almost certainly Elsie Mackay, his co-star in *Another Man's Shoes.* We can assume that Elsie was the temptation that caused the rift, because for

Another newspaper photo of Atwill and Frances Starr in *Tiger! Tiger!* (1918)

Atwill's next stage production, he chose her to be his co-star again. This new production would be a milestone in Atwill's career. In fact, it may well be the highpoint in a career that lasted more than 40 years. Its impact on critics and audiences in the early 1920s cannot be overstated, and yet today it is almost completely forgotten. The play was *Deburau.*

Chapter 4
Lionel Atwill's Greatest Triumph

Atwill's next theatrical venture was a play entitled *Deburau*, and it deserves its own chapter. For one thing, it may well represent the greatest triumph of his entire career—on both stage and screen. The play also deserves highlighting because it is almost completely forgotten today, yet in the 1920s it was a sensation. Atwill was acclaimed by the critics as one of the greatest stage actors of all time. It is time to put the record straight, look back on the play and put its importance into some kind of perspective.

The year 1920 would also prove to be eventful for Atwill in other ways. "Lionel Atwill Weds Miss Elsie MacKay," announced the *Sun* and the *New York Herald*. He had married his co-star from *Another Man's Shoes* on Saturday, February 7. The ceremony took place in Chicago, where Atwill was performing in *Tiger! Tiger!* The newspaper reported that he had been divorced from Phyllis "just 365 days," which means that he had petitioned for divorce exactly one year earlier and was legally free to re-marry.

Elsie Mackay was 26 when she married Atwill. She was born in 1894 in Roebourne in Western Australia. She first played on the New York stage in 1916 in *Grumpy*, starring Cyril Maude. When Atwill met her during *Another Man's Shoes*, he was probably not only impressed by her good looks, but also found they had something in common—they could enjoy reminiscing together about Australia, a country which must have made a huge impression on the young actor when he had toured in plays there for a year and a half in 1910 and 1911. Elsie had also scored successes in other New York plays, including *As You Like it* (1919), *Clarence* and *Poldekin* (1920).

(Note: There were *two* Elsie Mackays. Many sources, including many reputable ones, confuse them. The other one (1892 to 1928) was a British actress and pioneering aviatrix. She was also known as Poppy Wyndham. Because she starred in a number of British silent films, she is often mistakenly assumed to be the same Elsie Mackay who acted on the American stage with Atwill.)

After Lionel and Elsie married, they presumably took a honeymoon. Where they went is unknown and their whereabouts, for the next eight months, remain a mystery. Research has found no records of them acting on any stage, nor any records of entries on passenger lists which might indicate they went abroad for a long vacation. Perhaps they spent several months touring around America. What we do know is that toward the end of 1920, they were preparing for their next theatrical project.

Atwill chose Elsie to co-star alongside him in *Deburau,* which was to be produced by David Belasco. Belasco, who had previously starred Atwill in *Tiger! Tiger!,* was a major player in the New York theater scene. Not only did he produce, direct and write many plays, but also owned a number of theaters. He was a highly innovative talent, and a new play by Belasco was always an eagerly awaited event. Belasco's teaming with Atwill was significant in both their careers. The partnership began in late 1918 with *Tiger! Tiger!* and continued—with *Deburau* and two other successful plays—for five years until late 1923. The pair became friends as well as just professional associates and in 1925 Belasco referenced "my very good friend, Mr. Lionel Atwill." The Atwill-

Belasco pairing was mutually rewarding in other ways too—it may also have offered their personal lives some fringe benefits. Belasco had an apartment above his New York theater and in it he had a secret *priest's hole* in which he no doubt could hide young ladies when necessary. This was discovered when the theater was restored in 1980. He also had a peephole that allowed him to spy on the auditorium. It was rumored (and reported in Mank's *Hollywood's Maddest Doctors*) that he had a second peephole that allowed him to spy on the women's dressing room, and from what we know of Atwill in later life, there is a pretty good chance that it wasn't just Belasco who enjoyed a sly ogle at the disrobing ladies.

In the play-within-a-play of *Deburau*, the title character (Atwill) plays Pierrot, who murders an old man.

Belasco had a well-calculated strategy to ensure that *Deburau* would have a maximum chance of success when it was performed in front of the discerning New York audiences. It was a strategy in three phases. First, he would try out the play in an out-of-town theater to gauge audience reaction well away from the prying eyes of New York's theater reviewers. This he did with little ballyhoo at the Ford's Grand Opera House in Baltimore, where the play had its opening night December 7, 1920. It played for a few nights and this offered a chance to make some revisions, based on audience reactions, and iron out any technical problems.

A week later came the second stage in Belasco's strategy: The play would be performed in front of the slightly more sophisticated audiences in Washington, D.C. More minor changes were probably made to the production, hopefully ensuring that when the Broadway critics finally encountered it, everything would be fine-tuned.

Even before *Deburau* opened in Washington, there were eager notices about its imminent arrival. The *Washington Times* wrote in late November 1920:

> … one notes that Lionel Atwill, whose support of Frances Starr in *Tiger! Tiger!* was so brilliant, is coming to the Shubert Belasco in a comedy … called *Deburau* and it said to offer Mr. Atwill an excellent opportunity to make a successful start as a star.

Theatergoers were intrigued: a new Belasco production was always keenly anticipated, but what an odd title for a play. What could it mean? How was it pronounced? What would the play be about?

Tormented by the ghost of his victim, Pierrot kills himself.

A week later, the *Washington Herald* revealed some more advance information about the play and whetted theatergoers' appetites further:

> Elsie Mackay is leading woman for Lionel Atwill in *Deburau*, a comedy from the French [writing] of Sacha Guitry, adapted by Granville Barker, in which Mr. Atwill will be seen at the Belasco Theater next week, immediately preceding his engagement at the Belasco Theater, New York.

A day or so later the *Washington Times* explained that Atwill would be performing the title role that had been performed successfully in France by the play's author, Sacha Guitry. Atwill's many fans will have been excited to read that the play "will reveal his artistry in an entirely new light." It also gave details of the cast, which included a young Sidney Toler, whom Atwill would encounter many years later in two Charlie Chan movies. Farther down the cast list was one Fred Bickel, who later changed his name to Fredric March. The *Times* informed its readers that the play was based on the career of real-life French actor Jean-Gaspard Deburau, a successful pantomime artist.

Teasing ads were taken out in the Washington papers to entice readers to see the play.

> Tonight at 8.20 precisely … Owing to the elaborate nature of the production, it is imperative that the curtain rise at 8.20.

And:

Lionel Atwill

Every happiness, which the theater holds for those who love it, is to be found in *Deburau*. It has surging drama, delicious humor, exquisite music, poetical beauties, charm and innumerable surprises.

And:

Scenically the prologue and four acts will be a continuation of elaborate and atmospheric pictures on a scale equaled by nothing Mr. Belasco has done in years.

· L I O N E L · A T W I L L

Mr. Atwill, Shown Here in the Costume of Jean-Gaspard Deburau, Will Make His First Appearance in New York as a Belasco Star Next Thursday Night.

A cartoon portrait of Lionel Atwill from *Deburau*, published in the *New York Times*, December, 19, 1920.

At last, on December 13, the play opened at the Shubert-Belasco Theater in Washington. Next day, Belasco, Atwill and his new wife Elsie must have waited with bated breath to read the newspaper reviews and see what the critics made of *Deburau*.

"Triumph for Atwill," proclaimed the *Washington Times*. The paper admired the lavishness of the production, the skill of the cast and the poetry in the rhythm of its lines, but the reviewer did have a few reservations about the play as a whole. There was, however, nothing but praise for the star.

Lionel Atwill, through voice and gesture, gives a masterly interpretation to the role ... His reading of the rhythmic lines is a delight, and his portrayal of the conflicting emotions of the once great actor, now deposed, is flawless.

The *Washington Herald* wrote of the "hypnotic glamour" of the play that:

... introduces as a Belasco star, one Lionel Atwill, a young man with rather more than the usual share of actorial afflatus ...

(This verbose critic's vocabulary probably had many of the newspaper's readers reaching for the dictionary: afflatus is a divine creative impulse or inspiration.) The *Herald*,

Deburau is deeply in love with Marie, played by Atwill's second wife Elsie Mackay.

too, was not without reservations, feeling that the tragic scenes lacked "the majesty or grandeur of tragedy."

One feature enjoyed by 1920s audience members was a play-within-a-play device, whereby a mock stage was built on the actual stage, with members of the cast standing before it as if they are members of an audience watching a play. Also very effective was the dialogue. Most of the play is executed in verse with an irregular meter and rhyme, a technique that lends its dialogue a lot of simple charm.

The plot of the play revolves around Deburau, the successful Parisian pantomime artist, who is adored by his public. He is a stage Pierrot, with a sad, white-painted face, and a loose white costume. Although happily married and with a son, he falls in love with one of his many female admirers, Marie Duplessis (Elsie Mackay). She lures him away from his contented family life. But one day he finds Marie in the arms of a new lover, and the shock almost breaks his heart. Years pass and Deburau is a broken man who has abandoned his acting profession. But later, he finds within himself a desire to return to the stage and recreate his former glories. To his dismay he is hissed from the stage and is completely crushed. He realizes his career is over. However, all is not lost; he is reunited with his son who, now a young man, wishes to follow in his father's footsteps, carrying on the great name of Deburau on the stage.

This simplified summary of the plot shows the astonishing extent to which *Deburau*, Atwill's greatest triumph, is full of extraordinary parallels with his real life. The irony of some of these parallels cannot have been lost on Atwill himself. But other parallels to events that were yet to happen to him once again give cause to wonder if some strange workings of Fate were somehow involved.

For example, both Atwill and Deburau were successful actors, and both were happily married with a son. A female admirer tempts both away from a life of married bliss. A double irony exists in the play, as the same woman who, in real life, actually did cause Atwill's marriage to fall apart plays the temptress. All of this Atwill would have been aware of, and probably found some amusement in the similarities. What he couldn't have known is that the similarities didn't stop there.

Atwill would have been amazed to learn that a few years later he would indeed find his beloved in the arms of another. And he would have been horrified to learn that, a decade later, he would (metaphorically at last) be hissed from the stage when a court case destroyed his career. He would indeed become "the once great actor, now deposed." And, like Deburau, he found within himself the desire to combat this by recreating his former triumphs, returning to the Broadway stage in 1943. The saddest irony, however, is the parallel that never occurred—unlike Deburau, Atwill never did enjoy a happy reunion with his estranged son John, who died in his twenties in WWII.

Perhaps, given what happened to Atwill years later, he should have paid heed to a brief scene in *Deburau* in which a palm reader called Madame Rabouin reads his future:

> Deburau: I've a *wonderful* future … if nothing goes very wrong with it.
> Madame Rabouin: What a remarkably interesting man! So full of charm. I'm sorry he's coming to grief … written indelibly in his palm. Poor fellow!

A close-up of the legendary ring, made up of three intertwined bands, which Atwill wore throughout his career and can be seen in all his films. [Photo courtesy of Tony Atwill]

The play's last night in Washington was December 18. Finally, *Deburau* made its way to New York, no doubt after a few more minor adjustments were made to action and dialogue. It opened on Thursday December 23 at the Belasco Theater. This was the moment for which Atwill had been waiting. This, he hoped, would be the play that would transform him into a major Broadway star.

The *New York Tribune* was impressed:

> … there are moments when *Deburau* seems a great play, moments in which a thing now dead, which we call the grand manner, is animated so eloquently that it seems to be again the one true and perfect mood of the theater.

The reviewer was greatly stirred by Atwill's performance:

> Lionel Atwill without question gives a great performance, a performance, it seems to us, which is second to nothing seen in New York

in recent years except the Richard III of John Barrymore. Atwill is always graceful, eloquent when opportunity is offered, and in the final scene, above all others, profoundly and deeply moving.

The review continued by saying that there were occasions when the play's rhyming verse was distracting, but then resumed its praise of Atwill.

The greatest glory of the evening belongs to Mr. Atwill. [His performance] is actually one of those stirring and extraordinary things that happen in the theater now and again.

Other papers were equally complimentary. The *New York Times* thought that Atwill gave "a performance of distinguished beauty." The *Globe* said he gave "a memorable performance."

Atwill must have been thrilled. These were just the type of notices he had hoped for. He had invested a lot of his time and energy into *Deburau*, and it must have been satisfying to see it all paying off. The sheer number of lines that he had to learn must have been daunting during rehearsals. In fact, the play contains the single longest speech of Atwill's entire career. It's a wonderful scene in which he talks to his son and gives him advice on acting.

The love scenes between Deburau and Marie are a delight. Atwill's film career gave him few chances to play the romantic lover (unless you count his mauling of Kathleen Burke in *Murders in the Zoo* to be romantic), but in the early 1920s he was very much a matinee idol. In *Deburau*, it would have been a joy to see and hear him in throes of rapture as he idolizes Marie:

The has-been actor gives advice to his son.

At last I've discovered
Why one fine day,
Long ago, I was hurled
Into this quaint world.
Nobody ever told me why.
I've been guessing and guessing ever since;
And what is the use of life unless we
Know that one thing, unless Fate has uncovered
Our destiny?
But now that I know—
why, how simple it all is!
I was born
To love you, my dear.

Lionel Atwill

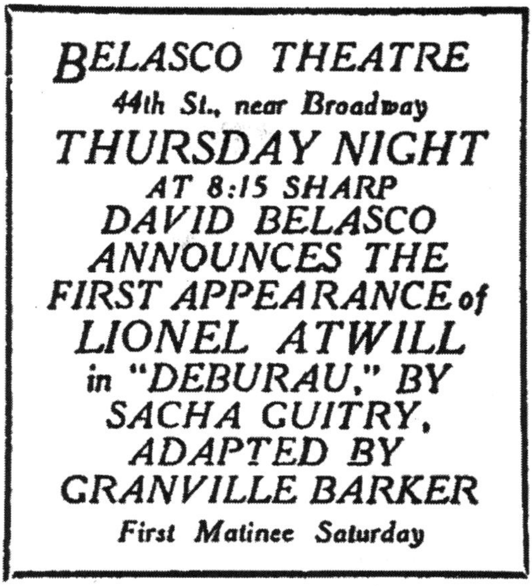

Deburau contains a number of scenes that greatly affected 1920s audiences. For example, in the scene where he is booed and hissed by his audience, he turns to address them. Although he is a mime artist, he attempts to speak but his grief so chokes him up that he cannot. So using a few simple gestures, he tells his audience that he is ill and cannot go on, and that he has performed on the stage for the last time. He asks their forgiveness and says goodbye. The stage direction says it all: "By this time, there is dead silence in the house. Deburau's tears are falling."

But perhaps the play's most outstanding sequence comes at the end, when Deburau speaks to his son, giving him advice about acting. He tells him all he has learned, tells him how to conquer stage fright, advises him on how to make specific gestures and much more. This long speech is Atwill's *tour de force*, a touching and charming discourse. Here is a short extract from it, as Deburau tries to describe the experience of being on the stage:

BELASCO THEATRE
44th St., near Broadway
THURSDAY NIGHT
AT 8:15 SHARP
DAVID BELASCO
ANNOUNCES THE
FIRST APPEARANCE of
LIONEL ATWILL
in "DEBURAU," BY
SACHA GUITRY,
ADAPTED BY
GRANVILLE BARKER
First Matinee Saturday

And the triumph of triumphs, to hold
A whole house breathless, to mould
Them to tears or to laughter!
Would I sell that power for a king's
Ransom? Picture it now.
The curtain has risen.
For a moment after,
Silence. Row upon row,
So silent you'd swear you could hear the shakings
Of the earrings that bedizen
That lady there.
Or the manager as he absconds with your share
Of the evening's takings.
All of a sudden you fling
Across the footlights to them
Some trivial thing
That takes their fancy.
Then it begins.
A whisper they sway to, a rhythm.
First it's only a smile you can see,
Like a ripple that has just
Been raised by that tiny gust

Of laughter. But the laughter will keep growing
Till a gale of it is blowing;
A gale that spins
Away with it, amid the silence it has broken
Into a thousand pieces, every token
Of dullness, of care,
Of trouble, of despair.
That's what they come hoping for…

Throughout his career, Atwill was drawn again and again to macabre subjects. He had already starred in stage versions of *The Invisible Man* and *The Lodger*. There was also a dark element in *Deburau*. Its play-within-a-play, performed on the mimic-stage, was an old pantomime called *Old Clo'*. It told the tale of an old clothes merchant, murdered and robbed by Pierrot to acquire the riches he needs to woo his beloved Columbine. Conscience-stricken, Pierrot sees the ghost of the old man and in a frenzy of terror stabs and kills himself. A dramatic still survives from this scene, a splendidly gruesome image of Pierrot in the act of stabbing himself, with the ghost looking on, gloating that he got his revenge.

A portrait still of Atwill taken at the time of *Deburau*.

The still is also of interest because it is the earliest image that shows the ring that Atwill always wore on the little finger of his left hand. If one looks carefully, the ring, made up of three intertwined bands, can be seen again and again in his films. The history of this ring and the story of where Atwill acquired it are unknown, but the fact that he wore it throughout his life suggests it must have had some special significance to him—a significance now lost. (It can't be a coincidence that his brother Stanley also always wore a ring on the same finger.) That Lionel wore it on his little finger seems to have been the inspiration for his nickname *Pinky*, a slang name for that finger. Another suggestion for the nickname, but which seems less likely, is that it came about because he may have had red hair when he was young.

The play went from strength to strength, as did Atwill's reputation. By January 1921, ads for *Deburau* in the New York newspapers featured his name in large letters that were twice the size of the font used for the play's title. Audience attendance was good through all of January, February and March.

On the evening of March 6, the Drama League of New York City gave a dinner "in honor of the 10 who have contributed most to the art of the theater in the last year." Atwill was included among the 10 for his work in *Deburau*. Others include Dudley Diggs, David Belasco and black actor Charles Gilpin (whose inclusion in the list caused some controversy). This was a big event, and 1,000 guests crammed into the Hotel McAlpine for this very popular occasion. The *Washington Herald* described Atwill and the other nine recipients as "the 10 entitled to wear the laurel crown of supreme achievement for the year."

By April 1921, *Deburau* was still going strong, and a theater reviewer in *Variety* named Lait relished the opportunity of being able to review it a second time, five months after his first review. He was ecstatic.

> *Deburau* is probably the finest play that has been done since Shakespeare died. Surely it is the finest done on this continent since the Bard laid down his quill.

He was just as gushing—in fact more so—about Atwill.

> Lionel Atwill … is excellent … he has the physique, the voice, the respectful touch of the artist and two bewilderingly eloquent hands, which, together with his every fiber of vehemence and his every vibration of artistic ecstasy, he throws into the personification of this egotistical, human, sympathetic lover, father, player, hero and clown.

This outpouring of praise continued:

> Atwill at once and beyond cavil justifies his presentation as a star and the trust in him to execute a role destined to become historic and carry him with it into the pauperized cabinet of recent contributors to the lovely things of the stage.

Deburau continued to be a great success throughout April and May, but Atwill did find time to be involved in some other ventures. Unusually, he was one of the financial backers of an operation to salvage a boat called *Isis* that had sunk off the coast of Florida. This was reported in the press on April 1, but whether or not anything of value was retrieved is unknown.

Meanwhile, the theater accolades kept coming. On the April 24, 1921, the Society of Arts and Sciences staged a dinner at the Hotel Biltmore to honor about 20 people associated with the stage. Channing Pollock acted as chairman and those honored included Atwill, as well as D.W. Griffith, Elsie Ferguson, Frances Starr and others.

Atwill took one day off from *Deburau* to appear for one night at the Equity Annual Show at the Metropolitan Opera House on May 1. The show featured a Shakespearian Pageant, which was made up of short scenes from a variety of Shakespeare plays, with numerous well-known actors appearing. What was Atwill's choice of role? Well, no

The only known photo of Atwill playing the leading role in *Hamlet* (1921).

less a figure than the tragic Dane himself, Hamlet. Laurette Taylor played his Ophelia. John Barrymore, Lionel Barrymore, George Arliss, Reginald Denny, Edmund Lowe and Norma Talmadge were among the many stars that gave up their time freely to support the cause of raising funds to assist actors less fortunate than themselves. Even Mrs. Atwill—still using the name Elsie Mackay—was involved, performing in an extract from *The Winter's Tale*. What a shame that no one thought to film the evening. Even without sound, it would be thrilling to see Atwill in full flow as Hamlet.

The first week of June 1921 was to be the last time *Deburau* would be performed onstage. Belasco and Atwill immediately began work on their next collaboration. Incredibly, *Deburau*, the play whose emotional power had moved audiences to tears, and whose central performance by Atwill had been regarded as one of the great theater performances of all time, gradually became only a thing of memory. The play, as far as can be established, has never been revived. By the time Atwill became a Hollywood star it was largely a forgotten entity. Certainly, if one asks a selection of his fans today, most of them will have never heard of *Deburau*.

There are, however, several footnotes connected with the play's descent into obscurity.

In February 1923, Belasco announced that he had made a deal with Warner Bros. to let them make a film version of *Deburau*, with Atwill starring. The film was eventually released in 1924 as *The Lover of Camille* ... but Atwill was nowhere to be seen. Very probably, he turned the part down—he knew from previous film experiences that an outstanding stage role does not necessarily transfer successfully to the silent screen. Instead, Monte Blue took on the title role. When Atwill saw a review of the film in the *New York Times*, he must have been secretly pleased by what he read:

> It will hardly appeal to those who witnessed the delicate, exquisite performance given by Lionel Atwill ... [the film version is] a vague and artless reflection of the superb Belasco production.

It would be fascinating to see the Monte Blue film, to get just a hint of what the stage version may have been like. But frustratingly it seems to be a lost film.

From the mid-1920s onwards, Atwill made several appearances on radio. In May 1928 it occurred to him that he could revive *Deburau* for this medium, bringing it to a whole new audience who had not seen it onstage seven years earlier. An hour-long

A distinguished portrait of the handsome Atwill probaby from the late teens or early 1920s
[Photo courtesy of Tony Atwill]

The Exquisite Villain

version of the play was devised and it was broadcast on station WGY on Sunday, May 27. Whether or not a recording of it survives is not known—if it ever turns up, it may well be the closest we will ever get to experiencing Atwill in his greatest role.

Another footnote to the history of *Deburau* is even more tantalizing. Atwill, having successfully adapted *Deburau* for the radio, now devised a way of bringing it to the screen. In 1928 he made a short seven-minute film for Fox-Movietone in which he recreated the play's most famous scene. The short is commonly known as *Lionel Atwill in The Actor's Advice to His Son* but an alternate title is *Deburau—Message to His Son*. When it was released in 1928, *Variety* enjoyed it:

> … as Mr. Atwill does it, the short cannot fail to interest an audience … Set in the bare stage of a theater, with the curtain dropped, cutting off the auditorium, Deburau speaks to his unseen boy, giving him a lecture on the elements and essentials of acting ... His delivery is beyond comment, while his screen appearance and presence for this role are … splendid.

So far, it has not been possible to trace this film.

Finally, those interested in getting a flavor of the character of Deburau may wish to watch *Les Enfants Du Paradis*, the 1945 classic French film directed by Marcel Carné, in which Deburau was the central figure.

Chapter 5
Broadway 1921 to 1925

After the giddy triumph of *Deburau*, which was last staged on June 6, 1921, it seems that Lionel and Elsie decided to take some time off from the stage during the summer. Even so, they still found time to support a worthy cause. On July 24, the *New York Tribune* reported on a Near East Relief benefit performance at the Rosemary Theatre, Huntingdon, on Long Island. Its purpose was to raise funds to help some 200,000 people in the Near East (an area today generally called the Middle East) who had been displaced after the war, and who had not been able to return home since. Atwill acted alongside his wife Elsie Mackay "in an act from Rostrand's *Romancers*." The occasion is just one of many examples that demonstrate the decent and generous aspects of Atwill's character—he was always willing to give his time for free to support a worthy cause.

A week later, the Atwills were spotted enjoying their summer break. "Stage Folks Flock to Seashore for the Breeze," reported the *Washington Times* at the end of July, and then gave a list of various actors who were seen taking the sea air at Atlantic City, including Lionel and Elsie.

In mid-August, the couple were back onstage again, albeit only briefly. For two days, August 12 and 13, they appeared at the Rosemary Theatre, Huntingdon, Long Island in a Dramatic Festival. It included some ballet, some Shakespeare and a prologue featuring Lionel, Elsie and several others. Such was the pull of this event that special trains were added so that New York's avid theatergoers could attend.

This remarkable make-up of Atwill in *The Grand Duke* (1921) convinced some audience members that they were seeing an understudy.

With a happy summer behind them, it was now time for the Atwills to get back to work. David Belasco had been working on another adaptation of a play by the author of *Deburau*, Sacha Guitry. This one was called *The Grand Duke,* and much of September and October must have been spent rehearsing for it. Belasco adopted his usual strategy

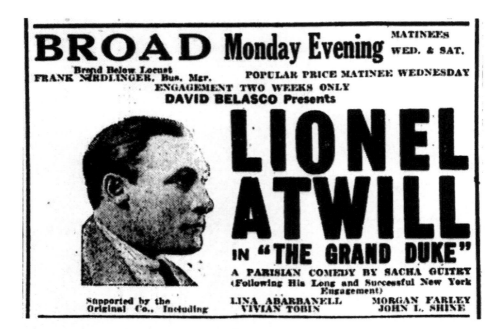

BROAD Monday Evening MATINEES WED. & SAT.

Broad Below Locust
FRANK NIRDLINGER, Bus. Mgr.   POPULAR PRICE MATINEE WEDNESDAY

ENGAGEMENT TWO WEEKS ONLY

DAVID BELASCO Presents

LIONEL ATWILL

IN **"THE GRAND DUKE"**

A PARISIAN COMEDY BY SACHA GUITRY
(Following His Long and Successful New York Engagement)

Supported by the
Original Co., Including

LINA ABARBANELL   MORGAN FARLEY
VIVIAN TOBIN   JOHN L. SHINE

---

of trying out the play in a provincial theater first, and it opened on October 17 at Ford's Theatre in Baltimore. Two weeks later, on November 1, it opened at New York's Lyceum Theatre on West 45th Street.

The play is a comedy in three acts and Atwill played Grand Duke Feodor Michaelovitch, a Russian nobleman who has been forced by political upheavals to flee to Paris. Here he takes pleasure in trying to arrange marriages for everyone around him, including a son whom he previously knew nothing about. Much amusement is derived from the way that the Grand Duke does his best to control his son's destiny.

Many critics singled out one scene in particular for high praise. The *New York Times* wrote:

> Only from Paris could have come that final and philosophic breakfast scene, where the haughty old émigré toys with his simple meal of Italian sausages, Russian caviar, French celery, brandied peaches from Spain and tea from India, the while he administers the social and romantic affairs of his son with justice and wisdom and humor.

Photos of Atwill in the title role appeared in some of the newspapers. At first glance, it is hard to believe that this lean, elderly gentleman, with streaks of gray in his hair, really is Lionel Atwill. He wore a false forehead and a wig for the part, which made the shape of his head much thinner and added about an inch to his height. Some subtle eye make-up further disguised his true appearance. As a result, several members of the paying public did not recognize him in the part. The *New York Tribune* reporter managed a quick interview with him during the play's interval and remarked to him that they hardly recognized him.

Atwill: It is a good make-up, isn't it? When we were out on the road, one woman went to the box-office and demanded her money back because she said she came to see Lionel Atwill and had seen an understudy play the part. "Nonsense," she replied when they assured her that I had played that Grand Duke that afternoon. "I think I know Mr. Atwill. Why, I've known him for years!"

The reporter, Harriette Underhill, was apparently more than a little excited to be finally in the presence of the great Broadway star, whom she described as "that very attractive gentleman."

The *Evening World* was extremely impressed with Atwill's performance:

A cartoon of Atwill from *The Grand Duke* appeared in the *New York Times* on November 13.

In this delightful Parisian comedy by Sacha Guitry, new honors were won by Lionel Atwill, whose Duke proved better than his Deburau ... Mr. Atwill was always the aristocrat of good taste and good manners, acting with admirable poise and skill.

The *New York Tribune* theater reviewer so enjoyed the role that he could not resist writing a long piece just about Atwill:

Lionel Atwill, as you know, is pre-eminent in the impersonation of distinguished men of 40. His mien and bearing are notable and quietly conspicuous, and he dominates all his roles by a sure urbanity, no matter how imposing their contents. Nobel Earls, members of Parliament, envoys, plenipotentiaries, major generals, a Pope, perhaps, or a Secretary of Commerce, beat upon him no light so fierce he cannot reflect it back. He treads with security the precarious rim between mere elegance and real distinction, and I suspect that he could have, the other day, paraded on Fifth Avenue in the place of Admiral Lord

This 1922 newspaper ad shows the extent to which Atwill's name could pull in audiences.

Beatty, and that few among the so-called cheering multitude would have hushed their, in a manner of speaking, hosannas, because they would not have discovered the counterfeit.

The same reviewer especially enjoyed some of Atwill's individual lines, such as, "I never feel what I think, and I never think what I feel"; and "Is she telling the truth? No. Why? Because she is a woman."

The Grand Duke kept Atwill busy throughout the latter part of 1921 and into early 1922. One short diversion took place on the December 9 when a group called Drama Comedy put on an afternoon social event at the Hotel Astor, in which Atwill was invited to be one of the guests of honor. A one-act play was staged as well as some singing.

The Grand Duke continued at the Lyceum until the third week of February 1922, after which it toured around a number of provincial theatres, including the Montauk Theatre in Brooklyn for one week, two weeks at the Broad Theatre in Philadelphia and finally (from April 3) at the National Theatre in Washington, D.C. A reviewer for the *Washington Times* singled out the breakfast scene for praise:

Does anyone recall a more intense scene of drama than the opening of the last act of *The Grand Duke*—with no one on the stage but Lionel Atwill and his breakfast? Here was drama reduced to highest nutri-

A *New York Times* ad for "Mr." Lionel Atwill's appearance in *The White-Faced Fool*

ment—the conflict between an epicure and his spices which was as packed with thrills as a conflict between a dope fiend and his vices. Atwill gave as much thought and deliberation to the dressing of his salad as Ziegfeld does to undressing his chorus.

Once again, it seems such a crime that no one thought to record this great scene on film (although, of course this was before the days of sound film). How unsatisfactory that today all we can do is imagine what the scene must have been like.

On April 24, 1922, Theoria (a club which supported the theater) held its annual Easter breakfast in the grand ballroom of the Hotel Astor. Yet again, Atwill found himself being invited along as one of the guests of honor. Other guests of honor included his wife Elsie Mackay, theater producer Earl Carroll, actor Harry Davenport, actresses Doris Kenyon and Blanche Yurka, playwright Channing Pollock and many others.

A few days later, on April 28, The New York League of Girls' Clubs held a Spring Carnival Fashion Show. The show followed a celebrity tea in the afternoon with Mr. and Mrs. Lionel Atwill, Adele Astaire (sister of Fred) and other guests of distinction. It was another example of Lionel and Elsie giving up their time for a worthy cause.

A month later, Atwill was investing his own money in what he considered to be another deserving cause. The Actors' Equity Fund, still in relatively early days, decided to raise money to run its own theater, and they took out a one-year lease on the Forty-Eighth Street Theatre in New York. Atwill was one of the 40 actors and actresses who gathered the money, so clearly he had amassed significant savings by this stage in his career. George Arliss was one of the other names giving financial support to the venture.

June saw Atwill taking a risk by temporarily forsaking the so-called legitimate stage and appearing once again in vaudeville theaters. He was nervous about the effect on his career of returning to vaudeville and asked David Belasco's advice (and in fact his permission too, since the actor was part of Belasco's company). The producer was all for it:

> Go and win another branch of the profession for yourself. Get another string to your bow … Give them your best in vaudeville, for the audiences are just as exacting as any who saw you in the Belasco and Lyceum theaters.

With this moral support, Atwill seized the opportunity. He assumed the role of producer again, and arranged for a new one-act sketch called *The White-Faced Fool*

Atwill with his wife and co-star Elsie Mackay in *The White-Faced Fool* **(1922), from a photo in** *Vanity Fair*

to be specially written for him. The author was Edgar Allan Woolf—possibly best known as the co-author of the script for *The Wizard of Oz* (1939). Craftily, Atwill chose to capitalize on his great success in *Deburau*, presenting himself once again as a white-faced clown. He was remunerated very handsomely; *Variety* reported that, "the Keith office has given the Belasco star 12 or 15 consecutive weeks … at $2,000 weekly."

The story of *The White-Faced Fool* concerned a clown named Davazet who despairs of ever giving a good performance onstage because he is so troubled by suspicions that his wife is cheating on him. He is driven into frenzy when he sees her staring at him heartlessly from the audience. The action of the play requires his character to strangle another character, but in his passion he chokes his victim with such force that he thinks he really has killed him. Later, he is in his dressing room, quaking with terror and remorse. He is astounded when the *victim* and his wife burst in and explain that everything was all a trick designed to inspire him to find the necessary emotions to give a great performance—a performance that is hailed by all as a triumph.

The sketch first played at B.F. Keith's Palace Theatre in New York in June 1922. Later it played at two other theaters owned by the same company in Washington and Philadelphia, as well as short spells at the Majestic, Orpheum, Royal and Riverside theaters, keeping Atwill busy until late September.

New York Times, November 29, 1922

ACTORS TO AID WET FIGHT.

Many Volunteer for Concert In Apollo Theatre Sunday.

It was announced last night that the Theatrical Committee of the Association Against the Prohibition Amendment, of which Daniel Frohman is Chairman, will give a performance Sunday night at the Apollo Theatre in support of the association's campaign against the prohibition amendment.

The entertainers will include Lionel Atwill, Frank Tinney, Ernest Ball, Eddie Dowling, Eddie Buzzell, Bert Levy, Lou Holtz, Mosconi Brothers, Savoy and Brennan, Paul Whiteman's Collegians, Jack Donohue, Dorothy Smoller, Paul Nelva, Gus Lessis, Edna Morn, Mr. and Mrs. Bert Lahr, Edna Fay, Frankie Heath, Leipsig, Eva Clarke, MacDonald, Watson and company in a scene from "Hunky Dory," Thelma Harvey, Dora Dubby and a host of others.

Will Morrissey will act as master of ceremonies. The array of artists, the announcement from the association says, "offers a sure indication of the opposition which Volsteadism has aroused among members of the theatrical profession."

Another instance of Atwill giving freely of his time and talent to help a cause, this time a benefit against the Prohibition Amendment, November 29, 1922.

The newspapers were enthusiastic. The *Evening Public Ledger*:

> Lionel Atwill is a Big Keith Hit ... Dramatic Star Offers Gripping Playlet—Lionel Atwill ... was the outstanding hit of the bill ... Nine curtain calls and a demand for a speech attested to the appreciation of the audience.

Variety said:

> Mr. Atwill achieved the miraculous in this vaudeville debut. He is giving a performance equaling at least anything that raised his presence among the highest on the dramatic stage.

The *Washington Herald* liked Atwill's performance and commented on one unusual facet:

> He also carries into his present characterization some of the peculiar neighing sounds that marked his performance in *The Grand Duke*.

Alas, today we can only imagine what that might have sounded like. *Variety* reported that when *The White-Faced Fool* played at the Royal Theater, "the star was accorded an ovation at the final curtain."

At the very end of September 1922, Atwill, ever the epicure, found another cause to support—this time it was the campaign against Prohibition! The theatrical profession was generally against this ban on the sale and production of alcohol, and Atwill was one of many entertainers who volunteered his services for free to appear at the Apollo Theater in New York to raise funds to fight the ban.

After one final commitment in 1922—where he gave a speech at the Molly Pitcher Club luncheon on October 17—Atwill decided he needed a long break. His bank balance was healthy after three months of continuous playing in vaudeville, and he was able to treat himself and Elsie to a lavish excursion. Back in late July, the *New York Tribune* reported that:

Lionel Atwill and Elsie MacKay in _The Comedian_ (1923) [White Studio/Billy Rose Theatre Division, The New York City Public Library for the Performing Arts]

Lionel Atwill

Caricatures of Atwill and Elsie Mackay from *The Comedian* appeared in the March 23, 1923 edition of the *New York Times*.

> Lionel Atwill and his wife, Elsie MacKay, are sailing for the Orient, to spend several months in Hawaii and China.

However, Atwill continued in *The White-Faced Fool* until late September, and it seems that the voyage was postponed for a few months. What a memorable trip it must have been. It would be fascinating to hear what adventures they had. The trip saw the couple enjoying a well-earned change of scenery, and Atwill was not seen onstage again until the end of January 1923.

The new play was *The Comedian*. It was another Belasco production, and again it was adapted from a French play by Sacha Guitry. Once again, Elsie Mackay, Mrs. Atwill, would co-star alongside her husband. It was the story of a stage actor and included a scene in which a play is rehearsed, giving audiences the feeling that they were being allowed a revealing glimpse into the world of the theater. In one standout scene, Atwill steps down into the stalls and stands among his audience as he directs the actors on the bare stage above him. This scene was singled out for special praise by *Variety*, who thought that:

> Above all it shows Lionel Atwill in a high stage of artistic perfection … Belasco's arrangement of the bare stage scene stands out and will become much talked of.

Audiences also thoroughly enjoyed the humor of this scene, with Atwill offering frequent words of encouragement to his wife on the stage, while she holds up the proceedings by rewarding him with a kiss every time he does so.

The Exquisite Villain

79

The dramatic crux of the story is that the hero must chose between his loyalty to the theater and his love for a beautiful young wife, Jacqueline. Out of love, he gives her a part in a play, but she turns out to be a dreadful actress. When she demands a part in his next play, he refuses, and (as explained by the *New York Times*):

> … she goes—leaving him desolate as a human being but proudly loyal to his art and his public. He has kept the Comedian's faith.

Of course, no play starring Atwill would be complete without some controversial element, and *The Comedian* is no exception. When the hero first falls in love with the "willful flapper" (*New York Times*), he whisks her off for "a little train ride." But decency is upheld—he marries her in the nick of time before any reputations are tarnished!

As ever, Belasco tried out the play quietly in obscure out-of-town theaters before risking it on New York playgoers. It played first of all in a theater in Wilmington in the last week of January 1923, then moved to Baltimore during the first week of February. The *Baltimore News* was enthusiastic:

> Mr. Atwill displays the best assortment of acting we have ever seen him do … There is high comedy in the first act … farce and vaudeville humor in the second act and excellent drama in the final one.

The play was also staged briefly in Boston in late February, and finally Belasco felt it was fine-tuned enough for New York's sophisticated theatergoers.

The Comedian opened in New York on March 13 at the Lyceum Theater. The newspapers were impressed with the star of the play. "Notably good performance by Lionel Atwill," wrote J. Rankin Towne in the *Evening Post*. "Atwill in Guitry play triumph," enthused the *Commercial*. "An evening of sheer delight. A perfect performance in a few golden hours," eulogized R.G. Welsh in the *Evening Telegraph*.

The *New York Times*, however, had mixed feelings:

> Lionel Atwill labors nobly and well … but the mechanism creaks … hardly convincing … his interpretation of the part is gorgeous, but the part is dull and uninteresting and frequently boringly platitudinous. The fault for all the unconvincing nature of the role lies not in him.

The same reviewer was impressed by Mrs. Atwill's performance too:

Close to Mr. Atwill in respect of excellence of performance is Elsie Mackay, as the girl newborn at the age of 18, with the fever of the stage in her veins.

Two weeks later, the same newspaper wrote about *The Comedian* again.

Mr. Lionel Atwill does remarkable work … He overplays to be sure, but it seems reasonable to believe that he does so because the author of the play conceived his role as being that of a man who does overplay … to Mr. Atwill's credit …

Reading some of these glowing reviews, it is, once again, impossible not to mourn the fact that today we will never be able to experience the pleasure of watching Atwill in this role. The last act in particular, with Atwill playing the broken-down old actor, must have been compelling.

During the run of *The Comedian*, Atwill also found time to be involved in a number of other theatrical events. On the April 17, 1923 the National Stage Women's Exchange at the Stage Door Inn at 43 West Forty-Seventh Street hosted an afternoon tea (how frightfully British!). Atwill and his wife were part of the reception committee, along-side actresses Alice Brady and Margaret Wycherly.

On April 29, David Belasco staged a one-off appearance by Moscow's leading actress Olga Chekova—widow to the Russian author Anton Chekov—at the Belasco Theater. She read extracts from her late husband's plays, and Atwill had the honor of introducing her. Two weeks later, Atwill enjoyed another honor—on May 13, he was invited to the Bayes Theater, where he was asked to present a cup to the East West Players of Manhattan, in recognition of being the best little theater organization.

The Comedian moved from the Lyceum to the Belasco theatre on May 7 and played there for three successful weeks, up to the end of the month. May proved to be a busy month for Atwill in other ways as well.

On May 1, 1923 he was one of many actors giving their services for free at a fund-raising benefit for the National Vaudeville Association at the Metropolitan Hotel. It was a sell-out attraction, with Atwill performing to a standing room

'THE COMEDIAN' IS DISAPPOINTING

A Play of the Stage in Which Lionel Atwill Labors Nobly and Well.

BUT THE MECHANISM CREAKS

New Belasco Production Is Well Acted and Staged, but Is Hardly Convincing.

THE COMEDIAN. A play in three acts, from the French of Sacha Guitry. Adapted by David Belasco. At the Lyceum Theatre.

The Comedian	Lionel Atwill
G. Maillart	A. P. Kaye
Jacqueline	Elsie Mackay
Leclerc	H. Paul Doucet
Bloch	Albert Gran
Robert	William Lorenz
A Stage Manager	Will Hindson
Mouret-Icombia	H. Cooper Cliffe
Antoinette Vivier	Itsne Winter
Marguerite Simonest	Evelyn Gosnell
Yvette	Marguerite Denys
Marcelle	Myra Florian
Alise	Edmonia Nolley
Henri	Jacques de Wolfe
Maria	Maquita Dwight
Lucien	Harold Seton

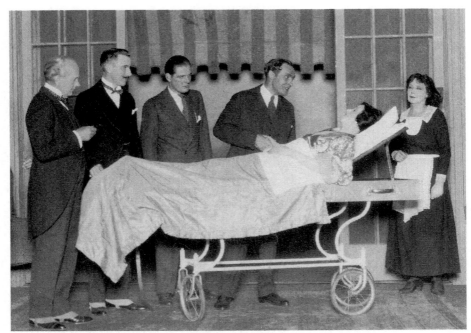

For the first time, the mad doctor with his patient. Atwill as Anton Ragatzy in *The Out-sider* (1924)—from left: Thomas Louden, Gilbert Douglas, Pat Somerset, Lionel Atwill, Ann Davis and Octavia Kenmore at the Plymouth Theatre, Boston. [Photo Courtesy The Billy Rose Theatre Division, The New York Public Library for the Performing Arts]

only audience. Later the same month, on Saturday, May 12, he presented *The David Belasco Trophy*, a silver loving cup, to the East-West Players, to reward them for having staged a play that was considered to be the best among 20 candidates. Atwill was also a member of The Friars, a club with theatrical interests, and in May he was nominated to be the club's Dean.

Barely taking a rest after *The Comedian* ended, Atwill was back in vaudeville again during much of June, reprising his role in *The White-Faced Fool* at B.F. Keith's Palace Theatre. He then appears to have taken another well-deserved vacation with Elsie—we can infer this from his absence from the theater pages of the newspapers for two months.

But in August *Variety* reported: "Atwill Leaves Belasco." After four and a half highly successful years together and four smash hit plays (*Tiger! Tiger!*, *Deburau, The Grand Duke* and *The Comedian*), the Belasco-Atwill partnership came to an end. Although he had two years to go on his contract, the star didn't want to go on tour with the company, preferring to stay in New York. He had other plans and decided to go it alone. It was not an acrimonious split; it was more a case of Atwill having the confidence to become his own producer once again. Two years later, in 1925, Belasco referred to Atwill in print as "my very dear friend Lionel Atwill," confirming no falling out existed between them.

Atwill's first solo production was *The Heart of Cellini*, a play by Anthony Wharton based on the life of the 16th-century Italian sculptor Benvenuto Cellini. Atwill took the

Lionel Atwill

title role. It is not difficult to see what attracted the hedonistic Atwill to this larger-than-life character, who was involved in all manner of reprehensible acts: He slept with his models, fathered illegitimate children and, on a number of occasions, took sadistic delight in maiming and murdering those who had wronged him.

The play went into rehearsals on September 17 and opened in Detroit on October 1. On October 21, 1923 the *New York Times* wrote of Atwill:

> It was when blades flashed that he appeared to best advantage—the Atwill Cellini, infrequently a hero, quick with the sword …

Clearly, it showcased an athletic side of Atwill that unfortunately was rarely seen in his later film career. To Atwill's disappointment, the play was not a success and it had a short life.

His final theatrical contribution in 1923 found him back at B.F. Keith's Palace Theatre, the headline act above several other vaudeville acts, including various musicians and comedians. *Lionel Atwill and Company* opened on the December 27 in a new 22-minute dramatic playlet entitled *By Right of Love,* written by the author of *The White-Faced Fool,* Edgar Allan Woolf. Atwill played a character called Clyde Worthing, "the reigning matinee idol." *Variety* described it as "a hectic dramalet" and it climaxed with a pistol duel. Elsie Mackay was also in the cast. It moved for one night only to the B.F. Keith New Amsterdam Theater for a "New Year's Eve Pre-Celebration" on December 30. During the week beginning December 31, it was at the Orpheum Theater in Brooklyn.

A series of four newspaper ads for *The Outsider* featured eye-catching cartoon images of Atwill.

Early in 1924, Atwill took the very first step in becoming "the maddest doctor of them all." The play was called *The Outsider* and its central character was Anton Ragatzy, an arrogant, self-proclaimed medical genius who has invented a device that can, he claims, work miracle cures on the crippled. Hailing from some un-named European country, he speaks in accented, broken English that gives him a sinister edge. He doesn't just speak his lines—he spits them out with venom. Many of his lines in the text of the play (written by Dorothy Brandon) are prefixed by the instruction "(snarling)." In *The Outsider*, Atwill gets his first-ever *mad doctor* speeches.

For example, there is a gruesome exchange between Ragatzy and two doctors who disapprove of his lack of formal training. One of them asks where he studied anatomy.

Ragatzy: In the stockyards in Chicago ... the slaughter house ...
Tollemache: Good God.
Ragatzy: Where was I, a poor boy, to get blood and bones? Ach, many
times I have been soaked in scarlet.
Helmore: Then, are we to understand, you began as a butcher?
Ragatzy: Butcher, no ... I go and cut up carcasses to find out how the
joints fit in the sockets, what holds them and what makes them bend
... But you are shocked, hey?
(The doctors leave.)
Ragatzy: Ach, I would like to cut them into joints for Sunday dinner!

And later, he gloats over his impending cure of a female patient:

I ... I shall be famous, rich, more great than any doctor—you shall
make them all bow down like Joseph's sheaves to me, because you
are my lovely, living statue that I have made perfect for myself!

His invention is a mysterious wooden rack that is powered by electricity and "pulls
one thousandth part of an inch an hour." It's a precursor to all the devices seen in labo-
ratories in Atwill's mad doctor films of the 1930s and 1940s. Adding a further macabre

touch, the text of the play describes
how his hands are made up so that
his fingers look unnaturally long.
His face is darkened with make-up
to give him a swarthy, exotic appearance.

It is not a very big leap from
Ragatzy to, for example, Atwill's
Dr. Benson in *The Mad Doctor of
Market Street* (1942), who will always be remembered for a legendary moment when, after accidentally killing a patient, he flees the
scene of his crime by clambering
out of a rear window, still dressed
in his surgeon's white gowns.

A series of four different advertisements for *The Outsider* were
placed in the New York newspapers, and each one featured a small
but eye-catching cartoon image
of Atwill as Ragatzy. One was a
silhouette of him in profile with a
stethoscope around his neck; the
image is Atwill's very first public
appearance in mad doctor guise.

**Artist Marcus drew this striking image of Atwill for
the *New York Times* at the time when *The Outsider*
was released.**

Lionel Atwill

Atwill followed Belasco's strategy of trying out the play first in an out-of-town theater. It opened on February 10 in Wilmington, before moving to New York's Forty-ninth Street Theater on March 3. The *New York Times* reviewer was impressed:

> Mr. Atwill plays well and with earnestness ... [the play] succeeded in holding its first New York audience in its seats for some five minutes after the final curtain.

Variety described Atwill's character as:

> A blatherskite roughneck without a medical license or degree, who practices nature healing by bone setting and stretching.

The *New York Times* enjoyed the play so much that they wrote about it again a few days after their first review, enthusing about Atwill's acting:

> He swells to bursting with the man's conceit and self-seeking, glares with the venom of his mind and spits forth the malice of his tongue. Here is the perfect bounder, if you will.

Atwill's co-star was Katherine Cornell, one of the greatest actresses of the American stage. She plays a crippled girl who has almost given up any hope of finding a doctor who can help her ... until Ragatzy arrives on the scene. Ragatzy "cold-bloodedly conceives a brilliant publicity stunt" (*Variety*) of healing her, and even blackmails one of his other patients into giving him a glowing testimonial. What follows, as described by *Variety*, sounds like a scene out of one of his later horror films: "He straps the girl to an elaborate stretching machine and the cure starts." But when she subsequently gets up from the table, she falls to the floor in a heap. However, all is not lost and "by sheer masculine electricity he cures her by taking her in his arms and making violent love to her." In other words, the real cause of her problem was sexual repression!

What a treat it must have been to be in the audience watching Atwill at his melodramatic best, and at the peak of his acting form.

The Outsider, which moved to New York's Ambassador Theater on March 31, was a great success. Daily

A magnificent portrait (by Roy Williams) of Atwill in costume for *Caesar and Cleopatra* (1925)

ads for it appeared in the newspapers and in all of them Atwill's name was billed in larger letters than the play's title, a sure indication of his pulling power. Another indication was displayed large and proud in the April 6 edition of the *New York Times*—a stunning half-page drawing of Atwill in close-up, his intense gray-blue eyes seeming to come alive on the page, even in black-and-white.

In March 1924, it was announced that Atwill would travel west to Los Angeles to star in a stage version of *The Moon and Sixpence* by W. Somerset Maugham, but the project seems never to have been realized.

Instead, *The Outsider* kept Atwill busy onstage throughout most of 1924—apart from a two-and-a-half month period from June to August when the Atwills sailed off on another of their long and exotic vacations. On the July 5 they sailed to England on the transatlantic liner the *Bergenland*. After a time there, visiting family and friends in London, they traveled farther afield. Passenger lists show that they sailed back from Batavia (the former name of Jakarta), the capital of Indonesia on the July 24. Refreshed from their trip, the couple arrived back in the States on the ocean liner the *Majestic* on August 12.

Very quickly, Lionel picked up more or less where he had left off: *The Outsider* opened at the Shubert-Riviera Theater (on 97th Street and Broadway) mid-September 1924. In early October it moved to the Bronx Opera House (on 149th Street, east of 3rd Avenue), where it played for a week until October 11. And in the last week of November, it was at the Garrick Theatre in Chicago, with Atwill still ranting and raving as Ragatzy.

Atwill with Helen Hayes in a dramatic scene from *Caesar and Cleopatra*

The Outsider was filmed three times. The first version in 1926 was directed by Rowland V. Lee, a director who would become significant in Atwill's later career. Whether or not Atwill was offered the film role is not known. It's very likely that he was, but if so he turned it down, having already found the medium of film did him no favors. A later film version in 1939 starred George Sanders in the Ragatzy role. It would be interesting to watch one of these film versions and imagine Atwill in the title role, but maddeningly all three versions seem to be lost.

At the very end of 1924, Atwill returned to vaudeville by putting on the same playlet that he appeared in over the New Year period the previous year, *By Right of Love*. He was still appearing in this on January 18, 1925, as evidenced by an ad in the *New York Times*. Elsie Mackay was his co-star. On the same bill

Lionel Atwill

Another cartoon of Helen Hayes and Atwill from *Caesar and Cleopatra* that appeared in the *New York Times*, April 12, 1925.

at the B.F. Keith's Palace Theatre was comedian Larry Semon. On at least one evening at the Palace, Atwill performed two different acts. On January 21, *Variety* reported that he not only acted in *By Right of Love* but also performed "the Clown's speech from the third act of *Deburau*."

On January 22, 1925, Atwill made his first foray into what for him was a new medium: radio. With his unmistakable voice, it was a natural venue for his talents. *Queens Night* was broadcast on New York's WNYC at 7.35 in the evening. All the artists and entertainers were from the Borough of Queens. The announcer and Master of Ceremonies was Ellis Parker Butler; those performing included Willie Collier, Andrew Mack and Lionel Atwill.

A month later, on February 28, he was donating his services for free yet again to help a worthy cause. A benefit show was staged at the Palace Theatre to raise money to help complete the building of the Cathedral of St John the Divine. Atwill was one of the stage managers. Will Rogers, Fannie Brice, Al Jolson and Sophie Tucker were among many stars that appeared.

On April 13, 1925 a new theater opened in New York. It was the Guild Theater on 52nd Street, and its first production was *Caesar and Cleopatra,* the famous comedy by George Bernard Shaw. In the title roles were Lionel Atwill and Helen Hayes. It seemed only right that Atwill, having just starred opposite one of America's two greatest stage actresses in *The Outsider*, should now star opposite the other one.

The *Stage* was impressed:

A distinguished portrait of Lionel Atwill from 1925

Mr. Atwill, giving a more careful and finished performance than I have seen from his lately, made of the Roman Commander a middle-aged sentimentalist.

However, the *New York Times*, although they thought it a fine play, had some reservations about Atwill, which must have caused him serious consternation.

> Many of the speeches last night disappeared partly because of enunciation and faulty diction but often because the accents did not strike where the sense lay. In Mr. Atwill's case this was particularly unfortunate, and point after point from Caesar's marvelous discourse was lost or failed to register.

For an actor who prided himself on his superior diction, this must have hurt. And if he restrained himself from throwing the paper aside in anger and read on, he would have been even more dismayed.

> Lionel Atwill looked very splendid in the part ... Now and then he was effective, but not often. A mere improvement in his reading, even as to making the lines entirely audible, would help. And he greatly needed more of what we may call the poetry of the role.

The play was a reasonable success, running for 128 performances until August.

On April 25 the American Legion staged a tribute to General Pershing, who had led the American forces during WWI. It was held at the Hippodrome, with Senator James J. Walker as M.C., assisted by Lionel Atwill, John Drew and other Broadway stars.

In October 1925, it was announced that Atwill was assembling a cast to appear in *Deep in the Woods*, which went into rehearsals the first week of November. Not much is known about this play, other than that it was "from the Hungarian" and was first staged by Atwill at the Baltimore Auditorium, then at the Belasco Theatre in Washington, D.C. *Variety* mentioned very briefly that, "reviews were not favorable." Atwill directed the play as well as acting in it.

The Fates conspired against *Deep in the Woods*. First, on November 18, 1925, Atwill was very nearly killed in a train crash. He was traveling with his business manager George Jordan on the Washington-to-New York express train when its rear end was struck by a St. Louis express train, just as it was passing through Plainsboro, New Jersey. The two rear Pullman carriages were completely demolished. Atwill, fortunately, was in the third Pullman. A beam that came through the window killed the occupant of the berth ahead of Atwill. Escapes don't come any narrower.

Despite this, Atwill did not miss a performance of *Deep in the Woods* in Washington, although the raising of the curtain had to be delayed slightly on his first evening back at the theater after the crash.

There was another more crucial reason why *Deep in the Woods* was doomed. Atwill's marriage was on the rocks. His wife Elsie was due to star alongside him in *Deep in the Woods,* but Atwill had reason to believe that she was becoming romantically involved with another actor in the cast, Max Montesole. Atwill's suspicions had been brewing for three weeks. One night during rehearsals, Elsie failed to return home to their house in Douglas Manor, Long Island. New York's *Daily Mirror*, in an interview with Atwill's friend Claude Beerbohm, tells what happened next.

According to the interview:

LIONEL ATWILL SUES WIFE FOR A DIVORCE

Charges Élsie Mackay With Improper Conduct With Actor He Once Employed.

SHE DENIES HIS ACCUSATION

Has Gone Abroad With Max Montesole, Lawyer Says—Trouble Long Brewing, Husband Asserts.

Lionel Atwill, actor, announced yesterday through his attorney, Charles S. Colden of Flushing, that he had sued his wife, Elsie Mackay, for divorce. Miss Mackay, the lawyer said, left New York last Friday in company with Max Montesole, an actor formerly employed by Mr. Atwill, for Boston, whence they sailed for Liverpool last Sunday. Service was effected, he said, fifteen minutes before her departure.

Mr. Atwill, who was in the lawyer's office when the statement was made, told reporters "this trouble had been brewing for a long time.".

"All possible attempts at reconciliation so far have utterly failed," he said. "Montesole is the direct antithesis of myself. He cares nothing about success. I am not emotional, and I am not going about crying over this affair or carrying a revolver."

Mr. Colden said Mr. Atwill discovered the attachment between his wife and Mr. Montesole three weeks ago.

"We made an investigation and we ascertained that Montesole and Mrs. Atwill were occupying an apartment in West Sixty-eighth Street, Manhattan," he continued. "There we caused a further investigation to be made, as a result of which a complaint and action for divorce have been prepared. On last Thursday night we found Mrs. Atwill with Montesole in the apartment. There were trunks all about the room being packed. One of the investigators who was in our party called for the janitress to have her sign a statement that Mrs. Atwill and Montesole had been living there under the name of Mackay. When the janitress came she hesitated and then Mrs. Atwill said: 'Oh, never mind; I will sign the statement.' She did sign it."

A *New York Times* newspaper article published December 17, 1925

Atwill prowled through the house. He found two revolvers. He fingered them nervously. He fondled them.

"He spoke of shooting Montesole," said Beerbohm. "He spoke of throttling him. He was furious. But gradually he grew calm. He decided not to put his hands on the man who had stolen his wife. He wanted to kill him. But what good would it do? ... Was a woman who left her husband worth dying for? Dying in the chair? And would it bring Elsie back to him—his killing Max?"

Instead Atwill decided on a solution that was more pragmatic but hardly less dramatic: He would catch the lovers red-handed in their Manhattan apartment. As witnesses, he recruited two detectives and, on December 10, 1925, accompanied also by his attorney and his chauffeur, he paid an unannounced visit to 59 West 68th Street. We can imagine poor Elsie's reaction when she heard Lionel angrily knocking at the door, especially as she knew he owned a revolver.

Inside, Lionel found her with Montesole, surrounded by packing cases, all ready to do a moonlit flit. The couple, it seems, had hoped to get as far way from Lionel as possible before he found out. A janitress was dragged into the affair and, encouraged by one of the detectives, signed a statement saying that Elsie had been staying in the apartment under the name of Mrs. Montesole.

Elsie pleaded later in her affidavit that Montesole was only in her flat to help her pack for her trip to Europe; it was a desperate attempt to salvage some dignity. But eventually she signed a statement admitting to being unfaithful because (as reported by the *New York Times*) she "feared scandal and desired to avoid arrest."

Elsie and Max sailed for Liverpool the next day on the *Samaria*.

The *Lima News* of Ohio picked up on another of those many coincidences that followed Atwill throughout his career. "Couple's Stage Play Now Role in Real Life" headlined the newspaper noting, "It was in the last act of *The Comedian*, in which the Atwills starred, that the wife leaves her husband as he seeks in vain to win her back."

If the high drama of the love-nest showdown sounds like a scene from some sensationalist movie—well, that's because it is. Several years later, an almost identical scene occurred in *Murders in the Zoo*, in which Atwill's character bursts into his wife's love-nest apartment and discovers her with her lover in the act of packing her things as she prepares to flee to Europe. A coincidence? Hardly, it is far more likely that Atwill had a conference with the director and suggested the whole episode as a way of spicing up the film.

When the divorce case came to court, Lionel alleged improper conduct on the part of Elsie, who denied it: She said she and Montesole were dressed when her husband and detectives entered her apartment at 59 West 68th Street" (*New York Times*). She also claimed to be almost financially destitute, asked for alimony of $350 per week and stated that her husband earned around $60,000 yearly. However, a few weeks later in mid-January 1926, her plea for alimony was denied, despite her claims that she was "without support and had only a small quantity of jewelry." It seems harsh that she didn't get a penny out of Lionel. He, on the other hand, probably felt that as he was the aggrieved party, she didn't deserve a cent.

As it turned out, a happy ending existed for Elsie. Montesole married her and they lived together in Paris for a while. Around 1930, the couple settled back in her home country of Australia, and there they even acted in theatrical productions together.

Chapter 6
Broadway 1926 to 1928

After the trauma of having his marriage to Elsie come to a messy end, Atwill now had to put all the emotional upheaval behind him and get back to work.

In late January 1926, he was in vaudeville again, this time at B.F. Keith's Riverside Theatre, performing in an 18-minute sketch entitled *The Song of Victory*. Written by Brian Marlowe, this was yet another French-themed play about the birth of *La Marseillaise*, or the French National Anthem. *Variety* was impressed:

> Mr. Atwill plays the role of the composer with delightful repression, at the same time incorporating the latter's moodiness and his tinkering upon the harpsichord until he has perfected the battle hymn … His performance was at all times superb.

In March he was rehearsing for a new play, *Beau Gallant*. It played in Buffalo and some other towns before opening in New York on the April 5 at the Ritz Theater. Atwill played the title role, with Marguerite Burrough and Dodson Mitchell co-starring. Atwill's reputation on Broadway by now was such that in one advertisement for the play, the letters of his name positively dwarfed the play's title, which was so small as to be almost illegible.

Atwill played Caton Beale Carrington, an upper class gentleman who is dubbed Beau Gallant, the proud, penniless and last remaining member of the aristocratic Carrington family. He is so poor that he often has to borrow money from his butler's daughter.

It gave him a good opportunity to try some light comedy again, and the *Evening World* was impressed:

> No more completely perfect work of characterization has been presented on the New York stage.

The *New York Times* also warmed to it:

RITZ THEATRE 48th St., West of B'way. 1st MAT. TODAY
LIONEL ATWILL
in "*Beau Gallant*"
"Stands out amid Broadway's gems." —Eve. Telegram.
"No more completely perfect work of characterization has been presented on the New York stage."—Eve. World.
—SEATS NOW SELLING 4 WEEKS IN ADVANCE—

By 1926 Atwill's status as a star was such that, in this newspaper ad for *Beau Gallant*, his name was in huge letters while the play's title was almost irrelevant.

With this perfectly tailored role, Mr. Atwill does just what he might be expected to do. He is urbane and suave as the romantic gallant, badly adjusted to this hopelessly mercenary and workaday world, but occasionally he curbs a natural desire to give full rein to the juicy part by an apparent bit of under-acting.

Beau Gallant ran for an unspectacular 26 performances.

Atwill made his second radio appearance on April 8 for station WGBS. It was an afternoon slot and he was the subject of a half-hour interview. Perhaps he spoke dryly about his attitude to acting, or perhaps he slipped in a couple of less-than-gracious remarks about how female co-stars don't make good wives.

May 2, 1926 saw Atwill once again donating his time and services for free to support a good cause. This time it was the NVA Show, put on to raise money for the National Vaudeville Artists' Benefit Fund. "5 Monster Super Shows ... 5 Largest Theaters ... The event you wait all year for" ran the ads. It was a one-night-only event, and Atwill was one of just hundreds of actors who took part.

Later that month he was one of many guests who attended a special dinner at the Hotel Biltmore, at which it was announced that the Greenwich Village Theater and the Actors' Theater would merge. Whether or not he was asked to speak is not known.

April 6, 1926, the *New York Times*

LIONEL ATWILL SUAVE IN PLAY 'BEAU GALLANT'

His Romantic Role Made to Order, but Stuart Olivier's Drama Is Lacking in Action.

BEAU GALLANT, a play in three acts, by Stuart Olivier. Settings by Henry Dreyfuss; staged by Clarke Silvernail; produced by The Playshop, Inc. At the Ritz Theatre.

Smithson	Wallace Erskine
Jessica Smithson	Marguerite Burrough
Bruce Fairchild	Robert Gleckler
Caton Beale Carrington (Beau Gallant)	Lionel Atwill
Holmes Carrington	Clarence Bellair
Clare Hoyt	Gypsy O'Brien
Sheriff's Man	Percival Jackson
Another Man	William Lawrence
Tom Beale	Dodson Mitchell
Mr. Ainsley	Leslie King

Lionel Atwill, divested of the robes of the mighty Caesar, but appearing in a part that permits him to retain many of the mannerisms, returned to town last night at the Ritz Theatre in a play called "Beau Gallant," by Stuart Olivier, last represented here by Peggy Wood's vehicle of two seasons ago, "The Bride."

No records have come to light to tell us what Lionel was doing between June and September 1926—presumably he was enjoying a long break somewhere.

On October 5 Atwill made his third radio appearance. At 9 p.m. that evening it was the *Eveready Hour* on station WEAF, and the station put on an hour-long version of *Show Boat*, "a musical narrative." Ads announced that: "The principal part will be taken by Lionel Atwill." Was it just a speaking part or is it possible that he sang? One could imagine Atwill having had a good baritone voice—if he ever used it. The show was broadcast on a number of different radio stations on the East Coast and the Central Time Zone.

Atwill's next venture in the theater saw a change of direction; he would direct a play but not appear in it. The production was *The Squall*, written by Jean Bart, who later would be involved with two of Atwill's films. The play was set in Granada in Spain and told the story of the Mendez family, with Blanche Yurka starring as Dolores Mendez. As its title suggests, a highlight of the play was an elaborate on-stage storm.

An ad for *The Squall* did its best to lure patrons in with a bit of titillation, describing it as—

> A passion-swept play in which all the emotions, good and base, are shown with camera-like fidelity.

Might it be that Atwill dreamed up that lurid catchphrase? We will probably never know for sure, but in his role as director, he might certainly have been involved to some extent in trying to promote the play. *The Squall* opened at New York's Forty-eighth Street Theater on November 11, 1926 and ran for a remarkable 444 performances until December 1927. Atwill must have been delighted.

Part of the reason for its popularity was due to *Variety* labeling it "among the dirtiest plays of this season" in an article called "New York's Dirtiest Plays." Today *The Squall* sounds tame, despite being the story of "a torrid Gypsy vamp who plays havoc in a righteous household" and included "a hot seduction scene of innocent youth, with other spicy trimmings."

Atwill attended regular social events at the Friars Club, of which he was a member. On November 13, 1926 a special evening was arranged (at their clubhouse on West 48th Street) to honor a comedy duo named Clark and McCullough. Atwill made a speech and fellow club member Irving Berlin got up and sang a song.

At the same time as *The Squall* was running successfully at one theater, Atwill was free to appear onstage at another. He was engaged by veteran theater producer William A. Brady to appear in *Slaves All*. The director was Lumsden Hare (who had a prolific film career that ran from 1916 right up to 1961). It opened at New York's Bijou Theater on December 6.

It is easy to see why *Slaves All* appealed to Atwill: it gave him a part he could really get his teeth into. He played John Rigordan, "a near-dipsomaniac who has been driven to seek refuge in stimulants by an iron-willed sister of inflexible code of ethics and morals" (*New York Times*). The climax of the play sounds like a prime example of Atwill doing what he always did so well—going crazy. His sister's behavior enrages him beyond all reason and he puts poison into her cup of soup. But at the last moment, he recovers his mental balance in time to snatch the cup away from her.

The *New York Times* again:

> Mr. Atwill, expert in various sorts of roles, gave a generally first-rate performance, although it was inclined to be a bit overblown at times.

For fans of the actor sitting in the stalls of the Bijou, it must have been a real treat. It doesn't get much better than watching Lionel Atwill being "a bit overblown."

Despite Atwill giving it his all, *Slaves All* was not a success and lasted for only eight performances.

Other stage productions were announced in 1927 for Atwill, including *Lady Alone* with Alice Brady, *The Guardsman* with Marjorie Rambeau and *Machiavelli* (by Lemist Esler)—but none of them ever materialized.

In early February 1927 it was announced that Atwill would both direct and star in *Penelope's Daughter*, set in ancient Rome. Adapted by Brian Marlowe from an Italian play called *The Web of Penelope*, it opened in Baltimore on February 28, co-starring Ernest Cossart and Hilda Spong. It also played for a while in Atlantic City, but it appears that it was never judged strong enough to be brought to Broadway. For Atwill as director, it must have been another disappointment.

On March 7, 1927, *The Adventurer*, written by Raffaela Carsini, opened at the Belasco Theater in Washington and later that month in New Haven. Atwill directed, and also took the starring role of Ulysses. *Variety* gave it a mixed review, dismissing its plot:

> It amounts to little more than a moderately interesting story of a returning husband who isn't wanted.

Even so, it took a healthy $7,000 in its first week, and as *Variety* noted, this was due almost entirely to the draw of its star.

It's not hard to see what the attraction was for Atwill's hordes of female admirers. In one scene he was lying on a couch and stripped to the waist, while being attended to by a "dancing girl and unashamed courtesan." *Variety* stated:

"I agree with Lionel Atwill Luckies are more enjoyable," says Paul Berlenbach

Popular pugilist tells his manager, Benedict Sterns, that Lucky Strikes are the finest cigarettes.

LUCKY STRIKE "IT'S TOASTED" **CIGARETTES**

MADE OF THE CREAM OF THE TOBACCO CROP

You, too, will find that LUCKY STRIKES give the greatest pleasure—Mild and Mellow, the finest cigarettes you ever smoked. Made of the choicest tobaccos, properly aged and blended with great skill, and there is an extra process—"IT'S TOASTED"—no harshness, not a bit of bite.

Lionel Atwill, Noted Dramatic Star, writes:
"I quickly adopted Lucky Strikes when I found they were kind to my throat, safeguarding it against irritation, and at the same time they were more enjoyable."

"It's toasted"
No Throat Irritation-No Cough.

Atwill happily sings the praises of cigarettes in this 1927 newspaper ad, unaware of the effect they would have on his health.

> The play is inoffensively improper. It is risqué at intervals … but it is handled delicately.

On April 22, 1927 he opened at the Ritz Theatre in *The Thief*, written by Henri Bernstein. Again Atwill directed, this time co-starring with Alice Brady and Gilbert Emery. The play is notable for a powerful second act that caused a furor when originally staged back in 1907. In the scene in question, only the two leading characters—a husband and wife—are onstage, and the husband very slowly and gradually causes his wife to break down and confess to having stolen money regularly from the family's cash drawer. It sounds like a choice bit of psychological persecution by Atwill.

The *New York Times* described this scene as "thoroughly shocking" and like "flying through Fifth Avenue traffic with a motorcycle escort." Karl K. Kitchen, writing in the *Evening World*, thought it was:

... one of those rare productions, both a fine performance and a fine play. If there has been any better acting on Broadway this season, I have not seen it.

Publicity photo of Atwill used to promote the radio play *Peer Gynt* in 1928

The *Wall Street Journal* thought the play was "a masterful piece of direct, devastating writing."

The Thief fared better than Atwill's other recent ventures. It lasted for 83 performances, ending in early July 1927.

In August 1927, Atwill was back in vaudeville again for five weeks in a sketch called *Close Quarters* by Oliver White. Nothing more is known about this production.

On August 9, 1927, the *New York Times* printed an article that clearly intimated far more than it actually said. It reported that Mrs. Douglas MacArthur had leased the entire 26th floor of the Beverly Hotel on Lexington Avenue. In the next paragraph, the article went on to say that Lionel Atwill had leased an apartment in the same hotel. No connection between the two events was stated, but astute readers will have put two and two together.

Mrs. Douglas MacArthur was originally Louise Cromwell, born around 1890. She became Louise Cromwell Brooks after her first marriage in 1911. She had two children and divorced in 1919. In 1922 she married again, this time to Douglas MacArthur, the distinguished soldier of WWI and, later, WWII. Louise was the stepdaughter of railway financier Edward T. Stotesbury—and hence the heir to a vast fortune estimated at around $100,000,000.

Exactly when she and Atwill first met or became close is not known—the news item about the Beverly Hotel is the first indication that something was going on. Of course, in1927 she was still married to MacArthur, so the newspapers chose to exercise some discretion. After all, no newspaper would want to make accusations that might lead to a legal battle with one of the country's richest families.

Like Atwill, Louise was an avid partygoer. She was also renowned for her quick wit, was rumored to drink too much and said to dance enthusiastically to the jazz music that was popular at the time. Perhaps we can imagine Lionel sometimes getting up and dancing with her. She was considered to be one of Washington's most beautiful women, and it is not hard to see why Lionel was attracted to her. But it would be another three years before the pair would make their relationship legally binding.

On October 31, Atwill was at his Friars Club again, this time attending a special dinner given in honor of the Mayor of New York. Other members of the club who were present that night included David Belasco, Al Jolson, Eddie Cantor and Irving Berlin.

Atwill's last theatrical appearance of 1927 was in *The King Can Do No Wrong*, a comedy-mystery written by F.S. Merlin. It opened at a theater in Allentown, Pennsylvania on November 3, and audience reaction was good enough for it to move to New York, where it opened on November 16 at the Masque Theatre on West 5th Street. Atwill was in the starring role as Baron Reus, supported by Felix Krembs and Leona Hogarth. Reus was the sort of character that Atwill always did so well, a nobleman who in this case was also the head of the secret police of some unnamed country. During the course of the play, he had to deal with various traitors and invaders, shield some innocent ladies from harm and solve a murder.

The *New York Times*:

> Most of the burden of *The King Can Do No Wrong* ... rested squarely upon the shoulders of Lionel Atwill, who played the leading part with a regal bearing. The sleuthing Baron, with shoulders squared, expressed contempt for villainy merely by tossing bonbons into his mouth as he strode angrily up and down the room.

Despite good reviews like this, the play only lasted 13 performances in New York.

On December 15 Atwill was a guest at a grand dinner event where Fanny Brice and a dancer from Berlin provided the entertainment. The other guests in attendance included Major General and Mrs. Douglas MacArthur. It must have been an interesting evening for Lionel, trying his best to conceal from the Major General that he was romantically involved with Mrs. MacArthur.

Early in 1928, Atwill was back on the radio again. He chose to perform some dramatic selections from *Peer Gynt* by Ibsen, the playwright whose works had been such an important part of the actor's earlier theatrical career. It was broadcast on January 22 at 9 p.m. during the *Eveready Concert* program on WEAF and 22 other radio stations. A full supporting cast, an orchestra and a mixed chorus assisted Atwill.

Atwill had high hopes for his next venture, *Napoleon*. The play, written by B. Harrison Orkow and directed by Robert Milton, got off to a bad start when rehearsals had to be delayed as a result of Atwill falling ill with a cold and congestion of the lungs. Eventually, *Napoleon* opened in a theater in Hartford, Connecticut in mid-February, then for one week played in Providence, Rhode Island, opening there on February 27.

Variety reviewed the opening night in Providence. They didn't think much of the play as a whole, considering it to be "almost too tiresome to be considered even good entertainment." But they gave the highest praise possible to the star:

March 4, 1928, the *New York Times*

The Lionel Atwill Napoleon, to Be Seen at the Empire on Thursday

Lionel as Napoleon in 1928

Mr. Atwill gave a performance that indicates his talent as being that of one of the best actors on the American stage. He was Napoleon from the first act to last, and saved the night.

Napoleon eventually opened in New York on March 8, 1928 at the Empire Theatre. The *New York Times* thought that:

> Most of it is flat and stodgy … Napoleon's elegant smugness is a little trying.

The *Stage* was even more hurtful:

> This was, from nearly every angle, a sorry affair. In the first place, Mr. Atwill did not look like Napoleon, and in the second he made very little effort to act like Napoleon.

The *Variety* reviewer not only thought the play "too long and tedious" but also chose to ridicule Atwill and the buckskin breeches he was wearing:

> On first entrance his costume hardly befitted him and he exhibited an unbecoming paunch.

What must Lionel, who had invested so much effort into this performance, have thought on reading that? The reviewer at least made up for this remark by declaring that Atwill "gave the best performance he has offered in years."

The play struggled to find an audience. Many had been put off by the negative reviews. As a result the play's producer, James W Elliott, was struggling to pay the salaries of the cast and staff. Atwill, still having faith in the play, came up with a rescue plan. *Variety* reported that in mid-March the play—

… went co-operative with Lionel Atwill, featured player, more or less in control, and the Elliott interests said to be out entirely.

But audiences failed to improve and the play ended after only 10 performances at the Empire. Atwill had already suffered many theatrical disappointments, but this one hurt more than most. After the final curtain on Saturday, March 17, Atwill made his feelings plain to his public, and he did it in grand style. The curtain was raised to find him still sitting in the chair in which Napoleon had died in his final scene. Atwill rose to his feet and addressed his audience:

> I have no bone to pick with the critics. They have their livings to get the same as we. I think it a shame, however, that so much energy and so much effort should be wasted on a production like this simply because of attacks made upon it by certain members of the critical profession, attacks which I feel, and we all feel, were unfair. It may be many months before I return to a New York audience. I may suffer from this talk. Nevertheless I feel that I should make it ... I thank you from the bottom of my heart for the generous enthusiasm you have shown here tonight.

To make up for this disappointment, Atwill returned to one of his earlier success, *The Outsider*, and put up some of his own money to stage a revival of it at the Ambassador Theatre. Atwill once again took the starring role, as well as directing the play and re-writing some sections of it. It opened on April 9, with Isobel Elsom in the role previously taken by Katherine Cornell. It ran for a respectable 56 performances, and Atwill even had the bright idea of giving the play a bit of extra publicity by arranging to have a version of it broadcast on radio. On April 27, *The Outsider* was broadcast on WJZ and two other stations.

During the run of *The Outsider*, Atwill also found time for other social and theatrical events. On Sunday April 15, his Friars Club held a testimonial dinner at the prestigious Hotel Astor on Times Square. There were 400 attendees, and the speakers included Atwill, David Belasco, Paul Whiteman, Eddie Cantor and the Mayor of New York. On April 22, Atwill gave a special performance of a selection of Ibsen extracts at the Hudson Theatre. The money raised went toward paying for a monument to the dramatist of whom the actor was so fond.

"Atwill Asks Divorce" ran the headline to a short article in the *New York Times* in May 1928, followed three weeks later by "Atwill Decree is Signed." His divorce from Elsie had come through.

Also in May, Atwill was back on the radio again, this time in an hour-long version of his great success *Deburau* (already referred to in the chapter on that play). It was broadcast on the evening of Sunday May 27 on station WGY.

An indication of Atwill's celebrity status came in a show called *Grand Street Follies of 1928* at the Booth Theatre. He wasn't in it, but it included impersonations of many stars including Mae West, Billie Burke, Dolores Costello and Atwill. It would be interesting to know exactly which of his stage acts they lampooned. James Cagney arranged the dance routines.

Lionel Atwill was yet again generously giving his acting services for free at a supper-dance in aid of the Children's Village, "where 600 problem children live." It was held at the private home of the Kendall family in Dobbs Ferry on June 16, and Atwill supplied some vaudeville sketches.

From late August until early October 1928, fans of Atwill could get a double-dose of their idol: He could be seen starring in two short films that played concurrently at different New York cinemas. At the Globe was *Lionel Atwill in The Actor's Advice to His Son* playing as part of the support for a film called *Mother Knows Best*, starring Madge Bellamy. (See the chapter on *Deburau* for more information on this short film.) Meanwhile, at the Gaiety was *The White-Faced Fool*, with Atwill recreating one of his biggest vaudeville successes. It was a 3-reel film, so it ran approximately 30 minutes and probably contained the full playlet. It supported a film called *The Air Circus*, starring Louise Dresser. Thomas W. Chalmers directed both of the Atwill shorts. It would be thrilling to watch either of them, but extensive enquiries have failed to establish if they still survive. Most likely they perished in a major 1937 fire, which destroyed a New Jersey storage vault containing most of the pre-1935 Fox negatives.

In October 1928, reports appeared which made it clear that the relationship between Atwill and Louise MacArthur had now gone public. On the 31, *Variety* reported that:

> Mrs. MacArthur, who has been seen about with Lionel Atwill, is a daughter of the fabulously rich Mrs. E.T. Stotesbury and the late Oliver Cromwell.

In November 1928, a play called *The Jealous Moon* featured a Pierrot—the same type of clown character that Atwill played in the play-within-a-play in *Deburau*. The play's director, Priestley Morrison, enlisted Atwill's help and the piece was staged "with supplementary program acknowledgment to Lionel Atwill for supervision of production." *Variety* thought: "It's all a long bore" and it soon closed.

In December, Atwill was recruited to try something different: advertising. At a convention of automobile dealers, a film was screened, its purpose being to demonstrate how people can address an audience "by screen instead of in person." The film included a prologue delivered by Atwill.

By the end of 1928, Atwill must have looked back with mixed feelings at all his theatrical ventures of the preceding three years. There had been some successes (such as *The Thief*) but nothing to compare with his earlier triumphs in *Deburau* and *The Outsider*. There had been a lot of disappointments, and one especially dismal failure, *Napoleon*. Fortunately his next stage role was in a lavish production that proved to be a great success.

Chapter 7
Broadway 1928 to 1931

In December 1928, Atwill was rehearsing for *Fioretta*, a lavish romantic musical with a Venetian setting. Earl Carroll staged the production and the three big-name stars were Leon Errol, Fanny Brice and Lionel Atwill. *Fioretta* played for the very first time on New Year's Eve 1928, at the Ford Theatre in Baltimore, and the house was packed. Newspaper reviews of Atwill's performance were all so glowing that it almost seemed as if the critics had felt obliged to make up for their previous harsh treatment of *Napoleon*.

The *Baltimore Sun* had high praise for Atwill:

> As Count Matteo, the Machiavellian Minister of State, Mr. Atwill gave an exquisitely shaded performance. Strange it is to see him making this Minister live, and utter poetry with sinister grace, the while surrounded by showgirls and clowns. His soliloquy in the park scene, given to music and dance by those lovely girls, lifted that scene into a class by itself, and made it something more than entertainment.

Fioretta opened at the Earl Carroll Theatre on Broadway on February 5, 1929. *Variety* described it as "an eye-filling production," in part because of the 56 scantily clad showgirls on display. Atwill no doubt found them all most agreeable. The review continued:

> Mr. Atwill gave a polished performance as the minister of state or something like that and wore a number of gorgeous uniforms in heavy golds and silvers.

The *New York Times* also had nothing but good words to say about the actor:

> Lionel Atwill, who can be more royal than a king, impersonates the minister of state with matchless elegance and aplomb, treacherous, suave, imposing. Better than anyone else in the performance, Mr. Atwill holds his own against the strut of vestments.

The play ran successfully for 111 performances in New York, but huge costs were involved in staging it. In late March 1929 it was announced that the three stars had all agreed to take a pay cut so that the show could continue running without making a loss.

In the figure of Earl Carroll himself, Atwill should have perceived another warning of what Fate had in store for him in later years. Just three years earlier, Carroll had staged a wild party whose excesses included a naked young woman lying in a bathtub full of illegal alcohol. The event was reported in the *New York Mirror* and Carroll was hauled up to appear in court before a grand jury, denying that the event had ever taken

THE PLAY

By J. BROOKS ATKINSON.

Mr. Carroll Puts On a Show.

FIORETTA, a "romantic Venetian musical comedy" in two acts and seventeen scenes. Book by Earl Carroll, adapted by Charlton Andrews, music and lyrics by George Bagby and G. Romilli and additional lyrics by Grace Henry, Jo Trent and Billy Rose. Staged by Clifford Brooke; dances and ensembles arranged by LeRoy Prinz; costumes designed by William H. Mathews and Charles Le Maire; scenery by Clark Robinson; produced by Mr. Carroll. At the Earl Carroll Theatre.

Duke of Venice	Theo Karle
Duchess of Venice	Ethel Jane Walker
Count Matteo Di Brozzo	Lionel Atwill
Captain of the Guard	G. Davison Clark
Julio Pepoli	Leon Errol
Fioretta Pepoli	Dorothy Knapp
Orsino	George Houston
Luigi	Giovanni Guerreri
Marchesa Vera Di Livio	Fannie Brice
Caponetti	Jay Brennan
Marquis Filppo Di Livio	Charles Howard
Harlequin	Nelson Snow
Harlequin	Charles Columbus

No musical entertainment can compete with such splendor on equal terms. And although Mr. Carroll has lured Fannie Brice, Leon Errol and Lionel Atwill under his canopy of pleasures, it is to assist rather than to lead. The book chronicles the high romance of the maiden who is loved by a count honorably, if that is possible, and by the Duke of Venice more illegally. The Count is shot in the first act, and, according to authentic tidings, restored to the human comedy of life in the second. Without being notable for novelty or subtlety, the book serves the purpose of keeping the pageant in motion. Lionel Atwill, who can be more royal than a king, impersonates the minister of state with matchless elegance and aplomb, treacherous, suave, imposing. Better than any one else in the performance, Mr. Atwill holds his own against the strut of vestments.

place. However, other party guests confirmed that it *had* occurred, and Carroll was prosecuted for perjury and sent to jail for six months.

This sequence of events is remarkably similar to what was to happen to Atwill many years later. If it was one of the many instances of Fate warning him to stay out of trouble, then, as we shall see later, he chose not to heed it.

During the successful run of *Fioretta*, Atwill found time on his few days off from the theater to engage in various social and charity events. For example, in February his Friars Club held a special dinner with 300 attendees, in honor of actor Louis Mann. Atwill provided the entertainment. In March, the British Commonwealth Club held a dinner in honor of author R.C. Sherriff, whose play *Journey's End* had just arrived in the States. Atwill was one of the guests but on this occasion didn't speak. In April he was onstage for one night at the Metropolitan Opera House for the annual show in aid of the National Vaudeville Artists' Benefit Fund. Fanny Brice, the *Fioretta* Chorus, Eddie Cantor and the Marx Brothers appeared onstage alongside Atwill.

Clearly, Atwill loved to socialize, to keep busy and to attract publicity. He was not one of those actors who, when not working, preferred to stay out of the limelight. The one-off appearances kept coming. On April 27 Atwill was one of several actors giving his services for free at a charity ball in aid of the Marshall Stillman Movement, which assisted men with criminal records. It was held at the Star Casino on Park Avenue. On May 19, his Friars Club held their "Friars Annual Frolic" at the Metropolitan Opera House, with attendees including Will Rogers and Eddie Cantor. It began with a minstrel show, and perhaps for Atwill it brought back memories of his first-ever stage appearance—as a 10-year-old schoolboy in black-face make-up.

Around this time, Atwill starred in another short film for Fox. It was a two-reeler called *The Knife* and, like his other two shorts, was directed by Thomas H. Chalmers. Atwill played a top surgeon who discovers that his wife is secretly having an affair with his close friend. He then finds himself having to perform surgery on this friend …

Atwill is clearly enjoying seeing his female costar wearing just her underwear in *Stripped* (1929). [Photo courtesy White Studio/Billy Rose Theatre Division, the New York Public Library for the Performing Arts]

knowing that he has the power, with one *accidental* slip of his scalpel, to rid himself of his love rival. This film has always been omitted from Atwill filmographies and there is something of a mystery surrounding it. No stills or publicity material from it are known to exist, and early articles on Atwill usually state that he made only two short films for Fox, not three. Certainly the film existed (and was registered at the Copyright Office in April 1929), but Atwill's part in it has not been completely verified.

Atwill's next play—which he produced, directed and starred in—had the sort of sensational title that, he hoped, couldn't fail to draw in audiences. It was called *Stripped*. Its original title had been the far-less risqué *The Eternal Quest*, and it's rumored that it was Atwill who came up with the title change. Described as "a smart comedy," its plot concerned a jewel robbery, and the play (written by Jane Murfin) derives its title from a scene where a woman accused of the robbery is asked to strip to her chemise. In other words, it was just the sort of titillating subject matter to which Atwill was naturally attracted.

It opened at the Apollo Theatre in Atlantic City on June 3, 1929. It did well enough there to move on to the Brooklyn Theatre on Flatbush Avenue on June 24. In late September and early October it was playing at the Maryland Theatre in Baltimore, where its title was temporarily changed to *Intrigue*. The reason for the change is unknown—perhaps some eminent Baltimorean had objected to it. After a spell at a theater in Wilmington, it eventually reached New York on October 21, opening at the Ambassador Theatre.

May 22, 1929, the New York Times

'STRIPPED' ITS TITLE NOW.

Lionel Atwill to Act Star Role in Jane Murfin's New Play.

The title of Jane Murfin's new play, previously called "The Eternal Quest," has been changed to "Stripped." Lionel Atwill, who is directing the production, will appear in the star rôle of a tryout production in Atlantic City on June 3. The company will also include Jessie Boyce Landis, Charles Trowbridge, Frederick Truesdell, Anne Sutherland, Ferdinand Hast and Mario Majeroni. "Stripped" is scheduled to open on Broadway next season.

Atwill played Monsieur Lazlov, a romantic and debonair prince-pretender to a Slavic throne, who is attempting to cash in on the crown jewels while agents from his now-communist country try to thwart him. The *New York Times* thought that the plot contained "some of the thickest plot ramifications in a long time." But they had good words for the star:

> Atwill, with suave artistry and ingratiating personality, succeeds in imparting interest to the character, if not to the play.

They described him as "savoring his lines with a relish worthy of Shaw at his best."

Variety thought it was "… just a boresome evening" and thought that Atwill—

> … was wasting his talents upon a trifle. It may be taken off this Saturday. If not, it should be.

It lasted 24 performances in New York.

Memorial Day, paying tribute to those who had died during WWI, fell during the run of *Stripped*, and Atwill was keen to offer his services. There was a parade through New York followed by a church service and finally a memorial held at the Mall in Central Park. It was here that Atwill recited *The Unknown Solider* and the occasion was broadcast over WNYC radio.

The last months of 1929 saw Atwill involved with two more plays, neither of which was especially successful.

The first was *A Strong Man's House*, written by Lee Wilson Dodd. It opened at the Ambassador Theatre on September 16 and ran for 24 performances. Atwill directed but did not act in it. The star was Mary Nash, whom Atwill would meet again many years later in *Charlie Chan in Panama*. The plot concerned "the exploits of a Middle Western adventuress," a euphemism for a woman of lax morals.

The *New York Times* was not impressed:

> A play that for all its rambling situations flares only fitfully into life behind the footlights … it has moments when it moves as laggardly as the stationary smoke issuing from the chimneys painted on the backdrop of its single set … In his direction, Mr. Atwill appears to have favored the performers rather than the play.

It was withdrawn on October 5 after only 24 performances—another disappointment for Atwill.

Before his next play, Atwill appeared for one night only on November 24 at a show produced by the Friars (of which he had been made one of 10 governors back in May). It was the club's Silver Jubilee Frolic, staged at the Majestic Theatre, where it played to a full house. Atwill was one of many "interlocutors" (that is, an announcer); the performers included Rudy Vallee and Eddie Cantor, and the evening featured a minstrel show.

The last of Atwill's three plays at the end of 1929 was *Seven*, which opened at the Republic Theatre on December 27. Again, Atwill directed but did not star, leaving the acting honors to Preston Foster. It was a WWI drama set on the Western Front in France, and it told the story of a group of doomed American airmen. It lasted for 35 performances, ending some time in January 1930.

Atwill's activities from February to April 1930 are unknown—perhaps he was touring in plays around the States, or, more likely, simply taking some time off and enjoying a life of leisure, making the most of his beach house and his yacht. As far as is known, his first theatrical work after this break was in May 1930.

Louise Cromwell Brooks becomes the wife of Lionel Atwill in 1930.

The Ackroyd Mystery, staged at the Copley Theatre by the Boston Stock Company, opened in that city on May 12. Information about this play, sometimes referred under the title of *Alibi*, is scant because it never reached the New York theaters. It was a version of Agatha Christie's *The Murder of Roger Ackroyd*, which had been a successful play in London in 1928 and 1929. Audiences were treated to the delicious spectacle of seeing Atwill playing Christie's Belgian detective, the great Hercule Poirot. The play was not a huge success and the *New York Times* wrote:

> In spite of Lionel Atwill's neat acting, *The Ackroyd Mystery* goes better in print than on the stage.

In June of 1930, the newspapers were full of details of a forthcoming grand society wedding: "Lionel Atwill to Wed Mrs. MacArthur," ran the *New York Times*, continuing,

> The marriage ... had been rumored for several months, but only a few close friends knew about the definite plans of the couple.

It had been announced six months earlier that the marriage would take place on New Year's Eve of 1929, but for reasons unknown, it didn't happen then and was postponed

The Exquisite Villain

A portrait of Atwill taken around 1928 or 1929

until the following summer. The ceremony took place in Louise's home, a vast house called Rainbow Hill in Eccleston, northwest of Baltimore, in Maryland. Then the couple sailed off for a honeymoon trip on their new yacht. When interviewed years later about her divorce and her new husband, Louise quipped, "I traded four little stars for one big Hollywood star."

In August of 1930, the *New York Times* referred to *Dice*, a play written by Artad Pasztor and announced that Atwill "shall come forth … to star in it." Whether or not the play ever materialized is not known, but there is certainly no record of it ever reaching Broadway.

The newspapers reported in early September 1930 that Atwill would be starring opposite Colleen More in *On The Loose*, a play to be produced and directed by Arch Selwyn. Again, little is known about this play, or even if it ever was staged. Later in September, the *New York Times* reported that Atwill would star in *On The Spot*, a play about London gangsters from an Edgar Wallace novel, but the part went to someone else.

In late 1930, Atwill was finally back on Broadway. He directed, but did not act in, *A Kiss of Importance,* and rehearsals began in late October. The play starred a 38-year-old actor named Basil Rathbone. It would be the first of many significant encounters between Atwill and Rathbone over the ensuing years. The pair had much in common. They were both Englishmen with an aristocratic demeanor and impeccable diction. Both had successful stage careers before abandoning the stage and embracing Hollywood. And both became typecast as villains, in their own unique ways (with, in Rathbone's case, a nice sideline in playing one particular detective).

Derived from a French play entitled *Monsieur de St Obin* by Andree Picard and H.M. Harwood, *A Kiss of Importance* was a comedy in three acts. What attracted Atwill to this play? Perhaps it was because of its reputation as: "One of those French plays supposed to be naughty" (according to *Variety* magazine). Atwill may have been particularly tickled by this "naughtiness," which involved the subject of divorce, a subject that the thrice-married actor knew much about. The story has a woman conspire to obtain a divorce from her aging husband by arranging to have a young man (Rathbone) pretend to make advances to her, thereby furnishing the necessary evidence for the divorce. Frederick Kerr, a fellow Londoner, played the aging husband, who a year later would be memorable as the grumbling old father in James Whale's *Frankenstein*. The play's last act had some very well played comic exchanges between Rathbone and Kerr.

The *Variety* review did not mention Atwill directly, but did comment on his directing skills when it said that one actress—

> Suddenly developed something akin to a French accent. She had not used it previously … Appears to be a distinct error in direction.

The *New York Times* spotted Lionel in the audience on the opening night:

> Mr. Atwill gave the play either too much direction or not enough … there were times when he seemed vicariously to be performing some of its antics.

A Kiss of Importance opened on December 1, 1930 at the Fulton Theatre, New York. It lasted 24 performances—not a complete disaster but nevertheless it must have been a disappointment to Atwill that it did not prove to be more popular. *Variety* described the play as "an expensive flop," blaming its demise largely on the excessive salaries paid to some members of the company, explicitly citing the $1,500 that Atwill was receiving every week.

When *A Kiss of Importance* closed, it left the way clear for Atwill to become involved with a play that would be of crucial significance in his career. It was *The Silent Witness,* and it opened on Monday, February 9, at the Majestic Theatre in Brooklyn. It was sufficiently well received that a week later it moved to the Broad Street Theatre in Newark, followed by four weeks at the Walnut Theatre in Philadelphia.

This engrossing drama, written by Jack Celestin and Jack De Leon, depicts the lengths a father (Atwill) will go to in order to protect his son from receiving a death sentence for committing a *crime passionel.* Kay Strozzi played the woman who is murdered, and Anthony Kemble-Cooper played the son who believes he has strangled her. The play included several scenes of considerable tension, especially a highly charged courtroom sequence. It had already been a hit on the London stage and, when brought stateside, proved to be a great hit in theaters on both the East and West Coasts. Its success was such that a year later it was turned into a film, with Atwill making his debut in a sound, feature-length film.

The director of the American stage production, Harry Wagstaff Gribble, worked alongside Atwill to make some important changes. Chief among these was the introduction of a revolving stage that allowed three flashback scenes, all written especially for the American version, to be depicted swiftly and dramatically. It certainly wasn't the first time such a device had been used, but it definitely increased audience enjoyment. *Variety* (March 18, 1931) wrote:

> They have removed the heaviness and quickened the pace and, thanks to the ingenuity of treatment, the quick changes are at present the sensation of the performance.

Variety reviewed it at the Walnut Theatre:

Lionel Atwill, the star, hasn't as showy a role as usual as the father, but he plays Sir Austin sincerely, understandingly and, in his one or two big scenes, impressively. The witness stand scene provides good opportunities for emotion, and the second cut-back [i.e., flashback], bringing father and adventuress together, is a well-written comedy interlude.

This second of the three new flashback sequences is a delightful encounter between Atwill and Strozzi, and Atwill may have had a hand in the dialogue. He has come to persuade her to stop seeing his son, and he is prepared to buy her off. She flirts brazenly with him, while he, with some difficulty, tries to remain aloof.

After four successful weeks at the Walnut Theatre, the play had to find another venue to make way for *Dracula*, the play that had made a sensation of its star Bela Lugosi. On March 23, 1931 *The Silent Witness* moved to New York where it opened at the Morosco, a Broadway theater on 45th Street. *Variety* reviewed it again (on April 1):

Seems something new for Atwill, but his polished manner and bearing give the definite impression of a cultured, thoroughbred Englishman.

Finally, after an absence of around a year, he was back on a Broadway stage in front of an appreciative audience.

The play was such a success that it was even featured in a very early television broadcast—or a *radio talkie,* as it was called at the time. On the evening of Sunday,

Sir Austin (Atwill) hopes his checkbook can persuade the "adventuress" (Kay Strozzi) to stop seeing his son, from *The Silent Witness.* [Photo courtesy White Studio/Billy Rose Theatre Division, the New York Public Library for the Performing Arts]

April 26, 1931, WGBS studio set up a number of special receivers, only 12 inches square, in Aeolian Hall, 5th Avenue, and several thousand interested spectators turned up to catch glimpses of a parade of stage stars. The show featured one scene from *The Silent Witness*, with Kay Strozzi flirting outrageously with Atwill. Bursts of static occasionally marred the performance, but it was still a milestone occasion. It was so popular that WGBS repeated it a week later, on May 3, this time increasing the wattage from 500 to 5,000 watts, thereby increasing the stability of the image. Presumably it went out live again, with Atwill and Strozzi in the WGBS studio once more.

After 80 well-received performances, *The Silent Witness* ended its very successful run at the Morosco on May 30—but only for a temporary

Lionel Atwill

summer break. Lionel took a well-deserved three-month vacation from the theater, heading back East to his new wife Louise and no doubt making the most of the two yachts they owned. The pair lived a very high-profile social life and entertained guests frequently. For example, on the last weekend in August they had Paul May, the Belgian ambassador, staying with them as a guest at Rainbow Hill, their palatial house, and hosted a dinner dance for him and other guests. Other notables who were present included the Cuban ambassador.

Recharged by his summer break, Atwill was back in *The Silent Witness* in September. The play opened in Albany, then toured around Rochester, Detroit and at the Selwyn Theatre in Chicago.

The Silent Witness moved to the West Coast in October 1931. Initially, it would seem that Atwill had not planned to move with it. However, on October 26 *The Los Angeles Times* published a still of Atwill looking very handsome in top hat and tails for his role as Sir Austin:

> Lionel Atwill has come to Los Angeles from his Eastern home to enact his original role in the mystery drama starting tonight at the Belasco Theatre. Atwill is replacing A.E. Anson, who was taken ill.

This remark suggests that Atwill had perhaps never intended to act in the play once it moved West, but he was encouraged to help out the Belasco production, which must have suddenly found itself in a tight spot as a result of Anson's illness.

For its West Coast production, some significant cast changes occurred. The adventuress was played by Olga Baclanova, a respected Russian actress who will be forever remembered as the villainess of *Freaks* (1932), Tod Browning's horror movie classic in which she ended up being transformed into a hideous half-bird monstrosity. Bramwell Fletcher played the son, who in 1932 would be driven quite mad by the sight of Boris Karloff coming to life in *The Mummy*.

Reviews were again good. *The Los Angeles Examiner* wrote:

> Mr. Fletcher's astonishingly beautiful work sets a hit pace, but when Lionel Atwill, Sir Austin, takes over the murder to save his son, by the Holy Poker! You see memorably fine acting.

The Fox film studio took notice and bought up the rights to film the play—and they wanted Atwill to recreate his stage role on film. The rest, as they say, is history.

Chapter 8
The Hollywood Years 1931 to 1936

LIONEL ATWILL TALKS

LIONELL ATWILL, who has trouped with the best of them from London to Broadway—and back again through the years—has apparently come to rest in Hollywood. This is not said in the spirit of requiem, by either the chief character or any one else. But the motion pictures, with their youthful garb, have a future in which Mr. Atwill wishes to share. And moreover—this admission was made with a bland unconcern:

"I'm one of those few stage actors who really like the films, and admit it."

On the pages preceding this, a biography of Mr. Atwill would be superfluous, and it is necessary to say here only that he has been in just two pictures. The first was "The Silent Witness," in which he portrayed a rôle he had taken on the stage. The second is the energetically satanic "Doctor X." Although this last is a current visitor—as is the actor—he hasn't seen it yet. He did remember, however, that the cast had a lot of fun in its making.

A tall man, well-groomed, whose manner and conversation suggest a friendly humor, Mr. Atwill looks upon his life and his art with a frankness that defies the worship of illusion. He is now connected with the film industry quite boldly because he likes it and because "every man should do what he can for himself." For the youngsters who never knew "The Wild Duck" and "Hedda Gabler"—well, let them talk until they have reached maturity. Mr. Atwill in the meanwhile will be in Hollywood, making pictures.

Two Methods of Acting.

He has some theories—as why does not?—certain ambitions and an excellent simile about the difference in acting technique for the stage and the screen. To take them in inverse order, life is not unlike a glance through a telescope. Looking in the correct way is the art of the theatre, expanding personality and voice so that the far stretches of those balcony seats feel that they are in on it, too. Looking through the wrong way is the screen, suggesting gently and paying close attention to microscopic things.

"There are two different techniques," he explains. "That is why some stage actors are not good in the pictures and some movie stars fail on the stage. It is easier for the former to learn the other mode than the latter."

His ambitions deal, naturally enough, with future parts that he hopes to play. He isn't much interested in "drawing-room drama," but rather he has a thirst for the adventurous. By this he does not mean something about the Riders of the Western Plains. He sees "adult entertainment" with adventure, enough sophistication to keep both the audience and himself from being bored in this mad age—in other words, a bit out of Kipling or Somerset Maugham. The career of Count von Luckner would also be a good one, he thinks.

Leaving For Coast Soon.

Among his theories is one that says, briefly, "the theatre type of play is not going to be the mode" in the moving pictures. The future will hold the scope, manners and customs of the old, silent days; and will have the further asset of the spoken word. And that, he is sure, is as it should be, for the screen is quite distinct from Broadway—the lines being parallel and not necessarily at right angles.

As to his immediate future; he is going back to Hollywood in a week or so. There is a script waiting for him, but he didn't want to say anything about that. He has not said farewell forever to the stage, for at most that is just a gesture. He likes the people out on the Coast, and the work, and presumably the climate, too. He likes the people in New York, and the work, but the gentle tribute must stop there. The heat, like the Twentieth Century Blues and Mr. Coward, is getting him down.

FILM FLASHES

VILMA BANKY, who has been absent from the screen for about a year, will have the leading feminine rôle in "The Rebel," which will be filmed this Summer in the Tyrolean Alps. Luis Trenker will be the star of the picture, as well as one of its directors, and Victor Varconi will also have a part.

William Powell is to do a picture called "The Mind Reader," from an unproduced play by Vivian Cosby. Just when work will start is not clear. The Warner office also purchased the screen rights to "Grand Slam," the novel by B. Russell Herts about a bridge whist expert. This one is planned as a vehicle for either Mr. Powell or Warren William.

The final title for the film which Douglas Fairbanks made in the South Seas during the Spring is "Mr. Robinson Crusoe."

In this August 14, 1932 article from the *New York Times*, Lionel Atwill discusses his transition to the movies.

Someone from the Fox Studio saw Atwill onstage in *The Silent Witness* and offered him the chance to star in a film version. The actor had previously been unimpressed with the medium of film, but a lot had changed since his last silent picture a decade earlier. Now audiences would be able to hear his voice as well as see him, and he decided to give the movies another try. He accepted the offer from Fox and reported for work at the studio in December 1931.

The film, released in February 1932, was a great success and allowed a much wider audience to experience Atwill's powerful performance as Sir Austin Howard, especially in the nail-biting courtroom scene. It's a shame that the film is so little known today because, despite some scenes and dialogue that have become dated, it still packs quite a punch. In the witness box, Atwill gives one of the best performances of his entire film career. This film and all of Atwill's other films are discussed in greater detail in the section entitled *The Films*, later in this book.

Atwill started working on his second sound film on March 2, 1932, and it would turn out to be one of the key films of his career; it saw him star for the first time in a full-blown horror film. *Doctor X* is regarded by many today as one of the classic horror films of the 1930s. It is also the first cinematic appearance of Atwill as a mad doctor, and he filled the role superbly. His Dr. Xavier is shaped very much from the same mould as Anton Ragatzy of his old Broadway play *The Outsider*, but taken to another level. In *Doctor X*, Atwill dons a white lab coat for the first time, stands at the controls of some outlandish equipment and gets to speak some marvelous pseudo-scientific mumbo-jumbo. He was perfect for the part.

His appearance in *Doctor X* begs the question: Why did Lionel Atwill, the revered Broadway star, so readily accept offers to star in lurid horror films? His

legion of fans today are all grateful that he did, but it seems odd that he did not turn down offers to star in low-budget chillers like *The Vampire Bat* and *The Sphinx* in favor of more *respectable* parts. He gave clues to his reasons in various interviews that appeared in the press over the next few years.

"Frankly, I've had my fill of art," he told the *New York Times* in 1934. He had already proved his worth to the critics, to the public and to himself a dozen times over on the stage. Now he had the self-confidence to decide that he would have some fun. All around him, Hollywood was making successful horror films—such as *Dracula* (1931, starring Bela Lugosi), *Frankenstein* (1931, with Boris Karloff) and *Dr. Jekyll and Mr. Hyde* (1932, with Fredric March)—and Atwill, who almost certainly would have seen these films, decided he wanted to be a part of the action. He had always been drawn to the macabre, and the film roles offered to him in the early 1930s gave every opportunity to play highly melodramatic parts, where he could really let rip with his particular brand of acting.

Other reasons existed why he liked the horror film roles. For one thing, the money

August 7, 1932, the New York Times

"Doctor X," which is at the Strand, is Lionel Atwill's second talking picture. He was lured away from Broadway late last year, to translate his talents and "The Silent Witness" to the films. He left behind him two columns in the "Who's Who in the Theatre," the souvenirs of a theatrical life that started in 1905. That was in London, and in the decade which followed he was seen in several Ibsen rôles and also in the original London production of "Milestones," in which he played throughout its run of 600 performances.

In 1915 he accompanied the late Lily Langtry to this country for a tour, and later repeated his London successes in "Hedda Gabler," "A Wild Duck" and "A Doll's House," with Alla Nazimova. Under the management of the late David Belasco he scored a success in "Tiger! Tiger!" in which he played opposite Frances Starr. Then followed "Deburau," and "The Grand Duke." "The Outsider," "Stripped" and "The Silent Witness."

He was born in 1885 in Croydon, England, and was intended by a fond family to be an architect.

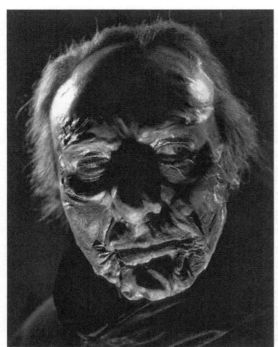

Atwill displays his remarkable make-up in *Mystery of the Wax Museum* (1933).

was good. For *Doctor X*, he received $2,000 a week, a significant increase on the $1,500 he was getting when he directed *A Kiss of Importance* on Broadway in 1930. By 1932, Atwill was already financially secure; he had amassed considerable savings and property, not to mention a valuable collection of paintings. On top of that he was married to an extremely wealthy woman. Even if the Hollywood paychecks had not been so attractive, he could still have chosen to ignore the *worthy* roles in favor of popular ones that allowed self-indulgence.

He also knew that he was no longer the young, good-looking Broadway matinee idol of the 1910s and 1920s. He was 46 years old when *The Silent Witness* was released, and he knew that if his acting career were to continue, he would have to take on other kinds of roles. Playing the "heavy" suited him and he enjoyed every minute of it. He was never one of those actors who try to play down their associations with horror films; he saw nothing to be ashamed of and rather enjoyed the notoriety.

Atwill's resonant speaking voice meant he was able to earn a little extra on the side doing narrations for film trailers. The first was *I Am a Fugitive from a Chain Gang* (1932), starring Paul Muni:

> Here he is—the man who preferred death to the tortures of the chain gang. His was the most sensational escape in chain gang history. Crawling through the thick brush, bloodhounds at his heels, hiding in swamps, he outwitted his pursuers at every turn. This man has lived a thousand lives in one—a hunted thing on earth.

It was Atwill's voice, too, that boomed over the trailer for *20,000 Years in Sing Sing* (1932):

> Imagine a motion picture where every scene is a big headlight of some colorful career that has made headline history … a picture that condenses the most dramatic moments from hundreds of sensationally dramatic lives into a single evening's entertainment. Such a picture is *20,000 Years in Sing Sing* … with Spencer Tracy … and Bette Davis.

Lionel Atwill

In 1932 he worked on two more horror films (both released early the following year), *The Vampire Bat* and *Mystery of the Wax Museum*. In the former, Lionel played a kindly physician who, in the last 10 minutes, turns into a fully-fledged mad doctor. The film is a lot of fun but is certainly no classic. *Wax Museum*, on the other hand, is one of his best-remembered films, giving him an opportunity to indulge his acting talents first as a dreamy-headed sculptor, then as a gray-haired, wheelchair-bound cripple and finally as a hideously scarred monster, wearing make-up that was as good as anything any of the other film studios—specifically horror specialists Universal—were creating.

During 1932, Atwill continued to be something of a party animal. He was on the Board of Governors of the Pierrette Dansante Club, whose members were mainly prominent figures in theatrical circles. They organized regular Saturday night supper dances, and records survive of Atwill attending at least one of these, at the Waldorf Astoria Hotel on September 30.

Atwill went to MGM for *The Secret of Madame Blanche*, released in February 1933. In this superior tearjerker, Irene Dunne played lowly showgirl Sally, and Atwill was a wealthy, tyrannical father. The film gave Atwill the cruelest scene of his entire career, as he forbids the desperate Sally from having one last glimpse of the baby that has been taken away from her. It is Atwill at his beastliest!

This was followed in March by *Murders in the Zoo*, which saw Atwill giving possibly his best performance in a horror film as the brutal Eric Gorman, disposing in most vicious fashion anyone who so much as dares to look at his wife—and then feeding her to some hungry alligators. It was Atwill at his most depraved and he seemed to thoroughly enjoy acting every nasty second of the part. He followed this with a magnificently dissolute performance in *The Song of Songs* (for director Rouben Mamoulian), playing a lecherous old Baron who lusts after innocent country girl Marlene Dietrich. The film's wedding night scene, with Atwill giggling like an excited schoolboy outside the bedroom door, is one of the highlights of Atwill's screen career. *The Sphinx*, also released in 1933, was a much lesser affair, a low-budget horror film with Atwill in the dual role of identical twins, one a deaf mute. At Universal, *The Secret of the Blue Room* was a very tame haunted house mystery, with Atwill in a forgettable red-herring role. Atwill's other 1933 release was *The Solitaire Man*, an unremarkable jewel-theft drama with Lionel playing a crooked detective.

After five high-profile horror movies—*Doctor X, The Vampire Bat, Mystery of the Wax Museum, Murders in the Zoo* and *The Sphinx*—it might be expected that Atwill would be hopelessly typecast in the same way that Karloff and Lugosi had become. But, remarkably, it didn't happen. He escaped typecasting. There were two reasons. On the one hand, the studios recognized that the theater-trained actor was a versatile talent and could fill a variety of roles. On the other hand, Atwill himself made a conscious decision to avoid typecasting, as he revealed in his *Film Weekly* interview from 1936:

> I had a long talk with my business manager and we decided that Karloff and Lugosi had already cornered the market. So I eased away from horror roles to menace parts.

In fact, he spent most of the rest of the 1930s performing very busily in non-horror films, with only two or three exceptions.

In a July 1933 interview with Atwill that appeared in *Motion Picture* magazine, the author referred to the actor's pet dogs as "mammoth hounds that greet you with hellish baying." A short while later, these same hounds metaphorically bit the hand that fed them because, in October of 1934, it was reported in *Variety* that he was being "sued for $10,000 damages on a charge of harboring vicious dogs. Plaintiff says he was attacked by four of the actor's pooches."

An indication of his celebrity status is found in a play called *The Dark Tower*, which played on Broadway in late 1933. Atwill had no connection with this play about show people, but there is a scene where one character, a stage manager, complains to another—

> Half of the time you were sitting on your prat in Hollywood, and the
> other half directing Lionel Atwill.

Atwill himself must have chuckled mightily.

As we have seen many times, Atwill never shunned the limelight and was always keen to have his fingers in as many show business pies as he could. Throughout the 1930s, he was heavily involved with the Academy of Motion Picture Arts and Sciences, serving as a member of the Actors' Committee from 1934 to 1939 (and perhaps other years as well), voting for the Oscar nominees. Other voting members at this time included Leslie Howard and Mary Pickford. Atwill's involvement extended to often leading the actors' contingent in negotiations, and he was nominated to be on their Board of Governors. All of this was not for self-serving reasons but to help his fellow actors.

Atwill always made the most of his spare time. He was heavily involved with the running of a farm on his Maryland estate (which covered a massive 160 acres in Green Spring Valley, just outside Baltimore) and in fact won four Blue Ribbon prizes for cattle at state fairs. What a sight it must have been to see Lionel Atwill leading one of his prize cows or bulls into the arena. And when he wasn't raising cattle, he found time to indulge another of his favorite pastimes: attending murder trials. We can imagine him sitting attentively in the public gallery, lapping up every gruesome detail and perhaps making notes whenever he heard something that he thought he could use in one of his "heavy" roles. He split his time between

A sinister early 1930s portrait

his Maryland home and another home at Lake Michigan. He also spent time sailing his 65-foot yacht called *Ricci*. It was a good life.

Early in 1934, Atwill was on the radio again, in a play entitled *The Finger of God*, broadcast by station WEAF on January 18. Originally a British play of 1924, it told the story of three people—a young couple and an older man—trapped in the pitch black tunnel of a Welsh mine, with water slowly creeping up around their feet. The dialogue was perfect for Atwill:

> Of all the incompetent idiots, turning the lights off just when a party of visitors was seeing the place! Call this a coalmine! A damned, dark rabbit-hole I call it, a rotten rat-hole, a dratted, wet smelly drainpipe ... The dithering fools!

But his gruff manner turns to noble heroism at the end, when he helps the young couple climb to safety, while he is carried off to his death by the water.

Also in January, the *New York Times* interviewed him in his hotel room. His comments included the quote referred to earlier in this chapter:

> Frankly, I've had my fill of art. It's all very well in its way, but there's an entirely different fascination to pictures that I haven't got over yet. No doubt I never will. It may be a little childish but the sheer mechanical ingenuity of the whole thing gets under my skin the way

In *The Firebird* (1934), Atwill gave a fine performance as a man whose family life is disintegrating around him. (With Anita Louise, Verree Teasdale and C. Aubrey Smith)

a mechanical toy fascinates a boy. I've been having a tremendous good time and I don't see why I should stop.

Atwill appeared in a remarkable seven film releases in 1934. MGM paid him $2,000 per week to star in *Nana* (directed by Dorothy Arzner), giving one of his most restrained performances as a military man who falls in love with the same woman (Anna Sten) as his brother. Monogram's *Beggars in Ermine* was low in budget but high in macabre melodrama. In one of Atwill's most gruesome scenes ever, molten steel burns his legs away, leaving him a helpless cripple for the rest of the film. At MGM, *Stamboul Quest* managed to sneak some very risqué scenes past the censor, with Lionel taking an intense interest in Myrna Loy's discarded underwear. In *One More River* at Universal, he worked for legendary horror film director James Whale, giving a superb performance as a flamboyant but relentlessly cruel prosecuting attorney. (Whale was sufficiently impressed with him to give him parts in two later films.)

Released September 1934 was RKO's *The Age of Innocence*, with Atwill in his element as a womanizing scoundrel. At Warner Bros. in *The Firebird*, he gave an outstanding performance as a husband who fears his wife (Verree Teasdale) has been cheating on him. No other Hollywood actor could look tortured and humiliated quite as effectively as Atwill. His final 1934 release was *The Man Who Reclaimed His Head*, a borderline horror melodrama made at Universal, with a horrified Lionel finding himself the target of an insane Claude Rains brandishing a sharp sword.

In 1934, two announcements were made of forthcoming films that were to star Atwill. One was *The Healer*, "one of Monogram's big production splurges," but eventually the leading role went to Ralph Bellamy instead. More mouth-watering was an announcement by Universal that they were going to film Robert Louis Stevenson's *The Suicide Club*, starring Boris Karloff, Bela Lugosi and Lionel Atwill. The film was never made.

Never a slouch when it came to self-promotion, Atwill offered his services to be the host to Manuel Quezon, President of the Philippines, at a dinner on the Paramount Studios lot in November 1934.

Some time late in 1934, he looked for, and found, a house to buy on the West Coast. According to Kenneth Anger (in *Hollywood Babylon II*), it was director James Whale, with whom Atwill had recently worked on *One More River*, who helped him find the property. It was located at 13515 D'Este Drive in the Pacific Palisades area of Los

This is all that remained of Atwill's Malibu beach home after a 1935 fire.

Angeles, and Whale himself lived not far away. This huge home came complete with a tennis court, a swimming pool, orchards and a view of the valley below. Around the same time, Mr. and Mrs. Atwill also splashed out $42,000 on a Malibu beach home.

He appeared in five film releases during 1935, all well worth seeing. In *Mark of the Vampire*, starring Lionel Barrymore and Bela Lugosi, he was a plain-clothes policeman with nice lines offering dry humor. The film was an attempt by director Tod Browning to recreate the success of his earlier *Dracula* (1931), but it misfired. In Paramount's *The Devil Is a Woman*, directed by Josef Von Sternberg, Atwill suffered unbearable torment at the hands of Marlene Dietrich, who kept him in a permanent state of sexual frustration, with the poor chap ending up a complete physical, emotional and financial wreck at the end of the film. At MGM, Atwill was one half of a kind of double-act with Spencer Tracy in *The Murder Man*, playing a jovial detective. Still at MGM, he was in *Rendezvous*, a good WWI drama in which he played the U.S. government's chief code-breaker. And finally, at the very end of 1935, he could be seen in *Captain Blood*, as the sadistic Colonel Bishop, owner of a West Indies plantation where he enjoys thrashing and branding his slaves (Errol Flynn among them). It is one of his best-remembered roles.

On September 26, 1935, Atwill was on the radio again. He co-starred on station WEAF with George Brent in *The Prince Chap*, a shortened version of a 1904 play by Edward Peple about artists and models.

In October 1935, the Atwills staged a party at their Malibu beach bungalow for 30 guests including silent film star Theda Bara and Jacqueline Wells (remembered by

Another 1930s portrait

horror fans for having acted alongside Karloff and Lugosi in 1934's *The Black Cat*, and at the time engaged to Lionel's stepson Walter Brooks). Just two weeks after the party, mountain brush fires swept through the hills behind Malibu, completely destroying the Atwill house and several other homes as well. It must have been a devastating blow to Lionel and Louise to see not only one of their homes, but also so many of their possessions, go up in smoke.

In the mid-30s Atwill was arguably at the peak of his Hollywood career, but in fact he had ambitions to go higher. A short news item in the British magazine *Film Weekly* in February 1936 stated:

Lionel Atwill, one of the soundest actors England has given to Hollywood, has been thinking seriously about his future. He has decided that he ought to be a star. He announces that, despite the fact that he no longer has the superficial appeal of youth, the parts he played in *The Devil Is a Woman* and *Captain Blood* prove that he could be as popular as [George] Arliss.

Atwill featured in three 1936 film releases. At Columbia, he was in *Lady of Secrets*, starring Ruth Chatterton, where he was at his coldest, cruelest and nastiest. For MGM, he starred in *Absolute Quiet*, playing a high-powered businessman whose doctor orders him to take a complete rest. Over at Paramount, he supported Herbert Marshall and Gertrude Michael in *'Til We Meet Again*, a WWI drama in which he played a stern German spymaster and suffered a particularly gruesome death scene.

In 1936, Atwill maintained his party animal lifestyle, and when he wasn't holding parties of his own, he was attending other peoples'. For example, in January he was a guest at a dinner given by Mary Pickford in honor of Lady Mendl. Also on the prestigious guest list were members of various foreign royal families, as well as Hollywood people such as Bette Davis, Miriam Hopkins, David Selznick and Leslie Howard.

Despite his appetite for the good life, it appears that Atwill didn't care much for the constant recognition that comes with being a celebrity. In his autobiography, director Josef von Sternberg commented on this.

I knew only one actor who shrank from being recognized, and that was Lionel Atwill. I was with him in a theater lobby when a woman tourist approached him and said, "Your face is familiar. Aren't you in the movies?" He turned pale and, mumbling, "Good God," vanished.

In May 1936, Louise's son from her first marriage, Walter Brooks, married Jacqueline Wells in Santa Barbara. Atwill spoke jauntily about the occasion in Britain's *Picturegoer* magazine:

> Lionel Atwill declared that, "Marriage is a woman's institution. I ought to know." He added, "I've been married three times. And now my stepson has just married. When he told me he was engaged and introduced me to his future wife, I gave him 25 bucks to buy a good dinner after the wedding and loaned him my beach home for his honeymoon. His wife was a nice girl, but I told him that if he wanted to get married he would have to learn about the responsibilities of life. So all he got was the 25 bucks."

In August 1936, Atwill was chosen from 28 candidates to play the leading role in a stage version of *Everyman* (the old morality play), staged by the California Festival Association at the Hollywood Bowl in Los Angeles. It was an elaborate production, staged by Max Reinhardt, with a chorus of singing angels who were dressed in attire that seemed less suitable for a heavenly setting and more at home in a Busby Berkeley musical.

Although Atwill was in the privileged position of being able to own more than one California beach home, he always seemed to have bad luck with them. One of them burnt down in October 1935 when fires in the Malibu Hills raged out of control. In 1936 he owned two beach homes, each worth around $60,000, but at the end of 1936, he had further bad luck when it was reported that both of them were badly damaged in heavy storms during the last weekend in December. Parts of the buildings were washed away into the sea, along with $12,000 worth of antiques. Presumably, he had at least one of the houses repaired, because in July 1937, *Variety* reported that he had been spotted "grunion fishing in front of his house at Malibu."

Chapter 9
The Hollywood Years 1936 to 1939

.On October 26 1936, Lionel and Louise sailed out of Baltimore, heading for England. He had arranged a deal to make a film in London, *High Command,* and it would give him his first chance to visit his home country in 12 years. On arriving in Southampton, his first task was to pay a visit to relatives living in the area—his brother Stanley, Stanley's wife Ethel and their 13-year-old daughter Diana. Today, Stanley's grand-daughter Leslie recalls how her mother Diana often talked about this visit, and how exciting it was to have her film-star uncle in the house, telling them all about his Hollywood adventures. She also remembered that the visit had to be cut short because Lionel and Louise had arranged to have tea with the Duke and Duchess of Kent. Thanks to his marriage, Lionel was socializing among the highest echelons of society.

Ahead of their visit, they rented a spacious apartment at 14 Waterloo Place, a very prestigious building in central London. During the 10 weeks they were in England, the couple split their time between here and an expensive hotel in fashionable Park Lane. At some point Lionel met up with his son John, who was studying to be a doctor. It is not known whether Lionel also had a meeting with his first wife Phyllis (John's mother), who was living in London and doing some occasional acting on the stage.

The British film magazines were overjoyed to have one-of-their-own back in England, and queued up to interview him. Articles appeared in *Picture Show, Picturegoer* and *Film Weekly*. The latter was delighted to find that "he is still typically British in looks, habit and speech." Max Breen, for *Picturegoer*, met Atwill in his Park Lane hotel. Atwill confided:

> The portrayal of black-hearted monsters has given me a kind of—well, you might almost say a brotherly interest in them.

Breen asked him if screen villainy paid well.

> Rather! The sympathetic character usually has to have the star billing, but the *heavy* is frequently better paid—and if you have been in the business as long as I have, you will appreciate the importance of *that!*

Breen closed by commenting on the possibility that Atwill could have made more British films had he wanted to.

> He crept into England unheralded; and since he arrived, three prominent directors have said to me [Breen]: "If I'd known he was coming, I'd have tried to get him for my new picture."

High Command gave Atwill one of his rare starring roles in a non-horror film. He was outstanding in it, portraying a stiff-upper-lipped Major General who must make

Lionel Atwill

FILM WEEKLY, January 30, 1937

ATWILL IN AFRICA

LIONEL ATWILL, one of Hollywood's most successful Englishmen, came home to England to make a picture about West Africa.

Atwill is part-hero, part-villain of *The General Goes Too Far*, which Thorold Dickenson directed for Fanfare Productions. It is a dramatic story of a stern and ruthless general, who goes to take up his duties in Africa, hoping to bury the unpleasant associations of a murky marriage. Among the white colony he finds the "other man," and tension grows in the close quarters of the fort with the bomb of the past threatening to explode.

The General's sensational solution to end complications with the least damage to all concerned provides an exciting climax.

Lucie Mannheim, who made a hit as the spy in *The Thirty-Nine Steps*, has an important part as one of those menacing white women.

Lucie Mannheim causes a good deal of consternation all round the European community immured in a West African fort. But General Atwill is stern enough to be proof against even her charms

Below : It looks like a honeymoon, but it's just the arrival in Africa of the General's daughter (Kathleen Gibson) and her fiancé (Tom Gill). On the right are Lucie Mannheim and her first victim, who is not Clark Gable, but James Mason

Above : Wally Patch offers welcome refreshment to the old enemies, Lionel Atwill and Steve Geray, who find it hot work keeping up appearances before Allan Jeayes, during an African picnic

Britain's *Film Weekly* magazine devoted an entire page to *High Command*, Atwill's only British film.

the ultimate sacrifice in order to protect the happiness of his daughter. It's a shame that Atwill was not tempted back to England for more film roles.

When the filming of *High Command* was completed, Lionel and Louise sailed back aboard *The Washington* to the States, arriving in New York on January 9, 1937.

The Exquisite Villain

The 1937 radio version of *The Song of Songs* starred Douglas Fairbanks, Jr., Marlene Dietrich and Atwill.

Back in Hollywood, Atwill was as busy as ever. Offers from the major studios to appear in prestigious films came thick and fast, and 1937 saw him in six film releases. Paramount cast him in *Last Train From Madrid* as Colonel Vigo, behaving unpleasantly to Lew Ayres, Dorothy Lamour, Gilbert Roland and others. At Universal he made his second film for James Whale, *The Road Back*, and, as in his previous Whale film, he featured in some key scenes as a cold-blooded prosecuting attorney. At 20th Century Fox in *Lancer Spy* he was (again) a British officer with a stiff upper lip, playing in some good scenes opposite a young George Sanders. In *The Wrong Road*, for Republic, he got a chance to act out of character, as a kindly private investigator that tries to reform two young kids played by Richard Cromwell and Helen Mack. He was even more out of character in *The Great Garrick*, his third and last film for James Whale, playing an over-dressed French fop and getting a chance to do some light comedy, something that he had rarely done since his theater days.

In 1937, Atwill also found time to appear in two radio shows that were part of the Lux Radio Theatre series broadcast on CBS. They were both adaptations of successful films, trimmed down to under an hour.

The first was *Under Two Flags*, broadcast on May 27. In the film version, Ronald Colman had starred alongside Claudette Colbert, Rosalind Russell and Victor McLaglen. For the 50-minute radio version, Herbert Marshall, Lupe Velez and Olivia De Havilland presented these roles, respectively, with Atwill in the McLaglen part. The shows all included interesting introductions and epilogues, and in *Under Two Flags*, the series' regular director, Cecil B. DeMille, introduced each member of the cast. After talking about Velez, he continued:

Lionel Atwill

Just as busy is Lionel Atwill, who like Lupe, is home from picture making in England. He's just finished *The Road Back* for Universal, and *Last Train From Madrid* for Paramount. We meet him tonight in the role of Major Doyle.

The show ends with an informal chat between the presenter, the four stars and Cecil B. DeMille discussing the origins of the story. It's a thrill to hear Lionel Atwill speaking informally, even if it is only a couple of pre-scripted lines.

In the story, Major Doyle is in love with Cigarette (Velez), who works in an Algerian café, but she flirts with him only to get what she wants. Asking a favor of him, she says suggestively that if he does what she asks, "I will love you so much more ..." It's Atwill in one of his trademark roles—the military man who is badly used by his lover. In his best scene, he complains that she has lost interest in him since meeting Marshall.

> Not a decent kiss have I had since that day ... You're lying to me! You're lying to me! Aren't you? Aren't you? ... I warned you once, Cigarette, that I'd never let another man take my place. No man ever shall ... I warned you, Cigarette.

He then orders Marshall into enemy territory where he knows he and his men will be killed.

Atwill, always surprisingly good at laughing convincingly on film, does some of his loudest and most raucous laughing in this show. For example, when de Havilland wonders why the soldiers don't have mosquito nets, he roars with laughter and quips:

> It is said in the Legion, when a fly bites a Legionnaire, the fly dies!

Atwill's second 1937 radio broadcast, also for the Lux Radio Theatre, gave him a chance to re-create one of his greatest screen roles, Baron von Merzbach in *The Song of Songs*. Marlene Dietrich reprised her role of Lily, and Douglas Fairbanks, Jr. took the Brian Aherne role. This 45-minute adaptation of the 1933 film was broadcast on December 20, and once again Cecil B. DeMille introduced the cast:

> From the film cast of *The Song of Songs* is Lionel Atwill, as Baron von Merzbach. This splendid character actor, most recently seen in *The Great Garrick* and *Lancer Spy*, has been host these past few days to his brother-in-law, James Cromwell, husband of the former Doris Duke.

(James Cromwell, an American diplomat, was the brother of Lionel's wife Louise, while Doris Duke, sometimes referred to as "the richest girl in the world," was the daughter of a wealthy tobacco tycoon.) The script was cleaned up for radio—there is no scene where Dietrich disrobes for the sculptor, and the legendary wedding night scene has been excised. But Atwill still shines as the lascivious old Baron and delivers two particularly good speeches: when he asks Lily to marry him and when he taunts Lily and the sculptor at the dinner table. Once again, we get to hear Atwill's wonderful bawdy laugh at its most obscene. There is a treat at the end: a five-minute section in

Rainbow Hill, the palatial Green Spring Valley (outside of Baltimore) Maryland home of Lionel and Louise.

which Cecil B. DeMille chats informally with Fairbanks and Atwill. It's pre-scripted but comes across like dinner party chat as Fairbanks tries to get de Mille to lend him his yacht and, when that fails, tries to get Atwill to lend him his. The joke is that Atwill seems more interested in talking about his stamp collection (did he really have one?) and eventually discloses that his yacht is in dry-dock in Maryland, so he couldn't lend it even if he wanted.

The year 1937 very nearly presented Atwill in a film role that has been enjoyed worldwide by millions over the last 80 years: the *voice* of Grumpy in Walt Disney's animated *Snow White and the Seven Dwarfs*. Today, his great-niece Leslie vividly recalls her mother telling her on more than one occasion about a letter which Lionel had written to her, in which he told the family that he would be the voice of Grumpy. However, in the finished film Pinto Colvig supplied the voice. Could it be that Atwill auditioned for the part but was ultimately turned down? And might the audition tape still be somewhere in the Disney vaults?

In between the West Coast filmmaking and radio broadcasts, 1937 had other highlights for Lionel. In April, he and Louise found time for another transatlantic excursion, and passenger lists show that on April 7 they boarded *The Washington* once again heading for England. For a period during the summer of 1937, they offered Rainbow Hill, their palatial Maryland house, to the Duke and Duchess of Windsor for a honeymoon stay. Back in Britain the Duke, formerly King Edward VIII, had abdicated the throne in order to marry the American Wallis Simpson, and since the British Royal Family disapproved of the marriage, the couple had to find non-royal residences in which to stay. August 1937 saw Rainbow Hill become the victim of burglars on two occasions—one can only begin to imagine the haul of jewelry and paintings the thieves must have gotten away with.

Lionel Atwill

The Great Waltz (1938) contained a pivotal scene with Atwill and Luise Rainer, both giving outstanding performances.

The year 1938 saw only two films featuring Atwill, but he had memorable supporting roles in both. In MGM's *Three Comrades*, he supported the stellar cast of Robert Taylor, Margaret Sullavan, Franchot Tone and Robert Young. Atwill played a wealthy German whose best scene sees him drunk at a nightclub, telling dirty jokes and behaving shamefully. It feels like we are getting a glimpse of Atwill the party animal, whose high living would get him into so much trouble three years later. *The Great Waltz*, a musical biopic about Johann Strauss, showcased Atwill's superlative acting in a four-minute scene in which he confronts Strauss' wife (Luise Rainer) with her husband's infidelity.

In mid-1938, Atwill signed a contract with 20th Century Fox, which seemed to promise great things for him. It was a four-way contract that stated: "He will work as an actor, writer, director and producer under the new deal." With Atwill's experience in all these roles in the theater, it seemed only natural that he would want to try out similar roles in film. Disappointingly, Fox never did give him any opportunities to do anything other than act, and in frustration Atwill concluded his contract two years later in August 1940 and left the studio. Fox's shortsightedness is our great loss; who knows what wonderful films Atwill might have made? With his penchant for the macabre and the risqué, they surely would have been intriguing and controversial productions.

In November of 1938, Atwill signed up with Universal to appear in *Son of Frankenstein*, and it gave him one of his best-remembered roles. As Inspector Krogh, the chillingly stern policeman whose false arm seems almost to have a personality of its own, Atwill created one of the great characters of the Golden Age of Horror. The film served another purpose: The horror film *genre* had been in the doldrums for around three years, but *Son of Frankenstein* revitalized it, thrilling a whole new generation of

Atwill as Dr. Mortimer with Nigel Bruce and Richard Green from *The Hound of the Baskervilles* (1939)

filmgoers and creating a market for the kind of films which would keep Atwill in steady employment over the next six years.

The year 1939 was a bumper one for Lionel: as well as *Son of Frankenstein*, he appeared in a further eight film releases. 20th Century Fox kept him busy in four pictures. In *The Three Musketeers*, starring comedy trio the Ritz Brothers, Atwill played the villain De Rochfort and looked splendid in a succession of fancy collars, lacy cuffs and leather boots. He was a superbly sinister Dr. Mortimer in *The Hound of the Baskervilles*, telling Sherlock Holmes (Basil Rathbone) about the legend of the Hound, and the history of Grimpen Mire. Atwill was a much less memorable red herring in *The Gorilla* (starring the Ritz Brothers again), and he was much better served in his fourth Fox film of 1939, *Mr. Moto Takes a Vacation*, in which he had another rare chance to indulge in a bit of light comedy as the excitable, blustering curator of a museum where Mr. Moto (Peter Lorre) comes to protect the crown of the Queen of Sheba.

Away from Fox, he acted in an obscure Mexican-U.S. co-production, *Carlotta the Mad Empress*, playing a stern, aristocratic military man. In *The Sun Never Sets* at Universal, he was allowed to really chew up the scenery as Dr. Hugo Zurof, indulging in some colorful mad doctor ranting while planning to rule the world and treat all its inhabitants as if they were mere ants. His role in MGM's *The Secret of Dr. Kildare* was a very low-key supporting part, and he was only slightly better served in a second 1939 film for MGM, *Balalaika*, playing a bearded Russian music teacher who is father to Ilona Massey.

Lionel Atwill

In March 1939, Atwill was on the radio airwaves again. The Gulf Screen Guild Theatre was a regular weekly slot that usually ran radio adaptations of successful films. But *The Bridge of Mercy* was unusual in that it was an original drama and, moreover, its controversial subject matter, assisted euthanasia, would not have been tolerated on the screen. It's Atwill's most powerful radio drama, both in terms of his performance and also in terms of the play as a whole. Directed by George Cukor, the play has Atwill, for the third time in his career, playing an aggressive prosecuting attorney. He tries to get Paul Muni convicted for murdering his wife, Josephine Hutchinson (with whom Atwill had recently co-starred in *Son of Frankenstein*). Hutchinson has been suffering the agonies of a slow death from cancer and Muni administered a fatal dose of morphine to put her out of her misery. Atwill gets a good speech at the opening of the play, addressing the jury and introducing the case, and later he conducts a series of tough cross-examinations of witnesses, interrupting them as they speak, and trying to twist their words. But his best speech is his summation. He delivers these lines with more passion than he put into any speech, before or since, often raising his voice very nearly to a shout as he rams home a point, determined to condemn a man to the electric chair.

> … And, ladies and gentlemen of the jury, in conclusion, Mary Carsons might have lived for some time still. But Defense claims she wished, *against all human instincts*, to die. But we have proved that the defendant *did* lie to the druggist about Dr. Morton having left the city, and *did* forge a deadly prescription, raising the amount of morphine prescribed by said Doctor Morton. Ladies and gentlemen, this man *murdered* his sick and helpless wife by administering to her a lethal dose of morphine …

It's a magnificent example of Atwill at his finest: bullish, nasty and irresistible.

In November 1939, Atwill must have been delighted when he heard news that his son John had received his doctor's degree. There was some other news about John, too, which Atwill must have greeted with a mixture of pride and trepidation: He was now a captain in the Royal Army Medical Corps.

The 1930s had been a golden decade for Lionel Atwill. He was one of Hollywood's most highly respected and sought-after character actors. He was earning substantial amounts of money that offered him a luxurious standard of living. He was married to an extremely wealthy woman. He traveled often from East Coast to West Coast and back again, making the most of his homes in both—a large house and beach homes in Los Angeles, and a palatial mansion out East in Maryland. He had two yachts, one on a lake near his Baltimore home, the other on the West Coast. He had a valet to look after all his domestic needs. In his social life, he met and entertained rich and important guests—some of them foreign royalty—whose presence gave him prestige and status. It was a dream life.

What could possibly go wrong?

Chapter 10
The Hollywood Years 1940 to 1941

The decade of the 1940s started off well for Lionel Atwill—at least in terms of his film career.

He was still hopeful that 20th Century Fox would honor his four-way contract with them, and on that year's Federal Census, he wrote that his occupation was "actor-director." (On the same census document, he stated that his annual income was "$5,000 plus" and that he was paying his butler Otis Hawkins $720 per annum.) The directing jobs did not materialize but Fox kept him busy during 1940, and he appeared in six film releases. But Atwill must have been frustrated to find that he only had minor supporting roles in all of them. He must have started to wonder if signing with Fox had been a big mistake. If he had continued to freelance, he might have been offered better roles. Still, he was no doubt enjoying all the money that was still rolling in.

Five of Atwill's 1940 films were at Fox. *Charlie Chan in Panama*, starring Sidney Toler in the title role, was an enjoyable entry in the detective series, with Atwill as one of the red herrings. In *Johnny Apollo*, a crime drama starring Tyrone Power, Atwill had an unimportant role as Edward Arnold's attorney. *The Girl in 313* was another crime drama, with Atwill as the crooked owner of a high-class jewelry salon. Atwill was better served in a second Charlie Chan opus, *Charlie Chan's Murder Cruise*, where he played another red herring but at least got plenty of screen time. His last Fox film of 1940 was *The Great Profile*, starring John Barrymore. This tale, set in the world of the theater, gave audiences a rare opportunity to see Atwill on a stage, but his scenes are so brief that this is very probably his least memorable film role.

Atwill's other 1940 release was in MGM's prestigious *Boom Town* starring Clark Gable, Spencer Tracy, Claudette Colbert and Hedy Lamarr. In this oil-prospecting drama, Atwill played a New York businessman, but it was yet another minor role that wasted his talents. Its most remarkable moment was an uncannily prophetic scene in a courtroom. Atwill is in the witness box, and Gable points a finger at him and shouts, "That's a lie!" It wouldn't be long before Atwill found himself living that scene for real.

While waiting for his next film role to come along, Atwill acted in another radio drama. Broadcast on November 10, 1940, *History Is Made at Night* was an episode in the Gulf Screen Guild Theatre series. It was a heavily condensed version of the 1937 film, cut down to a brisk 25 minutes, and featured Atwill in the role of the brutal husband played by Colin Clive in the film version. Charles Boyer repeated his film role; Greer Garson took on the Jean Arthur role.

The story tells of nasty Bruce Vail (Atwill) who wants to divorce his wife, and so arranges for his chauffeur to be caught in her room in order to provide the necessary evidence. The wife, however, runs off with a waiter (Boyer). Vail meanwhile alleges that the chauffeur was shot dead by the waiter. It all ends up in a courtroom scene.

Atwill's dialogue in court is remarkable. It's yet another foreshadowing of his own court case. During the proceedings, he suddenly cries out:

Hollywood's maddest doctor is clearly thrilled by the prospect of experimenting on pretty Anne Nagel from *Man Made Monster* (1940).

> Your honor! I believe I have something to add to the testimony that has a great bearing on this case … I wish to tell the court and the jury that your whole case … is built on perjured testimony. My story on the stand was a lie from start to finish.

It is simply astonishing that Atwill should find himself speaking these lines, in view of what happened later. After this dramatic outburst, it turns out that the chauffeur wasn't shot at all but fell and struck his head. Vail framed the waiter in the hope that, with him out of the way, his wife would return to him. But he has had a touching change of heart, and Atwill delivers his final lines with memorable theatrical poignancy.

> I can't fight a love like theirs. Let them go. Let them live.

The radio show makes no mention of whether or not Atwill's character ended up back in court on a perjury charge … but in just a few months he would certainly find himself in that very situation in real life.

After 1940's series of disappointing supporting roles, Atwill must have been delighted when, in December, Universal offered him a starring role in *Man Made Monster*. Here at last was a part that he could really get his teeth into, playing scientist Dr. Paul Rigas who pumps Lon Chaney, Jr. full of large doses of electricity, turning him into a glowing zombie. He then very nearly does the same to Anne Nagel. This was the *exquisite villain* at his best, with Atwill's insanity and evil scaling truly megalomaniacal

Is this a photo of Lionel Atwill at one of his wild parties? No, it's a frame enlargement of him playing a drunken character at a nightclub in *Three Comrades*.

heights. The intensity of Atwill's stare during his best scenes is something that audiences must see to believe. The dialogue is equal to the occasion and Atwill delivers some of the best mad scientist lines of his career, especially in one feverish outpouring—perhaps conceived or refined by Atwill himself—which is so risqué that, as he pins Nagel to his operating table, he makes it sound as if he is doing the groundwork for later research by Masters and Johnson into female sexual response.

During the Christmas holiday period of 1940/1941, Atwill held a party at his house on D'Este Drive in Pacific Palisades. He would spend the rest of his life regretting that it ever took place. Before saying more about it, let's recall scenes in two of Atwill's recent film releases. *Charlie Chan's Murder Cruise,* just referred to above, contained an entertaining scene in which Atwill's character stages an on-board party which gets out of hand, with drunken young ladies cavorting on wooden hobby horses, and an excitable Atwill egging them on from the sidelines calling out, "That's a hot one!" Two years earlier, in *Three Comrades*, audiences had seen another glimpse of Lionel Atwill the party animal, getting sozzled on champagne, telling a dirty joke and laughing drunkenly.

Both instances were, of course, fictitious. But with hindsight we can see that they are very revealing glimpses of the lifestyle that Atwill was perhaps leading offscreen. Back in November 1939, Atwill's marriage to Louise had finally broken down and (according to her) he had ordered her to move out of their Pacific Palisades home. Atwill now found himself single and fancy-free again. No longer having access to all of Louise's social connections, there would be no more parties attended by foreign dignitaries and other VIPs who were his wife's acquaintances. But never mind, now he was free to hold parties more to his own liking …

Unhampered by Louise's watchful eyes, he was free to invite whomever he liked to his parties—but unfortunately Lionel does not appear to have been a very good judge of character when it came to selecting his party guests. They included several shady people that Louise would probably never have allowed to walk through the front door.

What exactly took place at Atwill's uninhibited Christmas gathering is open to some conjecture. One alleged account of it can be found in Kenneth Anger's *Hollywood Babylon II*, and those wanting to grub around in the mire of lurid sleaze are referred to that book. However, since Anger gives no citations identifying any of his sources, the veracity of his account cannot be checked. Other *facts* elsewhere in his book have since been shown to have little basis in the truth—such as his *Murders in the Zoo* story about Lionel taking the snake home with him—and, as a result, one must question everything else.

By the sound of it, Lionel had a grand old time at this particular party and had no idea that it would come back to haunt him in a few short months. Meanwhile, he continued to enjoy both the single lifestyle, and the fact that he was still very much in demand in Hollywood.

Variety announced on January 8, 1941: "Atwill has signed [James] Whale to direct *Dark River*." He paid $25,000—an enormous amount—for the rights to film this romance about a young Englishman and a Tahitian girl. The cover blurb

Atwill in party mode again (extreme right)—though hardly wild. Here he waits for cake at the wrap party for *Balalaika* (1939). Left to right: director Reinhold Schunzel, cameraman Karl Freund, Nelson Eddy, Ilona Massey, producer Lawrence Weingarten, pianist Dalie Frantz and Atwill

described it as, "A thundering tale of adventure, love, mystery and danger in the South Seas." Whale had been good to Atwill in the past, featuring him in three of his films, so it was fitting that Atwill should want to return the favor. But for reasons unknown, the project never materialized.

On April 19, Atwill received a letter from his son John, reminding him that he had not seen his father for five years (that was in 1936, when Lionel had visited England to make *High Command*). John, a Flying Officer in the Royal Air Force, had written:

> Is there any chance dad that you may be coming over soon? I would like awfully to see you again—and one can never tell these days and nights.

The *Los Angeles Examiner* reported Lionel's reply:

> I'll wind up my affairs as soon as possible and I will be seeing you in May.

Clearly, John and his father were still close, writing letters to each other regularly. John's letter was a plea for some fatherly support in a time of distress, and Lionel's response, stating that he would travel to England in just a few weeks, shows the level of his fatherly concern.

But the visit never took place. On April 28, 1941 Atwill received the kind of news that any father dreads. A telegram from the Air Ministry in Whitehall, London, read as follows:

> Deeply regret to inform you that your son, Flying Officer John Arthur Atwill, is reported to have lost his life as a result of enemy action on April 26, 1941. The Air Council expresses profound sympathy. His mother has been informed.

The *Los Angeles Times* reported:

The father collapsed and was put under the care of a physician.

Somewhere at the back of his mind, Atwill must have recalled *Deburau*, his greatest stage triumph, in which the title character had become estranged from his wife and son, but at the climax enjoys a proud and tearful reunion with his son. Now, in his real life, no such reunion would ever take place.

Or perhaps he recalled that poignant scene in *The Secret of Madame Blanche* in which his character, following the suicide of his son, dictates letters to his valet thanking people for their notes of condolence:

I had such great plans for my son. I wanted him to amount to something so that my name could be carried on. Now I am alone, the last of my family. Thank you so much for your sympathy in my trouble. Yours very sincerely …

TESTIFYING—Sylvia Hamalaine, 16, took the stand yesterday against Virginia Lopez, 30, with whom she lived and who is charged with a statutory morals offense against her.

Film Colony Shakedown Hinted in Party Inquiry

Alleged Victim, 16, Testifies at Morals Trial; Grand Jury Pushes Investigation of Involved Actors

Newspaper photo of Sylvia Hamalaine in court. She seems to be enjoying being center of attention.

During this part of 1941, Hitler's Luftwaffe heavily bombed Britain. Having lost his only son, Atwill must have worried that the lives of his other relatives were also at risk. His great-niece Leslie recalls that Lionel wrote a letter inviting his three brothers and their families to come and stay with him in Hollywood, to be safe from the bombing. It was a grand gesture but they never took him up on the offer.

Wartime restrictions would have prevented Lionel from being told the full details of exactly what happened to John. Recent research, however, has uncovered the facts.

John was stationed near the east coast of England at RAF Coltishall (as was Douglas Bader, the famous legless airman played by Kenneth More in the film *Reach for the Sky*). As well as being a Flight Lieutenant, John was also the Station Medical Officer. A pub called the Ferry Inn, in the nearby village of Horning Ferry, was a favorite haunt of the RAF men, and John was there on the evening of Saturday, April 26, 1941 with two RAF friends. A number of customers all left at around the same time and the headlights of their cars, all starting up simultaneously, attracted the attention of a German Junkers Ju88 flying overhead. Fifteen bombs were dropped and one scored a direct hit on the pub. Twenty-one people were killed, including the three RAF airmen.

Lionel Atwill

Lionel Atwill, still reeling from the tragic loss of his son, was about to receive news that would shake him still further. It may well be that he first learnt of it on the morning of May 13, 1941, when he read his morning newspapers over breakfast. To his horror he found that his name had been mentioned in a court case in which a woman was charged with "contributing to the delinquency" of a 16-year-old girl. Atwill had no connection with this alleged misdemeanor, but the defense attorney dragged his name into the case in a desperate attempt to win his case. It was the first step in a nightmare, which would haunt Atwill for the rest of his life.

The Court Case—Part One

Let's begin by dismissing some of the untruths about Lionel Atwill's court case. He was *not* prosecuted for showing pornographic films. He was *not* prosecuted for holding a wild orgy. He was *not* prosecuted for raping someone. He was *not* prosecuted for holding a party at which someone was raped. He was *not* prosecuted for having sex with an underage girl. There are printed and online articles in circulation that have accused him of all of the above. The misinformed writers of these fallacies prefer not to let the facts get in the way of a good story.

The offense for which Atwill *was* prosecuted, on October 15, 1942, was that of committing perjury—i.e., lying—in court. His reason for lying had nothing to do with personal gain or concealing some other criminal offense. "I lied like a gentleman to protect my friends," he said, explaining that he had wished to keep the names of his friends out of the press. This is not to excuse the offense—lying in court is a serious crime. But reasons for lying come in different degrees of criminality, and Atwill's reasons were definitely at the lower end of villainy.

It was a cruel and unnecessary twist of fate that Atwill became involved in a trial at all. The affair started with a court case with which he had absolutely no associa- tion. There was an instance of alleged rape at a party. It had not taken place at Atwill's home, he was not present at the party and in fact he had absolutely no connection with it whatsoever. And yet he got dragged into the affair because the two women involved in the court case had attended one of Atwill's parties on *another* occasion.

The two women at the center of the alleged rape case were 30-year-old Virginia Lopez, a Cuban dress designer, and Sylvia Hamalaine, 16, a Minnesota girl who had come to Los Angeles to enter a Hollywood film school. According to the *Los Angeles Times*, Lopez, along with one Adolphe LaRue, was charged, with "having aided in the molestation of the juvenile girl." The incident took place at the Hollywood apartment where both women resided.

That might have been the end of things—except that Lopez' defense attorney, Donald MacKay, decided to adopt a strategy which he hoped would deflect blame from Lopez by performing a character assassination on Hamalaine, demonstrating that she was far from being an innocent young thing. He decided to tell the court that Hamalaine:

> … was present at several parties at the beach home of Lionel Atwill, character actor, last December and January, where asserted indecen- cies took place.

This bombshell was a gift for the press, who probably couldn't believe their luck. Judge Ambrose, presiding over the case, even did his best to keep this out of the public eye, sustaining an objection that this information was not material to the case:

> I am not saying that this evidence is not material, but I am saying that it is not wise to admit it in the broad sense of justice. You see, these newspaper people here are taking this down.

It was too late. The cat was out of the bag. It was the first step in Atwill's fall from grace. The revelation took place on May 12, 1941 and was reported in the papers the next day. We can imagine Atwill's reaction when he read his morning newspaper at breakfast.

The trial resumed on May 14, with additional witnesses testifying, but Atwill managed to avoid making a court appearance as he was "out East" in Washington at the time. The *L.A. Times* reported that from a distance he "vehemently denied all accusations and hinted at the possibility of a shakedown." In other words, he was claiming that he was the victim of a blackmailer who was setting him up in order to extract money from him.

Atwill Tells About Party

Grand Jury Hears Actor in Version of Asserted Wild Doings at Beach

After having heard almost everyone else present testify about the asserted "wild parties" at his Santa Monica beach home, the grand jury yesterday listened to Lionel Atwill's version of what, if anything, occurred.

The stage and motion picture actor, who returned from the East in order to testify, appeared alone at the grand jury chamber and was closeted with the inquisitors most of the day.

DENIES EVERYTHING

Leaving the grand jury rooms after three hours, Atwill declared:

"I have returned from New York to testify voluntarily, and intend to remain here until my name is cleared. I emphatically and categorically denied all charges that any improper acts occurred in my home or that any

TESTIFIES — Lionel Atwill, who denies story of wild parties in beach home.

The wheels of justice were turning and Atwill was inexorably caught up in them. Lopez was sentenced to one year in jail, and when this was reported by the newspapers, they couldn't resist dragging Atwill's name into the story one more time, stating that Lopez had earlier testified that Hamalaine "was mistreated at several 'wild parties' in the beach home of Lionel Atwill, actor" (*L.A. Times*).

Eventually he turned up to testify in court on May 21, 1941. He was wearing a black armband in mourning for his son John. "Atwill Tells About Party" screamed the *Los Angeles Times* the next day. For three hours he was "closeted" alone with the Grand Jury, giving his version of events. It may well have been the best performance of his entre career. On emerging, he made a more public speech.

> I have returned from New York to testify voluntarily, and intend to remain here until my name is cleared. I emphatically and categorically denied all charges that any improper acts occurred in my home, or that any indecencies took place in the presence of the Hamalaine girl.

Lionel Atwill

Hamalaine herself seems to have done her best to keep Atwill out of things. When cross-examined, she refused to implicate Atwill in any wrongdoing, and, in fact, stated that at the beach house party she had not been molested by anyone. Two photographs taken of her in court show her smiling broadly and apparently lapping up all the attention.

On June 2, the jury announced that due to lack of evidence, the investigation should be wound up. The foreman of the jury stated:

> It is indeed regrettable that the names of certain prominent people were bandied about so freely and apparently without facts to back up the assertions.

Atwill must have breathed an enormous sigh of relief. Clearly his testimony to the Grand Jury, denying that any "wild parties" had ever occurred, had been believed. Now he probably just wanted to forget about the whole distasteful business and get back to work.

Chapter 11
The Hollywood Years 1942 to 1945

For the next year, Atwill was indeed able to get back to work. He threw himself into his work in a string of films, and appeared in no fewer than eight films, which were released in 1942. He was given good parts in some of them, but was wasted in others. Such is the lot of the supporting actor.

At Universal he had one of his best mad doctor roles in *The Mad Doctor of Market Street*, which included the marvelous sight of him absconding through a back window in his lab coat after accidentally killing his patient. He was underused in the Ernst Lubitsch comedy *To Be or Not To Be*, starring Carole Lombard, released just after her death in a plane crash. At MGM he played opposite Jeanette MacDonald in *Cairo*; it was another unremarkable villainous role for him.

"I made a slight miscalculation," says Dr. Bohmer (Atwill) to a fellow scientist (Barton Yarborough) in *Ghost of Frankenstein* (1942), perhaps making a cryptic reference to his recent court appearance.

Still in 1942 and back at Universal, he was shamefully wasted as a red herring in *The Strange Case of Dr. Rx*. He was more prominent, but scarcely more memorable, as the villain in *Pardon My Sarong*, a comedy vehicle for Abbott and Costello. Publicity for Universal's *Night Monster* held the promise of seeing Atwill in a good horror part, but disappointingly he appeared once again as merely a minor red herring. In the wretched 1942 serial *Junior G-Men of the Air*, Atwill sported one of his oddest make-ups, an oriental criminal mastermind, wearing prosthetic eyelids and dark spectacles.

He was memorable in Universal's *Ghost of Frankenstein*, and perhaps used the film as an opportunity to send a cryptic message to his public about his court appearances, playing a character that has been brought low by some undisclosed misdemeanor, and declares bitterly, "I made a slight miscalculation." Atwill's *miscalculation* was that he had been caught. There was no shortage of highly paid celebrities in Hollywood who were staging wild, no-holds-barred parties, but most of them managed to keep it out of the press. Atwill had not been so lucky.

His final 1942 release was something of a return to form. In *Sherlock Holmes and the Secret Weapon,* he played the detective's arch-nemesis Professor Moriarty, and Atwill did it superbly, adding depths of depravity that other screen Moriartys have lacked.

The Court Case – Part Two

To Atwill's dismay, the "wild party" trial came back to haunt him in mid-1942. On July 1, he was indicted on a charge of perjury. It was alleged that his testimony before the Grand Jury a year earlier was at variance with other facts that had subsequently come to light. In reports the next day, the *Los Angeles Times* referred for the first time to the fact that at the earlier trial, Atwill had denied showing "immoral motion pictures" at one of his parties.

Other papers were not so restrained. The *Moorhead Daily News* went so far as to name the "lewd films" that Atwill had allegedly shown as being *The Plumber's Girl, The Daisy Chain* and a sequel to the latter. This newspaper wrote of "wild revels by nude guests" on a tiger-skin rug. Atwill kept his cool, and when quizzed on what happened on this rug, suavely replied, "Nothing, nothing at all." In fact he "denied there even was a tiger skin—only an old, moth-eaten bear skin."

Atwill denied all wrongdoing and had his attorney read out a statement that said:

> Mr. Atwill is innocent and wants the trial set at the earliest possible date, so that the true facts may be known.

Again, Atwill claimed he was the victim of an attempted shakedown. On July 2, 1942 he entered a plea of not guilty to the charge of perjury and was ordered to face trial on August 17.

As if things weren't going badly enough, he then found himself being charged on a second count of perjury on August 11, six days before his impending investigation. In fact the case was postponed until September 24, presumably so that further evidence against him could be gathered.

Finally, on September 24, he attended court and decided that the evidence against him was too strong. He asked for his plea of not guilty to be changed to guilty. Although he again denied all charges of immoral acts by persons in his home, he admitted to possessing and showing lewd films to a select group of friends at his Pacific Palisades home.

At the witness stand, he was asked to explain why he committed perjury, and spoke one of the greatest lines of his whole career. We all can imagine he took a deep breath, pulled himself up to his full height, and said to the judge, with as much dignity as he could muster:

> I lied like a gentleman
> to protect my friends.

What an occasion it must have been to be present in the courtroom and hear this legendary star of Broadway and Hollywood utter, in his best theatrically trained voice, such a dramatic line. There's a catch however—it *never* actually happened.

Its delivery might have potentially sounded like a scene from one of his films, recalling his thrilling courtroom outburst in *The Silent Witness*. What *really* happened is less colorful. Much as we would all like that scene to have occurred, in fact Atwill *never* did utter that legendary line. The line was indeed spoken in court, but not by Atwill; he had his attorney read it out for him. Still, if anyone ever makes a film of his life, the delivery of that line will make an exciting moment!

Photographs in the papers showed him looking very glum as he discussed matters with his two attorneys. No doubt Atwill recalled the case of Earl Carroll, who had produced Atwill's 1928 stage production *Fioretta*, and who had also been charged with perjury after a wild party, and ended up serving six months in jail.

A date was set for him to be sentenced on October 15. After three nail-biting weeks, Atwill attended for sentencing on that date. To his great relief, he escaped a jail sentence and instead was given five years probation for perjury. Part of the reason for escaping a jail sentence was the fact that the judge recognized that all the witnesses testifying against Atwill—Virginia Lopez foremost among them—were unsavory people with criminal records, and there were suggestions that their actions had all been motivated by a desire, not for justice, but perhaps to extract money from the actor. The judge also felt that Atwill had already suffered sufficiently through adverse rumor and publicity. The fact that he had "lied like a gentleman" was rumored as perhaps another reason why the judge decided to apply a certain amount of leniency. In addition, numerous people had sent in character-reference letters in support of Atwill, including Assistant Attorney General Thurman Arnold and a number from people with whom Atwill had worked in the film industry. One of these is rumored to have been Josef Von Sternberg.

Although no doubt relieved that the trial was finally over, it was a terrific fall from grace for Atwill. His status as a popular socialite with would-be aristocratic origins was ruined forever. He was now the subject of derision by many in the film business and by members of the public, who like nothing better than to read about the scandalous ruinations of celebrities. Adding further misery was a condition of his probation that required him to report once a week to the local police station. The final blow—and perhaps the harshest one—came when he discovered that the Hays Office had instructed the film studios not to hire him, since the actor was now a convicted felon.

His reputation was shattered, he could not work and he had no money coming in. It must have seemed like the end of the road for Atwill.

Despite his tribulations in court, Atwill enjoys a lively dance with Ilona Massey in *Frankenstein Meets the Wolf Man* (1943).

The only glimmer of light was that just three days before the sentence was announced, Atwill had begun work on *Frankenstein Meets the Wolf Man* at Universal. Although there were rumors that the studio would fire him, to their credit they kept him on. Atwill gives a surprisingly spirited performance in the film—including a scene in which he does some lively dancing with Ilona Massey—and watching the movie today, it is hard to imagine that he was in the throes of the most dreadful episode of his life. Either he was such a good actor that he could conceal his inner turmoil, or else the distractions of working meant that he was able to forget his worries for a while.

It would be his last film work for a long time. November and December came and went, but no film offers appeared from any of the studios. Perhaps he hoped that once into 1943, something might turn up. But nothing did. Throughout January, February and March, Atwill must have been genuinely wondering if he would ever work again. For an actor who had been continuously in work for nearly four decades, it was a heavy blow. In the past, the only periods in his life when he had not worked had been when he had chosen to take a vacation. Now he wanted to work but could not. A small consolation to him was the knowledge that most cinemagoers would have been oblivious to this state of affairs, since the many films he had made in the previous year were still being screened at cinemas across the States during 1942 and 1943.

In April 1943, he decided something had to be done and spoke to his attorneys. On April 16, he submitted a plea to the court asking that his sentence be terminated, on the basis that the stigma surrounding it was preventing him from finding employment. His attorney also cited that Atwill had suffered "abject humiliation" and felt "the ends of justice have already been accomplished" (*Los Angeles Times*). Furthermore, Atwill's probation officers informed the judge that Atwill's conduct had been exemplary while on probation. In other words, there had been no more wild parties.

The judge asked Atwill if it was a rule of the Hays Office to refuse employment to persons on probation. Atwill replied:

> The studios don't want to offend you, but they put you off. It's a sort
> of unwritten law.

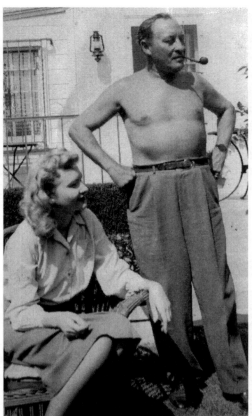

A week later, the judge had considered all the evidence. He was "convinced that the ends of justice had been met" (*L.A. Times*). Atwill was allowed to alter his original plea of guilty to one of not guilty, which was then dismissed by the judge. The judge told him:

> You are now in a position, Mr. Atwill, where you can truthfully say you have not been convicted of a felony.

Atwill responded:

> I am deeply touched, Your Honor, and want to thank you.

If Atwill expected that there would now be offers of work from Fox, MGM and the other studios, he was sadly mistaken. As far as the studios were concerned, he was still *persona non grata*. He had tarnished the squeaky clean image that Hollywood wished to promote. Today, the fact that a celebrity might hold wild parties or show pornographic films would hardly make the news. But in the 1940s it could not be tolerated.

A shirtless Lionel enjoys life at his home in the Pacific Palisades with his new wife Paula.

His fall from grace affected not only his ability to find acting work, but his social life too. For decades he had always embraced the whirlwind social life that surrounds a Broadway and Hollywood celebrity. He had been Guest of Honor at countless social events, and often entertained important guests—such as foreign ambassadors—in his own home. But many of his previous friends and associates no doubt now avoided him for fear of being caught up in any adverse publicity. And we can be sure that the wild parties stopped too.

News of the scandal affected his relatives over in England as well. Lionel's great-niece Leslie recalls her father mentioning that in the 1940s he regularly used to visit the local pub with her grandfather Stanley. Over the years, Stanley had very probably enjoyed telling his drinking buddies about his brother's successes in Hollywood. But on several occasions around 1943, he and her grandfather would visit the pub only to find that they were now on the receiving end of some embarrassing remarks:

> I remember Dad saying that people in the pub used to give Grandpa stick about young girls.

Lionel Atwill

Meanwhile, there was other unpleasant business in Atwill's private life that required attention. On May 6, 1943, his wife Louise sued him for divorce, claiming that the couple had been separated since November 1939. She stated that Lionel had "a surly character" and "desires to live his life without her." She alleged that back in November 1939 according to the *New York Times*—

> Mr. Atwill compelled her to leave their Pacific Palisades home in California. She asked for no alimony but requested division of their California estate.

Lionel, Paula and one of Lionel's pet hounds

In Washington, on June 18, the divorce was finalized, with Louise being granted 10 percent of Lionel's income (which at the time must have been negligible), with a condition that she should not receive more than $2,400 in any one year. Atwill did not attend the court proceedings, instead submitting an affidavit in which he admitted the separation, but denied charges of cruelty and mistreatment.

Unable to find work in films, Atwill decided he would try to return to where his career had begun—the stage. He headed back East, hoping to make a return to Broadway where he had been so celebrated in the 1910s and 1920s.

He first attempted to re-establish his career by directing and starring in a version of Molnar's *The Play's the Thing,* a romantic farce set in the world of the theater. The central theme of this 1926 play concerns the way that civilized behavior can triumph over life's usual chaos—and Atwill had certainly had more than his fair share of chaos in the last two years. He took the part of quick-witted playwright Holbrook Blinn. The play opened on May 17 at the Plymouth Theater in Boston, and Atwill must have been delighted with the reviews.

Variety stated:

> Lionel Atwill scored a distinct personal success in Max Brown's revival of *The Play's the Thing.* Supported by Virginia Peine … Atwill handled the playwright role and the directorial assignment deftly throughout.

The writer also praised the way that the drama built to an "uproarious climax." A week later the same paper reviewed the play again:

The return to the stage of Lionel Atwill in Molnar's slightly faded *The Play's the Thing* found neither that veteran's stage technique nor his personal appeal diminished by his long absence.

At the end of the play, when the cast returned to the stage to take applause, members of the audience cheered Atwill. Presumably many were veteran theatergoers who had fond memories of him in *Deburau, The Grand Duke* and all his other triumphs. The 58-year-old actor and former Broadway legend must have been very gratified to find that he was still welcomed.

Atwill relaxes in the orchards of his Pacific Palisades home.

The play moved later to the Playhouse Theater in Boston and, in June, to the Locust Street Theater in Philadelphia. The latter reported better-than-average weekly takings of $7,000. Atwill must have been hopeful that the next step would be to take the play to Broadway. Unfortunately, it was not to be. No Broadway theater would take the play, all claiming to be fully booked with other successful productions. He must have wondered if the real reason was that all his old Broadway friends had turned against him as a result of the court case. It must have hurt him deeply.

However, Atwill was not one to give up easily. In a previous time of crisis, he had turned to an old friend. He turned to that same old friend now—the mad doctor Anton Ragatzy, leading character in the play *The Outsider*. Back in 1928, *Napoleon*, a play that Atwill had expected to be popular, had failed on Broadway. To make up for this disappointment, Atwill had staged a revival of one of his greatest successes, *The Outsider*. Once again, in 1943, he turned to that play in the hope that it would revive his flagging fortunes and put him back on Broadway.

The Outsider opened on July 8, 1943 at the Playhouse Theater, Providence. This time, however, it made little impression and Atwill again was unable to take it to Broadway.

In August of 1943 he tried one more time to revive his former stage glories. He chose a play called *My Dear Children*, which had been a hit on Broadway three years earlier with John Barrymore in the starring role. It had been a hit for all the wrong reasons: Audiences went along to see the ailing, alcoholic Barrymore messing up his lines and doing some wild ad-libbing. In other words, it was like a real life version of the play-within-a-film in *The Great Profile*, the film in which Atwill had supported a drunken Barrymore in 1940.

My Dear Children opened on August 17, 1943 at the Flatbush Theater in Brooklyn. It played there for a week, and then played a week at the Audubon Theater in Manhattan. But again, Atwill was unable to find a theater on Broadway that would take the play. He had made three attempts at a Broadway comeback and all had failed. In an interview, he seemed to accept his fate with philosophical good humor [from an uncited newspaper clipping held by the Billy Rose Theatre Archive, New York]:

> Here I am, in my mellow years, trouping like a beginner, roughing it in a suitcase and getting along without a valet ... Wonderful land of opportunity, this America. That's why I became a citizen. But the war has wreaked havoc—especially for the poor, maligned rich man.

The proud father: Lionel with his son Tony

It's remarkable that he was able to take things so well. His only son had recently died, his marriage had ended, his film career appeared to be truly finished and now his attempt at a Broadway comeback had failed. He decided to abandon his efforts to return to the stage. But Lionel Atwill was not the sort of person to give up without a fight. He traveled back to his West Coast home and hoped that a few film offers would come his way, even if it meant accepting offers to appear in the type of low-budget films that he previously could afford to turn down.

Some film offers did indeed materialize, but they were from the Poverty Row studios that made cheap films aimed at the lower half of double-bills. PRC starred him in *The Lady in the Death House*, a 55-minute B-picture with Atwill playing, not a heavy, but a criminologist who tries to save Jean Parker from going to the electric chair. Republic Pictures, a slightly more prestigious studio than PRC, featured him in *Captain America*, a 15-chapter serial in which he played the Scarab, a criminal mastermind. It was a well-made cliffhanger and Atwill gave it his all, smiling with manic glee at all the right moments and, in one legendarily brutal scene, whipping an elderly man with unrestrained gusto. Also for Republic in 1944, Atwill was in *Secrets of Scotland Yard*, playing a murderous Nazi masquerading as a wartime codebreaker.

Fortunately one of the major studios still valued Atwill's talents and was prepared to offer him work. It was Universal, for whom he had recently done such good work in *Son of Frankenstein, Man Made Monster* and others. In April of 1944, Atwill began work on *House of Frankenstein*, the sixth film in the series, and a Monster Rally with

PRC's creepy 1945 chiller *Fog Island* shows Atwill and George Zucco overseeing events with intense eyes.

Dracula and the Wolf Man joining Frankenstein's Monster. Atwill must have been pleased to be working for Universal again, but his contribution was woefully brief; his Inspector Arnz got only nine lines of dialogue and less than four minutes of screen time. It was a low point in the Atwill *oeuvre*.

In May of 1944, it was announced that Atwill might star alongside Mae West in a stage play called *Catherine Was Great*. This, at last, could be his great opportunity to return to Broadway. The play lampooned the story of Catherine the Great of Russia, and Atwill would probably have played some Russian general. The idea of Lionel Atwill engaging in a witty sparring match with Mae West, the great sex symbol, is a concept to cherish—but unfortunately, and for unknown reasons, it never happened. The play went ahead (and was very successful) but without Atwill in the cast.

Also in May of 1944, Atwill started working on another production at Universal, the 13-chapter serial *Raiders of Ghost City*. It was repetitive nonsense, with Atwill playing a Prussian villain trying to steal American gold. The actor looked tired and unwell in many of his scenes. More often than not he was filmed seated behind a desk, as if unable to do anything that required greater physical effort.

Atwill was bitter about the way his career was going, but things started to look up in his personal life. In Las Vegas on July 7, Lionel, now 59 years old, married for the fourth time. His bride was 27-year-old Mary Paula Pruter, a radio singer and producer. Despite the age difference, Paula was besotted with the aging actor. She was too young

Lionel Atwill

to have been aware of him during his great days on the stage, but it may be that she had seen him on the screen many times, and as a teenager been impressed by him in some of his classic film roles, such as *Doctor X* and *Mystery of the Wax Museum*, or perhaps a classic "weepy" such as *The Secret of Madame Blanche*.

Atwill's first 1945 release was *Fog Island*, another PRC cheapie and a dreary film, enlivened only by good performances by Atwill and George Zucco. *Crime Inc.*, another PRC release of 1945, was a forgettable gangster melodrama and another shameful waste of Atwill's presence. In August 1945, Atwill was over at RKO making *Genius at Work,* a low-budget crime film starring comedy duo Wally Brown and Alan Carney. What might have been another forgettable cheapie turned out to be one of the most amazing and most enjoyable films of Atwill's career; he plays a standard villain but at the climax decides to dress up in drag and stomps around in high heels! Atwill never got to find out what audience reaction was to the film, as it was not released until after his death. Back at Universal, he was in *House of Dracula*, another gathering of monsters, and it gave him more screen time than he had in the previous entry in the series—but not by much.

October 14, 1945 was a happy day for Lionel—he became the proud father of a baby boy, naming him Lionel Anthony Guille Atwill. Lionel, Sr., who had lost his only other child back in 1941, was delighted, and by all accounts doted on his baby son, spending as much time with him as he could.

At last, after several turbulent years, life seemed to be improving. At age 60, he was blessed with a personal life that many younger men would envy. Several photographs taken of Lionel and Paula at their D'Este Drive house show the couple looking happy and healthy in their garden, with a shirtless Lionel enjoying the California sun.

Above all, Atwill was doing the thing that he loved most—acting. The quality of the film roles may not have been anything like those of his glory days in the 1930s, but acting was in his blood and he must have been pleased that offers of work were regularly coming his way.

Although he was disappointed by the standard of many of the films offered him, the paychecks were now regular, he had an attractive, young wife and he was a proud father. He was looking forward to seeing his son grow up. On balance his life was pretty good, and he looked forward to many more happy years of the same.

Chapter 12
The Hollywood Years:
The Final Curtain

The year 1946 started off well for Atwill. On January 14, he began working on the Universal lot again, this time playing the villain in a 13-chapter serial entitled *Lost City of the Jungle*. He was to be paid a respectable $1,250 a week, with a three-week guarantee. He worked tirelessly for nearly three weeks, completing a lot of scenes as Sir Eric Hazarius, an evil warmonger who is determined to find the location of a mineral called Meteorium 245, the only defense to the atomic bomb.

His early scenes give no indication that all was not well. In his first scene he is riding in the back of a car, as he puffs away enthusiastically on a fat cigar. What he didn't know was that cancer was eating away at his lungs. This was during the days when most people thought the only ill effect of smoking was a bad cough.

But on February 5, he failed to turn up for work. "No call due to illness" was noted in the daily report sheet. When Universal realized that the illness was serious, they came up with a scheme to introduce a new villainous character (played by John Mylong) and re-wrote many of Atwill's scenes to feature the other actor instead. For scenes where it was not possible to do without the presence of Eric Hazarius, a stand-in (George Sorel) was used. Some latter-day articles written about Atwill give the impression that very little of Lionel is to be seen and that most shots use George Sorel. This isn't the case. In fact, Sorel is only seen on a handful of occasions, and Atwill gets plenty of screen time. Even so, it was a sorry end to his film career.

Back at the grand house in Pacific Palisades, Atwill was struggling with lung cancer, complicated by pneumonia. At some point, his doctor must have broken the news to Paula that Lionel's condition was terminal and that he didn't have long to live.

In the center, Atwill's character Dr. Hazarius (with beard and glasses) is played by double George Sorel in *Lost City of the Jungle*.

In his last two months, as he lay dying of cancer, he must have wondered how future generations would regard him and his career. Did he fear that he might not be remembered at all? After his fall from grace in the courtroom, he almost certainly would have regarded all of his films of the last five years to be wretched affairs, which he imagined would be quickly forgotten … and perhaps he would be forgotten along with them.

Lionel Atwill

Did he fear that, if he were remembered at all, it would be for all the wrong reasons? Would he be known only as the actor whose reputation was besmirched by a court case that made a criminal of him? Or would he be remembered only as the actor who appeared in cheap horror films and serials that gave him no chance to shine? Did it pain him to think that all his wonderful stage triumphs would be forgotten?

Film director Reginald LeBorg, a friend of the actor, visited him as he lay on his sickbed and recalled in a 1987 interview (related by Greg Mank in his book *Hollywood's Maddest Doctors*) that Atwill was bitter about the way that events had transpired.

> I saw Lionel when he was very sick with cancer, at the end, shortly before he died. He must have lost 30 pounds; he was pale and lying in bed at the Palisades house. Then he was very bitter—he knew he was going. He was bitter about his treatment in Hollywood after the scandal ...

Lionel Atwill stands beside his final curtain, tears rolling down his cheeks, from *Deburau* (1920)

As Atwill lay in bed, his mind disordered by the morphine which was probably administered to help with the pain, did he relive those glorious curtain calls on Broadway in the 1920s, a time when he could do no wrong and was adored by critics and theatergoers alike? Did he drift into reveries where he imagined himself to be once again the white-faced clown Deburau, the tearful audience of the packed house of the Belasco Theatre hanging on his every word? I hope so.

In those last months his wife and son would have been foremost in his mind. Reginald LeBorg also recalled that—

> He wanted to live because of his baby son—and he loved Paula.

As a bedridden Lionel held six-month-old Tony in his arms, did the actor's memories of his greatest speech in his greatest triumph again come flooding back? For a moment, was he Deburau again, giving advice to his young son before sending him out into the world?

Perhaps, as he struggled through his final days, one particular speech from *Deburau* played out in his mind, a speech that he had performed hundreds of times on Broadway a quarter of a century earlier. It is the scene when the unwell, has-been actor recalls that a fortune-teller had predicted his final curtain:

> She said that one day it would break of itself,
> And never rise again for me;
> From that day on I'd be laid on the shelf.
> It has come then, you see ...

Oh, faded curtain for me
The emblem of the whole
Of life's beauty and mystery.
In the book of my life you bound,
I have turned the final page;
Sleep is stealing on me,
I let it fall to the ground.
They throw on the soldier's bier
The flag that he held so dear.
When I've to be carried away
Don't stifle me with the pall.
Of a solemn funeral.
Fling over me
This curtain, carelessly,
That the people you meet on the way
May look and smile and say,
"Why, at last that poor buffoon
Of a Pierrot's flown back to the moon."

That "poor buffoon" died on the evening of April 22, 1946. Paula sat with him as he faded away. The death certificate stated that he had been suffering from bronchial cancer for 18 months, but the newspapers reported that the cause of death was pneumonia—this was in the days when cancer was still very much a taboo word. He *had* also suffered from pneumonia, but it was the cancer, a result of a lifetime of chain-smoking (both on- and offscreen), that dealt the fatal blow.

What a trying time it must have been for young Paula, coming to terms with losing her beloved Lionel after less than two years of marriage. Now she faced the prospect of bringing up their young son alone. And how awful it must have been for her, at the young age of 29, to have to cope with the ordeal of making funeral arrangements for her husband. Hopefully some of Lionel's friends rallied round and helped her. On Thursday, April 25, Lionel was cremated at the Chapel of the Pines in Los Angeles.

LIONEL ATWILL, 61, NOTED ACTOR, DIES

Veteran of Stage and Screen Made London Debut in 1904 —Star in Shaw, Pinero

HOLLYWOOD, Calif., April 22 (P)—Lionel Atwill, veteran stage and screen actor, died at his Pacific Palisades home tonight of pneumonia. His age was 61.

Born in Croydon, England, he was educated at Mercer's School in London and started on the stage there in 1904. After a long career in the legitimate theatre, Mr. Atwill came to Hollywood and entered motion pictures in 1932.

The obituaries had the decency to avoid mentioning the court case. The *Los Angeles Times*, for example, recalled the highlights of his 41-year career as "actor, producer and manager," and his success in *Deburau*.

Over the next decade, his achievements on the stage and the theater began to fade slowly from the public's consciousness. At the time of his death, a few of Atwill's later films were still playing at cinemas across the United States, giving audiences

Lionel Atwill

a last chance to see a performance by the veteran actor. July 1946 finally saw the delayed release of *Genius at Work*, and one wonders what audiences made of this low-budget, unfunny comedy, containing one of Lionel's most bizarre performances. Many of the films which he had made during the 1940s (such as *Ghost of Frankenstein* and *Mad Doctor of Market Street*) had not received a release in Britain because of the war, and they eventually had their European premieres in the late 1940s and early 1950s, thereby giving Atwill a measure of publicity over there for a few more years. No doubt some of Atwill's relatives in England (who were not able to attend his

Many of Atwill's horror movies were re-released in the late 1940s and early 1950s by Realart. Here *Man Made Monster* has been re-titled *The Atomic Monster.*

Los Angeles funeral) made special trips to the cinema to pay their last respects to him.

Atwill himself probably expected most of his films to be quickly forgotten. In the 1930s and 1940s, films usually had their initial period of general release and then were often never seen again. Films were not revived and made freely available like they are today. Public tastes were changing fast in the mid-50s and the old horror films were already beginning to be perceived as very old-fashioned. Even so, a number of Atwill's films enjoyed a brief renaissance in the late 1940s and early 1950s.

A company called Realart, newly formed in 1948, bought up the rights to most of Universal's older films, with a view to re-releasing them. With the major film companies making few, if any, new horror films, the re-releases proved to be very popular. In 1948, Realart re-released *Ghost of Frankenstein* and *Sherlock Holmes and the Secret Weapon*. In 1949, *Night Monster* and *The Sun Never Sets* were both back on cinema screens. The following year, 1950, saw *House of Frankenstein* and *House of Dracula* both doing the rounds and keeping Atwill's name alive. In 1951, *Lost City of the Jungle* was screened again. And finally, in 1953, Realart revived two of his greatest roles: *Son of Frankenstein* and *Man Made Monster* (the latter being re-titled *The Atomic Monster).*

At the time, the Realart re-releases must have seemed like they were the last gasp for the popularity of Lionel Atwill and his movies. But a few years later, in 1957, a new and developing medium breathed fresh life into the old films: television. In fact, Atwill had been in the vanguard of this medium way back in 1931 when he had starred in two experimental television broadcasts of scenes from his stage success, *The Silent Witness*. Little could he have known back in 1931 that this same medium would prove instrumental in reviving interest in his films and introducing him to a whole new generation of film lovers.

In late 1957 a television subsidiary of Columbia Pictures put together a package of 52 old Universal horror films and screened them nationwide under a series title of *Shock Theater*. The films shown included a number featuring Atwill: *Son of Frankenstein, Frankenstein Meets the Wolf Man, Mad Doctor of Market Street, Man Made Monster, Night Monster* and others. The series was a huge success and was followed quickly in

Is this how Atwill might have looked if he survived into old age? Atwill appears in age make-up in *The Great Waltz* (1938).

1958 by *Son of Shock*, which added a number of old Columbia horror films to the roster. A large audience—including huge numbers of pre-teens and teenagers—encountered the films of Lionel Atwill for the first time. And they loved them.

This new interest in the old horror films was so great that it spawned a magazine devoted solely to films of this genre—the very first of its kind. First published in February 1958, it was called *Famous Monsters of Filmland* and its pages were full of information about the classic horror films, with in-depth articles on genre stars Boris Karloff, Bela Lugosi, Lon Chaney and others. Edited by horror film aficionado Forrest J Ackerman, the magazine was devoured eagerly by a vast readership across the United Stated, in Britain and elsewhere.

Many of these readers were learning about the old films for the first time, and they were fascinated to read about the hideously scared Ivan Igor of *Mystery of the Wax Museum*, the hate-filled, one-armed Inspector Krogh of *Son of Frankenstein* and the disturbingly insane Dr. Paul Rigas of *Man Made Monster*. The magazine was partly responsible for creating a whole new generation of film fans who grew to respect and care about the horror films of the 1930s and 1940s.

Atwill himself would have been very surprised to learn that more than a decade after his death, these old films had attained a durability and just refused to be forgotten. He would have been even more astonished to learn that today, over 60 years later, interest in these old horror classics shows no sign of waning.

This chronicle of the life story of Lionel Atwill, the *exquisite villain*, has been a saga filled with incident, acclaim and notoriety. His remarkable career as actor, writer, director and producer spanned over 40 years. It began with his early stage successes in England, achieving its pinnacle with his glory days on Broadway, followed by his 15 years as one of Hollywood's leading character actors. His private life saw the high drama of four marriages and some high-profile divorces that followed. It was unarguably a life that was lived to the full.

His character was a complex one. On the one hand, he was always willing to help those less fortunate than himself. Time and again throughout his career, he demonstrated his generous nature, donating his time freely in support of a host of worthy causes. On the other hand, a darker side is hinted at by allegations about his private life. Two of his marriages ended amid accusations of surliness, infidelity and cruelty, all suggesting a nature that could at times be less than gallant. And the court case revealed a party-animal lifestyle so hedonistic that it could sometimes cloud Atwill's judgment, seeing him associate with disreputable people and indulging in activity that over-stepped the

Lionel Atwill

mark. These aspects of Lionel Atwill have all been referred to in this book, but the emphasis throughout has been on his professional career and his unforgettable acting.

I hope that if Lionel Atwill is up there somewhere, looking down on us now, he is actually rather pleased with the way things turned out. He could never have imagined that many of those low-budget horror films would achieve classic status and be adored by fans too young to have seen them when they were originally released. Although most of his superb stage work and even many of his mainstream films have been forgotten, his horror films have assured him a kind of immortality which will bring him to the attention of generations still to be born.

What a shame, though, that death claimed him at the relatively young age of 61. Other *genre* actors, such as Boris Karloff and John Carradine, lived on into their eighth decade and continued to delight fans with their own particular brands of acting. The prospect of seeing an elderly Lionel Atwill in sinister supporting roles is a mouth-watering one, but for chain-smoking Atwill, it was not to be. A glimpse of what the elderly Atwill may perhaps have looked like can be found in the closing minutes of *The Great Waltz* (1938), in which, thanks to some very credible make-up, he played a character in his seventies or eighties.

Atwill's contribution to the horror genre is enormous. Among all the stars who became typecast in horror films—including Karloff, Lugosi, the Chaneys, Price, Lee and Cushing—Atwill was, in this writer's opinion, the finest *actor*. He had learned his craft thoroughly on the stage over a period of 27 years, so that by the time Hollywood beckoned him, he knew his trade thoroughly and was a master of his craft. But it wasn't just his training and his experience that made him such a fine actor. In film role after film role he showed that he was a *thinking* actor who cared deeply about the parts he played, imbuing the characters with great depth of feeling, albeit often hidden behind a cold exterior. His superb performances in some of his non-horror films, such as *The Silent Witness, The Song of Songs* and *The Firebird,* demonstrate his enormous talent.

Within the ranks of horror film fans, Atwill is often regarded as being in the *second division* of those actors who specialized in the genre. In his horror roles, many fans will say that Atwill never portrayed a character as iconic as Karloff's Frankenstein Monster or Lugosi's Dracula. But I disagree, and cite Atwill's Inspector Krogh in *Son of Frankenstein* as being one of the classic horror performances of the 1930s. Too many think of him as no more than a supporting actor—the man who played the policeman or the doctor or the assistant scientist. But let's not forget that he was the top-billed star of many horror films, including *Doctor X* and *Mystery of the Wax Museum.* If we compare him with other horror actors, he could outdo them all in terms of the sheer *intensity* of his portrayals: just think of Dr. Paul Rigas in *Man Made Monster*. Within his repertoire of horror film roles, he showed great versatility—for example, the characters he played in *Murders in the Zoo* and *Son of Frankenstein* could not be more different. The pages that follow will look at each of Atwill's film roles in depth and will discuss in detail exactly why I consider him to be such a fine actor, and why he should properly be regarded as being, in my humble estimation, one of the genre's *first division* performers.

It is the horror films that will keep his name alive but I hope this book has gone some way to encouraging an appreciation of all the other aspects of this extraordinary man and his often glorious career.

The Exquisite Villain

The Films in Analysis

Eve's Daughter (1918)

Lionel Atwill's first-ever film (now believed lost) was an adaptation of his successful 1917 stage play of the same name. Again he played monocle-wearing cad Courtenay Urquhart, who treats the ladies abominably—but does it with style and panache. Billie Burke played the vulnerable girl who runs away with Urquhart after he has plied her with champagne. Thomas Meighan was the hero who steps in just in the nick of time to save her from Atwill's dastardly intentions.

Scriptwriter Margaret Turnbull transferred the setting from England to America to make it more palatable to local movie audiences. The film ran for 50 minutes and Atwill got one or two favorable reviews.

One review in particular made some telling remarks that could also well be applied to almost every subsequent film in which Atwill appeared. The *Evening Public Ledger* (a Philadelphia paper) wrote:

> Lionel Atwill is the real star of this production, and his character work is capital. It is not often that an auxiliary player is allowed to do such good work. Director Kirkwood's wide experience has made him realize the possibilities of his minor characters.

In other words, this was the first time in which Atwill, in a supporting role, had shown that he could be a scene-stealer.

The *New York Tribune* also thoroughly enjoyed Atwill's acting, describing him as—

> The most delightful he-vampire we have seen in a long time.

Scene from Billie Burke's latest Paramount success, 'Eve's Daughter,' at the Colonial.

This poor quality photo from a 1918 newspaper is the only known surviving image of Atwill in *Eve's Daughter*.

Variety was less impressed, calling the film:

> ... dull and uninteresting ... There is no drama. Thomas Meighan as the hero and Lionel Atwill as the heavy, handled their respective roles adequately ... a commonplace picture.

On the other hand, many reviews failed to mention Atwill at all, most preferring to praise the film's charming female star, Billie Burke, and the ever-changing frocks she wore. Even the newspaper ads for the film mentioned only Burke, with no credit given to Atwill. It may well be that, since a silent film could not benefit from Atwill's distinctive theatrically trained voice, his role could not achieve the impact it had onstage. Perhaps that was why, despite the favorable reviews, Atwill has been quoted on a number of occasions as saying that during this period of his career he wasn't impressed with the movies.

Newspaper ads for the film show that it played at cinemas in February, March and April 1918, and then again in October. Exactly when Atwill filmed his scenes it is not known.

For Sale (1918)

Atwill's second film was *For Sale*, starring comedienne Gladys Hulette and Creighton Hale. Directed by Fred Wright and written by Fred Jackson, it

was a 5-reeler, so again ran for about 50 minutes. It played at various cinemas in June and July of 1918, and newspaper ads mentioned Gladys Hulette but not Atwill. Like his previous film, it is believed that no prints of *For Sale* have survived.

Very little is known about this film. It doesn't appear to have made much of an impression, and was quickly forgotten. Once again, it is not difficult to see why Atwill remained unimpressed by the medium of moving pictures.

The Marriage Price (1919)

Atwill's third motion picture was a 50-munute 5-reeler from Paramount starring popular star of stage and screen, Elsie Ferguson. Scripted by Eve Unsell from a story by Griswold Wheeler, it tells the tale of a society girl who is engaged to Kenneth Gordon (Atwill), a cad and an idler.

By all accounts, Atwill gave a bizarre performance. The *New York Tribune* described it in some detail:

> The only thing that bites like vinegar through this oily preparation is Lionel Atwill's performance of the cad. He plays with a kind of brisk physical wit in which every quirk of his lip suggests something unedifying and refreshing, and which makes us long to ask him how he dare do so much with his face and do it so quickly without blurring himself in the photography.

If Atwill read the review in *Variety*, he must have been mortified:

> There is so great a lack of action, it tires ... Lionel Atwill as the heavy was always acting and when he wasn't doing that he was overacting.

The reviewer went on to complain about his performance in more detail:

> The habit of slapping his hands together immediately on entering a door to attract attention to himself is one that his next director should break him of.

A 1919 newspaper photo of Atwill in *The Marriage Price*. This is the only known still known to exist.

Of course, what *Variety* could not know is that today, nearly a century later, Atwill's fans love him all the more when he overacts. It's a shame that *The Marriage Price* cannot be viewed today.

Dismayed by the reviews, Atwill vowed to stay clear of films from now on when interviewed in July 1919 by *Motion Picture Classic* magazine:

> I, for one, will never play in pictures again, until I am assured that the director is broad-minded enough to present a villain who has loveable qualities, or a hero who has a few weaknesses.

The Eternal Mother (1919)

Atwill's fourth film saw him co-starring with Florence Reed, who (according to the *Washington Herald*) had "a powerful dramatic role" in a story that told of "a young society girl whose disposition is changed by the influence of the men she is with."

Atwill shot the film in July of 1919, and spent the best part of a week on location in the Adirondack Mountains north of New York. A trade magazine stated that director William S. Davis "promises some striking novelties in the exterior setting." That may be so, but the film seems to have made little impression, and the press largely ignored it.

Once again, Atwill must have been left wondering if he was ever to make a name for himself in films. His only mention came in a brief item in the *New York Tribune* in December 1919, which referred to him in connection with his work on this film, stating that he had "the distinction of being the highest salaried non-star in pictures." Presumably, the writer was referring to Atwill's supporting role in *The Eternal Mother*, and his status as the industry's highest paid supporting actor.

United Picture Theaters originally released the movie, and newspaper ads show that it was playing at cinemas in 1919. Pioneer Film Corporation later picked it up, who re-released it in September 1921 under the new title of *Indiscretion*, presumably in an attempt to fool audiences that it was a new film.

This ad for *The Highest Bidder* shows Atwill with Madge Kennedy in the bottom right corner.

The UCLA holds a copy of *The Eternal Mother*, and it may be the only one of Atwill's silent films to have survived. Frustratingly, it does not seem to be possible to view the UCLA print.

The Highest Bidder (1921)

In Atwill's fifth and final silent film, he starred opposite Madge Kennedy. A few reviews of the film survive in old newspapers, but none of them mention him. For example, *Bemidji Daily Pioneer* described the film as:

> One of the best of the numerous good Kennedy vehicles that have
> been supplied to the star by Goldwyn.

It was adapted from a *Saturday Evening Post* story called *The Trap* by Maximillian Foster.

Again Atwill must have been disappointed to find that neither the film nor his performance in it made much impression. As result, he now decided to stick with the theater, and it would be several years before he made another film.

Atwill discussed *The Highest Bidder* briefly in an article he wrote about Josef Von Sternberg that appeared in the British magazine *Film Weekly* in 1935. In this fascinating article, designed to tie in with the recently released *The Devil is a Woman*, Atwill wrote primarily about his friendship with both Von Sternberg and Marlene Dietrich. He included a reminiscence about earlier years and revealed that Von Sternberg was assistant director on *The Highest Bidder:*

> I first met Josef Von Sternberg at the MGM studios in 1920, when I was playing a leading role opposite Madge Kennedy, and he was the young assistant director. In those days, he was a rather quiet, timid little fellow who seemed to have to screw up courage to go around asking people's views on this or that new book.

In the article, Atwill went on to recount how he got to know Von Sternberg better while working on *Devil Is a Woman.* Many years later, when Atwill was badly in need of help during his court trial, Von Sternberg was one of the people willing to stand by him and offer support.

The Silent Witness (1932)

Lionel Atwill's first sound film is rarely seen today and yet it contains one of the great Atwill performances. *The Silent Witness* is also the closest we can get to experience a flavor of his stage skills, as he recreated one of his big Broadway and West Coast theater triumphs. It's a thrilling affair for three reasons.

First, it is a taut, superbly acted murder melodrama with a long and riveting courtroom scene. Second, it contains much evidence of Atwill's talents as a writer. He and Harry Wagstaff Gribble (the director of the American stage version) both felt that the pace and tension of the original British play could be improved. To those ends they devised new scenes or altered existing ones to heighten the drama, and these revisions are also in the film version. A third reason why *The Silent Witness* makes such gripping viewing is that it contains an uncanny foreshadowing of events that would come to haunt Atwill many years later.

In the film's courtroom scenes, as we watch Atwill committing perjury in the witness box to protect his son, it is impossible not to feel that we are looking through a window into his actual court case of a decade later. We see Atwill go through the whole gamut of emotions—confusion, fear, desperation, fatigue, a final wild outburst, etc.—

Atwill and Greta Nissen in *The Silent Witness*

and surely these are the same stages that Atwill must have gone through in 1942 when he lied to protect his friends, only to be exposed later when accused of lying in court.

At the time of his trial, Atwill himself could not have been blind to the irony. The plot and dialogue of *The Silent Witness* were ingrained in him, because he had performed it so many times onstage as well as in the film version—he must have thought about it a great deal in 1942 as he squirmed in the witness box.

It is even conceivable that the film was the inspiration that made him believe that he could lie in court and get away with it. Or was this yet another example of some higher power trying to warn Atwill: Don't even think about committing perjury, because if you do, you will become horribly unstuck.

The drama begins when Bramwell Fletcher strangles the woman (Greta Nissen) who has been cheating on him. Back home, the thought of what he has done turns him into a wild-eyed, nervous wreck—a state he would find himself in again a year later after witnessing Karloff's bandaged corpse come back to life in *The Mummy*. He confesses to his father, Sir Austin Howard (Atwill). Sir Austin takes

"I did it! I did it! I did it! I did it!" proclaims Atwill in *The Silent Witness*.

control of events magnificently, swiftly deciding that he must save family and reputation at all costs. Atwill is superb here, ordering his wife and son to bed, ushering in the police detective and holding his nerve as he is questioned. With a gesture or a stare he conveys all the inner tension convincingly.

Protecting his son, he allows himself to be accused of the murder and ends up in court. The courtroom scene that follows is irresistible high drama, and it becomes one of the most gripping scenes in Atwill's screen career. The sequence with Sir Austin in the witness box lasts a formidable 14 minutes. Not only does it feature Atwill at his tortured best, but it also has a deliciously venomous performance from Alan Mowbray as the aggressive prosecuting counsel who shouts at Sir Austin, "You've said enough to convince any sane man that you've been lying in the witness box!"

Sir Austin still thinks he can wriggle his way out of the charge. And why wouldn't he? After all, he has committed no murder. He begins by answering confidently, but as the questions become trickier, the tension mounts, as Sir Austin flusters and hesitates, unsure of some of his responses. The prosecuting counsel becomes more aggressive and produces evidence that seems to demolish Sir Austin's alibi, proving that he was not at the theater on the evening in question. Sir Austin rubs his brow. He looks like he might even collapse.

The prosecuting counsel produces a collection of tickets stubs from the theater where Sir Austin claims he was on the night in question. They prove that the seat Sir Austin claims he sat in was in fact empty. Nearly at breaking point, Sir Austin begins to lose control. Determined at all costs to save himself and his son from the hangman's noose, he shouts out, "I *was* in the theater that night!" In a dramatic moment he starts to collapse and drops all the ticket stubs, which fall to the floor. This visually striking moment is not in the original play but is a device added either as part of the rewrites done by Atwill and Harry Wagstaff Gribble for the U.S. stage version, or by screenwriter Douglas Doty. No proof exists, but I sense that Atwill was significantly involved in devising this dynamic bit of action. In distress, Sir Austin runs his hand through his hair, leaving it in a wild and untidy state—in stark contrast to Atwill's normal appearance, which is always impeccably coiffured. The long sequence climaxes when the court is disturbed by a man rushing in shouting that Sir Austin must not be found guilty because he can identify the real murderer! To shut the man up, Sir Austin makes a last, desperate attempt to save his son. He turns to the judge and shrieks: "I did it! I did it! I did it! I did it! I did it! I did it!"

For me, this thrilling outburst is Lionel Atwill's equivalent of Colin Clive's great speech in *Frankenstein* a year earlier: "It's alive! It's alive! It's moving! It's alive!" The repetition, the brevity of the phrase and the almost hysterical delivery are similar. What a shame that *The Silent Witness* is so little known, because this is one of Atwill's great moments.

Interestingly, in the original play, Sir Austin says, "I did it!" only once. Perhaps it was *Variety*'s review of the stage version, which said that Atwill's role wasn't as "showy" as usual, which inspired the decision to repeat the line so many times. It's another of the enhancements to which Atwill (or the director?) very probably made a significant contribution, and it certainly has the desired effect: It's a positively electrifying moment.

After this brilliant scene, it's a shame to have to report that the rest of the film, as it works its way to a happy ending, is less satisfying, and its plot twists and developments are too contrived.

However, there are still some fine moments. A police inspector (Montague Shaw) gathers all the crucial cast members into a room. Sir Austin tries to prevent his son from confessing but is unable to stop him handing over a written statement to the inspector. A long and powerful silence follows, with Sir Austin realizing that his son will go to the gallows.

"Father, I don't know what to say to you."

With painfully understated emotion, Sir Austin grips his son's arm and says quietly, "That's all right ... all right, old boy." (This is another powerful line that is not in the original play, but is part of the re-writes initiated by actor, screenwriter or director.)

Sir Austin recounts, via a flashback sequence (not in the original play but written by Atwill and stage director Harry Wagstaff Gribble) that he had visited the murder victim with the intention of buying her off so that she will stop seeing his son. The scene is illuminated by moments where Nissen tries to entice Sir Austin to stray from his purpose by flirting with him and encouraging him to make a play for her. Nissen rubs her foot up against Sir Austin's foot, then asks if he "approves" of her (i.e., finds her physically attractive), and this gives rise to the first occasion in the actor's screen career where we hear that wonderful Atwill laugh. It's a difficult thing for an actor to do convincingly, but Atwill had mastered it.

Subsequently, a key witness (Billy Bevan) reveals (in a clumsy plot twist) that he was hiding behind curtains in the victim's apartment and saw that she revived after the younger Howard fled the scene, only to be killed by Weldon Heyburn, the victim's low-life former husband.

Great relief appears all round, and the film ends with Sir Austin speaking of the power of family love. He closes the film by explaining why he felt compelled to lie in court: "Why, self-sacrifice is one of the greatest luxuries in life ... for someone you love very deeply."

Lionel Atwill

The Silent Witness has a number of other delights. Although filmed in Hollywood, it feels entirely British: It is set in London and almost all the cast are British. Another pleasure is a hilarious performance by Herbert Mundin (who died at the young age of 40 in a car crash) as a taxi driver called to the witness stand. Some early 1930s comedy in other films has dated badly, but this is still laugh-out-loud funny. Also the many pre-Code risqué lines of dialogue, which would not be tolerated after 1934, are very funny.

Doctor X (1932)

Doctor X is one of the highlights of Lionel Atwill's film career. His first horror film is also among his finest, featuring some of his most spectacular mad doctor scenes. He is a commanding presence throughout, appearing in virtually every scene. He looks magnificent. Ray Rennahan's glittering two-strip Technicolor makes the most of the photogenic star, and even the costume department rises to the occasion, providing Atwill with some good costumes, including a lab coat snappily offset by shoes adorned with white spats and a heavy-duty overcoat with a huge furred collar.

Preston Foster, Fay Wray and Lionel Atwill in *Doctor X.*

The film is full of memorable sequences, in particular two frantic, high-tension laboratory episodes that rank among the best moments of 1930s horror cinema.

Atwill plays Dr. Xavier, head of the Academy of Surgical Research. Ghastly, cannibalistic murders have been occurring in the vicinity, and Xavier and all his researchers and staff come under suspicion. Atwill, naturally, is Suspect Number One.

Eventually he turns out to be a red herring, but it's the best red herring role of his career. In a dozen subsequent films, Atwill played murder suspects who turn out to be quite harmless, but none of them ever came close to the high melodrama of *Doctor X*. Atwill's skill here is that, although he is not the guilty party, it is necessary throughout the film for the audience to suspect that he might be the killer, and to this end he embellishes his performance with all manner of sinister stares and hints of unwholesome desires—such as when he seems to take a perverse pleasure in watching Professor Wells (Preston Foster) remove his false arm, or when he seems to stare at his daughter (Fay Wray) with a more than fatherly interest.

Atwill and the rest of the cast and crew were required to put in long 10-hour days, made even longer by the fact that two versions of the film were shot concurrently, one in the new process of Technicolor that required additional lighting. In an interview (by Rick McKay in *Scarlet Street* #27), Fay Wray described the conditions:

> That was difficult. It was just too hot. They had to use so much light
> to photograph color that it was almost unbearable. Awful experience

… I was just sweltering like I was in an oven … Awful! Awful! … They left the lights on, because a lot of scenes were so sustained that you needed quite a bit of time. But, it was an unhealthy kind of feeling that we all had to go through. Our clothes just felt like they were too much—like we just wanted to rip everything off!

Atwill's opening scene, set in a morgue in a seedy dockside back street (creepily designed by Anton Grot) sets the tone perfectly. Dr. Xavier performs a post mortem on the corpse of the latest murder victim, and around his head is a leather band with a light attached that helps him perform his grisly work. It's a contraption that makes him look every inch the mad doctor.

"This … is cannibalism!" he declares.

The mad doctor at the controls of his laboratory in *Doctor X*

Xavier even has a nice line in dry humor. When he tells a policeman his theory on the type of person capable of carrying out these murders, the cop reacts with a laugh, "It's hard to believe that."

"Yes, for a policeman, I suppose it is," responds Xavier.

His first scene with his daughter Joanne (Fay Wray) takes place in the Academy's library, a nightmarish set with medical papers occupying shelves that reach up to dizzying heights. When Xavier kisses Joanne and bids her good night, he looks back over his shoulder at her with a sinister expression. The shot is designed to reinforce our suspicions that he may be the murderer, but it also hints that incestuous thoughts run through his mind.

When Xavier reveals to the police that one of his colleagues is a student of cannibalism, the police are ready to jump on the suspect, but Xavier defends him. "I'm very *fond* of Dr. Wells," he says with an inflection so sinister it gives the word new meaning.

Xavier takes two policemen on a tour of his "strange, uncanny place" (as they call it) and what follows is a fine piece of the *Grand Guignol*, with Atwill the impeccably well mannered yet menacing guide. First they meet Professor Wells peering into a glass jar containing a heart, which he has kept alive for three years, and then Wells treats them all to the sight of watching him remove his false left arm.

They meet the rest of Xavier's social-misfit researchers. Professor Rowitz (Arthur Edmund Carewe) is a gaunt, scar-faced man wearing a tinted monocle and a bloodstained lab coat. The police are almost convinced he must be the Moon Killer, but Xavier's dry humor puts them right. "He has such a lovely nature. Why, he's the author of several volumes of poetry." They also meet Professor Haines, who gets a kick out of looking at dubious "French Art" magazines and has sadistic tendencies. Finally, they encounter bad-tempered, club-footed Professor Duke, sometimes to be seen in a wheelchair, and other times hobbling about with the aid of crutches.

Lionel Atwill

The action now shifts to Xavier's cliff top mansion, where he intends to carry out a series of weird experiments to uncover the identity of the Moon Killer. The creepy old mansion, first seen from a distance in an eye-catching miniature shot, is another fabulous Anton Grot creation, full of enormous wooden doors, huge stone arches, crazily carved banister rails and low, overhead beams.

The Moon Killer (Preston Foster with his "synthetic flesh") in *Doctor X*

In two scenes, Dr. Xavier subjects all his researchers to weird scientific tests designed to identify the Moon Killer. These scenes are the film's highlights, staged by director Michael Curtiz with a sure understanding of the importance of imaginative camera angles and fast editing. The film began life as a play (in fact, it was playing on Broadway at the same time that Atwill was in *The Silent Witness*) and could have become a very stage-bound film, but Curtiz avoids this. The design of the "mad lab" equipment is a thrilling combination of Art Deco and nightmare, with bulbous, almost fleshy, glass receptacles strung up next to arrays of narrow glass rods and tall cylinders full of bubbling liquids.

In the first laboratory scene, Dr. Xavier and Professor Wells (eliminated from being a strangler-suspect because he is one-armed) handcuff the three suspects to their chairs. The nervous dialogue between the suspects includes an exchange where one character makes references to another's sado-masochistic proclivities. Curtiz includes a grotesque shot of Duke's clubfoot, twitching uncontrollably.

Xavier subjects them to a theatrical recreation of one of the murders, the theory being that the killer's metabolism will react violently and the liquids in the equipment will reveal him. Xavier explains the workings of his strange devices in a long speech full of enjoyable pseudo-scientific mumbo-jumbo: "Your pulses are now connected with the magnetic rotators ... and each variation of your heartbeat reaction is amplified 4,000 times!" These scenes are a feast for the eyes and ears, and all the more effective for the lack of any background music. All the participants get intense, extreme close-ups, their eyes wide with anxiety, their brows glistening with the sweat of fear. Atwill, eerily lit from below, never looked better than he does here, as he takes control of the dials and begins the experiment. Suddenly the lights go out, and the tension is cranked up another level, with all the suspects shrieking out.

"The lights!"

"Somebody get my crutch!"

"Don't move!"

"Look at that tube!"

The lights go back on and Rowitz is discovered dead on the floor, killed by a scalpel incision to the back of the neck. The paralyzed Duke is up on his feet, the extreme fear

Doctor Xavier (Atwill) and his daughter Joan (Fay Wray) in *Doctor X*.

of the moment having caused a hysterical reaction in him that gives him the ability to walk a few steps.

Ten minutes before the end of the film, the identity of the Moon Killer is revealed in a superb sequence in which Preston Foster smothers his face in "synthetic flesh." This is actually a series of make-ups—all devised by Max Factor—with Foster going through various phases of frightfulness as he smears on more and more of the fake flesh. In his final make-up, his mouth slowly opens and closes in a particularly ghastly manner that suggests a fish struggling for oxygen.

The second lab scene is just as exciting as the first. Wells handcuffs Xavier, Haines and Duke to their chairs. This time Joanne plays the victim in the murder reconstruction ... and now it's the real Moon Killer who will walk onstage and try to strangle her. With one gruesome hand grabbing Joanne's neck, the Moon Killer reveals his identity to the three scientists, who all try desperately to break free from their handcuffs—but in vain. Shots of them all straining at their shackles and screaming at the murderer are all edited with great gusto by George Amy and director Curtiz.

Xavier cries out: "Run, Joanne!"

Duke (his clubfoot straining pathetically to reach the keys on the floor that will unlock the handcuffs): "The keys! The keys!"

Haines: "Look at his hand! Horrible!"

Wells delivers a neat mad doctor speech in which he explains all about the synthetic flesh and how it has enabled him to fashion a replacement arm: "What difference could it make if a few people had to die?"

In a fiery finale which 1930s audiences found genuinely thrilling, Wells goes up in flames, is sent crashing through a window by Lee Tracy, then plunges like a fireball onto rocks at the foot of the cliffs. It's a dramatic end to a terrific film.

The film does have its faults. At the time, most reviewers were full of praise for Lee Tracy's comic performance as a wisecracking newspaper reporter. Today, however, it seems just like an unnecessary distraction from the real business of the film, full of cheap unfunny devices such as a handshake buzzer and an exploding cigar. The film makes a major misjudgment in one of Tracy's early scenes, in which the Moon Killer

Lionel Atwill

sneaks up behind him only to be frightened when Tracy's cigar explodes. In this scene, the frightful face of the killer is revealed in a very drab, unimaginative way which, considering Curtiz' skill in the later laboratory scenes, is a major disappointment.

Good prints of both the two-strip Technicolor version and the black-and-white version of *Doctor X* are available today. Some horror purists may prefer the creepy stylishness of the black-and-white version, but there is no denying that the color version at times looks breathtaking.

Doctor X is crying out to be remade as a modern horror film. The concept of synthetic flesh is still a novel one and, with CGI effects, some amazing sequences could be created. But who would play the Lionel Atwill role?

The Vampire Bat (1933)

The early 1930s are full of classic horror films, but this is not one of them. It remains something of a mystery why Atwill should have accepted this role. This is far from being his greatest film. At this stage in his career he was still a highly regarded stage actor and did not have to take roles in low-budget horror films made by Poverty Row studios (in this case Majestic)—that would come later in his career.

For the first 75 percent of *The Vampire Bat* Atwill plays the kindly local doctor and has no dialogue or scenes that are anything other than routine. After he has been revealed as the villain, it is only in the last 10 minutes that his role livens up. He becomes a fully-fledged mad doctor and at last has the chance to deliver some juicy lines. Perhaps it was these last scenes that attracted Atwill, and perhaps he took on the role simply because he thought these scenes would be a lot of fun (and bank him a nice paycheck).

Atwill would also have been very aware of Bela Lugosi in the stage play of *Dracula* and how its recent film version had catapulted Lugosi to enormous fame and popularity. Perhaps Atwill felt that *The Vampire Bat*, which had also been a successful stage play, might do the same for him.

The film is not without merits and is a lot of fun throughout, albeit seriously flawed. Dwight Frye is magnificent as the dim-witted Herman, who loves to play with bats: "They soft … like cat … they

Dr. Niemann (Atwill) charms Maude Eburn and Fay Wray in *The Vampire Bat*.

not bite Herman." There is a wonderfully creepy opening passage, backed by sinister music, in which a limping night watchman (George E. Stone) does his rounds beneath a tree in which dozens of bats are nesting. And the sets of Anton Grot are occasionally impressive, such as the musty old steps that lead down to Dr. Niemann's laboratory.

Occasionally Atwill is given a half-interesting line, such as when he spouts his expert knowledge of the undead: "According to accepted theory, the vampire dematerializes

Dr. Niemann (Atwill) has Ruth (Wray) in his clutches in *The Vampire Bat*.

its body and reintegrates it outside the grave." Or, later: "Our saner, calmer judgment tells us such things can't be. Yet here, for instance, in this ponderous tome are cited 1,000 and one phobias and complexes that human beings are heir to. Some of them as strange, more untenable even, than werewolves and vampires." All good fun but it is nothing special, and all recounted in his less-interesting benevolent guise before he has revealed his true colors.

Things liven up when we at last see Dr. Niemann in his mad doctor's white gown, applying a nasty spiked contraption to the neck of a woman victim … and the camera pans right to see blood dripping into a glass bottle. Later there are good close-ups of Dr. Niemann telepathically giving instructions to his assistant Emil, who carries out the abductions. Neither the scriptwriter nor the director makes enough of Atwill in these moments … and neither bother to explain how he has suddenly gained telepathic powers.

The film only really comes to life in the closing five minutes in which Atwill menaces Fay Wray, who plays Ruth. She has overheard one of his telepathic sessions and puts two and two together. Niemann waits for her beside a door and, when she steps out, he grabs her arm. He subjects her to the legendary Atwill stare! Their dialogue is worth quoting, as it features one of Atwill's classic mad doctor speeches—all delivered in dinner jacket and bow tie.

"You! You're the one!" she cries out. "What mad thing are you doing?"

"Mad? Is one who has solved the secret of life to be considered mad?" responds Niemann. "Life … created in the laboratory. No mere crystalline growth, but tissue, living, growing tissue. Life … that moves, pulsates and demands food for its continued growth!"

Ruth looks horrified.

"Ha!" mocks Niemann. "You shudder in horror. So did I, the first time. But what are a few lives to be weighed in the balance against the achievements of biological science?" He stares off into space with all the zeal of a twisted mind: "Think of it! I have lifted the veil. I have created life! Wrested the secret of life from life! Now do you understand? For the lives of those who have gone before, I have created life!"

He moves in close so that his face is almost touching Ruth's face as he tells her that she will be his next victim. It's the best scene in the whole film.

Immediately afterwards, he is found in his lab coat, with Ruth tied up in a chair, as he tends lovingly to his blob of tissue. However, the scene does not develop satisfactorily and in fact the ending is rushed. Emil suddenly decides that he has had enough of Niemann, and as Fay Wray and Melvyn Douglas run from the lab, the sound of two

Lionel Atwill

gunshots is heard, and when next seen, both Emil and Niemann are dead, lying on the floor of the lab. The script has failed to come up with a suitably dramatic death for its chief villain and has fallen back on a lazy, offscreen shooting.

Too many elements simply do not work. A pulsating football-sized blob of tissue kept alive in a tank is glimpsed a few times, but nothing is made of it. The character of Emil, Dr. Niemann's assistant (Robert Frazer), is never developed, so his climactic change of allegiance just seems painfully contrived. The film ends with a pitiful joke in the realm of *toilet humor*, the only effect of

The U.S. six-sheet poster (81 inches by 81 inches)

which is to make one wonder why scriptwriter Edward T. Lowe could not come up with something better. Overall, one wishes fervently that director Frank R. Strayer had been a more inventive craftsman and had made *The Vampire Bat* the classic it could and *should* have been.

The Secret of Madame Blanche (1933)

Audiences will need a box of tissues nearby when watching this classic tearjerker. Today, some situations and lines of dialogue are, of course, hopelessly dated, but this is still an enormously enjoyable melodrama. Atwill plays a wealthy, tyrannical father who forbids his son (Phillips Holmes) from seeing the woman he loves (Irene Dunne) because she is a lowly singer in a nightclub. From there on, plot developments get progressively more and more tearful.

For most of the film, Atwill plays the kind of cold, stern and scary character that he does so well. But his very first appearance is enlivened by a marvelous flourish that really brings the upper class Aubrey St. John to life. Looking grand in his top hat, he pays a visit to the apartment where his son is keeping Sally (Dunne), and while waiting for her to emerge from the bedroom, he spots one of her stockings on the sofa, lifts it into the air with his walking stick, brings it close to his face—and breathes in its scent, closing his eyes as he enjoys the sensual pleasure of the moment.

Atwill, Irene Dunne and Phillips Holmes in *The Secret of Madame Blanche*

A dab of blood on St. John's (Atwill) shirt tells him his son committed suicide, in *The Secret of Madame Blanche.*

Atwill almost certainly dreamed up this memorable incident, even though I can offer no actual proof. Circumstantial evidence can be found in the fact that similar moments exist in several of Atwill's other films, including *The Sphinx* and *The Man Who Reclaimed His Head.*

What St. John does next is equally risqué. He walks to the doorway of the room in which Sally, still unaware of his presence, sits on a bed and adjusts a stocking and garter. He stands there for several seconds, admiring the view, before she turns and is startled to see him.

"My son told me about you last night, so I thought I'd come and take a look at you," he says, placing a monocle in one eye and looking her up and down. Whatever else we might think of St. John in later scenes, we certainly know that he is no prude.

Thinking of his reputation, St. John is horrified to learn that his son has married Sally and so cuts him off without a penny. Eventually the penniless son comes crawling back to father, who convinces him to give up Sally. Minutes later a gunshot is heard—the son has shot himself. The discovery of the body is well done—we don't see the corpse but a maid comes out of the room, tries to prevent St. John from going in and, in so doing, her hands leave bloodstains on his shirt. When St. John looks down and sees the bloodstain, a look of horror crosses his face as he realizes the truth.

The film cuts cleverly to a scene in which St. John paces up and down in front of his valet, dictating thank-you notes to all the people who have sent him letters of condolence. It is difficult to watch this scene without reflecting on the fact that eight years later Atwill would indeed lose his son in tragic circumstances. In subsequent scenes, St. John wears a black armband, just as Atwill did in real life after the death of his son John.

The dastardly St. John becomes ever crueler when he learns that Sally, now living in France, is pregnant. Having lost his only son, he is determined to acquire the grandchild. He plots to take the baby away from Sally and does just that in

In the courtroom, St. John offers his grandson (Douglas Walton) stern-faced support in *The Secret of Madame Blanche.*

Lionel Atwill

a potent scene that could have descended into Victorian melodrama. Instead, the sequence manages to be sentimental and powerful at the same time.

The most heartless scene of Atwill's career follows. Sally pays him a visit in the hope that he will let her have the baby back. He won't. Then she pleads for him to just let her see the baby once in a while. No, he won't. Finally, she begs him to let her see the baby just once. No, he won't allow even that. He instructs his butler to show her to the door. The camera

St. John realizes that the woman in the dock is his grandson's mother, from *The Secret of Madame Blanche.*

lingers on a shot of St. John, teasing the audience by making us expect that surely just a little hint of remorse will cross his face. It doesn't.

Twenty years pass—it is now 1918—and Leonard, the grandchild (Douglas Walton), is serving in the Great War. Sally, gray-haired and hardened, runs a French café of dubious repute and hasn't seen her son since he was taken away from her. The inevitable happens. Leonard is serving nearby, falls for a local beauty and brings her to the café, hoping to spend the night with her. But the girl's brutish father gets wind of it, tracks them down and, in a fight, Leonard accidentally shoots and kills the father.

Sally, initially unaware of the identity of the British soldier, realizes that he is her son, but she does not tell him. She helps him to escape from the café without being seen and decides to take the blame for the killing herself. Inevitably, the film ends with a dramatic courtroom sequence.

Atwill's film career is full of dramatic courtroom scenes, and this is a memorable one, even though Atwill's contribution is relatively minor. Sally is in the dock. St. John, now silver-haired and looking very grim-faced, sits behind his grandson and gives him occasional encouraging taps on the shoulder. Gradually St. John realizes that the elderly woman on trial is the mother of his grandchild, and there is a superb shot of Atwill's face as the realization dawns on him.

Eventually the truth comes out in court, and there is a terrific moment when young Leonard, having learned she is his mother, rises to his feet to approach her, with St. John trying in vain to pull him back. Of course, mother and son are reconciled and it all ends (relatively) happily. All that is missing to make this a perfect ending is a scene in which St. John, moved by the affection between mother and son, also experiences reconciliation. But unfortunately the film focuses on Sally and Leonard, and St. John gets forgotten at the end.

Mystery of the Wax Museum (1933)

Along with *Son of Frankenstein* and *Doctor X,* this is the film for which Lionel Atwill is best remembered today. And with good reason—it offered him some wonderful

Atwill as Ivan Igor, the kindly ownr of a New York wax-works, in *Mystery of the Wax Museum*

acting opportunities in a variety of guises.

First, he is a sweet, head-in-the-clouds sculptor. Second, 12 years later, he is gray-haired, wheelchair-bound and outwardly respectable, but is he hiding some sinister secret? Third, he is a ghastly, scar-faced creature who skulks around darkened morgues and basements. And finally, after an unmasking scene that Atwill must have known would hit all the headlines, he becomes a frenzied, energetic madman who runs around his secret lair like some wild animal. When Atwill read the script for this, he must have thought: Who cares that this isn't the serious drama I'm used to on Broadway? I'm going to have a lot of fun making it and it will be a sensation!

Atwill had always been interested in the art of make-up, as was shown by his comments in the early 1920s about his make-up for *The Grand Duke*. He may even have been an admirer of Lon Chaney. *Mystery of the Wax Museum* would give him the chance to wear a make-up that would rival the sensational, groundbreaking disguises of Karloff in *Frankenstein* and *The Mummy* (which Atwill had very probably seen at the cinema). His co-star Glenda Farrell recalled (in a 1990 interview by Scott MacQueen in *American Cinematographer* magazine):

> It was a frightening make-up! It took about four or five hours to get on every morning. I know he [Atwill] had to be up around three o'clock in the morning and at the studio ... It was a dreadful make-up—dreadful from the standpoint of horror. But he was a darling man and it didn't seem to bother him.

Britain's *Picture Show* magazine reported that on one occasion Atwill collapsed on the set because of the heat.

In a 1934 interview with the *New York Times*, Atwill gave further insights into his dedicated preparations for the film:

> They fooled me in the *Wax Museum* thing, though. Or rather they let me fool myself. I'd been practicing before a mirror for weeks, learning how to keep my face as stiff as a board and just wiggle my jaws in talking, eyes set and staring—a grand effect. But then in the finished picture I looked so much like a stone image that they had to cut all those close-ups for fear of giving away the fact that my face was supposed to be a wax mask.

Mystery of the Wax Museum is a film of great moments and great scenes, but it does not hold together as satisfactorily as the best horror films of the early 1930s (such as *Frankenstein* or *Dr. Jekyll and Mr. Hyde*).

For example, the opening 10 minutes are very well done. Rain pelts down on a grubby London back street, while inside an equally grubby wax museum, two odd characters—one an unsavory businessman, the other a dreamy-eyed sculptor—argue about their failing enterprise. And even better

... but he turns out not to be so kindly after all, as Fay Wray discovers, from *Mystery of the Wax Museum.*

are the film's last 20 minutes, set in the underground lair of Ivan Igor, a nightmarish place of shadowy corridors, oddly slanting doorways and giant steel staircases ... a movie set seemingly designed by a madman.

Unfortunately between these two episodes there is much that is routine and muddled. For a director of Michael Curtiz' standing, it is surprising that so many scenes pass with negligible impact or purpose. To cite just one example, look at the scene in the morgue when we encounter the scar-faced villain for the first time. The morgue set (designed by Anton Grot) is superb; it looks like the bell tower of a grand Gothic cathedral. But Curtiz fails to employ it to good effect. Does he imbue the scene with any dramatic build-up to the encounter, or does he make use of any inventive camerawork to heighten the tension? Neither—the figure simply appears in a dull long shot. Again, compare this with the imaginative scenes in *Frankenstein* or *Dr. Jekyll and Mr. Hyde* when their monstrous characters are first encountered.

Curtiz, not unwisely, wanted his attempt at a horror film to differ from most of the other films in the current horror boom by placing them *not* in some vague, mythical European location but in early 1930s America, complete with fast cars, criminal bootleggers, pushy cops and a fast-talking, hard-drinking girl-reporter (Glenda Farrell). This is a fine idea but it is not realized with any particular style or dramatic cohesion, being rather a muddle of half-realized characters and snide remarks. For example, when Farrell is describing the hideous character she saw lurking in a basement, she says, "I don't know what he was, but he made Frankenstein look like a lily." A line like that only serves to emphasize that the scriptwriters were more concerned with appearing glib than they were with fashioning a coherent work of art.

Weaknesses aside, one of the great pleasures of the film is that it *looks* marvelous. Fortunately, some very fine prints of the two-strip Technicolor version of this film are in circulation, and they really sparkle, with close-ups of Atwill and Fay Wray looking particularly ravishing.

Mystery of the Wax Museum features one of the key roles in Atwill's film career. As Ivan Igor he looks striking, one lock of abundant gray hair hanging down to suggest his artistic, Bohemian nature. For most of the film he sits in a fabulously antiquated

Director Michael Curtiz (seated on right) prepares Atwill for the morgue scene.

wheelchair. One of its features is a leather guard above each hand-rest, discreetly placed so that his guests don't have to see his ugly, fire-scarred hands. ("Look! Look at these claws … It is a cruel irony that you people without souls should have hands.") Another feature of the wheelchair is a handy pouch at the back that holds his crutches. This creates the expectation that we are going to see Igor hobbling around on them at some point, but unfortunately, Curtiz misses a trick and no such scene ever appears.

Although Atwill must have been tempted to portray Igor as a raving madman, he instead skillfully underplays in most of his scenes. For example, one of Igor's finest moments is an encounter with Charlotte (Fay Wray) on the opening night of his new wax museum. He finds himself alone with her for a few fleeting seconds.

"You're very beautiful," he says with remarkable simplicity, yet imbuing the phrase with an inflection suggesting not just an artist's appreciation of beauty but also unspeakable depths of perverted lust.

Later Florence (Glenda Farrell) sneaks into the basement beneath the museum and has to hide behind some barrels, when she sees a ghastly figure coming down the stairs toward her. It's Atwill in a wide-brimmed black hat, long black cape and that amazing scarred face make-up created by Perc Westmore. In fact, the studio could have used a stand-in and few people would have noticed—but the body language and facial gestures are definitely those of Atwill. The scene provides a scare but also typifies the script problems of the film's mid-section. The action serves absolutely no purpose: Atwill pushes a box 10 feet across the floor, but then leaves the basement. This is lazy scriptwriting.

Another example of lazy scripting—or perhaps evidence of a missing scene—also takes place in the basement, when Florence sees a large crate swing back from a wall, presumably because some kind of secret passage exists behind it. But the scene ends there, no passage is ever seen and we never find out who made the crate move. In other words, it's just a cheap, poorly thought-out scare.

But all shortcomings can be forgiven once the film's final sections are underway, and they are a treat. Charlotte arrives at the wax museum one evening hoping to find her boyfriend Ralph. Instead she meets deaf mute Hugo (Matthew Betz), who mumbles incomprehensibly at her. She is relieved when Igor appears, and he tells her to go look for Ralph down in the basement.

She walks through a series of nightmarish sets (more excellent work from Anton Grot) whose stark angles and shadows would look right at home in *The Cabinet of Dr. Caligari*. She reaches a bulky steel doorway, which illogically leans back at an angle of 45 degrees. The doorway slides open in front of her like a portcullis, and she walks through it. On the other side, she finds herself at the top of an elevated steel walkway that leads into a cathedral-sized laboratory for making wax dummies. Here, Grot has abandoned Expressionism in favor of a mad combination of industrial architecture and Art Deco. At the center of the lab is a huge, bubbling cauldron of molten wax.

Charlotte nervously walks down a steel staircase. When she reaches the bottom, a door slides open and Igor wheels through it. Initially she is relieved to see him ... but then events take a turn for the worse. This is the film's key sequence, one that has been discussed and analyzed many times in the eight decades since it was filmed.

Igor stands up from his wheelchair, without the aid of his crutches. Charlotte realizes that all is not as it seems. He steps toward her, a mad glint in his eye, and takes her in his arms.

"My Marie Antoinette!" he says ecstatically. Atwill adds a degree of mania to the moment by looking not into Charlotte's eyes; instead, he seems to stare through her into some insane world of his own imagining. Charlotte backs away from him with a terrified wail.

"My child, why are you so pitifully afraid?" he asks, as he advances on her. "Mortality has been the dream, the inspiration of mankind through the ages. And I am going to give you immortality!"

"No, please! Oh, please!" she cries desperately. "I've done nothing to hurt you."

An ingenious and risqué ad for *Mystery of the Wax Museum*

"I have no desire to hurt you. You will always be beautiful. Think of it, my child! In 1,000 years, you will be as lovely as you are now. Come! Come!"

He takes her in his arms. She resists: "Let me go! Let me go!" She batters on his face with her fists. Shockingly, his face splits and sections peel away. She pauses for a moment, horrified by what is revealed underneath, but some strange force impels her to continue battering at the rest of his face, and to pull off his wig.

What she sees is blackened skin, patchy hair, a deformed nose, a bulbous upper lip, a mutilated chin. Surely, along with Lon Chaney's similarly shocking unmasking in *The Phantom of the Opera*, this has to be the most gruesome sight that had ever been seen in any horror film up to that time.

Revealed in all his ghastliness is the fire-scarred madman (Atwill) in *Mystery of the Wax Museum.*

Fay Wray lets out one of her legendary, ear-piercing screams.

Lionel Atwill, on the other hand, does a brilliant bit of underplaying: He just turns his head slightly away from her, looks at the floor and says nothing for several seconds. It's a moment of resignation for him, as he is finally revealed to her in all his ugliness.

"Your face was wax. You fiend!"

"My Marie Antoinette! You must not say that to me!"

She faints and he ties her down under a contraption that will cover her in molten wax. Igor, previously the mild-mannered, inactive cripple, now becomes a frenetically energetic evil force. A stunt double is used for some of these shots, but it is Atwill himself in many of them. When Ralph enters the lab, Igor runs up the staircase and slugs it out with him. When the police break in, there is a truly inspired touch when Igor picks up his wheelchair and throws it at them. He sprints up the stairs to escape, but one of the policemen shoots him and he falls back into his own cauldron of molten wax. Charlotte is rescued in the nick of time, just as she is about to be mortally sprayed.

It's a thrilling climax and rewards repeated viewings, especially the mask-splitting scene, which still packs a punch today.

But some reviewers feel it was mistake to have shown the make-up in two earlier scenes, weakening the impact at the cli-

Igor prepares a syringe to immortalize Fay Wray in wax, in *Mystery of the Wax Museum.*

Lionel Atwill

max. I tend to agree. It would have been far better in those scenes just to have shown a glimpse of part of that face—perhaps from the side or the back, thereby letting the audience know that the character was hideously disfigured, but saving the full impact until later.

Back in 1933, how must audiences have reacted? Today's viewers all know that the scar-faced man was Atwill behind a wax mask, but in 1933, how many theatergoers were genuinely surprised when the mask split? With Atwill's recent Broadway reputation, did many think he actually was playing a kindly sculptor, and that the mystery fiend was a separate character altogether? It would be grand to get in a time machine, attend a premiere and find out.

The Warner Bros. publicity campaign for the film hyped the risqué angle, and the ad-men came up with some titillating phrases to adorn the posters. "Images of wax that throbbed with human passion! Almost woman! What did they lack?" and "When he wanted a woman he made her … with wax!" Back in 1933, it must have been quite a sight to see massive, full-color, 48-sheet posters pasted up around towns, depicting Atwill working feverishly on the bare-breasted sculpture of a female model.

Warner Bros. remade the film in 1953 as *House of Wax*. Despite an energetic performance by Vincent Price in the Atwill role, it was a mediocre production with a surprising lack of understanding of the importance of atmosphere, style and pace.

Murders in the Zoo (1933)

This film has a legendary opening sequence but it only achieves its full horror when it is watched a second time. We are deep in the jungles of French Indo China. Eric Gorman (Lionel Atwill) is crouched over a prostrate man, with two locals helping to hold the man down. Gorman is stitching something up, pulling the thick cord with firm, determined gestures. On first viewing, we think that he is perhaps tending to a wound. But on a second viewing we know the reality; he is stitching the man's lips together. The noises coming from the man are horrific. They are not screams but loud, pained sighs that suggest genuine suffering. Those firm, determined gestures are not those of a kindly surgeon—they are the brutal work of a vicious sadist. As he wraps up his devilish work, he tells his victim, "You'll never kiss another man's wife!" The full horror is revealed to us after Gorman leaves. The victim stands up and staggers toward the camera, so that his hideously stitched mouth can be seen in its entire gory splendor.

This is one of the most depraved scenes in Atwill's career, ranking up there with the molten steel episode of *Beggars in Ermine* and the underwear-inspecting moments of *Stamboul Quest*. A satisfying coda occurs next. Back at camp, Gorman's

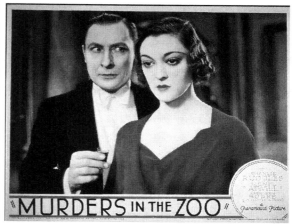

Lionel Atwill and Kathleen Burke

wife Evelyn (Kathleen Burke) asks after the missing man. Gorman says he has seen him. "What did he say?" she asks.

Lighting a cigarette with casual abandon, he replies, "He didn't say anything."

Murders in the Zoo may well be a modestly budgeted film with no big-name stars, but it scores full marks in the horror and sleaze departments, and the film gives Atwill one of his best roles. It revels in pushing the boundaries of what could be depicted on screen before the Hays Code was enforced in 1934. Although Gorman claims

Eric Gorman (Atwill) treats his wife (Kathleen Burke) as if she were an animal to be caged and dominated, in *Murders in the Zoo*.

to love his wife Evelyn (Kathleen Burke), in reality he is just a sadistic pervert who gets his kicks by mistreating her and subjecting her to his lusts. To him, his wife, with her panther-like looks, is just another animal to be owned, caged and mistreated.

A key scene exists when Gorman takes Evelyn home from the zoo after her lover has died from a mamba bite. Visually, it has all the ingredients of a glossy 1930s Hollywood love scene, yet at the same time highlights Atwill at his most cruel and lascivious. It is only two minutes long, yet it is one of the finest in Atwill's long career, and is worth looking at in detail.

Evelyn accuses Gorman of killing her lover Hewitt. Gorman delights in protesting his innocence: "Evelyn, you don't think I sat there all evening with an eight-foot mamba in my pocket, do you? Why, it would be an injustice to my tailor!" And he chuckles at his own joke. As she becomes more distressed, he enjoys slowly and sensually running his hand up her arm in a way that suggests a crawling tarantula. (This was a bit of business that most likely Atwill dreamed up.)

She pulls away from him, disgusted: "Oh, don't touch me!"

Her reaction only serves to arouse Gorman more: "I never saw you look more beautiful." One hand strays dangerously close to one of her breasts.

"Yes, Eric, now, I know—now you're going to make love to me." Burke puts a wonderful nervous tremble into her voice that suggests she has endured her husband's unwanted attentions many times. In fact, it may be that the intensity of Atwill's lascivious acting caused Burke to fluff her lines. Surely the word "now" is only meant to occur once in the second part of this line, and not in the first part.

"I never wanted you more than I do at this moment!" he coos.

"Oh—you're not human!" she says desperately.

He takes her in his arms. "I'm not going to kiss *you*—you're going to kiss *me*!" He runs his hand through her hair and grins wickedly.

"Kiss you?" she replies. "I hate you!" She tells him that she had been planning to run away with Hewitt.

A look of intense anger crosses Gorman's face, but then he composes himself and pretends to become the charming gentleman again. He takes his hands off her and offers her a kindly open-handed gesture, adopting a mock-understanding tone of voice: "My dear ... why didn't you come and tell me? You know I have too deep an affection for you to ever stand in your way." She turns away from him, a look of disgust on her face. It's enough to bring out the animal again in Gorman. He grabs her again and starts pawing her, one hand straying to her breast. "What is it...? What is it that makes me love you so?"

"I hate you!" she shouts at him and runs off ... and Gorman smiles. He has thoroughly enjoyed the whole encounter. Evelyn locks herself in a bedroom but her husband will not be denied his conjugal rights so easily. He tries to open the door.

A full-page feature from the British magazine *Picture Show* devoted to *Murders in the Zoo.*

"I'm coming back in five minutes and I expect to find this door open."

It's one of the classic Atwill scenes, superbly acted by him.

The film has another classic slice of Atwill high drama to offer us. At the climax, Gorman frees all the big cats from their cages but then finds that he is on the receiving end of their attentions. He flees, locks himself behind an iron gate and thinks himself safe. What he doesn't see is the 20-foot python slithering up behind him. It bites his leg, then wraps itself around him, slowly choking the life out of him. As has been well documented elsewhere, the scene was staged first with a rubber prop snake, but it looked unrealistic. So Atwill agreed to have a real living python wrapped around him. It certainly paid off. The scene is extremely grisly, especially the final shot of wide-eyed Atwill gasping his last breath as the snake coils round his neck. That final shot is one of the classic images of Atwill.

Atwill told the full story of the snake scene when he was interviewed in Britain in 1936 for *Picturegoer* magazine.

> They asked me whether I would mind wearing the real brute,
> just for the close-up, if he were unconscious.
> How unconscious, I asked.

"Gassed," they said.

Well, gas him and I'll have a look at him first, I suggested.

So they gassed him and also tied his mouth up with adhesive tape, in case he woke up too soon, and I must say he looked extremely dead. So I said I'd do it; but I didn't altogether bargain on his weighing three hundredweight. Doing my death-agony like anything, I bent my legs, and the coils of the python weighed so heavily on me that I couldn't support it and crashed down on my knees. Fortunately the floor was covered with sawdust or bark, so I didn't break any bones but I had tender knees for weeks. And the stench of that brute—*pah!*

In his *Hollywood Babylon II*, Kenneth Anger recounted all manner of alleged factual details of Atwill's lifestyle. One of these was a claim that the actor was "infatuated" with the python, a female called Elsie, and that Atwill took it back to his Pacific Palisades home, thereby causing friction with his wife. But in fact contemporary publicity material went to some pains to explain that the snake was a male called Oswald, and was owned by a Texas snake handler. Additionally, Atwill's stated revulsion at the snake in the *Picturegoer* interview is evidence—if any were needed—that Anger's story is a fiction. And the fact that it *is* a fiction calls into question many of Anger's other statements.

Murders in the Zoo is full of other memorable moments and rewards repeated viewings. One of these moments has Atwill at his most brutal, when he throws Burke off a bridge into a lake full of hungry alligators. He tips her head over heels in a way that has an almost casual nastiness to it. Another moment to relish is a brief shot of him in close-up, planning the mealtime murder; his eyes have a truly fiendish look in them.

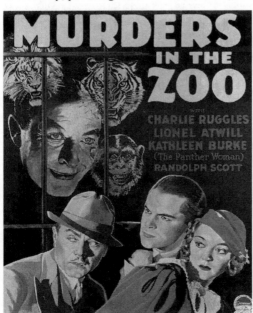

The U.S. Window Card poster

Absolutely no one in films, before or since, could *stare* like Atwill could. Other enjoyable sequences include one in which Atwill pretends to be upset when he hears about his wife's death and another scene that is both funny and chilling, when he tries to sneak up on Randolph Scott in order to jab him with his fake mamba head. But Scott keeps looking round at all the wrong moments.

On several occasions in Atwill's film career, he played out scenes that had extraordinary parallels with events in his real offscreen life. Eight years earlier he had suspected his wife, Elsie Mackay, of infidelity and tried to catch her red-handed with her lover one night, just before she was about to sail off for Europe. In *Murders in the Zoo*, Eric Gorman pays a surprise visit

Lionel Atwill

on Hewitt (John Lodge) while Evelyn is there. She is planning to flee from her husband to Paris. This probably cannot be mere coincidence—it is far more likely that Atwill may have had some input.

Edward Sutherland's workman-like direction is all that prevents *Murders in the Zoo* from being the classic it could have been in the hands of a more imaginative director. The comic relief provided by Charlie Ruggles was well received in its day and must have made a welcome change of tone from

A giant python suffocates Atwill in *Murders in the Zoo*.

the film's grimness, but today it seems weak. Another negative is that during the climax, where the big cats are freed and fight among themselves, there can be no doubt that some serious injuries were inflicted on leopards by lions, etc. It wouldn't be allowed today, and quite rightly so.

Young lovers Gail Patrick and Randolph Scott look pleasant but don't have a great deal to do. Wide-eyed, beautiful Kathleen Burke, who just the previous year made her name as the Panther Woman of *Island of Lost Souls*, has a meatier role here as the tormented wife.

The film and especially Atwill's performance outraged Will Hays and his censorship office, and they were equally disapproving of his next film, *The Song of Songs*. We may imagine that they placed a disapproving mark against his name in some little black book. Several years later, as we shall see, they were able to get their revenge.

The Song of Songs (1933)

Although Marlene Dietrich sizzles as the star of *The Song of Songs*, this is Atwill's film. He must have been delighted at having landed the part, and no one could have played it as well as he did. His Baron August Von Merzbach, a colonel in the Prussian army, is a bully, a sadist, a letch and a drunk. In fact, he's a dirty old man, even chuckling indecently on a number of occasions.

The film, directed by the great Rouben Mamoulian a year after he made the magnificent horror film *Dr. Jekyll and Mr. Hyde*, stars Fredric March, Atwill's old acting buddy from his days in *Deburau*. Mamoulian makes the film a joy to watch and it rewards

A distinguished portrait by Freulich circa 1933 [Courtesy of Tony Atwill]

With suggestive intent Baron von Merzbach (Atwill) blows cigarette smoke over a sketch of a naked Marlene Dietrich in *The Song of Songs.*

repeated viewings. Some wonderful sets are on display (especially the vaulted ceiling of Von Merzbach's Baronial home) and this is one of the sexiest pre-Code films audiences will ever see, with Marlene Dietrich featured in some extremely erotic scenes.

The plot is essentially simple: Lily (Dietrich), an innocent country girl, moves to the big city (Berlin), falls in love with a sculptor (Brian Aherne), the sculptor rejects her, she is swooped up by a lecherous old Baron (Atwill) and ultimately a happy ending rewards the viewer. This simplicity of plot gives the film much charm, but it is also one of its few short-comings: *Song of Songs* is held back from becoming the classic it might have been because the linear plot lacks more substance. That aside, it is a film to treasure.

This is Lionel Atwill in one his finest film roles. In an accurate recreation of a Prussian military uniform, he wears a high bearskin hat emblazoned with skull and crossbones. He sports a memorably brutal haircut, cropped short and gray (to emphasize the age difference between him and Lily). Complete with the inevitable monocle, he looks resplendent.

He has commissioned Waldow (Aherne) to sculpt a life-size statue of a naked girl. It is made clear from the dialogue that Von Merzbach is no appreciator of art—he just wants to own an erotic statue that he can ogle. Shamelessly, he convinces Waldow to give up Lily (Dietrich) so he can have her himself. The long wedding night sequence is one to treasure. Von Merzbach primps and preens, quietly singing as he contemplates the pleasures to come. Listening outside Lily's bedroom, he hears her crying, and this only excites him further, eliciting a thrilled laugh.

Treating Lily likes he owns her, he has her learn to speak French, to dance, to sing and to play the piano, so that he can show her off to his guests. His most manipulative scene is a treat. He invites Waldow, who has not been seen for some time, to join him and Lily for dinner. The atmosphere is fraught, on account of Waldow having previously rejected Lily. But Von Merzbach delights in the tension, because his very reason for inviting Waldow was to impress him how he has molded Lily into becoming his willing slave.

Lily runs off into the night followed by Waldow. To punish him for rejecting her, she rushes into the home of Von Merzbach's farm manager (Hardie Albright), offering herself to him. But the place catches fire, and all the local people see Lily being brought out, thereby humiliating her husband. Although hopelessly drunk, Von Merzbach runs out brandishing a pistol, intending to shoot her. But he is talked out of it and she is allowed to leave his life forever. It's the last we see of Von Merzbach; what a shame there was not some dramatic scene in which he got his comeuppance.

It is fun to look at the sexual content of some of these scenes in more detail. It is remarkable for the period and sneaked in just before the Hays Code clamped down on such antics.

After her father's death, Lily is sent to stay with her crotchety, rum-swilling old aunt (Alison Skipworth). Lily tells her she used to read the

The sculptor (Brian Aherne), the Baron and the life-sized naked statue of Dietrich in *The Song of Songs.*

Song of Solomon to him every night. "Knowing your father," the aunt replies, "I imagine there was something dirty in it." She tells Lily to undress and go to bed. As Lily undresses, the aunt's reflection is seen in a mirror, watching and commenting on her. Lily steps out of several layers of underskirts and petticoats. "I've never seen a girl unpeel herself like an onion before!" quips the aunt, enjoying the spectacle (as indeed are all male viewers). The aunt continues to chuckle delightedly—so delightedly that a hint of lesbianism surfaces—as Lily continues to strip, standing eventually in just a lacy slip and bloomers. "A figure like that will get you into trouble, if you're not careful!"

Next day, Waldow enters the aunt's bookshop and catches an enticing glimpse of Lily's stocking-clad leg revealed accidentally as she dusts the shelves. He asks her to model for him in his studio. Of course she refuses but she can't resist sneaking out to pay him a visit. In his studio she finds herself surrounded by dozens of statues of nudes, both male and female, and they add a charge to all the subsequent scenes in the studio. Waldow asks Lily to strip down, and they speak to each other from either side of a life-size nude statue of a young girl, but she resists his requests to disrobe. Eventually she agrees and goes behind a curtain. In one amusingly deft moment, Lily starts to unpeel a stocking and Mamoulian pans round to the legs of a statue whose legs are gradually revealed, as Waldow moves a lamp.

As Lily unbuttons the last of her clothes, Mamoulian pans again, this time to Waldo pulling a sheet off another nude sculpture. When she stands before Waldow wearing only a smock, the outline of one of her nipples can be plainly seen. Finally, in a rapturous moment backed by similarly rapturous music, Lily eventually throws off the smock and stands naked and proud before Waldow. Just her head and shoulders are in the frame, naturally, but our imaginations do the rest.

A little over 20 minutes into the film, we meet Von Merzbach for the first time. He arrives at the studio just after Lily has gone behind the curtain to dress. He looks impeccable in military peaked cap and long coat. He admires Waldow's sketch of her naked. "Hmmmm … not bad!" he says, fingering his monocle appreciatively, "She's a little beauty!"

The Exquisite Villain

On seeing Lily, now fully dressed, he discreetly says to Waldow, "Ah ha! A pretty face as well as the … er ... hidden charms." After a brief exchange, Lily leaves. "A lovely girl," coos Von Merzbach, extracting a cigarette from his cigarette box and placing it between his lips with an almost lascivious pleasure. "Lovely!" he tells Waldow, "She interests me very much … Very much!" Who can forget the sensual way he blows smoke over the sketch of her naked?

When we next see Lily in Waldow's studio, a highly charged scene occurs in which he watches a silhouette of her undressing, at the same time as he caresses the shoulders of his naked statue of her. We sense that he really wants to grab the statue's breasts! When she stands naked in front of him, he walks toward her and she grabs the smock and holds it up in front. He takes her in his arms and kisses her, only the flimsy smock between them. There isn't a more erotic scene—at least not one that I know of—produced by Hollywood in the 1930s.

This is followed by another stunning moment—a shot of them in the countryside, running up a hill lit by bright sunshine, and it must be one of the most romantic and picturesque images of all time, suggesting the idyllic happiness of young love.

Von Merzbach visits the bookshop and tries to convince the aunt to let Lily come and live with him. She protests and he assures her, "All the proprieties would be observed."

When this approach fails, he tries bribery, offering her 1,000 marks for a 3-mark book. "Understand me, Frau Rasmussen, when I set my mind on a thing, I usually get it ... one way or another."

In his next scene, Von Merzbach craftily convinces Waldow to give up Lily, so that he can marry her. Atwill has a lot of lines in this scene, all impeccably delivered with militaristic persuasiveness.

The Baron marries Lily (Dietrich) in *The Song of Songs*.

In the next scene, Von Merzbach is in Waldow's now-deserted studio and tells Lily that Waldow has gone to Italy. She breaks down and, as she falls to the floor, she pulls off the cloth covering the statue of her, revealing it in all its nakedness. Von Merzbach hovers over her, offering support—even though we know what is really on his mind. He stoops and reaches out to her but can't bring himself to lay his hands on her. His murky motivation here is that he genuinely feels sorry for her, yet at the same time the proximity of the nude statue makes him lust after her.

He sits Lily down and tries to console her. He tells her he loves her and wants to make her the Baroness von Merzbach. "I'll make you my wife, Lily," he says with a manic stare. It's a great sequence.

The two are married in grand style and Lily is taken back in a horse-drawn carriage to the Baron's vast chateau. Von Merzbach escorts her into the antechamber of his house, a vast room with dizzying vaulted ceilings and three giant statues of knights in armor. The staff is lined up to greet them. "This is Fraulein von Schwertfeger, the ... er ... housekeeper," he says, clearly implying that she is much more than that and has been keeping her employer sexually occupied. Von Merzbach can hardly wait to get down to the business of the

Outside the bedroom on his wedding night, the Baron sniggers filthily as he anticipates what awaits him, from *The Song of Songs.*

wedding night, cancels supper, instead offering his new bride champagne.

"To our wedding night!" he toasts bluntly, finishing off a glass.

"I'm not used to champagne," says Lily. "It'll make me dizzy."

"All the better," he replies, "all the better!"

Unable to constrain his excitement, he actually lifts Lily's glass to her mouth, to make her drink more quickly. As he escorts her to the bedroom, Atwill adopts a slightly decrepit walk, to remind us that Von Merzbach is old enough to be Lily's father. Showing her into the bedroom, he says he will join her shortly. Closing the door, he hears Lily sobbing on the other side. The sound of it only serves to make him even more excited and he giggles like an excited schoolboy.

In his own rooms, he changes into a dressing gown, brushes his hair, slicks down his moustache and applies some scent, all the while humming to himself. He takes a look at the pencil sketch of Lily naked, which is on his dresser, and chuckles obscenely once again.

Mamoulian cuts to the exterior of the building and we see Von Merzbach's silhouette crossing the room toward Lily. This might have been the expected place to end the scene, but the director (or perhaps the scriptwriters) can't resist adding a further note of perversity. Standing outside and looking up at the window is Von Merzbach's servant (Hardie Albright), who has fallen for Lily and presumably detests the thought of his boss ravishing her ... yet nevertheless wants to be a spectator. Enough depravity? No, Mamoulian piles it on. The housekeeper, now feeling rejected and jealous, is also outside looking on, and she is observing Albright, who she has noticed is attracted to Lily. Talk about voyeurism.

Months later, Von Merzbach invites Waldow to visit him. He then enjoys gloating about her in front of him, and taunts them both.

"You modeled her in marble. I modeled her in the flesh, so to speak," he boasts with a filthy laugh. He delights in the knowledge that Lily is his, and that Waldow cannot have her. Boasting about how well he has trained her, he even slaps her face several times, as if she were no more than a dog to him. Getting drunk on port, he mercilessly

After the wedding, Lily resists the Baron's advances, from *The Song of Songs*.

drags up the past, recalling that he and Lily first got together thanks to Waldow.

"The noble Waldow graciously steps aside so that his old friend might ... *renew his youth!*" He puts indecent emphasis on the last three words and chuckles filthily at his innuendo. Lily has heard enough and storms out.

In his last scene, he staggers outside drunkenly brandishing a pistol intending to shoot Lily for her indiscretion with the farm manager. Just in time, the housekeeper talks him out of it. The character is not seen again and deserved a better final scene—it would have been satisfying to see him die in a fire or in a duel.

Lily gets a job in a nightclub and takes up smoking cigarettes and drinking champagne. One customer asks her back to his apartment and, when she declines, his next line has been blanked out and drowned out by music—did he say something that really went too far? This being an early 1930s Dietrich vehicle, she naturally sings a song. And what a suggestive song it is.

> Johnny ... when we're all alone, we'll have a lot to do ... There's something wrong with me, I can't say no ... I need a kiss or two, or maybe more.

Throughout his career, Atwill gave many Hollywood actresses a run for their money in terms of his wardrobe; he seemed to insist that the various costume departments dress him in a manner that was as impeccable as his diction. In *Song of Songs*, he wears a varied succession of striking outfits. He is first seen in military peaked cap and long coat; then in full Prussian officer's attire, complete with the skull and crossbones hat; then in a silk dressing gown and finally in white bow tie and tails.

To sum up—this is, in all respects, one of the *great* Atwill performances. I would suggest entirely seriously that Atwill deserved an Academy Award nomination for *The Song of Songs*. But the Academy probably found the role too distasteful.

The Sphinx (1933)

Lionel Atwill in a dual role—it sounds too good to be true! And, sure enough, it is too good to be true. This Monogram cheapie is unimaginatively scripted and slackly directed. Even at an hour's running time, it drags. This is one of very few films in the Atwill *oeuvre* that is disappointing. Anyone expecting a lurid horror film will instead find they have to sit through a very tame murder mystery. It does, however, feature a few good sequences.

Things begin promisingly. A superb painted image of Atwill's face adorning a sphinx-like statue provides the eerie background for the opening credits. Then the actor emerges from an office building, dressed in a dapper suit. He asks the night janitor for the time and a match and walks off jauntily. Because it is Lionel Atwill, we know he has been up to no good and, sure enough, the janitor discovers a dead body. We soon learn that other recent murders share the same characteristics, with the departing murderer making the same two requests: He asks for the time and a match. The janitor identifies the man to the police as Jerome Breen, a wealthy benefactor.

The Sphinx opens with this striking image of Atwill's face adorning the eponymous Egyptian carving.

But Breen has the perfect alibi—he is a deaf mute so he could not possibly have asked for anything!

When we first meet Breen in his huge mansion, Atwill does a bit of convincing sign language to his butler (a good smirking performance by Lucian Prival). Atwill may have gone to the trouble of learning some sign language for this scene, but in all subsequent scenes, his hands are kept just out of the frame when he signs—a clumsy and unsatisfactory device. The deaf-mute angle gives the film the feel of an old Lon

The impressive U.S. one-sheet poster

Chaney melodrama (as would be the case in the following year's *Beggars in Ermine*), and the device adds interest to scenes in which Breen flirts with Sheila Terry, sometimes signing to his butler, at other times writing his thoughts on notes of paper. It says a lot for Atwill's acting skills that even when he is deprived of opportunities to use that distinctive voice, he still steals every scene in which he appears.

Immediately after committing another murder, Atwill takes great delight in saying a few words to the victim's mother. Atwill stares at her with a sadist's relish as she puts two and two together and promptly faints. He casually lights up a cigar as she slides to the floor!

A well-staged moment occurs when a policeman fires a pistol to see if he can get Breen to reveal that he really can hear. But Breen's butler has tipped him off with a hand signal, so when the bullet is fired, there is

a delicious shot of Breen calmly smoking a cigarette and showing no reaction.

A couple of deft moments occur, which are little bits of business that I feel were most likely thought up by Atwill. They are evidence that Atwill, a former theater director and writer, was always alert to ways a scene could be improved. Breen, as if to com-

The deaf-mute Jerome Breen (Atwill) flirts with Jerry (Sheila Terry) with the aid of his notebook, while sinister butler (Lucien Prioval) looks on, in *The Sphinx.*

pensate for the loss of hearing and speech, has a heightened sense of smell. On one occasion he wafts his cocktail cigarette under his nose so as to smell it, and later he moves in close on Sheila Terry and breathes in the smell of her hair, his eyes closing in delight. It's a sensual moment, and a similar moment occurred a year later with Joan Bennett in *The Man Who Reclaimed His Head.*

The plot's mysteries are all eventually revealed. If the right note is struck on Breen's piano, a wall panel slides back to reveal a secret room in which his identical twin is hiding. In a climactic scene, creepily devoid of both dialogue and music, Terry finds herself in between two Lionel Atwills, both walking toward her with evil intent. It includes a great shot of Atwill in extreme close-up. The scene (which uses split screen to achieve the dual image) could almost be the inspiration for that very similar moment in *Targets*, when Tim O'Kelly finds himself between two Boris Karloffs.

Terry is tied up and kept in the secret room, but he is rescued in the nick of time, with one twin getting shot and the other taking his own life using a ring (on his pinky, naturally) that injects him with poison.

It probably all sounds far more exciting than it actually is. Atwill is as polished as ever and is particularly good in the early scenes at adopting facial expressions which suggest he just might be guilty … but then again, he might not. Why he is nicknamed the Sphinx is never explained; presumably the difficulty of pinning the murders on Breen is akin to the unsolvable riddle of the Sphinx.

(Note: This critique is based on a print that runs just under 60 minutes. Other sources claim the running time may be as long as 64 minutes. Is something missing? I notice that one of the murders (of a suspicious cop) is only referenced but not actually seen. Also, a still on the DVD cover showing Atwill tying up Terry has no counterpart in this print.)

The Secret of the Blue Room (1933)

With Lionel Atwill in the starring role, and after the thrills of *Doctor X* and *Mystery of the Wax Museum*, horror fans probably went to see this one expecting something similar. How disappointed they must have been. It's a very tame and unimaginative haunted house story, and Atwill is very much a forgettable red herring.

Guests who sleep in the Blue Room of a huge old mansion are being murdered or disappear, and of course the scriptwriters want us to think that Atwill is the culprit. They go so far as to feature a couple of shots of Atwill in a large flat cap, so that when we see the actual murderer from behind wearing a similar hat, we will of course assume it is Atwill. It is all so clumsily done that only the most gullible members of the audience will have been fooled.

All the action takes place, very stagily, inside the mansion, and mostly in two rooms. The opening scene looks marvelously dated today, with the four major male protagonists all sitting in a living room in dinner jackets listening admiringly to pretty Gloria Stuart singing at a piano. When each gives her a kiss to celebrate her 21st birthday, is it my imagination or does Atwill, playing her father, hold her to his lips for just a second or two longer than one would expect for a fatherly peck? It's no surprise to discover years later that Stuart recalled (as quoted in Mank's *Hollywood's Maddest Doctors*), "Lionel was really darling! He was crazy about me."

The drama is heightened when Atwill, playing Robert Von Helldorf, owner of the creepy mansion, recounts the story of the Blue Room and the three mysterious deaths that have occurred in it. "Three persons met death there … under strange and peculiar circumstances… I'd rather not speak of it. It's long ago now… and better left forgotten."

But he is persuaded to tell at length how his sister stayed in the Blue Room many years ago and how, after a scream was heard, her body was found in the moat below. He continues his tale, and recounts how a few months later his best friend was found in the Blue Room, dead from a gunshot, " ... in the same room … at the same hour… one o'clock." The long dialogue continues, with Von Helldorf describing the events of the third death, a detective who chose to spend the night in the Blue Room. "His face

Robert von Helldorf (Atwill) acts suspiciously, but is he just a red herring in *The Secret of the Blue Room*?

was still frozen in a look of agonized horror. The physician claimed that death was due to heart failure, caused by great fright. Now you understand why I never want to go in that room again."

If only the script had maintained this level of interest—and this amount of Atwill screen time—but it turns out that this is the best scene and dialogue that Atwill gets. Disappointingly, most of his scenes after this are very short and perfunctory.

His only other substantial scene is a long exchange with police detective Edward Arnold, in which von Helldorf

TERROR. For twenty years the sinister blue room of the castle had been locked up. Von Helldorf (Lionel Atwill) told the story to his guests and one of them offered to spend the night in it. But it was no empty legend, the others—Faber (Onslow Stevens), Brink (Paul Lukas) and Irene (Gloria Stuart) found in the morning. From Universal's *The Secret of the Blue Room.*

A still from *The Secret of the Blue Room* appeared in a British film magazine.

reveals that he isn't really Gloria Stuart's father after all (that explains the lingering kiss at the film's start) and that her real father is a mysterious figure who has been skulking around outside the house.

As with *The Vampire Bat* the year before, *Secret of the Blue Room* is a case of Atwill appearing in a film that was unworthy of him. But, as he said in an interview in the *New York Times*, after years on the stage, he now thoroughly enjoyed the whole process of filmmaking and was fascinated by it. And if Hollywood was willing to pay him exorbitant amounts of money to make substandard films, then he was quite willing to go along for the ride and enjoy every moment of it.

The only time that director Kurt Neumann comes to life is in the climactic scene in the shadowy tunnels below the house, with Paul Lukas chasing the killer. Just one year earlier, Universal had made the classic *The Old Dark House*, a film with many similarities to *Secret of the Blue Room* (they shared some of the same sets), yet the two could not be more different in terms of quality. And it's hard to believe that William Hurlbut, who wrote the uninspired script for this film, also wrote the script for Universal's *Bride of Frankenstein* two years later.

This was the first of many films that Atwill made for Universal Pictures. One of the great pleasures of watching the old Universal films is the charming opening studio logo sequence with a small propeller-driven plane circling a model of the Earth as

Atwill as Inspector Wallace, playing *The Solitaire Man*

clouds scud by in the background. By the late 1930s—around the time of *Son of Frankenstein*—the logo sequence had changed to a more glamorous (but equally charming) image of a glass globe surrounded by twinkling and rotating glass stars, all backed by the rousing studio theme music.

The Solitaire Man (1933)

This is an engaging if largely unremarkable jewel-theft drama, starring the unremarkable Herbert Marshall, an actor who in his day was surprisingly popular, although today it is hard to understand why. Having been filmed just before the Hays Code was enforced, the

HE COULD EVEN STEAL A LADY'S HEART!

Here is a melodrama that is new and exciting every moment! A Raffles of the Riviera, outwitting, single-handed, the whole continental police, snared at last in the arms of a lovely woman!

THE **SOLITAIRE MAN**

Directed by **JACK CONWAY**

with

HERBERT **MARSHALL**
MARY **BOLAND**
LIONEL **ATWILL**
MAY **ROBSON**
ELIZABETH **ALLAN**

A Metro-Goldwyn-Mayer PICTURE

film contains a lot of fun, risqué dialogue, the sort of thing that would disappear a year later. What also makes this film entertaining is the setting of the majority of the action. About 40 minutes of the 66-minute running time take place onboard a 1930s 12-seater bi-plane, in the gloriously free-and-easy traveling days long before regulations made us all wear seat belts and stay in our seats. The plane door is even opened on several occasions and, at one point, Ralph Forbes (a shell-shocked WWI veteran who is hooked on drugs) commits suicide by jumping out.

Third-billed Lionel Atwill has a significant role, but it's certainly not a classic one. He isn't seen at all during the first 30 minutes, but after that he is in every scene. He appears just as the plane is about to take off. In dark suit and bowler hat, he reveals himself to be Inspector Wallace, who is on board the plane to arrest Marshall. But then the plot becomes enjoyably convoluted: Atwill isn't a police detective after all, he's another jewel thief. Or is he? Was that a double bluff and is he really a detective?

Eventually it turns out he is a detective but a crooked one who is also a jewel thief! In fact it is revealed that he was the silhouetted figure seen earlier who shot another policeman (although a stand-in appears to have been used for that scene to prevent the audience from guessing the outcome).

Throughout, Atwill delivers his dialogue impeccably (apart from a gaffe when he calls Marshall "Wallace," his own character's name). Some of the exchanges between him and Marshall, both actors with wonderfully trained voices, are lively and enjoyable. For

Herbert Marshall, Elizabeth Allan and Lionel Atwill in *The Solitaire Man*

example, in one droll moment, Marshall searches Atwill and reads a letter he finds in his pocket. Atwill looks sheepish as Marshall says, "Amazing love life, Wallace."

"Think so?" he replies with a hint of pride.

Atwill's character also exhibits a fine line in wry humor, such as when he enjoys taunting Forbes about his drug habit. But he is given no meaty lines to compare with his best sinister and/or tortured roles.

The climax provides him with a memorable death scene. The plane lands, the passengers all walk to an airport building and the truth is finally revealed. Atwill, brandishing a pistol, tries to make a break for it through a window. But his pistol isn't loaded and a bullet thwarts his escape, as he falls backwards through the window. With a neat bit of unintended irony, the plane lands at Croydon airport, the borough where Atwill was born back in 1885. So Atwill dies where he was born!

Nana (1934)

"*Nana*, Zola's sordid novel of the rise and fall of a street-walker … has been transformed into a romance of the Parisian music halls," wrote a reviewer in Britain's *Film Weekly* magazine in 1934. It was no coincidence that Atwill was so often attracted to roles in films that were sordid, risqué or macabre. Many other actors turned these roles down, fearing that their reputations might be harmed. Atwill, on the other hand, lapped them up and thoroughly enjoyed himself.

After his magnificent no-holds-barred performance in *The Song of Songs*, Atwill's acting in *Nana*—whose plot treads in similar territory—is an exemplar of restraint. It's almost as if he wanted to prove that he *could* be restrained when it was needed. One critic of *The Song of Songs* had accused him of "doing a Von Stroheim," and it may be that Atwill wanted to show another side of his talents. There are scenes when he really could have let rip, such as when he allows himself to be seduced by Anna Sten, or when he confronts his brother at the climax. But Atwill made a conscious decision to keep his character, Colonel André Muffat, stern and cold throughout.

As such, Atwill fans should make a point of watching this just to see how he could portray a character that keeps all his turbulent emotions hidden. Britain's *Film Weekly* thought that, "Lionel Atwill is at times brilliant."

Anna Sten and Lionel Atwill in *Nana*

This was a major non-horror role for him and in 1934 he was, arguably, at the peak of his fame, having only recently starred in *Doctor X* and *Mystery of the Wax Museum*. In some ways it was a tricky role. Initially, he has to appear detached and pompous, disapproving of the flirtatious title character. But subsequently he changes track, falls in love with and lavishes money on her, even though his love is not reciprocated. He could have made Muffat vicious and unpleasant in the early scenes and milked later scenes for their sympathetic potential. But Atwill does neither. The lid on Muffat's emotional pot is kept firmly secured throughout. *Film Weekly* rightly observed that he "manages some very awkward scenes quite brilliantly."

Impressive though this approach is, it's a fact that Atwill's many fans enjoy his performances most when he throws restraint to the wind and attacks a role by the throat. Inevitably these fans will be disappointed by *Nana*.

The climax is gripping. Nana realizes she has gotten into an impossible situation, being loved by both Colonel Muffat and his brother. (In fact, she seems to be bedding most of the male cast at some point.) She chooses the only way out and commits suicide.

The two brothers: Atwill with Phillips Holmes in *Nana*

Sten is a delight in the title role. One of her streetwalker friends is well played by Mae Clarke of *Frankenstein* fame, here sporting dark hair. *Nana* was released just four months before the Hays Code was rigidly enforced, and hence plenty of risqué dialogue about prostitution and men's desires occur (directed by female Dorothy Arzner no less). Even so, it was still a very watered-down version of Emil Zola's original novel.

Despite it merits, *Nana* (released in the U.K. as *Lady of the Boulevards*) was a financial failure.

Beggars in Ermine (1934)

This obscure 1934 drama very nearly gives us a classic Lionel Atwill performance ... but not quite. He gets one of his rare top-billed roles in a non-horror film; he usually is billed third or lower. Non-horror it may be, but the plot reads like a combination of elements from *Mystery of the Wax Museum, Freaks* and one of the old Lon Chaney/Tod Browning melodramas involving cripples and amputees.

Atwill plays John "Flint" Dawson, general manager in a steel mill, who loses his legs when a disgruntled worker deliberately pours molten steel onto him. This is a gruesome sequence

Dawson (Atwill) is reunited with his daughter (Betty Furness) in the presence of the blind Marchant (Henry B. Walthall) in *Beggars in Ermine.*

that is cut very much from the same cloth as the opening scenes of *Mystery of the Wax Museum*, when Atwill is burnt in a fire caused by his business partner. Then, lying legless in his hospital bed, he is brought the news that his wife has run off with the executive director of the mill (Jameson Thomas), and if that wasn't bad enough, all his investments in the company have been wiped out. The camera lingers on a close-up of Atwill's face as the desperation of his circumstances sinks in. Surely, now he will be driven into madness and plot his revenge ...

For the rest of the film, Atwill performs from a wheelchair (very reminiscent of *Wax Museum*), and the prospect of terrible revenge looms large. But—unfortunately—the script chooses not to go down the horror route and instead Atwill's character remains sane and decent throughout. He plots and enacts revenge all right, but in a restrained and perfectly legal way. He teams up with a blind man (Henry B. Walthall) and creates an investment bank for beggars, which becomes so successful that he can live in a big house and plan a share take-over of the steel mill.

Numerous scenes follow in which various crippled beggars feature, and most of them appear to be genuine—armless men, blind men and a legless man who wheels himself along on a trolley (another image that links this film to the old Lon Chaney films). It seems that in just the same way that Tod Browning rounded up real freaks for his film of that name, so the makers of *Beggars in Ermine* rounded up genuine cripples. And is it a coincidence that in *West of Zanzibar*, Chaney's wheelchair-bound character was called Dead Legs Flint, and here Atwill's character is John "Flint" Dawson?

Adding to the Browning-Chaney link is a plot element involving Atwill's daughter (Betty Furness), which could have been lifted straight out of any one of those films. She was whisked away when her mother deserted Atwill, believes her father to be dead and has no idea that he is her mysterious benefactor. In one memorable scene, Furness spies on Atwill through a window and realizes he is her father.

"Did you see the hate in his eyes?" she says. "It frightens me." It's a marvelous line and an epithet that niftily sums up much of Atwill's appeal. It's a shame that this sequence is not more powerful, but director Phil Rosen (*The Sphinx, Return of the Ape Man, Spooks Run Wild*) lacks the talent to pull it off.

In this original U.S. lobby card, Atwill, now a double-amputee, is cared for by his daughter (Betty Furness) and her boyfriend (James Bush), in *Beggars in Ermine*.

A fine dramatic moment occurs at the end when Atwill, in wheelchair, wheels himself into the boardroom to confront his nemesis Jameson Thomas, and long lingering stares erupt between the pair. In a showdown between the two men, Atwill accuses him of having murdered his wife. He leaves a loaded pistol on the table and exits the room; a few minutes later, a shot is heard: Thomas has committed suicide.

The film closes with Atwill triumphantly wheeling onto a first-floor balcony and telling the workers below that all will be well from now on. A happy ending, but Thomas deserved a far more gruesome comeuppance. After all, it was he who incited a worker to pour molten steel onto Atwill, he who ran off with Atwill's wife, he who bankrupted Atwill and he who murdered Atwill's wife.

The film runs 70 min-

The actual shot of Atwill's legs being burned away by the molten steel was perhaps too gruesome for the lobby card set, so a tamer shot was used instead (a shot not included in the film), from *Beggars in Ermine*.

utes but there is evidence of some cutting. No scene exists where Atwill and his daughter are reconciled, merely a spoken reference that such a scene occurred. After the scene at the window described above, the daughter is next seen being loving and affectionate toward her father, now that he has explained everything to her. Was a more powerful scene filmed, perhaps an emotional confrontation between father and daughter that was subsequently dropped? Have we possibly lost a great bit of acting by Atwill? And why did Jameson murder Atwill's wife? It is never discussed, suggesting additional cuts. And midway through the film, Atwill has taken on a false identity, after he was believed killed in a railroad crash, yet there are no scenes of the crash or the adoption of the new identity. More cuts? The original novel on which this is based, by Esther Lynd Day, was presumably much more involved; extra scenes may have been filmed but then discarded, or perhaps never filmed at all.

Along the way are various memorable moments, such as a tearjerker scene in the hospital. Told that his wife has signed away his stake in the mill, Atwill gets dreamy eyed and melancholy: "She couldn't have known what she was doing," he says with great melodramatic restraint, still in love with her even though she has ruined him. "She was very young. Younger than I by 15 years." Soon, the penniless Atwill realizes he can no longer afford to stay in the hospital's private ward. He asks to be transferred to a charitable ward, but he puts on a brave face to his tearful nurse, by pretending that his reason for wanting to change wards is that he could do with some companionship. A brief scene appears, told in flashback, jumping forward 15 years to when Atwill has become successful again, in which Walthall wheels Atwill to the address where he believes his wife is living, only to see her corpse being carried out on a stretcher by police.

In a climactic confrontation with Thomas, we see a glimpse of the more traditionally nasty Atwill. He gloats that the angry mill workers would like to throw Thomas into a vat of molten steel: "If I turned you over to them, you'd be buried with a lot of metal into which they would throw you. Perhaps you'd rather die that way ... the way you tried to kill me." Then he takes great pleasure in leaving Thomas alone with a loaded revolver, knowing that he will shoot himself rather than face trial for murder. In this scene, one senses that Atwill was secretly longing to turn really nasty but had to hold back to remain true to the character.

Overall, this is an intriguing, off-beat drama and a must-see for Atwill fans, but director Rosen's style is simply too lackluster to raise it above the average.

Stamboul Quest (1934)

It's fun to watch lovely Myrna Loy parading about in a succession of slinky dresses and huge hats as a German spy in this obscure and exotic WWI spy drama. Co-star George Brent, however, is dull and irksome as the American who flirts endlessly with her. An example of the level of his humor is his description of the character played by third-billed Lionel Atwill: "Tough old baby. He probably eats nails for breakfast." Is that really the best line the scriptwriter could come up with to describe Atwill's memorable character?

The first 10 minutes are the film's best. Atwill's presence dominates, and he enacts the most perversely erotic scene of his career. He plays Von Sturm, a monocled German spymaster, immaculately dressed in long coat and spats. Early on, a superior officer tells him that he must resolve a tricky situation in Turkey and that the fate of Germany rests on whether or not he is successful. As the importance of his task dawns on him, Atwill's eyes open wide and he gives one of his legendarily intense stares.

One of his spies, nicknamed Fraulein Doktor (Loy), has gone missing and it is implied that a relationship exists between them. When she reappears, a great scene occurs that is so rich in sexual suggestiveness that it's a wonder it got past the censor. The Hays Production Code had only just begun to be enforced around the time of this film's release (mid-1934), so the filmmakers were still able to sneak a few risqué moments past the board.

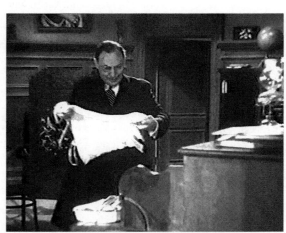

Von Sturm (Atwill) takes geat interest in Myrna Loy's discarded underwear, from _Stamboul Quest_.

The scene begins with Von Sturm being so pleased to see Loy again that he emits a long, loud laugh, which goes beyond being hearty and becomes positively dirty. She says she needs a bath and Von Sturm tells her she can use his bathroom—just why a bath exists in the room adjoining his office is unclear, but it certainly makes for a memorable scene.

"We can talk while you scrub," he says.

She does a sexy striptease while she talks to Von Sturm, throwing items of her clothing

Evidence (though a playful *long* stretch) of Atwill as the *unofficial* director? This behind-the-scenes still, taken on the set of *Stamboul Quest,* shows Atwill in the director's chair, while actual director Sam Wood is apparently on the left in the rear. [Photofest]

and underwear in his direction. The casualness with which she undresses in his presence clearly tells us a sexual relationship exists between them. Von Sturm picks up each item of clothing and examines it—ostensibly not for sexual kicks but because code words are hidden in the garments! Stepping out of her last item of clothing, a lacy slip, and throwing it at Von Sturm, she says, "The aircraft department would love to play with that," and Von Sturm chuckles delightedly.

As she talks lightheartedly about her last assignment, Von Sturm sniggers at everything she says, and Atwill manages to imbue his sniggers with a *timbre* that suggests a sexually excited schoolboy. Atwill specialized in roles as the slightly perverse lover, and they all take on an extra edge in light of what happened to him later in his career.

Another moment occurs that is an uncanny foretaste of what was to happen to Atwill. Leo G. Carroll, in a small uncredited part as a German spy, is given his orders by Von Sturm, who tells him he must masquerade as an Englishman and, even if caught, must not reveal his true identity. "Whatever happens," Carroll says with an ironic smile, "I promise to die like an English gentleman." Did Lionel remember this line when, in court, his lawyer delivered his statement, "I lied like a gentleman to protect my friends"?

Von Sturm has Brent brought before him, and the contrast between Brent's chirpy wise-cracks and Von Sturm's stern manner is adeptly staged. When Loy enters the room, Von Sturm lets out a long laugh that is even dirtier than his earlier one. The reason is that he plans to send Loy to spy on Brent by becoming *romantically involved* with him. She

The two spies, Fraulein Doktor (Myrna Loy) and Von Sturm, enjoy one another's scheming in *Stamboul Quest.*

clearly has a reputation for inciting men to fall for her, and Von Sturm no doubt enjoys hearing all the lurid stories she tells about it afterwards.

The action switches to a train, then to Turkey, and Von Sturm is not seen for about 40 minutes. [Note: Some prints of this film are missing Atwill's next two scenes and give the false impression that he does not reappear until the closing scenes.] Von Sturm arrives in Turkey, and pays Loy a morning visit. Polishing his monocle and chuckling, he is full of praise for Loy's clever intrigues when she requests that he have Beal executed—but use someone else as stand-in. In the second of the two missing scenes, the Turkish commander (C. Henry Gordon) suggests to Von Sturm that Loy may be Fraulein Doktor, the famous German spy. But Von Sturm keeps his cool, letting out a hearty laugh at the suggestion.

Brent is sentenced for execution by firing squad and there is an eye-catching shot of Von Sturm watching the execution through the ornate bars of a window (camerawork is by James Wong Howe). One can't help sensing that he actually *enjoys* watching the execution.

Things become quite deliciously perverse at the climax. Loy tricks Gordon into revealing details of the German mines—by persuading him to write them in invisible ink on her back. As he helps her replace her dress, he says very suggestively, "At our next meeting I hope this process will be reversed." But Atwill marches in and accuses Gordon of treason against Germany, taking great pleasure in dabbing a heated cloth onto Loy's exposed shoulder to reveal the secrets written on her. Gordon tries to talk his way out of it with some flowery words. This gives Atwill an opportunity to deliver one of those lines that he always spoke with such relish.

"I'm afraid His Excellency's passion for literary composition has been his undoing," he says, preceding it with one of his evil chuckles, as the words beneath are revealed clearly to all.

Having caught Gordon red-handed, he follows up with another crisply authoritative line: "It is the general misfortune of traitors to underestimate the intelligence of honest men."

Von Sturm takes voyeuristic pleasure in watching an execution in *Stamboul Quest.*

A powerful moment occurs when Atwill has to admit to Loy that, contrary to her understanding, he was not able to substitute Brent with someone else just before the execution. Then in a cruel twist that takes Atwill's villainy to an even greater level, he reveals (but not to Loy) that in fact he *did* save Brent at the last minute, but chose not to tell Loy, because he doesn't want his spies forming romantic attachments.

"When a spy is in love," he says with a note of regret, "her usefulness for us is gone."

The apparent death of Brent sends Loy into madness. Atwill, suddenly realizing this, says, "The girl has lost her mind," and he says it with an inflection that is extremely sinister. It is Atwill's final scene in the movie.

One More River (1934)

James Whale, who directed this drama adapted from John Galsworthy, is a legend in horror film circles. He made four of the greatest horror films of all time: *Frankenstein, The Old Dark House, The Invisible Man* and *Bride of Frankenstein.* He directed over 20 other films but few of them, if any, match the quality of his horror films. *One More River* is a case in point. It is a very engrossing, well-acted drama about a wife (Diana Wynyard) who flees from a brutal husband (Colin Clive) and ends up in a divorce court. But it never scales the heights of Whale's horror films, the subject matter of which seemed to inspire him.

The highlight is a superb courtroom scene (or rather three consecutive scenes) in which Atwill gives a bravura performance as Mr. Brough, an aggressive, posturing barrister employed by Sir Gerald Corven (Clive). In the courtroom, Lady Corven (Wynyard) is subjected to questioning by Brough that is scarcely any less brutal then her husband's treatment of her. Atwill gives one of his most bullish and intense portrayals. His scenes do not appear until nearly an hour into the film, but they are well worth waiting for.

The three scenes last over 15 minutes and Atwill gets a lot of screen time and some excellent dialogue. The part gives him a chance to really shine, and there are moments when he rolls his eyes in feigned exasperation and other moments when he is genuinely piqued when things don't go his way. He mops his brow after some particularly tough exchanges of dialogue, and at another point during the proceedings, he leans back theatrically onto the woodwork, triggering a double-take by the defense barrister (Alan Mowbray), who is alarmed by this false posturing.

The courtroom, designed by Charles D. Hall, is a magnificent setting for this legal duel, with a dizzyingly high ceiling and ornate wood paneling covering all the walls. Hall, who designed the sets for *Dracula* (1931), does similarly impressive things with the family home of Lady Corven, full of giant windows and Gothic arches. During the courtroom passages, Whale consciously tries to prevent the action from appearing static; he keeps his camera moving, pans with characters as they walk to the witness box, and in one audacious shot, he pans a full 360 degrees around the room.

Mr. Brough, in barrister's wig and gown, begins by summarizing the case and referring to the fact that Wynyard had been seen in the company of Frank Lawton. Wynyard denies that she is guilty of any misconduct with Lawton.

With more aggression in his voice, and one hand cockily placed on his hip, Brough launches into his attack: "Lady Corven, you, a married woman, wouldn't call inviting a young man to your cabin, entertaining him alone in your room at half past 11 at night, spending a night with him in a car and going about with him continually in the absence of your husband … misconduct?" When Wynyard asserts that on the occasion of one of Lawton's visits, he did no more than show her some photographs, Brough cannot resist throwing a knowing glance in the direction of the judge and using a pencil to showily scratch under his wig.

When Brough impertinently asks Wynyard how she was dressed when Lawton visited her, she replies, "I'm sorry to have to inform you that I was fully dressed."

Brough closes his eyes in a show of feigned vexation and turns to the judge.

"My Lord, may I ask to be protected from these sarcasms?"

Whale has his cameraman John Mescall make the most of Atwill's presence. For example, some shots linger dramatically on his profile as he fires off his questions. Another is angled from below to heighten the theatrics and the camera pans around him as he unleashes further accusations.

Brough raises the issue of a night the couple spent together in Lawton's car, which had broken down. Brough finds it hard to believe that nothing happened between the couple.

"He had beautiful manners, hadn't he, this young man who was in love with you?" says Brough, with extreme sarcasm in his voice.

As he speaks, Brough playfully taps his pencil on his chin, and when Wynyard asserts again that nothing occurred in the car, he looks toward Heaven in exasperation and melodramatically drops his pencil, which lands on the floor with a loud clonk. It's a delicious moment of colorful acting from Atwill.

Brough calls Sir Gerald to the witness box for a key episode in which the matter of him raping Lady Corven is examined. This being 1934, the language is carefully chosen, but even so it is surprisingly explicit for the time, given that stricter enforcement of the Hays Code had just begun. Brough clearly enjoys the opportunity to tread in such dangerous territory.

"On that occasion," he asks, "besides any conversation that took place between you … what else occurred?"

"My wife and I were reunited," replies Sir Gerald.

"You mean," intercedes the judge, "the marital relationship between you was re-established?"

"Yes, my Lord," say Sir Gerald.

"Thank you, that is all I wanted to ask," gloats Brough with a self-satisfied grin.

Lady Corven is recalled to the witness box and denies that anything took place. Brough seizes the moment.

"So your husband has gone out of his way to commit perjury?"

One of them must be lying.

(Is it just a small coincidental irony that this sequence has Atwill accusing others of committing perjury—or is it Fate stepping in yet again to warn Atwill of things to come?)

Brough raises his voice and roars an accusation at her. "Isn't it true, that you have made this answer, in order to spare the feelings of the co-respondent?"

She denies it, and Brough sits down, mopping his brow melodramatically.

Lawton is called to the witness box. Brough remarks on his unlikely statement that although the pair spent a night in a broken-down car, nothing took place between them.

"Tell me, did you sleep at all that night in the car, when her head was on your shoulder?"

"Yes."

"Hmm! Considering your feelings, wasn't that ... singular?" Brough enjoys the chance to put a tone of mockery into his voice, and, with another flourish, scratches his head again with his pencil.

"Do you seriously expect us to believe, that you took no advantage but just went to sleep?" Lawton asserts again that nothing happened, and eventually

Mr. Brough (Atwill) is the posturing prosecuting attorney of *One More River*.

Brough sits down, having tried his best, but failing to get his victim to admit to some indiscretion.

It is tempting to imagine the film with Atwill not playing Mr. Brough but instead in the role of Sir Gerald. As a bullying, violent husband who rapes his wife, Atwill would seem to have been the natural choice. There is even a speech made by Colin Clive that is almost tailor-made for Atwill, and which makes one wonder if at some stage Atwill had been lined up to play Sir Gerald:

> What I want you to understand is that I'm two men. One—and the one that matters—has his work to do and means to do it. And the other man ... well, the less said about him the better. You see, I'm honest—or shameless, if you like that word better.

It's almost as if the scriptwriter were paraphrasing something which Lionel had said in an interview in *Motion Picture* magazine in July 1933:

> See, one side of [my] face is gentle and kind, incapable of anything but love of my fellow man. The other side, the other profile, is cruel and predatory and evil, incapable of anything but the lusts and dark passions.

A coincidence?

In fact, Atwill is better served by the role of Mr. Brough, which in many respects makes more of an impression than the Colin Clive role. Atwill milks the role for every bit of theatrical impact that he can, and as a result it is one of the best things about the film. His opposing barrister, played by Alan Mowbray (who had been such an unforgettably vicious lawyer in *The Silent Witness*), is but a pale shadow.

The Age of Innocence (1934)

This enjoyably creaky drama holds the interest but is let down chiefly by the fact that Irene Dunne and John Boles give performances that are far too restrained. A bit more passion would have enlivened things no end.

Third-billed Lionel Atwill is Julius Beaufort, a disreputable scoundrel who cares little for what society thinks and is more interested in pursuing women, specifically Countess Ellen Olenksa (Dunne)—even though she is already married. He has three enjoyable, substantial scenes, but they are not enough to make Beaufort a genuinely memorable entry in Atwill's *oeuvre*. Beaufort is suggestive of the kind of role he had often played onstage: the well-dressed, monocled, gentleman bounder.

"I can't pretend," the Countess tells us, "that I'm like the other women over here … they never seem to feel any … needs. I'm not mincing words … I'm one of those women who must have … love." Beaufort is only too happy to satisfy her needs, and she becomes his mistress. Beaufort himself is married and is quite open about his delight that his wife has gone away on a long trip abroad, leaving him to enjoy himself. "It's hard for a man to keep track of his wife these days," he says flippantly.

There is much to enjoy in a scene in a posh living room in which various characters have been discussing the Countess' inappropriate behavior with Beaufort. An idea of what the other characters think of him is given in this line from Helen Westley: "I told her no nice woman would be seen walking up Fifth Avenue in broad daylight with Julius Beaufort. And what do you think she said? 'Would you rather I walked with him at night'?" The Countess and Beaufort arrive, and the latter is clearly aware that he is

Lionel Atwill (as Julius Beaufort), Julie Haydon, Irene Dunne, Helen Estley and John Boles in *The Age of Innocence*

Lionel Atwill

disapproved of, but holds his own. When offered some tea, he quips, "I never drink between meals … tea that is." Then he laughs heartily at his own joke. (Another fine example of how good Atwill was at laughing realistically.)

The Countess informs them that she is planning to rent a house and live on her own. The others are horrified that a young woman should live alone without "protection," and when that word is stressed again, the camera lingers on a shot of Beaufort looking smug, swinging his monocle playfully.

When she says that the house is on West 23rd Street, the others are even more horrified. "You told me it was respectable," says the Countess to Beaufort, who has chosen the house for her.

"Well, in my experience, I've always found it very respectable," he replies rather sheepishly, suggesting that he has had numerous colorful experiences there.

The scene ends comically when the Countess mentions that she is seeking a divorce from her husband, and at the mere mention of the word *divorce,* one of the stuffy guests, an elderly man, nearly has a fainting fit.

Atwill's other good scene is a confrontation with Boles, the latter regarding Beaufort as a low-life who treats women despicably. It is a confrontation of words, all done while Beaufort admires a statuette, and then tucks into some caviar. All very civilized—what a shame the pair of them could not have become a bit more vicious with each other. Beaufort leaves the room with a wide, self-satisfied grin, intended to let Boles know that his words have had no effect on him.

There ought to have been a scene in which Beaufort gets his just desserts and is publicly humiliated for his disgraceful behavior but, oddly, no such scene appears. The rest of the film concentrates on Boles and Dunne, and Beaufort is largely forgotten.

The theme of the film is the harshness of an upper-class society (in this case in late 19th-century New York) that, for the sake of so-called decency, forces people to behave in a way that often makes them give up any real chance of happiness. Atwill's character represents the kind of person who doesn't give two hoots for decency or what society thinks.

Like other RKO films of the period, this has a few links with *King Kong.* Max Steiner composed the jaunty music that backs the opening sequence, a thrilling montage of shots in which the very mobile camera takes us into the swinging decadence of 1930s New York: the skyscrapers, the bright lights, swanky cocktail bars and nightclub acts, with newspaper headlines screaming about divorce and other scandals. One quick shot of a nightclub act shows some African dancers who look remarkably like the natives of Skull Island.

In 1993, the film was re-made, with Martin Scorsese directing and Stuart Wilson playing Julius Beaufort.

The Firebird (1934)

If you think Alfred Hitchcock was the first filmmaker to have a leading character killed off after half an hour (as he did in *Psycho*), then watch *The Firebird.* Here, smooth-talking, womanizing Ricardo Cortez, who is the central figure, is discovered with a bullet in his brain after 25 minutes.

What follows is a highly enjoyable whodunit, and naturally, Lionel Atwill is one of the suspects. One of Atwill's great strengths was his ability to look tortured. He made a string of films in which his lovers cheated on him or humiliated him, and this is one of them. He has several opportunities here to don expressions suggesting great inner torment and anguish.

At first he is a mere supporting figure playing His Excellency John Pointer, a retired Austrian cabinet minister, who just happens to live in the same apartment block as Cortez. He is seen in a few early scenes enjoying a happy family life with wife Verree Teasdale and daughter Anita Louise. In one of these he is seen playing a viola (less than convincingly), and in another he instructs his servant to burn a book which has been given to his daughter as a gift, a copy of Tolstoy's *Resurrection* that he considers wholly unsuitable for his darling daughter. Later he dons top hat and tails and goes to the opera with his family.

On returning, they find the place swarming with police and the real drama begins. Police Inspector C. Aubrey Smith arrives on the scene and Atwill now becomes a central character. A gripping series of scenes unroll in which Atwill tries to establish the identity of the mystery woman who was seen sneaking into Cortez' apartment one night. In one key moment, he is forced to eliminate the family's governess from his inquiries and, judging by the intense expression on his face, it is the first moment when it crosses his mind that his own wife could be the guilty party.

"Oh, I'm very sorry. I beg your pardon," he says to the governess, and his eyes seem to stare off into a world of nightmarish possibility.

He starts to interrogate his wife. He hunts through the drawers of a cabinet, and then in an exchange of dialogue shot slightly from below to heighten the tension, he says to her, "That diary of yours, I'd like to see it."

Teasdale tries to sneak off with the locked box that contains the diary.

"Give me the key or I'll wake the entire house!" he barks at her. He reads the diary entry for the day in question, realizes that another candidate is eliminated from his inquiries, and then the truth creeps up on him. The book drops to the floor with a clatter. He sits down and the camera films him in close up. He starts to talk to himself: "In that case, there's only one woman left ..." With a pitiful tremor in his voice, he calls out

John Pointer (Atwill) begins to suspect his wife (Verree Teasdale) of infidelity in *The Firebird*.

his wife's name: "Carola!" It is impossible not to feel sorry for the poor chap at this moment.

Then, in his best stony-faced, cold-voiced manner, he accuses his wife of having visited Cortez' apartment.

"It was you who went to Brandt's apartment," he says, then shouts at her: "You and nobody else!"

She finally admits it, and he stares at her in horror. Then his eyes slowly close as despair overtakes him.

Lionel Atwill

A long and powerful silent passage follows as Atwill walks slowly away from the camera and Teasdale follows him. We see only their backs; the expressions on their faces are left to our imaginations.

Teasdale says, "Please believe me when I tell you I've always loved you."

In response Atwill lets out a pained gasp. It's a skillful piece of acting. "How do I know what else has happened during all these years?"

It's a superb seven-minute sequence and the best in the film. It is also Atwill at his finest. Immediately following this, Teasdale goes to the police inspector to admit to the murder, but Atwill follows her, a look of absolute horror on his face as he tries to convince Smith that his wife

Pointer tries to stop his wife from confessing to the police inspector (C. Aubrey Smith) in *The Firebird*.

doesn't know what she is saying. A few minutes later, the Inspector has worked out that Teasdale has only been pretending to be the killer, in order to protect someone else. Atwill looks bewildered and can't think who that person might be. The Inspector says he wants to speak with Atwill's daughter. Now Atwill looks even more bewildered and horrified. By this time, any right-minded viewer should be thinking: Atwill deserves an Oscar for this performance!

Atwill now realizes his daughter could face the death sentence. A magnificent and eerily-lit close-up of him appears, shot slightly from above: "But Inspector, tell me, they won't ... she won't be ... ?."

He also participates in a touching exchange of dialogue in the film's closing scene. "It passes my understanding," he says shaking his head. "My little girl ... We've always sheltered her so ..."

"It's modern youth," responds C. Aubrey Smith philosophically, "trying to grope its way through the moral chaos that's all around us."

"Has it been our fault?" Atwill pleads, still bewildered by events.

"You wouldn't think so," says Smith, "if you read all the secrets that are locked up in my records."

The film then closes poignantly with Atwill and Teasdale embracing silently.

This is a terrific film with well-written dialogue, a strong performance from Teasdale and an even stronger one from Atwill.

The title of the film, by the way, refers to Stravinsky's *Firebird Suite*. It has symbolic significance because the over-protective Teasdale bans her daughter from listening to it—all part of the theme of repression leading to extreme behavior—and it is played by Cortez as a signal to the daughter that he wants her to come to his apartment.

The Man Who Reclaimed His Head (1934)

Atwill's career is full of gruesome moments and this film contains one of the most sensational. The head of the title is his, and it has been hacked from his body by Claude Rains, who caught him red-handed with his wife. Naturally, Rains stuffs the disembodied head into a large bag and walks with it through the streets of Paris.

Such is the film's opening sequence and this, combined with the macabre title, creates the expectation that this 1934 opus from Universal Pictures is going to be a horror film. Instead, however, it's a powerful drama (told by Rains in flashback after the opening sequence) set in the years leading up to WWI, with Pacifist newspaper writer Paul Verin (Claude Rains) exposing a conspiracy by the munitions manufacturers who want to make money out of war.

Atwill is third-billed as Henri Dumont, a newspaper owner for whom Verin works. It's a substantial role for him, as prominent as those of the two leads, Rains and Joan Bennett. Dumont doesn't have Verin's scruples and uses the newspaper for more self-serving purposes, switching sides in support of war when the owners of the munitions companies offer him wealth and status. Showing even fewer scruples, he makes a move on Verin's wife Adele (Bennett) as soon as Verin goes off to fight in the war. In fact he even arranges for Verin to be kept longer at the front, giving him more time to have his wicked way with Adele.

Adele Verin (Joan Bennett) doesn't look too happy about being snared by Henri Dumont (Atwill) in *The Man Who Reclaimed His Head.*

Atwill thoroughly conceives and executes Dumont's growing interest in Adele. Their first meeting is a chance encounter during a Paris festival. She wears the fancy dress outfit of a clown and follows a group of drunken revelers, also in fancy dress. Playfully, they all step into Dumont's parked car and then step out of the door on the other side. Adele is the last of the group, and Dumont invites her to step into the car. She looks in nervously, fearing that she will end up alone in it with Dumont. A few seconds later, one of the other revelers (Wallace Ford) pulls her safely through the car … but not before Dumont has clearly pondered the pleasures of the liaison that very nearly occurred.

Dumont is later introduced more formally to Adele by Verin, and his intentions become clearer: His light kiss of her proffered hand is just a little too warm, and his later "au revoir" is just a little too charged.

He arranges to meet her in a fancy restaurant where, as part of his charm offensive, he takes her onto the dance floor. The couple enjoy a waltz, Dumont's face hovering just a little too close to hers for decency, in view of the fact that she is a married woman.

"I'm a little afraid of you," she says, with good reason.

Later he takes her to the opera, and heightens the intimacy between them a little more. He suggests, in veiled language, that she has every right to indulge herself and not be held back by a dull, workaholic husband. In their plush box at the opera house, Dumont cannot restrain himself. He leans forward and kisses her on the back of the neck, his eyes closing as he thinks of the pleasures that may be in store for him. This may very well have been an idea added by Atwill, who had done something very similar to Sheila Terry in *The Sphinx*.

At the film's memorable climax, he visits Adele one evening and, in her shadowy drawing room, puts his arms around her roughly and plants a kiss on her as she tries to fend him off. Just at that moment Verin walks in. Up to this point, director Edward Ludwig's direction has not been remarkable, but during the next few minutes, he displays some inventive flourishes and some very mobile camerawork.

The U.S. one-sheet poster gives the impression that Atwill is strangling Claude Rains, when the reality is very different.

Adele exclaims "Paul!" and Ludwig's camera pans with dizzying speed from her startled face to Paul standing in the doorway. The camera then cuts back to Dumont, a look of extreme horror on his face.

"My wife," says Paul in a menacing close-up, "was not included in our bargain, Dumont." He walks forward with a mad glare in his eyes, the camera dollying backwards with him.

"Stop him! Stop him!" cries Dumont offscreen. "He's gone mad! Mad!"

Paul draws his sword, pushes Dumont down onto a windowsill and tries to run him through. Meanwhile, Adele screams, "Paul—no!"

The two men struggle in the half-darkness, and the camera lingers on Paul's madly grimacing face in extreme close-up several times. Ludwig also gives Atwill what is probably the most extreme close-up of his career, a look of sheer wild-eyed terror on his face as he realizes that he is going to be decapitated. When Adele sees what is happening, she faints.

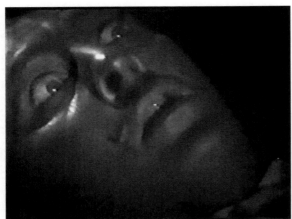

The look of horror on Atwill's face occurs when he realizes he is about to be decapitated, in *The Man Who Reclaimed His Head.*

It's a thrilling finale that places the film firmly back into the territory of the horror genre.

Atwill is also outstanding in an earlier scene, a long dialogue between Rains and him, in which, as part of his pandering to the munitions bosses, he tries to convince Rains to tone down his Pacifist rhetoric. His ingratiating attempts to sweet-talk Rains, and the fact that deep inside he actually sympathizes with the Pacifist aims, are delicately portrayed by Atwill.

The odd title is explained by the fact that Verin feels that Dumont has taken away all that he values: not just his career and his wife but, more importantly, his mind. In his madness, he imagines that by walking around with Dumont's head in his bag, he has reclaimed his mind.

The film began life as a Broadway play and, rumor has it, the original intention of playwright Jean Bart had been to cast Atwill in the role of Paul Verin. But Atwill instead went to Hollywood to make the screen version of *The Silent Witness*. In the film version of *The Man Who Reclaimed His Head*, how wonderful it would have been to see Atwill slowly losing his mind. He would have been terrifying—far more so than Rains—in the scene where he discovers Dumont with Verin's wife, advances on him and decapitates him.

Trivia (1): In some scenes Atwill stands a good three or more inches higher than Rains, whose modest height of 5 feet 6 inches was usually cleverly disguised in his other films.

Trivia (2): Horror fans will enjoy seeing Edward Van Sloan, uncredited, making a brief appearance as one of the munitions bosses.

Mark of the Vampire (1935)

This is director Tod Browning's attempt to recreate the glories of *Dracula* (1931) but, although it has many enjoyable sequences, it is badly let down by its insubstantial plot which, even in 1935, must have seemed far too much like a creaky old thriller from an earlier age.

Lionel Atwill plays Inspector Neumann, called in to investigate the murder of Sir Karell Borotyn (Holmes Herbert) in a huge Eastern European castle. For once, Atwill dispenses with the uniform and this time does all his sleuthing in plain clothes, sporting a fetching Homburg hat, bow tie and a flower in his lapel at all times. He has a lot of screen time and adopts his usual authoritarian persona, giving pompous instructions to the timid local doctor (Donald Meek), bossing the servants around and dismissing the supernatural beliefs of the local people.

Halfway through the film, Professor Zelen (Lionel Barrymore, top-billed) is called in to help with the investigation. Barrymore gives an excellent performance, and his eccentric style of acting makes one wish he could have appeared in more horror films. But for Atwill fans, it means that Inspector Neumann must now take something of a back seat to Zelen.

There are a couple of occasions when the script develops Neumann's character by injecting some dry humor into his

Professor Zelen (Lionel Barrymore) and Inspector Neumann explore the castle in *Mark of the Vampire.*

remarks. For example, timid Donald Meek, reluctant to admit his fear of vampires, explains why he didn't come to the castle on the night of the murder, but waited until the next morning. Neumann observes: "Oh, I see. You're no moon-flower, you're the morning glory!"

And at the coroner's inquest, a character explains how the locals believe that the inhabitants of the nearby castle can transform themselves into bats and back into human beings again. Neumann sniffs at the flower in his lapel and then quips, "How versatile!"

These are adroitly flippant bits of dialogue, but unfortunately the scriptwriters don't develop this aspect of Neumann's character and these are the only such occasions of this type of clever dialogue. (It's possible that there was more to Neumann's character originally; the film was trimmed from 80 minutes to just over an hour before being released.)

One of the film's more memorable scenes has Neumann accompany Baron Otto Von Zinden (Jean Hersholt) on a nighttime visit to the mausoleum where Sir Karell has been interred. They want to make sure that his body is where it should be and, sure enough, when they enter the crypt, they find that the coffin is open and empty. James

Lionel Barrymore, Holmes Herbert, Elizabeth Allan and Lionel Atwill in *Mark of the Vampire*

Wong Howe's elegant camerawork and the absence of dialogue add punch to this scene.

Atwill stamps his mark on this film with his fine performance, but it has to be said that he never gets any scenes that are of special note, nor any dialogue that stands out.

Carroll Borland is unforgettably sinister as Luna, the vampire girl. Lugosi looks good but is very poorly served, getting almost no dialogue. In fact, he got more dialogue in the film's trailer than he did in the film itself.

The Devil Is a Woman (1935)

"They were perverts," said Atwill (in a 1936 issue of *Film Weekly*), "but we couldn't show this. Will Hays' representative was there all the time to see that we didn't stray." He was referring to the characters played by Marlene Dietrich and he in *The Devil Is A Woman*, a prestigious production from Paramount, directed by the legendary Josef von Sternberg. The film is full of hints that both characters are sado-masochists, with Dietrich's Concha taking a beating from Atwill and then coming back for more the next morning, and with Atwill's Captain Pasqual Costelar enduring humiliation after humiliation from Concha, yet unable to give her up.

The film gave Atwill one of his most high-profile roles and he turns in a terrific performance, full of intense stares and bottled-up emotion. It has much in common with his role in *Nana*, in which he also played the long-suffering lover of a woman of dubious morals, and gave a restrained performance of great power.

Concha is a beautiful Spanish girl with a string of male admirers and she plays them off, one against the other. Atwill's Pasqual falls for her and is cruelly exploited for his passion. She leads him on mercilessly, usually just to extract money from him. One of the film's highlights is a scene in which his exasperation boils over and he physically assaults her—all done tastefully offscreen with only the sound of a series of loud slaps informing us what is going on.

Concha (Marlene Dietrich) flirts with Pasqual (Atwill) in *The Devil Is a Woman.*

In fact, that tasteful restraint is one of the few weaknesses of the film. It was released not long after the Hays Code had started to be rigidly enforced, and as such many of its more risqué elements had to be toned down.

Atwill is scarcely off the screen during the first 45 minutes, and he appears at key moments during the rest of the film. As such, this is the antithesis of so many of his other films where he was relegated to a minor supporting role.

The film has an engaging structure. During the first two-thirds of the film, Pasqual recounts a series of flashbacks in which he tells his friend Antonio (Cesar Romero) of his encounters with Concha and how she has mistreated him. The final third is set in the present day, with Antonio falling in love with Concha, despite Pasqual having tried to warn him off. Inevitably, the two friends clash and their friendship climaxes in a grim pistol duel at night in a rain-lashed forest.

The first flashback takes place on a snow-bound train where the passengers start fighting among themselves. Pasqual intervenes and holds Concha back—holding onto her just a little too enthusiastically, much to her delight. The second flashback has Pasqual and various dignitaries being taken on a tour of a cigarette factory where Concha just happens to work. Pasqual is delighted to bump into her again and asks suggestively, as he tickles her under her chin, if she will "sell me one of those cigarettes you roll with your pretty hands."

The third flashback is more substantial, a long and entertaining scene in which Concha invites Pasqual back to her humble lodgings at the top of a rickety flight of steps. Her money-grabbing mother (Alison Skipworth, who had been so memorable in *The Song of Songs*) provides much amusement, but when the mother leaves the room, the relationship between Pasqual and Concha starts to heat up. She sits on his lap and kisses him passionately—and then

Concha asks Pasqual for more money, in *The Devil Is a Woman*.

a second later pulls away angrily and tells him to keep his hands off her. It is all part of her strategy to lure a man in and then frustrate him.

Pasqual doesn't see her for three months, when she suddenly appears unannounced. He tells her he wants to marry her and is appalled when she dismisses his offer casually, telling him she has only come to see him because her mother needs money. Von Sternberg makes the most of Pasqual's genuine bewilderment by filming him in extreme close-up.

Back in the present day, Pasqual tells Antonio about how, apparently by coincidence, he bumped into Concha again months later: "I don't believe Destiny is controlled by a throw of dice ... but it couldn't have been merely a succession of accidents." The same remark could be applied to Atwill's real life—where time and time again scenes in his films seemed to mirror, or give warnings of, what was to happen to him later in his own life.

In the next flashback, Pasqual encounters Concha in a nightclub, where she sings a risqué song. He speaks to her, revealing that he knows perfectly well that she is stringing him along, yet he is helpless to do anything about it.

"You play with me as if I were a fool. What I gave gladly, you took like a thief." He orders champagne and the pair kiss. But once again she withholds her favors from him, a situation that is made fairly explicit when, back in the framing sequence, he explains that he spent the night walking the streets "in a fever."

The next flashback is one of the best, with Pasqual in Concha's changing room in a dingy bar-cum-brothel. She undresses in front of him and, just when it looks like he is going to have his wicked way with her, there is a knock on the door. It is one of Concha's lovers, a bullfighter. Pasqual's jealousy almost disturbs his outer calm, with Von Sternberg moving in for several extreme close-ups of Atwill's face, his tortured eyes looking daggers at his rival and saying all that needs to be said. This part of the scene ends with Pasqual taking Concha in his arms and kissing her.

The scene gets even better. Concha says she is going to lie down for a while and goes up to her room. Pasqual waits downstairs for a while but then gets suspicious,

A pistol duel at night features a grim Pasqual, from *The Devil Is a Woman.*

goes upstairs (in the rain) and violently bangs on her door. When there is no reply, he kicks the door in. Von Sternberg depicts Atwill in a superb shot, standing in an angry pose in the doorway with his back to the camera, clearly having interrupted something that confirms his suspicions. Concha appears, her hair all ruffled.

"Come on," barks Pasqual, his face dripping with raindrops. "You're going with me. I'm not going to hurt you, but come on!"

The bullfighter walks smugly out of the room past Pasqual.

"Well, what have you to say?" says Pasqual to Concha, almost shouting. "Invent something! Defend yourself! Lie some more! You lie so well! You've gone too far. You're not going to play with me any more."

There is a crack of thunder. Concha tries to kick him out but he won't go. He grabs her by the throat. She screams. The camera pans away as a series of around 12 slaps are heard, with Concha still screaming. The rain continues to beat down outside.

It's a terrific scene.

Another flashback takes place the next day. To Pasqual's surprise, Concha pays him a visit. She is bright and cheerful, despite the previous night's events.

"Want another beating?" asks Pasqual, still exasperated. "Haven't you had enough? I'm through with you. Why did you come here?"

But she is far too devious to be brushed aside so easily. She flirts with him, knowing he will be unable to resist her. "I know I've been cruel," she says, putting her arms around him, "but I'll make up for it. Tell me what you want me to do."

Back in the present day, Antonio pays Concha a visit and cannot resist her charms. He takes her in his arms and kisses her. Just at that moment, Pasqual throws open the doors and walks in, grim-faced at finding them together. He stands in front of a spectacular painting of a bull throwing a horse into the air, a matador on its back. Despite everything that he has said, Pasqual is still unable to give up Concha. She has just read aloud his letter to her.

"I hope," says Pasqual with a coldness that suggests inner torture, "it provided you both with amusement to know that I still love her."

Antonio calls Pasqual a fool for not having the strength of will to give up Concha.

"You young puppy! How dare you talk like that!" He slaps his face with a glove. Inevitably, this challenge leads to an agreement to meet for a duel the following morning.

"Weapons?" asks Pasqual bluntly.

"Pistols!" replies Antonio.

On his way out, Pasqual gives a display of his shooting prowess, firing a bullet straight through the heart symbol on a Queen of Hearts playing card.

Von Sternberg stages the duel with great visual flair in heavy rain among the delicate trees of a forest. Pasqual appears to be as cold and emotionless as ever. An extreme close-up teases us to try to imagine what is going through his mind. We find out a few moments later when the two duelists take 12 paces away from each other and turn to fire.

Atwill as Pasqual looks dashing in this U.S. lobby card from *The Devil Is a Woman.*

Pasqual keeps his pistol raised, making no attempt to shoot, allowing Antonio to have a clear shot at him. Pasqual is hit and falls to the muddy ground.

He is rushed to hospital with a bullet wound to his head. A short while later, Concha pays him a visit as he lies on the hospital bed, his head bandaged. He is annoyed that she has come and tells her he wishes he had died. Even on his sickbed, she still torments him.

In a 1936 interview with Britain's *Film Weekly* magazine, Atwill gave some insights into the film—

> I consider this the most interesting picture I've ever made … The result was not so happy as it should have been. But it was not Von Sternberg's fault. The script was magnificent. But we had so much censor[ship] trouble. We were not allowed to portray the characters as they had been drawn … and Von Sternberg was pulled up again and again.

It would be fascinating to see a copy of the original script and find out exactly what had to be left out. The sado-masochistic angle was more explicit in the novel (fittingly called *The Woman and the Puppet*), with Concha taking pleasure in the beating that Pasqual gives her and coming back for more. Scenes which were apparently filmed but dropped include one in which Pasqual puts out a cigarette on Concha's shoulder.

The Devil Is a Woman, despite its remarkable sets, costumes and photography, and the electrifying performances of Dietrich and Atwill, proved to be a commercial failure. Audiences wanted their love affairs to be more conventional.

The Murder Man (1935)

This is a thoroughly enjoyable detective story set in a newspaper environment, with Spencer Tracy as a hard-drinking reporter who, in a very unexpected and surely novel twist, turns out to be the murderer. A tense courtroom scene appears and an even more fraught episode when Tracy confronts the man who is going to the electric chair for a

Lionel Atwill, Spencer Tracy, Virginia Bruce and William Collier, Sr. in *The Murder Man*

murder which Tracy committed. A young Virginia Bruce makes a good platinum blonde, and James Stewart makes his debut in a supporting part.

Lionel Atwill, third billed (yet again), plays the non-sinister role of Captain Cole, the detective who is always one step behind Tracy's own deductive powers, and the pair makes a good double-act. Bowler-hatted and a few pounds overweight, Atwill is a commanding figure. By turns he is authoritative and jovial, snapping at an underling one moment, then chuckling about the electric chair at another. In a short nightclub scene in which Atwill gets a chance to don his dinner jacket and bow tie, he chats with Tracy: "He'll go to the chair protesting his innocence," he says with a laugh, "They always do! See you at the next murder!"

In one amusing moment during the courtroom scene, Atwill realizes, with the sort of confounded stare that only he can give, that his assistant is fast asleep, so he gives him a prod. In fact, on several occasions Atwill demonstrates that he was a dab hand at comic gestures, something that the rest of his career has largely overlooked.

At the climax, Tracy goes to Atwill's office and confesses to him, in a long scene with well-written dialogue. Atwill even delivers the film's closing lines. As Tracy is led off under arrest, Atwill puts a consoling arm round both Bruce (Tracy's girlfriend) and William Collier, Sr. (Tracy's father), advising them that a jury may look kindly on Tracy due to attenuating circumstances. It's an occasion where closing remarks serve to weaken the drama, since it detracts from the force of anticipating that Tracy is going to the chair. But perhaps studio bosses insisted on a happy ending.

Rendezvous (1935)

Here's an interesting trivia question. In which film does Karloff shoot and kill Lionel Atwill? No such film, you might well answer.

In this WWI spy drama, Binnie Barnes plays a spy called Olivia Karloff. Atwill, playing codebreaking expert William Brennan, has been having an affair with her and suspects she may be a spy working for the Germans. To expose her, he stages an elaborate trap in which he pretends his briefcase is lost, then arranges for her to find it. This

Brennan (Atwill) suspects his lover Olivia Karloff (Binnie Barnes) of being an enemy agent in *Rendezvous*.

is a long and well-staged sequence entirely devoid of dialogue or music. When Atwill is re-united with his briefcase, he finds it is empty. Realizing that Barnes must have taken out a classified document, he crosses the darkened room with great portent, finally opening a door to the kitchen where he catches her red-handed steaming open a letter. He gives her one of those legendary Atwill stares, then, with his back to the camera, stalks toward her into the room where she is standing and closes the door behind him with great portent. The sound of gunshot is heard. We assume he has shot her ... but moments later we see Barnes walking away and realize the truth. Karloff has shot and killed Atwill!

Unfortunately this is halfway through the movie, so of course Atwill is seen no more. But in the first half he is an imposing presence as Major William Brennan, the U.S. government's chief codebreaker. In his memorable opening scene he is halfway up a ladder, pointing at a large map of the Atlantic and telling his audience about German attacks on ships. The star of the film is William Powell, with whom Atwill had acted on the stage way back in 1918. They share a long scene in which Atwill talks Powell into deciphering some German code. In other scenes, Atwill looks dapper in hat and long overcoat. It's not a sinister role, yet Atwill can't help coming across as having some hidden dark side.

While not one of Atwill's great roles, this is still worth seeing. It's an agreeable 1935 drama, with Powell in good form as a codebreaker, being distracted by flighty Rosalind Russell (in something of a thankless role).

Incidentally, not only is there a character called Karloff, but another of the film's characters is a Russian whose first name is Boris. The film is based on a 1931 book; had the author just seen *Frankenstein*, I wonder?

Captain Blood (1935)

This is a classic slice of Michael Curtiz action on the high seas. Erich Wolfgang Korngold's music is stirring, Anton Grot's sets are full of striking detail and the black-

and-white camerawork positively glows. The film runs for a mammoth two hours but time passes quickly.

Lionel Atwill, re-united with the director of *Doctor X* and *Mystery of the Wax Museum*, is third-billed as chief villain Colonel Bishop, owner of a Jamaican sugar cane plantation manned by white British slaves and who becomes Governor of the island. Atwill gets to dress in a succession of flamboyant costumes and floppy wide-brimmed hats, and he looks marvelous.

In one memorable scene, he inspects the new slaves, slapping them around, prodding them and ordering them to open their mouths, looking inside as if he were inspecting horses. When Bishop inspects Guy Kibbee's mouth, Kibbee bites his finger and Atwill gives him one of his legendary stares. Naturally Errol Flynn (as Captain Blood) refuses to open his mouth, and Bishop slaps him twice in response. He actually slaps him hard, so Flynn must have come to some agreement with Atwill that, in order to make the scene look realistic, he would let Atwill strike him hard.

A superb establishing scene at Bishop's plantation kicks off with two shots of a magnificent, gigantic waterwheel, powered by slaves who push a smaller wheel at its base. It's like a shot out of *White Zombie* and is backed by Korngold's sinister themes. From here, the camera cuts to inside the plantation compound, where a slave has been strung up and is being whipped. Bishop, on a horse, looks on with keen interest.

"Last night, this dog attempted to escape," he tells the assembled slaves. "Show him the iron, Kent," he orders an underling, and the letters "FT" are branded into the right side of his face. "Whoever wears that brand," Bishop spits out with sadistic venom, "is known as a fugitive traitor. Burn those letters into your brains … lest they be burned into your hides too!"

Dressed in the height of fashion is slave owner Colonel Bishop (Atwill), in *Captain Blood*.

He even takes great delight in doing some of the thrashing personally, brandishing a five-foot-long rod and striking Flynn across the stomach.

In one scene, Atwill shows himself to be a competent horse rider—he probably rode horses around his Maryland farm.

Bishop discovers Blood tending to a man who has been thrashed. When he tries to stop him from helping the victim, Blood pleads, "In the name of humanity—if you know the word!"

"You dare take that tone with me?" Bishop barks back. "I've been too soft with you, but that shall be mended … Kent, tie him up!" Blood is strapped to the whipping post and Bishop picks up a five-foot rod. "Now I'll take this rod to you until there's not an inch of hide left on your dirty carcass!" It's one of Atwill most villainous lines.

Bishop gets his comeuppance when he boards a ship, expecting to find himself surrounded by good-hearted local citizens who have saved his town from an attack by the Spanish. Instead, he finds himself surrounded by Blood and all his other slaves. A good bit of comic bluster erupts from Atwill when he realizes that all his money has been saved from Spanish hands, and he sits down

Bishop inspects a new consignment of slaves, including Dr. Peter Blood (Errol Flynn), from *Captain Blood*.

on the treasure chests. Guy Kibbee gets his revenge and, in an amusing moment of role reversal, examines Bishop's teeth, arms, and chest. Bishop is then dragged toward a hangman's noose, a look of terror on his face. At the last minute Blood, disappointingly, talks his men out of this and instead has Bishop thrown overboard. There are two shots of him in the sea, angrily shaking a raised fist at Blood and shouting that he will get his revenge.

"Peter Blood, I'll make you pay for this," he spits, "if I spend the rest of my life doing it."

Bishop is thrown overboard by Blood and his men, in *Captain Blood*.

What would have been even more dramatically satisfying would be seeing Colonel Bishop stripped to the waist, tied to the mast and given a good whipping by Blood.

After this first hour, in which Atwill is very prominent, he is in only a couple of brief scenes, including a final scene which, although it wraps up the plot tidily, neglects to give Atwill a good closing line—instead he just nods his head acceptingly on finding that Blood is the new Governor. Why on Earth was such a foul villain allowed to get off so lightly?

Colonel Bishop is one of Atwill's finest non-horror roles, but the actor had reservations about the character. In an interview in *Film Weekly* in 1936, Atwill said:

> One of the parts I have found most difficult to play was Colonel Bishop in *Captain Blood* ... He was simply a hateful beast. His hardness and lust for thrashing people were never explained. You had no grain of sympathy for him—you could find no reason for him being like that at all. So he was not quite real—not a human being at all.

Basil Rathbone's French pirate makes a good villain in the film's second half, but surely, rather than introducing this new character so far into the film, it would have been more satisfying to concentrate on developing Atwill's character, keeping Bishop's lust for revenge against Blood center stage. No doubt all Rathbone fans will disagree emphatically.

Lady of Secrets (1936)

Lady of Secrets gives Lionel Atwill the kind of role which he could play better than any other 1930s Hollywood character actor: a cold, stern, self-serving authority figure, in this case a father who likes to rule his household with an iron hand.

He plays Mr. Whittaker, a successful banker, and when first introduced he is a silver-haired man of around 60 years, very well to do and living in a lavish house. Very soon, his daughter Celia (Ruth Chatterton) is daydreaming about a love affair she had way back in 1914, and this long flashback passage features Atwill as a much younger man.

In the flashback, he does everything he can to stop Celia from seeing lowly bank clerk Michael (Lloyd Nolan), and after an accidental shooting, he arranges for Michael to flee to Canada. But Celia is still hopelessly in love with him and, furthermore, is carrying his child.

This being made at a time when the Hays Code was being strictly enforced, the scandalous illegitimate pregnancy is never explicitly mentioned, and audiences could be forgiven for not catching on to the state of affairs. Whittaker, however, quickly realizes what has happened, and is not backward in letting Celia know what he thinks of her: "You common, miserable, little - - -." His wife interrupts him before he can utter the word, and he turns on his wife: "If you take her part, you're as bad as she is! I wish I never had to set eyes on her again."

Whittaker decides that, in order to preserve the family's reputation (or more accurately, his own), they will all move temporarily to France, where the baby will be born. Atwill delivers a gem of a speech when Whittaker telephones his wife to tell her what he has planned. The self-centered bully speaks every syllable with intense sarcasm and hatred, so much does he despise his wife and daughter for putting him in the predicament

The cruel Mr. Whittaker (Atwill) has his daughter (Ruth Chatterton) locked up in a cottage in *Lady of Secrets*.

in which he now finds himself. As he speaks, the camera moves in ever so slowly until his face is in extreme close-up, subtly heightening the intensity of the speech.

"Hello? Emily? Remember that trip to France you didn't take? Well, you're taking it now. And I'm going along ... Oh, it's very kind of me, is it? I'm simply delighted that you think so ... Of course, it means giving up my chance for the Governorship. But I'm glad to do it for you and that lovely daughter of yours. What's that? You're very sorry, are you? Well, that won't make me Governor. I haven't any more time to talk. Start packing, please."

It's Atwill at his coldest and cruelest.

He has more memorable dialogue when the family arrives at the French chateau they are renting. Here he makes sure that all the servants are paid enough to keep their mouths shut about the impending birth. An amusing exchange occurs between Whittaker and the French butler, whose accent and gestures exasperate the Englishman, allowing Atwill to indulge in a couple of comical double takes.

His self-centeredness is so extreme that when WWI breaks out, he regards it as another infuriating inconvenience that interrupts his own plans. "All I needed was this confounded war on top of all my other troubles—that's all I needed."

"Stephen," replies his long-suffering wife, "do you really think the war was declared just to annoy you?"

Surprised that his meek wife should be capable of such sarcasm, he unleashes one of the legendary Atwill stares on her.

In this U.S. Window Card, Atwill hovers over the young lovers (Ruth Chatterton and Otto Kruger) with what appears to be voyeuristic interest.

When the family head off back home, the penny should finally drop for any viewer who still has not quite grasped what is going on, since a baby makes an appearance in the arms of the family's maid, and Whittaker announces that the baby girl shall be referred to as Celia's sister.

Back in the present day, Celia's relationship with her "sister" Joan (Marian Marsh) now takes on new dimensions, especially when Celia tells her father that she is going to reveal all to Joan. In a well-played scene, Celia tells Joan the truth only to have Whittaker intercede by telling Joan that Celia is not in her right mind and that she should not believe her. If this all sounds very much like a soap opera, that's because it *is*—1930s style.

Worried that Celia will prevent the marriage of Joan to David Eastman (Otto

Atwill does some more voyeuristic hovering, this time over Kruger and Marian Marsh, from *Lady of Secrets*.

Kruger), Whittaker has Celia locked up in a country cottage. He and Eastman pay her a visit. When Celia tries to let Eastman know she is being held a prisoner, Whittaker tries to laugh it off, giving Atwill another chance to demonstrate his ability to act out a hearty laugh convincingly.

There is a happy ending for all concerned, featuring a double wedding. All that is missing from the finale of this very enjoyable melodrama is a scene where the brutish Whittaker gets taught a lesson. Unfortunately the character suffers the fate that so often befell supporting characters—he is forgotten about in favor of tidying up all the loose ends surrounding the principal players.

Atwill as businessman G.A. Axton with two criminals on the run, played by Bernadine Hayes and Wallace Ford, in *Absolute Quiet*.

Absolute Quiet (1936)

"One of my favorite parts," said Lionel Atwill in a 1936 interview with *Film Weekly* magazine, "was in a picture which you've probably heard very little about. It was called *Absolute Quiet*."

Atwill has a major starring role in this MGM production from 1936, but it is a film with a plot of so little substance that we find ourselves wondering how the go-ahead was ever given to make it. And even though it is not adapted from a stage play, it feels like it is, because so much of the action (if it can be called that) takes place in one room.

Atwill is high-powered businessman Gerald A. Axton. After a health scare, his doctor advises "absolute quiet" and so he retreats to his ranch for some rest. Once there, his rest is interrupted by the arrival of two criminals on the run (Wallace Ford and Bernardine Hayes) and a plane crashes nearby, the survivors of which take refuge at the ranch. The interplay between all these various characters makes up the rest of the film.

You only have to think of a film such as *The Desperate Hours* (starring Humphrey Bogart as an escaped convict who terrorizes a family) to see the potential in such a plot, but *Absolute Quiet* lacks any dramatic punch, is overly talky and filled with ineffectual characters. Any number of scenes might have been suspenseful, but director George B. Seitz simply doesn't appear to know how to create tension.

In the 1936 interview in *Film Weekly*, Atwill stated that he liked his character because:

> He was very understandable and very shrewd. Although he was horrible, cold, hard and mean, his psychology was sound.

That all may be so, but the part never really amounts to much—however, there are a few interesting moments.

For example, when Axton hears that the Governor has blocked a business deal, he loses his temper, giving Atwill a chance to do some full-blooded acting: "The fool! The pompous, over-bearing nincompoop! I helped put that stuffed shirt where he doesn't belong! ... I'll tear him down again! I'll smash his re-election, if it's the last thing I ..." He stops abruptly in mid-section, sways on his legs, then collapses onto the desk.

Lionel Atwill, Ann Loring and Louis Hayward in *Absolute Quiet*

To recover from his breakdown, he takes his secretary Laura (Irene Hervey) with him to the ranch, and he clearly has more than a professional interest in her. He tries his moves several times, but each time she rebuffs him. This gives rise to several entertaining moments.

For example, there is a hint of the old Lionel that we know and love when, after she says she is going to her room to freshen up, he says: "Leave your door open."

"Why?"

"Oh—so that I can talk to you."

"All right—four year old!" she quips, thinking that he is acting like a nervous young child who wants to keep talking to its mother. But his real reason is clear from the loaded close-up of Atwill that follows: He's hoping he might catch a glimpse of her *freshening up*.

A short while later, Atwill and Hervey share another good little scene. She turns on the radio, which plays some soft music. He walks up to her until he is standing just a little too close.

"You're very beautiful, Laura," he says. "There's something about your eyes, your hair, the line of your throat."

"What is this—an anatomical survey?" she replies looking, sheepish and trying to diffuse the situation.

He places his hand at the base of her neck, and says lovingly, "It's a very beautiful throat, Laura ... " For a brief moment it seems there is a chance that Atwill is going to turn into some kind of strangling sex-fiend. "But it's crying. Crying for pearls."

"I'm afraid it'll have to settle for beads," she answers, walking away from him.

A few minutes later, they hear on the phone that a plane will be crash-landing in their ranch. When Laura says she is frightened, Axton seizes the opportunity by taking her in his arms, under a pretense of comforting her.

This relationship could have led to further interesting scenes, with Axton pursuing the reluctant Laura, but the script drops the idea half way through the film.

Throughout Atwill's character adopts an air of amused superiority, apparently unconcerned by the loaded guns and fistfights all around him. He treats the whole af-

fair as something to be exploited for his own personal gain, and all the characters merely as pawns in a game. At various turns of events, he chortles and chuckles, something which Atwill has done very convincingly in many other films. This air of detachment is a change of pace for the actor, and a world away from the intensity of his best roles.

After Atwill has snubbed another character, Hervey utters a line that sounds like it has escaped from one of his mad doctor films: "Why do you like to hurt people?" A great line that is completely undeveloped by the scriptwriter.

The film ends with a bit of high drama involving Louis Hayward, who plays one of the plane crash survivors. Disgruntled because the crash has facially disfigured him, he shoots dead the two criminals, Jack and Judy.

A smirking Atwill looks on at the stagey interplay of other characters, in *Absolute Quiet*.

The film ends feebly and abruptly when Governor Pruden, mopping his brow, says, "I'll never be the same again."

"Then Jack and Judy haven't lived in vain," intones Atwill, getting the film's closing line.

J. Carrol Naish appears briefly as a worker on Atwill's ranch. An entertaining comic performance by Raymond Walburn as blustering Governor Pruden brightens things up.

Till We Meet Again (1936)

This is one of Lionel Atwill's rarely seen films. In this WWI spy drama from 1936, he is Ludwig, a plain-clothes German spymaster, sporting a monocle and flamboyant moustache. It's a significant role and he is stern and cold throughout, of course, almost relishing the fact that the war gives him an opportunity to separate lovers Herbert Marshall (playing an actor who becomes a spy) and Gertrude Michael (as a Viennese actress who also becomes a spy, but for the other side).

Ludwig is chief villain, ever giving orders to Michael and pursuing Marshall. At the end of the film, he shows a spark of decency and gets a memorable death scene. He has fallen from a train and as a result lies prostrate with a broken back. There are cuts on his face and the pain makes him sweat profusely. Finally he recognizes something good in the relationship between the two lovers. His last command to his underlings is to send them away in the wrong direction in order to allow the lovers to escape.

It's a shame that Ludwig's villainy was not made more vicious, and also a shame that his frustrated feelings for Gertrude Michael were not developed more, apart from one brief moment when he moves to kiss her, then stops himself.

A few tense scenes occur, including one on a train that is well staged, but overall the direction by Robert Florey lacks real drive. Hans Dreier was art director, but there are no sets of special note. Marshall, who lost a leg in WWI, shows few problems here, doing plenty of walking around (although a stand-in is used for a shot of him running upstairs).

A contemporary newspaper item added a personal touch to the publicity for the film. In a short piece entitled "Papa Atwill Stumps Sonny With Monocle," the writer related

Ludwig (Atwill) discusses his plans with Torben Meyer (left) and an identified player (right), from *Till We Meet Again*.

how Atwill enjoyed wearing his monocle in films so much that he often wore it at home too. During one family dinner, his stepson Walter asked, "Why is it that in the pictures your monocle always stays on, but at home it always falls in the soup?"

Last Train From Madrid (1937)

This 1937 Paramount drama, set in Spain during the then-raging civil war, has a formidable cast that includes Lew Ayres, Dorothy Lamour, Gilbert Roland, Robert Cummings, Anthony Quinn, Helen Mack and Karen Morley. Billed fifth is Lionel Atwill as Colonel Vigo. It's very much a supporting role and Atwill appears in five scenes, usually growling unpleasant orders at his underlings. He's the bad guy who wants to prevent our heroes from escaping on the last train out of Madrid; those who aren't on it fear they will all perish in bombing raids.

Delightfully, the script gives Colonel Vigo a few sympathetic moments. In one scene he berates Cummings for cowardice after he was unable to do his duty, refusing to execute an old man as part of a firing squad. But Vigo is visibly touched when Cummings explains emotionally why he couldn't do it. "Now, now, now, don't become hysterical" Vigo says, as he nervously reaches for a cigarette. For a moment it seems that Vigo is going to crack and become emotional too. It's a deft bit of understated acting from Atwill.

Vigo knows that military rules mean he has to punish Cummings and orders him to Cardozo, a battle zone where death almost certainly awaits him. But, showing a spark of decency, he gives Cummings some money and tells him to take two hours off before reporting for duty.

In another scene, he orders the court martial of Quinn, sending him to a firing squad. This scene begins with a superb shot of Atwill lit up by candles (there is no electricity due to the bombings), as he broods over his next dastardly action. It's a set-up worthy of a Von Sternberg movie. He confronts Quinn and accuses him of freeing a friend from prison. "Your ideal of friendship," Atwill says in his best clipped, military tones, "is no

doubt noble and sacrificial, but it leaves me but one course—to hold you for court martial." However, in a touching final gesture, he places his hand on Quinn's shoulder, offering moral support and showing that he wishes he didn't have to do it: "Sorry, Alvarez," he says.

Atwill's last scene is memorable. Quinn has forced his way into Vigo's office and, at gunpoint, commands his superior officer to order the train to leave the station, even though Vigo wants it held until Roland is found. But then Quinn is shot by one of Vigo's men, giving Vigo the opportunity to order the train to be held. However, Vigo's sense of decency surfaces—he has come to understand the nobility of Quinn's devoted friendship to Cummings and instead gives orders that the train is free to go. It recalls Atwill's final noble gesture at the end of *Till We Meet Again* when he helps Herbert Marshall and Gertrude Michael to escape.

Anthony Quinn, Helen Mack and Atwill relax between takes on the set of *Last Train from Madrid*.

The Road Back (1937)

This is the second of three films Lionel Atwill made for James Whale, the supreme director of horror films. A sequel to the WWI drama *All Quiet on the Western Front*, it's a frequently grim tale of the struggles of German soldiers to fit back into society after the horrors of war. It could have been a classic, but it fails to pack the punch that the director intended, despite a few powerful sequences. Even worse, Universal executives, who thought its original running time was far too long, edited down Whale's original cut. We will probably never know how much better the full version was, as all complete prints seem to be lost.

One of the returning soldiers, Albert (Maurice Murphy), discovers that the girl he loves has been messing around with other men. One evening in a bar, he catches her red-handed with one of them and shoots him dead. He is arrested, and the courtroom scene that follows features Lionel Atwill as the prosecutor. The courtroom, with vaulted ceiling, a Gothic window and ornately carved wooden seats, looks like something out of a Von Sternberg film.

Atwill was probably attracted to the role because, even though he doesn't appear

The heartless Prosecutor in *The Road Back*

Lionel Atwill

until the film's last 10 minutes, the prosecutor is a memorable figure, and the sequence is key in spelling out the problems faced by returning soldiers. Atwill, using all the skills learned over many years on the stage, would have known that he could make the character a charismatic one. His monocled prosecutor, in legal gown and collar, smirks confidently as he cross-examines the witnesses, interrupting them aggressively when he thinks it appropriate. Generally, he is a nasty piece of work, with no sympathy for the plight of the returning soldiers.

In James Whale's *The Road Back*, the Prosecutor (Atwill) is not swayed by Ernst's (John King) plea for him to show some humanity.

He even belittles the defendant's acts of courage during the war, suggesting they were done merely because he was following orders.

He asks one witness if, at the time of the shooting, the defendant was calm and knew what he was doing. When the witness hesitates, the prosecutor barks, "Answer my question—yes or no?" Atwill spits out the line with real venom.

And when the defendant compares his killing of one man in a bar with the many killings he committed on the battlefield, the prosecutor is outraged. "This is monstrous!" he exclaims, disgusted that his beloved legal process should be sullied by comparisons to the war.

The next witness, another soldier Ernst (John King), suggests that the girl in the bar was drunk and partially naked, thereby provoking the killing. Atwill's prosecutor thinks things have gone too far. He rises to his feet and roars out, "The dignity of the court!" He clenches his fists and continues, "This is a most monstrous disorder!"

A few minutes later, the members of the jury return from their deliberations and the defendant is found guilty. Atwill's prosecutor has a self-satisfied smirk on his face and throws his monocle down onto his desk triumphantly. Ernst, in a final gesture of disgust at the way his fellow soldier has been treated, rips the Iron Cross from his own uniform, approaches the prosecutor and throws it down on his desk. "I think you should have this. You be the hero."

It's a powerful scene and gives Atwill a chance to be seen at his overbearing, malevolent best. It's yet another of his many fine courtroom scenes, which include *The Silent Witness, One More River* and *High Command*. A small bonus for horror film fans is the sight of Dwight Frye in a small role as one of the townsfolk who attend a mass rally.

The Wrong Road (1937)

Republic's eye-catching one-sheet poster for this film depicted a huge, blue-tinted, glowering close-up of Atwill hovering above smaller images of Helen Mack and Rich-

Kindly insurance inspector Mike Roberts (Atwill) in *The Wrong Road*

ard Cromwell. If this sweet young couple were going astray down the wrong road, then the poster suggested that it was Atwill who was going to lead them there.

Unfortunately, the film turns out to be a rather inconsequential melodrama in which likeable lovers Richard Cromwell and Helen Mack take the wrong road, by deciding to rob a bank of $100,000.

Atwill, unusually, has a good-guy role, a private detective who knows that these are basically good kids who just made a foolish mistake, and he tries to talk them into handing over the money and going straight. He has plenty of screen time as the avuncular Mike Roberts, forever turning up at crucial moments to point out the error of their ways and how the money will only bring them misery, not happiness.

For once Atwill avoids even the slightest hint of the sinister. It must have been an enjoyable change of pace for the actor, but surely he would have fared much better if he had instead been cast in the role of the heavy (played by Horace Macmahon), an ex-con who tries to get his hands on the money, and who makes regular appearances throughout the film threatening to murder Cromwell if he doesn't give him a share.

Lancer Spy (1937)

This is an entertaining 20th Century Fox espionage drama set during WWI, with a young George Sanders in the double role of an English officer who impersonates a German Baron. He gets into various scrapes with an assortment of German characters, which include Peter Lorre and Sig Ruman performing an amusing double act as a pair of officers with brutal cropped haircuts. Dolores Del Rio—is she a spy or isn't she?—is the romantic interest.

Lionel Atwill (taking over a part originally intended for Colin Clive, who was too ill to appear) has a very prominent supporting role as an English officer who masterminds the impersonation plot. He plays solid, stiff-upper-lipped Colonel Fenwick of Military Intelligence, who appreciates that difficult sacrifices have to be made in order to fight a war. He even delivers a morale boosting speech at one point, which would give Winston Churchill a run for his money.

Atwill also enjoys the privilege of appearing in a framing episode set on board an airplane many years after the war. Now gray-haired, he tells his daughter (Lynn Bari) the story of one of their fellow passengers ... and so, in flashback, the adventure begins. "I can remember the day when it all started," he says with a fond twinkle in his eye, as he lights up his pipe, "the day there must have been so much in his life ... my life ... in the life of every Englishman ... "

In the body of the film Atwill plays the cold, uniformed type of character that he always did so well. Unfortunately in *Lancer Spy*, the role is not fleshed out with any further dimensions, but there is much to enjoy. This includes a droll scene in which he invites the captured German Baron to have breakfast with him, and Sanders is mystified as to why he is being so well treated. The reason, of course, is that Colonel Fenwick is checking him over to see how much he resembles Lieutenant Michael Bruce (Sanders' other role).

One especially dramatic moment occurs when Bruce realizes that Fenwick has told his wife that he has died at sea. He is horrified and refuses to go through with the charade.

Fenwick gives instructions to Lt. Bruce (George Sanders), who is masquerading as a German officer in *Lancer Spy*.

"The whole thing's off," he exclaims, getting to his feet, and becoming almost hysterical. "I won't do it! I won't do it! I won't do it!"

"Attention!" barks Fenwick. "Attention! Attention! You'll obey my orders, Lieutenant Bruce!"

What makes this dialogue especially potent is the fact that Atwill speaks his lines over the top of those spoken by Sanders, until the latter does eventually quiet down and stand to attention.

Fenwick then delivers his marvelously patriotic speech: "Listen to me, man. The slightest factor one way or the other may decide the war. It isn't only your safety ... nor your wife's ... nor my own, that's at stake. It's England ... our freedom ... our people ... our Empire. It's far from impossible that you hold their fate in your hands. That's your first loyalty and your only duty." Atwill delivers the speech beautifully and it's a shame no other similarly dramatic moments occur in the film.

After another substantial scene for Atwill, in which he gives Bruce his final orders before sending him off to Germany, Colonel Fenwick isn't seen again for quite a while. He reappears in a strong scene with Bruce's wife (Virginia Field) who, believing her husband to be dead, is wearing a widow's black clothes and veil. She suspects her husband may still be alive but Fenwick refuses to disclose any information. She gets more and more impassioned

"Michael's alive, isn't he? Tell me it's true!"

Fenwick's stern exterior eventually cracks for a moment.

"Yes, he's alive."

She is disgusted that he would let her believe he was dead. "What decent, human excuse have you got for that?"

"Your husband is alive and well," says Fenwick taking the criticism on the chin. "Beyond that, I can tell you nothing. Mrs. Bruce, in wartime there are no decencies ... no humanity ... and no rights. You'll just have to trust me."

It's another dramatic speech, marvelously delivered by Atwill.

The elderly Col. Fenwick (Atwill) reminisces about World War I in *Lancer Spy.*

Atwill closes the film in an epilogue, where we are back again on the plane. He explains poignantly that the reason Bruce is on the same plane is that once a year he flies to Germany to place flowers on the grave of Dolores Del Rio's character, executed by the Germans. Presumably, the opening and closing scenes are set in the present day—i.e., 1937—in which case Atwill's character is meant to be 20 years older than he is in the flashback scenes of 1917. He was 52 when he made *Lancer Spy*, so perhaps his make-up is intended to suggest he is more like 72 years old.

The Great Garrick (1937)

How fitting that Lionel Atwill, whose acting debut had been at a theater named after actor David Garrick, should, over 30 years later, appear in a film about that man's life.

The third of three films Atwill made for James Whale is an overly theatrical indulgence. The frivolous subject matter is unworthy of such a talented director. In 18th-century France, a company of actors decides to teach English actor David Garrick a lesson. They take over a roadside inn, playing the parts of innkeeper, serving girls, blacksmith and even all the fellow customers. However, their plan to terrify and humiliate the visiting Garrick backfires because he has gotten wind of their plot and undermines it to his own advantage. Along the way he falls in love with Olivia De Havilland, whom he initially mistakes for one of the actors, but subsequently learns that she really is in love with him.

Lionel Atwill plays a key role in the film's first 15 minutes, but subsequently is not seen at all, apart from a very brief and insignificant appearance at the end. He plays Monsieur Beaumarchais, dressed in the height of French fashion, complete with silk coat, lacy neckerchief and cuffs, a white wig with tight curls and even a black beauty spot on one cheek. The part gives him a rare opportunity to do some light comedy on film.

We first encounter Beaumarchais in a box at the Theatre Royal, Drury Lane, during a performance of *Hamlet*, with a lady companion. His constant frown and the way he taps his fingers on the balcony rail let us know that he is neither impressed by Garrick's acting, nor by his proposed trip to France to teach the French how to act.

The action cuts to the theater of the *Comedie Francaise* in Paris. The entire company is gathered to discuss Garrick's insults and his impending visit. Beaumarchais, who is the theatrical company's playwright, is present, taking a pinch of snuff and drawing on an absurdly long and ostentatious clay pipe. His other accoutrements, equally flamboyant, are two long sticks, one with an eyeglass at the end, the other with a small brush that he uses to scratch the occasional itch. In fact, he is every inch the effeminate dandy.

He is called on to address the gathering and thoroughly enjoys being the center of attention. It is he who comes up with the scheme to humiliate Garrick. Atwill milks the role for every camp expression and gesture he can muster.

Ironically, Atwill's long speech to the acting company contains several lines that are a prophecy of things to come. "Nothing in the world is so fatal to the actor as to be found ridiculous. Actors are idols. Idols must be admired. The moment your public starts to laugh *at* you, instead of *with* you, your hold on them is destroyed. Public opinion is cruel—it changes fast. There's an old saying that ridicule kills—and it's true!"

Atwill delivers the speech beautifully, oblivious to what Fate had in store for him.

The foppish playwright Beaumarchais (Atwill) in *The Great Garrick*

As would be expected in a James Whale film, a number of good supporting actors in eccentric roles appear. As well as Atwill, 81-year-old Etienne Girardot submits a hilarious performance as an excitable prompter. Melville Cooper is also good as the pompous president of the theatrical company who takes on the part of the innkeeper. In fact, Atwill might have been better served if he had been given this role—it's a more prominent role and would have suited him perfectly.

High Command (1937)

In his only British film, Atwill gets a strong starring role as Major General Sir John Sangye, a stern military type who deals with intense personal dramas with a quiet but powerful dignity. The film contains yet another of Atwill's many fine courtroom sequences, and also boasts a nail-biting climactic scene that will have audiences on the edges of their seats. The plot is enjoyably convoluted and is enlivened by an assortment of colorful characters. It was the first film directed by Thorold Dickinson who, 11 years later, directed one of the greatest horror films of all time, *Queen of Spades* (1949). Unfortunately in *High Command* he was still learning his craft and only on a few occasions does he raise the film to an above-average level.

John Milford, writing in Britain's *Film Pictorial* magazine, had high praise for Atwill.

> Lionel Atwill ... gives a magnificent performance in this film ... I have always thought him worthy of better parts than Hollywood has given him, and certainly his acting in this film puts him in the front rank of screen players. He gets inside the skin of the man. Every word, every inflexion [sic], every gesture, contributes something to your knowledge of the general, that crusty old disciplinarian who will do what he considers his duty at any cost. You are aware that, if you knew him, you would think him a pig-headed old martinet, with a

redeeming streak of greatness in him. Atwill makes you see all that. He does not sentimentalize, nor rant, nor go through a series of mock-heroics, as he might so easily have done. His whole performance is quiet and intimate and beautifully consistent. I believe that, in its way, it is likely to be one of the best pieces of screen acting of the year.

A 15-minute opening sequence is set in Ireland in 1921. Officer Challoner (Philip Strange), who is bitter after discovering that his wife had a previous relationship with General Sangye and that the daughter he thought was his own is actually Sangye's, confronts General Sangye. Challoner draws a gun and Sangye shoots him dead in self-defense. The Irish rebels are blamed for the killing.

In the present day, General Sangye is stationed in Africa, living with his *stepdaughter* Belinda (Kathleen Gibson) who, unknown to her, is his actual daughter. A montage sequence, designed to convey an impression of ex-pat life, includes a brief shot of Atwill in a polo helmet swinging a mallet while riding a horse (the horse of course being out of shot). He is now gray-haired, bad-tempered and his hearing is starting to fail him. On a couple of occasions, he barks, "What's that?" at someone who has had the temerity not to speak loudly enough.

A British doctor comes to join the British ex-pats and it transpires that he had known Sangye back in 1921 and has harbored suspicions all along that it was Sangye who had killed Challoner.

One night a shot is heard and the doctor is found dead in his bed, with Sangye standing beside him, gun in hand. A court martial follows, but it is Captain Heverell (a young James Mason) who is accused of the murder. This long courtroom episode is divided into two sequences, with Sangye being called to give evidence in both sections. The audience is reasonably convinced that Atwill must be the real murderer, and hence he appears to be committing perjury when questioned under oath, denying any blame.

This is one of many instances in Atwill's career when a script required him to enact fictional events that uncannily foresaw real-life circumstances that would entangle him in a few years. In *High Command*, Atwill seems to commit fictional perjury, and watching it today, it appears that Fate was providing a dress rehearsal for later events.

In the courtroom, the prosecutor decides to bring up the subject of the murder of Challoner many years earlier. He suggests that this gives Sangye a motive for the present murder. Atwill gives him one of his legendary cold stares and tells him, with a sneering intensity in every syllable: "I must decline to follow you into such vague speculations." Atwill delivers the line beautifully.

In this U.S. lobby card Sangye (Atwill) greets Diana Cloam (Lucie Mannheim). In the center-background is a young James Mason, from *High Command*.

Lionel Atwill

Sangye realizes danger exists if the truth comes out—Belinda will discover the reality of her past. Dickinson gives Atwill three extreme close-ups, in which a sense of Sangye's inner struggle is almost palpable.

He deduces that the real murderer is Cloam, a German trader jealous of the fact that his wife (Lucie Mannheim) had flirted with the doctor. There is a well-written scene in which Sangye confers with Cloam, playing a game of cat-and-mouse with him as he intimates that he knows the identity of the murderer without actually naming him.

By this point, Sangye has decided that there is only one way to resolve this tangled situation and keep Belinda ignorant of her true parentage. Later that day Belinda is about to leave for an evening's engagement with her boyfriend. When Sangye says goodbye to her, it is clearly no ordinary goodbye.

Major-General Sir John Sangye, in *High Command*

"You remind me more and more of your mother every day," he says. "She was beautiful."

"I'll see you in the morning," says Belinda.

Sangye closes his eyes just for a second, straining to prevent his emotions from betraying him. This scene only packs its full punch when the film is watched for a second time and the outcome is known. The restraint in Atwill's acting in this scene is remarkable.

Sangye discusses various options available with the Governor (Allan Jeayes), in a striking lobby card from *High Command*.

Sangye lays a trap to entice Cloam to his quarters that night. Sure enough Cloam breaks into the shadowy bedroom, hoping to find Sangye asleep in bed and then kill him. But Sangye is behind him, sitting at a desk, seen in an eye-catching shot in which a shaft of moonlight catches just the top half of his face. He taunts Cloam, so that the German reaches for his gun. Turning his back on Cloam,

Sangye takes a few calm steps away from him and waits for the bullet. It seems to take an eternity. Eventually a shot rings out. Sangye falls to the floor dead.

It's a powerful ending to an enjoyable film.

While working on the film at Ealing Studios, Atwill was visited on the set by writer O. Bristol of *Picture Show* magazine. Bristol was impressed by what he saw of the actor: "… never before have I seen such a genius for detail." Bristol's comments are the best evidence we have that Atwill, the former stage director, was always keen to contribute far more than just his acting talents to a film.

> Although everyone else on the set seemed perfectly satisfied with the particular *shot* they were engaged upon, Mr. Atwill insisted on it being done again and again. Then, when everything appeared to be all right, he noticed that the jacket of his military tunic was made to flounce out by the tightness of his belt. According to Mr. Atwill, no uniform that behaved in this un-military-like manner would be tolerated by a general in the British Army, and the production was held up for nearly a quarter of an hour while a fresh hole was punched in his belt.

Bristol also commented on another directorial flourish by Atwill:

> In this particular *shot*, a telegram was being used, and to avoid the crackling of the paper from sounding like peals of thunder when picked up by the mike [sic], Mr. Atwill insisted on it being sprinkled with water after every shot.

"I am quite certain," said Atwill to his interviewer, "that the secret of making good pictures is the ability to take infinite pains."

He went on to discuss the kind of roles he was getting in films.

> True, I nearly always appear as a rather severe sort of chap on the screen, but it's surprising the amount of variety you can get into this type of role … To be a good heavy man you must be a bit of a comic as well … you must have a sense of humor to be a menace!

"Off the set," concluded the interviewer, "he is a most delightful man with whom to talk."

Three Comrades (1938)

Audiences are given an unforgettable glimpse of Lionel Atwill the party animal in *Three Comrades*. In a scene at a late-night bar, he is as drunk as a skunk on champagne, dances to some jazz music, tells a dirty joke, slurs his words and laughs far too heartily at the misfortune of another character. Is this how he behaved at his own *wild* parties which got him into so much trouble just a few years later?

This MGM film tells the story of three young German soldiers (Robert Taylor, Franchot Tone and Robert Young) returning from WWI and having problems fitting into society. They meet Margaret Sullavan, and Taylor falls in love with her only to find she is suffering from an incurable illness. It becomes a classic *weepy* as tragedy follows tragedy. The film is always very watchable, thanks to the cast, but it is overlong and the screenplay (co-written by F. Scott Fitzgerald) is frequently slow moving.

Atwill plays monocle-wearing Herr Breuer, a wealthy German who is determined to have a good time despite his country's post-war economic and political problems. "I tell you, I don't know what to do with all my money," he moans.

"May I steal her from you for just one dance?" asks a drunken Atwill of Robert Taylor. Margaret Sullavan is center in this U.S. lobby card from *Three Comrades*.

He makes a memorable entrance. At first we don't see him, we hear him. The three comrades are driving a car through the German countryside and they hear a car behind them sounding its horn aggressively. Somehow, without even seeing a shot of the driver, you just know that it is going to be Atwill at the wheel.

What follows is a race between the two cars, with Breuer trying to pass the other car but eventually being out-maneuvered. To film it, Atwill—and his passenger Patricia (Sullavan)—sat in a car in front of a rear-screen projection in a studio. The two parties both pull up at an inn where they share a meal together. Patricia explains that Breuer is "just a friend"—whatever that means. Breuer drinks far too much even though he is driving. "He drives the same, drunk or sober," says Patricia. At the meal, Breuer turns out to be something of a loud-mouthed bore. "Too many people think they have a right to opinions nowadays," he says. "What Germany needs is order—discipline." Gottfried (Young) has had enough of his pompous opinions, stands up and knocks over Breuer's drink. "Oh, sit down, sit down! You shell-shocked fellows give me a pain with your hysterics." Gottfried grabs him, ready to punch him, but his friends pull him back.

Later, Breuer, Patricia, Erich (Taylor) and two of Breuer's lady friends are all dressed in their best evening attire at an American-style bar offering free champagne all night. This is where we see Lionel Atwill the party animal. Breuer takes Patricia onto the dance floor and the pair performs a lively dance to a band called the Tennessee Yankee College Jazz Boys, with Breuer adjusting his monocle in mid-step.

A few minutes later we catch Breuer telling the punch-line of a dirty joke: "... And she fell right off the horse!" He laughs heartily at his own joke as he takes another gulp of champagne. When Patricia tells him it's two o'clock in the morning and they should be going home, the insatiable Breuer replies, "Let's go on to another place!" Starting to slur his words, he asks Patricia for another dance.

Erich gets up to dance with Patricia but his dinner jacket and waistcoat, both borrowed and too small, start to split on him. Breuer and his drunken friends find it hilarious as bits of thread appear and the collar snaps.

Breuer can't resist making a joke at Erich's expense. "Ah! I've just placed that coat. My grandfather was buried in it!"

Atwill, one of the greatest *laughers* of Hollywood, unleashes his longest and loudest laugh in *Three Comrades*. But in this film, he outdoes himself, unleashing a long, drunken laugh that lasts for a full minute. Within the Atwill canon, it's a scene to cherish.

Unfortunately, Breuer has very little to do after this choice scene. He is seen for just a second or two when he buys a car from the three comrades, but the lack of dialogue here makes one wonder if the scene were cut prior to release.

The film has a bonus for horror fans: George Zucco has a brief uncredited scene. He is intended to portray a kindly surgeon, but inevitably he comes across as a sinister mad doctor as he explains the treatment to Patricia: "We take a little piece of bone from one of the ribs and collapse the lung. There's no danger!"

The Great Waltz (1938)

The first 75 minutes of this biopic of the life of Johann Strauss are eminently watchable, featuring a number of high-spirited (if slightly contrived) sequences full of smiling faces and lively musical segments. It is kept afloat by a fine performance from Miliza Korjus (*gorgeous Korjus*, as she was known) who has an amazing voice, which surely could shatter glass at a hundred paces. Not only that but she has the uncanny ability to sing at the same time as mentally undressing Fernand Gravet with her eyes, which exude pure lust (as does some of the careful dialogue).

This mood may be just a little *too* cheerful for some audiences, and fortunately the tone changes dramatically mid-way through the film. The tension heightens and the directorial inventiveness increases.

This improvement begins when Lionel Atwill, playing Count Anton "Tony" Hohenfried, knocks on the door of the Strauss house. Atwill has already been seen briefly in four or five scenes, largely as a background menace. Dressed in military garb, he is the lover of singer Carla Donner (Korjus), and is none too pleased that Fernand Gravet is also interested in her (although most of the moves are coming from the man-hungry Carla).

Count Hohenfried and Carla Donner in *The Great Waltz*

Strauss' wife Poldi (Luise Rainer) greets him. He has come to encourage her to compel her husband to end his affair with Carla. The encounter begins with some splendidly discreet opening lines, as Atwill looks sheepishly at the floor: "Perhaps something of what I am about to say is known to you … Madam, for some time now Madam Donner and your husband have … they have been together constantly … They will destroy each other … She is a woman of violent feelings, of strange whims, of irresistible impulses."

Lionel Atwill

Poldi does not want to hear the truth, so Hohenfried changes the tempo. "Madam, you must face the facts." Director Julien Duvivier, moving his camera in closer on the two faces, matches the increasing intensity. Poldi admits she has known about the affair all along but has decided to do nothing about it. "What would you have me do?" she implores Hohenfried.

Duvivier moves in even more for a series of extreme close-ups of Hohenfried's dramatically lit face.

The singing of Carla Donner (Miliza Korjus) delights her love, Count Hohenfried (Atwill), in *The Great Waltz.*

"Fight!" he spits out, like the military man he is. "What anyone wants in this world, one has to fight for, like the beast in the jungle! If you want to keep him, if you want to save him, don't leave it in his hands, you must *fight!*"

But he realizes that Poldi won't fight. "Oh, this humiliation," he mutters, mainly to himself, and the alarmed look on his face suggests he senses that all this grief has mentally unhinged the frail Poldi. He kisses her hand politely, dons his cap and walks out.

It's a magnificent four-minute scene, the best in the film and one of Atwill's best. If only there could have been more scenes like it.

There is another scene that is remarkable (albeit minus Atwill), and it follows almost immediately.

Poldi has placed a small pistol in her bag and goes to the opera house, presumably to shoot Carla. She walks to the entrance to the auditorium while the show is in full swing. As she stands in the doorway, Duvivier makes an astonishing series of 10 cuts (each accompanied by a crash of cymbals), each one the same shot of her but each from increasingly farther away, so that she gets smaller and smaller and smaller, eventually seemingly dwarfed by the huge auditorium and the hundreds of people in it. The technique makes us share her feeling of isolation, and of being intimidated by her surroundings.

This being a musical, it is tempting to speculate whether there were ever any plans to include a scene in which Atwill bursts into song. In May of 1938 (probably when he was shooting this film), *Variety* reported, "Lionel Atwill taking singing lessons." Was this a coincidence, perhaps?

For Atwill fans, *The Great Waltz* offers a bonus. The film ends with a sequence "43 years later," and we see him in a credible old-age make-up (no make-up artist is credited). He has a brief dialogue with Emperor Franz Josef—played by gravel-voiced Henry Hull, also in an elaborate old-age make-up and sporting some flamboyant whiskers. Is this how Atwill might have looked had he lived another 20 years? Is this the Lionel Atwill we never got to see—the Atwill who lived until his 80s and carried

"If you want to keep him ... you must *fight!*" Hohen-fried tells Poldi (Luise Rainer), in *The Great Waltz.*

on playing character parts in horror films, in the way that Karloff and Carradine carried on until their 80s? But regrettably chain-smoker Atwill succumbed to lung cancer at age 61, depriving his fans of the possibility of another few decades of filmmaking.

Son of Frankenstein (1939)

In *Son of Frankenstein*, Lionel Atwill's Inspector Krogh, with his scene-stealing prosthetic arm and gruff, intimidating manner, is one of the truly unforgettable characters of the Golden Age of horror films.

Basil Rathbone, Boris Karloff and Bela Lugosi may get top billing in this, the third of Universal's *Frankenstein* series, but Atwill is as much a star of the film as any of them. His Inspector Krogh is a major recurring character, encountered in the film's first few minutes and still there right at the end, appearing in the film's closing shot and even getting the final line of dialogue.

Inspector Krogh is also as much one of the film's bogeymen as are the Frankenstein Monster or Ygor. Even though, as the local police inspector, he is ostensibly a force for good, his every word seems to exude bitterness and menace. In an early scene, he explains to Wolf von Frankenstein (Rathbone) the reason for this bitterness. When he was a child, the Monster tore his arm out by the roots. From then on, the audience knows that every fiber in his being has been twisted by this traumatic event and, as a result, he might at any moment be capable of enacting some ghastly act of cruelty or revenge.

Atwill's dialogue in *Son of Frankenstein*, always incisively delivered in clipped, harsh tones, is very well written by Willis Cooper (and I can imagine with contributions by Atwill himself), full of occasions when Krogh, suspicious that Frankenstein has been up to no good in his laboratory, makes veiled insinuations which threaten to turn the highly-strung scientist into a nervous wreck.

Krogh's many conversations with Frankenstein, as he attempts to pressure the scientist into revealing if he has revived the Monster, build in intensity to the extent that

Two legends of the horror genre pay tribute to the portrait of a third. Lionel Atwill, Basil Rathbone and Colin Clive in *Son of Frankenstein*. Where is the portrait now?

Lionel Atwill

their battle of wits develops into one of the film's core themes. The charged dialogue between them is one of the film's great pleasures—a pleasure that could be experienced again three years later when Atwill and Rathbone were arch-foes in *Sherlock Holmes and the Secret Weapon.*

Rathbone is excellent as Baron Frankenstein, and Lugosi is full of malevolent mischief as Ygor. Karloff has his moments, but this time the Monster lacks the force that he had in *Frankenstein* (1931) and *Bride of Frankenstein* (1935). The film's greatest achievement is

Basil Rathbone, Lionel Atwill and Josephine Hutchinson posed in Jack Otterson's Expressionistic set in *Son of Frankenstein.*

its set design. This may well be the most visually striking horror film of the 1930s. Art director Jack Otterson had studied the Expressionistic sets of German silent films such as *The Cabinet of Dr. Caligari* (1919) and decided to recreate the look. The result is a nightmarish world of slanting ceilings, dizzying staircases and shadowy corridors.

Back in 1933, a reporter for the fan magazine *Motion Picture* dubbed Atwill "the mental Lon Chaney." The implication was that where the legendary silent film actor had achieved gruesome and terrifying effects by depicting himself as physically deformed characters, Atwill could achieve the same impact purely through the force of his personality. With *Son of Frankenstein*, Atwill demonstrated that he could match Lon Chaney when it came to disfigurement too. Atwill's Inspector Krogh, with his unforgettable false arm, features in so many notable scenes, and has so many memorable lines of dialogue, that it is worth looking at some of them in detail.

After a dazzling opening shot using a superb matte painting of the Castle Frankenstein at night, we find a gathering of the town's notables, including Krogh, discussing the imminent and unwelcome arrival of Wolf von Frankenstein. It's a very low-key introduction to Krogh, who only has a few lines, and the false arm is barely noticed.

By contrast, his next scene is a real showcase for the character—a prolonged and masterful six minutes in which George Robinson's skillful camerawork really shines, extracting the maximum visual impact out of Krogh, supported by Atwill at his cold, militaristic best.

The scene begins dramatically with a shot of Krogh walking through a rainstorm at night, past the huge stone buttresses of the castle and approaching the enormous door. He grasps one of the huge metal doorknockers and bangs it three times. Its echoing thuds alarm those inside, causing Elsa von Frankenstein and a maid to run about anxiously. The servant Benson (Edgar Norton) opens the door and, as Krogh walks through it, we see that the door is at least twice as high as any man.

Not waiting to be invited in, Krogh strides purposefully into the hall, then throws his rain-soaked cape over his shoulder. He introduces himself to Frankenstein, using his

"One doesn't easily forget, Herr Baron, an arm torn out by the roots," Inspector Krogh (Atwill) recalls a childhood incident, from *Son of Frankenstein.*

good arm to push the false arm into a salute. The arm makes a disturbing squeak when it is raised, and an even louder one when it is lowered. Krogh keeps his cold eyes on Frankenstein throughout the ritual. Was there ever a more chilling introduction in film history?

The squeaks may be sound effects that were added later, but they may also have been generated on-set. It is clear that, in order to make the false arm look convincing, Atwill wore some kind of rigid contraption under his uniform, with a hinge at the elbow. It is just possible that this device really did produce a loud grinding sound.

Frankenstein invites Krogh into a large room with two huge curving beams in the ceiling, where a portrait of his father (an oil painting of Colin Clive) hangs, a fireplace raging below. Krogh stands near the fire to warm himself. The pair conducts a heavily loaded conversation before flickering flames. Krogh explains the purpose of his visit.

"I've come here, Herr Baron, to ensure you of protection ... from a virulent and fatal poison."

The subject of the Monster is broached. Frankenstein suggests that stories about it have been grossly exaggerated over the years. So confident is he of this that he makes the mistake of asking a question which he very soon regrets.

"Do you honestly know of one criminal act that this poor creature committed?" There is an ominous crash of thunder. "Did you ever even see him?"

The camera moves in for a close medium-shot of the pair.

"The most vivid recollection of my life," replies Krogh, turning slowly to look Frankenstein in the eye. The false arm is raised with a squeak. "I was but a child at the time ... about the same age as your son, Herr Baron ..." He removes his monocle with his good hand and places it between the thumb and forefinger of the false hand. "The Monster had escaped and was ravaging the countryside ... killing ... maiming ... terrorizing." A handkerchief is brought out, Krogh breathes on the monocle and wipes it. These little gestures make for a grand bit of theater, and we can be almost certain, from what we know of Atwill's contributions to other films, that he most likely dreamed up these flourishes. "One night he burst into our house. My father took a gun and fired at him, but the savage brute sent him crashing to a corner. Then ... he grabbed me by the arm ..."

Krogh pushes his false arm down again, and it hits a wooden pillar with a superbly melodramatic thud. "One doesn't easily forget, Herr Baron, an arm torn out by the roots."

"No, I ..." says Frankenstein, taken aback, struggling to think of something to say.

"My lifelong ambition," continues Krogh, "was to have been a soldier. But for this, [pointing at his false arm] I, who command seven gendarmes in a little mountain village, might have been a general."

It's one of the most memorable speeches of Atwill's career.

The scene continues with Krogh explaining that there has been a series of murders in the village, and again offers his services to protect the Baron. The scene ends delightfully with

Hutchinson, Rathbone and Atwill in another of Jack Otterson's remarkable sets, from *Son of Frankenstein.*

Krogh meeting Elsa on his way out. She extends her hand to shake his, and he takes it in his left hand, momentarily confusing her. After Krogh has gone, she says to her husband, entirely accurately, "Wasn't he odd?"

The next day finds Krogh in a long scene that begins with him taking tea with Elsa at Castle Frankenstein in a room that, with its profusion of curving overhead beams, looks like an Art Deco nightmare. Frankenstein joins them and the dialogue becomes very charged as Krogh tries to establish if the scientist has been working in the laboratory. The subject of the bubbling sulphur pit beneath the old laboratory is mentioned, and how the Romans may once have used the site as mineral baths. Krogh can't resist making a joke: "One of the first health resorts, perhaps," and he chuckles as he thinks of the bubbling inferno that the site has since become. Frankenstein responds with a joke of his own, suggesting that one day he will invite Krogh to come and visit the sulphur pits, and will "par-boil" him. Krogh isn't amused but eventually sees the funny side, letting out a long, hearty chortle. It's another example of Atwill showing his skill as one of the cinema's great *laughers.*

Little Peter Frankenstein (Donnie Dunagan) enters and the scene that follows is surprisingly full of deft touches, which are designed to embellish Krogh's character with greater depth.

"You're not supposed to shake hands with your left hand," complains Peter after Krogh greets him.

"I'm sorry. That was very rude of me," replies Krogh diplomatically.

"You're not supposed to wear gloves in the house either," says Peter, noticing the glove of Krogh's false hand.

"I'm sorry about that too. But you see, I only have one real arm. This one isn't mine."

"Well, whose is it?" asks little Peter.

Krogh is momentarily confused and not sure what to say next. Frankenstein comes to his rescue. He tells Peter that Krogh lost his arm in a war. "He's a soldier."

The Exquisite Villain

This U.S. lobby card records a sequence not in the actual movie, showing Atwill and Donnie Dunagan horsing around on the set of *Son of Frankenstein.*

"Oh, are you a general?" asks Peter, unaware that he is treading in dangerous territory. Krogh once again is lost for words. Frankenstein again comes to his rescue.

"He's more than a general. He's an inspector."

Krogh is grateful for the generous gesture, and bows to show his thanks. It's a shrewd little exchange and does much to make the audience warm to Krogh's situation.

Little Peter goes on to tell everyone that his afternoon nap was disturbed when a giant paid him a visit. "And he had a hold of my arm!"

The remark startles Krogh, his good arm involuntarily reaching out for his false one.

A tense dinner scene follows, set in one of Jack Otterson's crazy Expressionistic sets, with fanged gargoyles overlooking the three diners: Frankenstein, his wife and Inspector Krogh. Frankenstein has become increasingly jumpy and becomes even more so when he is told that his butler has gone missing. As he sips at his soup, Krogh never takes his beady eye off the scientist, waiting to see if he will give something away. When Krogh gets up to leave, he snaps his heels together loudly. A clever minor moment of suspense occurs as Krogh refuses to depart until Frankenstein has responded by clicking his own heels together.

Next morning, another tense exchange between Frankenstein and Krogh occurs. The latter greets him on the castle steps and tells him about a mysterious murder in the village. Was it Atwill who dreamed up the bit of business of having Krogh take out a box of matches while they talk, and impale it on the end of a false finger so that he can strike a match with his good hand? (The moment includes a shot that gives us one of the best opportunities to see the legendary Atwill ring which adorns his little finger. The design, made up of several intertwined gold bands, can be clearly made out.)

Krogh continues to feature strongly in the following two scenes. In the first he places Frankenstein under house arrest in his own home, and in the other quizzes little Peter about the giant that he claims visited him in his room. The latter scene includes a shot of Atwill that clearly shows the contraption worn under his costume.

Later that day another excellent battle of wits occurs between Krogh and Frankenstein. Another strong scene that is enlivened by good dialogue, with Frankenstein hurling darts angrily at a dartboard as Krogh tells him there has been another murder and informs him that he is under arrest. Krogh suggests that the Monster has been revived. Trying to wriggle his way out of this, Frankenstein suggests that the killer is actually

Ygor. Krogh laughs heartily at the suggestion, swinging his false arm round to his back with a loud squeak and grasping it with his other arm.

"Everybody wants to hang old Ygor again," he says, knowing that Ygor is not the culprit. "It would be too simple to hang old Ygor."

The pace picks up as Frankenstein heads off to his laboratory, where he shoots Ygor dead. Meanwhile Krogh explores a secret passageway and discovers the body of Benson the butler. Immediately afterwards, Krogh and Frankenstein, the two archenemies, reconvene in the room with the dartboard.

Impaling a matchbox on a prosthetic finger, Krogh lights a match and also allows a good look at the legendary "pinky" ring he wore throughout his career, from *Son of Frankenstein.*

The fire throws flickering shadows onto the room's Expressionistic ceiling. Frankenstein is a bag of nerves, hitting the brandy as Krogh shows him the evidence of Benson's murder. At last Krogh can unleash all the suspicions that have been growing in him.

"But Ygor didn't do it. Nor did you," barks Krogh, staring malevolently at Frankenstein. "Nor was it done by any ghost. There's a monster afoot and you know it! He's in your control! By heaven, I think you're a worse fiend than your father. Where is this monster? Where is he? I'll stay by your side until you confess." Krogh's tone gets louder and more vicious. "And if you don't, I'll feed you to the villagers—like the Romans fed Christians to the lions!"

It's a superb 20-second speech, delivered immaculately by Atwill with all the venom and intensity that he can muster.

Frankenstein, refusing to be intimidated by Krogh, offers him a brandy and asks him if wants to play a game of darts. Krogh takes up the challenge, the aggressive game promising to become a symbolic extension of their verbal sparring. The match begins, both participants unaware that even as they play the Monster is strangling the maid and abducting Peter.

Frankenstein, having taken his turn at the dartboard, hands the darts to Krogh. Instead of merely placing them on a table and picking them up one at a time, Krogh takes them in his good hand and sticks them in his false arm. He then pulls one out and throws it. This superbly macabre flourish may potentially be another bit of business that Atwill (and perhaps the director?) dreamed up.

Elsa's screams interrupt them. Frankenstein runs one way. Krogh runs upstairs, opens the secret doorway in Peter's room and rushes through it. In the laboratory, the Monster holds Peter under one arm, threatening to throw him into the bubbling sulphur pit. Amid a cloud of smoke and steam, Krogh emerges in the background, having climbed through the caves and up the side of the pit.

In this trade ad for *Son of Frankenstein*, Atwill, previously billed only as supporting actor, has been elevated to being one of four stars.

What follows ranks as one of the most gloriously gruesome incidents in Atwill's career—a career that has not been short on gruesome moments. The Monster grabs him by his false arm and rips it off, leaving Krogh with just some hanging threads of torn cloth where his arm was. The Monster brandishes the false arm like a club. Krogh goes down on one knee and fires repeatedly at the Monster, but his bullets seem to have no effect. Up on a ledge, Frankenstein grabs a hanging rope, swings into the Monster and kicks him over the edge and into the sulphur pit below.

It's a visually dramatic climax, giving the Monster his best death scene in the entire Universal *Frankenstein* series.

Surprisingly, Inspector Krogh survives the ordeal. Given the sinister nature of his character throughout the film, it would have been entirely fitting if he too had ended up in the sulphur pit. Instead, he makes a few perfunctory appearances in the closing scenes (his false arm and damaged uniform now restored) as Frankenstein, Elsa and Peter all board a train and leave town.

Universal's *Son of Frankenstein* opened in mid-January 1939, and very quickly the studio realized they had a big hit on their hands. At the end of January they took out a full-page, green-tinted ad for the film in *Variety*. It depicted an unusual drawing of the Monster with a happy grin on his face, alongside a list of eight cinemas across the U.S. where the film had been so popular that it had been held over for extra weeks. More crucially, the ad also makes it clear that Universal had realized the importance of Atwill's contribution to the film. Whereas before only the names of Karloff, Rathbone and Lugosi had appeared above the ad title, now Atwill joined their prominently displayed names. A small photo of each of the four stars appeared in the ad, each with a catchy caption: "The Menace of Basil Rathbone! The Fright of Boris Karloff! The Horror of Bela Lugosi! The Hate of Lionel Atwill!"

No discussion of Lionel Atwill's role in *Son of Frankenstein* could be complete without mentioning Mel Brooks' *Young Frankenstein*, effectively a comic remake of the Universal film. Made 35 years after the original, it also contained affectionate *homages* to scenes in the first two Frankenstein films. Kenneth Mars played Inspector Kemp, an over-the-top parody of Inspector Krogh, with an incomprehensible German accent thrown into the mix for good measure. Ironically, many people today are familiar with *Young Frankenstein* but have never seen the film that inspired it. As a result they don't realize that the false arm, the monocle and the darts-in-the-arm gag all featured in the original.

"By heaven, I think you're a worse fiend than your father!" Krogh rants in *Son of Frankenstein.*

Brooks lampooned the scene where Krogh lights a cigarette from a matchbox impaled on one of his false fingers, but he took the gag even further and had Kemp actually set light to his false finger. Also parodied was the dart game sequence, the joke being that every time Frankenstein is about throw a dart, Kemp raises his voice deliberately, with the result that the darts fly everywhere except into the board. Most audiences probably don't realize how close to the original this gag is. Watch Atwill as he pulls one dart out of his false arm, takes aim and throws the dart. Eagle-eyed viewers will spot that the dart lands nowhere near the dartboard but, in fact, about a foot above it. Atwill was right-handed and the shot required him to throw with his left hand—clearly something he simply could not do with any accuracy. Probably several takes of this shot occurred, with Atwill getting increasingly flustered, before Rowland V. Lee instructed his cameraman to angle the shot such that the dartboard is only partially seen, thereby disguising Atwill's inaccuracy. The question is: Had Mel Brooks spotted this when he made his 1974 *homage*?

It's satisfying that the spirit of Atwill's character lives on in *Young Frankenstein*, and the film may even encourage some viewers to seek out and enjoy the older film and the incomparable Inspector Krogh.

The Three Musketeers (1939)

This is a light-hearted but lavishly mounted 20th Century Fox costume drama, with elaborate sets of 17th-century France and glittering aristocratic costumes. This could have been a classic adventure of the old-fashioned school but it is let down by Allan Dwan's pedestrian direction and the uninspired comic and musical routines of the three Ritz Brothers. Presumably they amused people in their time, but seem rather dull today.

Alongside the Ritz Brothers is an impressive collection of actors: Don Ameche, Binnie Barnes, Gloria Stuart, Joseph Schildkraut, Miles Mander and Douglas Dumbrille. Better still, John Carradine and Lionel Atwill are also in the cast.

Carradine is rather wonderful in three very brief sequences. Playing the nervous owner of a guesthouse, he opens his front door dressed in a white gown, floppy nightcap and holding a candle. Later, this lecherous old chap is seen peering through a hole in the floorboards at the bedroom below. And finally he is seen telling all he has witnessed to Cardinal Richelieu (Mander), while De Rochefort (Atwill) looks on.

As De Rochefort, the Cardinal's aide, Atwill has a larger role than Carradine—although not much larger. In a way that recalls *Captain Blood*, he has shoulder-length hair and wears an assortment of flamboyant costumes—all fancy collars, lacy cuffs and leather boots—and looks marvelous in all of them.

De Rochefort (Atwill) with Cardinal Richelieu (Miles Mander) in *The Three Musketeers*

In his first scene, he doesn't have a great deal to say as he takes orders from Richelieu to obtain a brooch which the Queen has unwisely given to the Duke of Buckingham (Lester Matthews) as a love token. He is better served in his second scene in which he is seen in close-up giving instructions to Binnie Barnes on how to obtain the brooch. At the end of the scene, he mounts a horse and rides off, but a double is used (even though, as seen in *Captain Blood*, Atwill knew how to ride a horse). In a third scene he is infuriated to learn that the brooch has slipped through his grasp. In a fourth scene (and in his third costume), he confers again with Richelieu, telling him he will stake his life on the brooch not eluding him again.

Finally, he has a sword-fighting showdown with D'Artagnan (Ameche). This is no classic Michael Curtiz sequence, and it appears that a double was used in most of the long shots, with Atwill only seen in medium shots. Presumably he was untrained in the art of fencing and there wasn't time to teach him. After some extended swordplay, De Rochefort, not surprisingly, is killed by D'Artagnan and slumps to the ground dead.

It's very much a supporting role, but Atwill conducts himself with dignity and presence throughout. Incidentally, the same role would be played many years later by horror star Christopher Lee in the 1973 version.

A special treat exists for those who enjoy old matte paintings. The film boasts eight eye-catching paintings of a castle, two chateaus, an old townscape and the decorative ceilings of various grand buildings, including a banqueting hall

Binnie Barnes and Atwill in *The Three Musketeers*

Lionel Atwill

and the room and corridor of a palace. One even features what may be a miniature rear projection of a character looking out from a window in the side of a (painted) chateau.

Hound of the Baskervilles (1939)

This, the first of the series of Sherlock Holmes films starring Basil Rathbone, may well also be the best movie ever produced about Conan Doyle's detective. It has a sparkling cast of colorful British actors (plus John Carradine putting on a Scottish accent). Almost as sparkling is the art direction of Hans Peters and Richard Day, who created a remarkable Hollywood version of Dartmoor complete with hills, crags, ancient stone monuments, quicksand, plenty of fog and even an ancient graveyard thrown in for good measure.

Among the collection of Brits are the ever-watchable Rathbone and Bruce as Holmes and Watson, as well as Morton Lowry as a so-nice-he's-scary neighbor and Eily Malyon as Carradine's creepy wife (and she actually looks like a female Carradine).

Best of all among the Brits, though, is Lionel Atwill as Dr. Mortimer, looking every inch the sinister villain chiefly because he wears round glasses that distort his eyes and seem to hide all kind of unsavory thoughts. He also sports a bushy beard, an unusual Atwill accoutrement. It's a prominent role for Atwill who, during the film's first 40 minutes, is in almost every scene. But ultimately it's a red herring role, meaning that he is deprived of any high-powered dialogue or moments of drama that really stand out.

His first scene makes it clear that he may not be all that he seems. He is just about to throw some light on the death of Sir Charles Baskerville, when his wife tugs at his coattails and stops him talking. This serves to add some tension to his next scene, when he visits Holmes in London to ask him to come to Dartmoor to protect the young Sir Henry Baskerville. The audience can't help wondering if this is a genuine plea for help or could there be something more that Mortimer is not telling Holmes? During this memorable six-minute scene, Atwill adds plenty of sinister overtones as he tells Holmes about the legends of Dartmoor.

"I am in mortal fear," he tells Holmes, "that Sir Henry's life will be ... snuffed out."

He proceeds to reveal more about his fears concerning Sir Charles' death, and tells of some footprints near the body.

"They were," he says dramatically, "the footprints of a gigantic hound!"

He then pulls out an ancient document and reads its contents aloud to Holmes— it is the legend of the Hound, and the film shows us a flashback of past events. Dr. Mortimer doesn't leave

The sinister Dr. James Mortimer (Atwill) in *Hound of the Baskervilles*

Dr. Mortimer and Sherlock Holmes (Basil Rathbone) in *The Hound of the Baskervilles*

out any of the gruesome details: "Before they could get at him, Sir Hugo was dead, his body literally torn to shreds."

An enjoyable exchange occurs when Holmes quizzes Mortimer about the bite marks on his walking stick, despite the fact that he denies owning a dog. "I used to have a dog ... a small spaniel ... but it died." The last three words seem innocuous enough, yet Atwill puts a macabre emphasis on them, suggesting all manner of evil wrongdoing. What other actor was capable of adding such force with a mere change in his tone of voice?

In a classic slice of Holmes action, Mortimer and Sir Henry walk along a cobbled street at night, unaware that a horse-drawn carriage is trailing them, and through its curtains someone is pointing a revolver at them.

A fine scene exists in which Watson, Sir Henry and Dr. Mortimer are all seated in a small horse-drawn trap, which takes them across the moor toward Baskerville Hall. As they travel through the bumpy terrain, Mortimer tells them all about the history of the malevolent moor and the prehistoric ruins that are found in it. "And over there," he continues, "beyond that hill, those dark spots, that's the great Grimpen Mire, as treacherous a morass as exists anywhere. Thousands of lives have been sucked down into its bottomless depths."

In Baskerville Hall, we learn that Dr. Mortimer's wife is a medium, and a séance is duly arranged. One of the participants belittles the idea.

"They'll not answer scoffers or skeptics," says Dr. Mortimer to him aggressively, adding: "If that's your attitude, Mr. Frankland, perhaps you wouldn't mind leaving us?" It's the bombastic, bullish Atwill that we know so well from many other films.

As Mrs. Mortimer tries to contact a dead Baskerville, Peverell Marley's camera lingers in delicious close-up on each of the participants, and includes a wonderful portrait of Atwill, eerily lit by the flickering firelight.

After this halfway stage, Atwill features less significantly, with the focus shifting to Holmes, Watson and dastardly deeds on the moor. But he is still around to make the occasional appearance, and is even given a decent piece of dialogue at the close of the film, thanking Holmes for his good work: "Mr. Holmes, we've admired you in the past, as does every Englishman. Your record as our greatest detective is known throughout the world. But this ... seeing how you work ... knowing that in England there is such a man as you ... gives us all a sense of safety and security. God bless you, Mr. Holmes." With England on the brink of war in 1939, it's a speech tinged with warming patriotism.

The Mad Empress [aka Carlotta The Mad Empress] (1939)

It was a real coup for Hispanola Continental Films to secure the services of Lionel Atwill to play the chief supporting role in this obscure and rarely seen Mexican-U.S. co-production. To have one of Hollywood's most bankable *heavies* in the film was sure to help its U.S. release. The role suits Atwill perfectly; it's one of his archetypal roles as a European military officer.

He plays Marshall Bazaine, a commander of the French army occupying Mexico in the 1860s. He was always perfect for such roles: He knew exactly how to exude an air of military rigidity tinged with a stiff-upper-lipped aristocratic edge.

Billed third, he is always a supporting character rather than a protagonist. But he nevertheless is given a decent amount of screen time and appears in a number of crucial scenes. Scriptwriter Jean Bart (who had earlier written the play on which Atwill's *The Man Who Reclaimed His Head* was based) even gives him some memorable dialogue too.

The local people—Juarez is their leader (played by Jason Robards, Sr., who in every shot is seen, oddly, only from behind)—are not thrilled to have their country occupied by the French. General Bazaine leads the French army in its continued struggle against the locals, and he reports to the French puppet-monarchy, which has installed Emperor Maximilian (Conrad Nagel) and his wife Empress Carlotta (Medea de Novara, who had already played the part of Carlotta in a 1934 all-Mexican version of the story).

Bazaine is first encountered in his office, seated at a grand table. He sports a goatee and is dressed in full military finery, including epaulets and a high collar embroidered with gold designs. He is surrounded by various army officers and informs them of

the appointment of Maximilian and Carlotta to the crown of Mexico. The scriptwriter—with perhaps Atwill's contribution—gives the character an amusing moment of light relief when he reaches for a pinch of snuff, takes it and then sneezes in mid-sentence. From the onset, he makes the brutal nature of his character plain with an ominous statement: "Gentlemen, I intend to secure the popular election of the Arch-Duke as emperor—even if I have to use force to achieve it."

There is an elaborate parade to welcome the new emperor and his wife, complete with army escort. The sequence includes a brief but memorable shot of Bazaine in plumed hat on horseback (although the horse is out of frame).

Later Bazaine speaks with Maxmilian and tries to get him to sign a decree that will make it a capital offence for any Mexican to be in possession of a gun. Maxmilian fears that to sign the decree will provoke further rebellion, but Bazaine laughs off his concerns (with one of those laughs that Atwill was always so good at). When

General Bazaine (Atwill) in *The Mad Empress* [photo courtesy Tony Atwill]

The Exquisite Villain

243

Bazaine, Empress Carlotta (Medea Novara) and Maximilian (Conrad Nagel) in *The Mad Empress*

Maximilian refuses to sign, Bazaine accepts that he has been defeated, bows and respectfully walks backwards out of the royal chamber.

In his next scene, his character is developed further. As he sternly tells his officers about his concerns that the rebellion is gaining strength, he is delighted when his pretty young Mexican wife Paquita (Graciela Romero) walks in. She is young enough to be his daughter. Bazaine adjusts a flower in her hair, telling his officers, "Gentlemen, war is so dull, when one has such beauty in the home. Mexico has been kind to me." He turns to his wife, playfully tickling her on the nose: "What brings you here, little rogue?" She tells him he will be late for the ball if he doesn't hurry. "Oh, that would be terrible, *ma petite*, terrible!" he exclaims with a very hearty laugh. It's only a brief exchange but it really brings the character to life and also recalls the way Baron Von Merzbach treated his young wife Marlene Dietrich in *The Song of Songs.*

At the ball, the royal couple and their guests, including Bazaine and his wife, all enjoy dancing to a Strauss waltz. How splendid to see Hollywood's maddest doctor enjoying so refined an entertainment. Suddenly the sound of cannon fire is heard and all the dancers stand still and listen. The emperor and his wife resume dancing, hoping to calm the situation.

Maximilian, Carlotta and Bazaine retire to another room to discuss the situation. Bazaine tells them he will take measures to stamp out the rebellion. When Carlotta reminds Bazaine that she and her husband are in power to protect the people, not to crush them, he starts to lose his temper.

"The people?" he barks. "It's time your majesties realized that two-thirds of the people are your enemies!" He then bows, apologizing for speaking out of turn.

Days later, there are more violent attacks on the French troops. Bazaine still wants to come down hard on the Mexican people, but he is in conflict with Maximilian and Carlotta. He says he must act in the best interest of Emperor Napoleon III back in France. To Carlotta he says (in his best clipped tones, tinged with a hint of contempt), "May I respectfully remind your majesty, that unless I am allowed to proceed in my own way, I shall advise the Emperor to withdraw from an impossible situation that can only lead to disaster."

At last, Maximilian agrees to sign the decree forbidding the people from bearing arms. Maximilian wants an assurance that Bazaine's actions won't inflame the situation and are just.

"Whoever deserves justice … will get it," replies Bazaine ominously, suggesting that wholesale slaughter is just around the corner.

Carlotta travels back to France to see if she can talk Napoleon out of withdrawing all his troops from Mexico. But the stress of her impossible situation causes her to topple over into insanity. Maximilian, still in Mexico, hears of her distress and decides to abdicate, leaving Mexico. But his loyal soldiers talk him out of it, and he realizes that he must do his duty and stay in Mexico to protect the empire that he has built there.

Bazaine is horrified that Maximilian has chosen to stay behind and face possible disaster. "It's madness, sire!" he says with a wide-eyed stare.

Bazaine makes a last-ditch attempt to talk Maximilian into leaving Mexico. It's an opportunity for Atwill to indulge in a memorable little speech. "One last word, Your Majesty, as man to man. Don't be foolhardy. There's no heroism in sacrificing everything to a pitiful farce that may turn into tragedy. Return with me to Europe—I

A foreign movie poster for *Carlotta the Mad Empress*

beg of you. There's no place for you here … and the Empress needs you. Come, sire."

But Maximilian refuses and Bazaine returns to France without him. Emperor Napoleon grills Bazaine about his failure to bring Maximilian with him, leaving him to almost certain death. The scene between the two gives Atwill more effective dialogue. Napoleon asks Bazaine why he didn't use force to bring Maximilian back to France. "Your Majesty, he is an emperor. You made him an emperor … and with simple dignity, he plays his part."

Napoleon is concerned with his people's reaction if Maximilian is executed. "History will call me a murderer!" he exclaims, a remark that Atwill reacts to with a marvelous wide-eyed stare. Bazaine delivers the scene's dramatic closing lines: "Your Majesty, making kings and emperors is an ungrateful task. As I recall, your illustrious uncle also had similar … difficulties." And the camera tilts to show a bust of Napoleon Bonaparte on a desk.

The film ends with two powerful scenes. In one, Carlotta has gone quite mad and sits at a table, imagining that Maximilian is dining with her. And in the other, Maximilian is marched off to a firing squad, and just before he dies, he utters his last words: "Long live Mexico!" then looks up to the heavens and, with a tear in his eye, cries out, "Carlotta!"

The film's plot is ambitious in its scope but unfortunately the direction by Miguel Contreras Torres lacks the drive and excitement that a Michael Curtiz or a John Ford could have given it. Medea de Novara and Conrad Nagel are adequate in the leading roles but the script never really gives them scenes that develop the full tragic force of their predicament. *Juarez*, a Hollywood version of the same story, starring Paul Muni and Bette Davis, was also released in 1939, with Donald Crisp in the role of Bazaine.

The Gorilla (1939)

Bela Lugosi, Patsy Kelly and a worried-looking Lionel Atwill in *The Gorilla*

This haunted house ape-on-the-loose horror comedy can be a struggle to watch. Not only have the comic antics of the Ritz Brothers dated badly, but we are also subjected to the endless squawking and screaming of Patsy Kelly as a terrified maid. Sadder still, poor Bela Lugosi is reduced to playing a sinister butler who does little more than turn up at odd moments and adopt a knowing smirk (apart from one amusing moment when he performs a nifty martial arts move on one of the brothers). The scriptwriters couldn't even think of a better name for him than Peters.

Hopes are dashed that things will liven up with the appearance of the gorilla when the Brothers encounter it in a shadowy cellar. Director Allan Dwan shows a complete inability to make anything of the occasion, which in the right hands could have been genuinely creepy. The film's only memorable image occurs when the ape is spotted on a roof, gripping Anita Louise by one arm as she dangles beneath him perilously.

Lionel Atwill plays Walter Stevens, the wealthy uncle of Anita Louise and owner of a huge old house riddled with secret passageways. It was the third of seven films in which Atwill would act alongside Bela Lugosi. He figures prominently in the film's first half hour after receiving a note from the gorilla telling him that he will be the next murder victim. But is he the affable uncle who extends a hearty welcome to Louise and her fiancé (Edward Norris), or is he somehow involved in the recent spate of mysterious gorilla murders? Although he gets plenty of dialogue, unfortunately most of it is perfunctory and, while his polished delivery still makes him something of a scene-stealer, he is given little opportunity to shine.

Dwan shows more flair when he gives Atwill a series of extreme close-ups as the appointed hour of his murder approaches, with Atwill looking nervously to left and right as the seconds tick down. The lights go out and when they come back on again, Atwill has disappeared. In fact he isn't seen again until the closing minutes of the film.

Atwill (in handcuffs) surrounded by Lugosi, Paul Harvey, Joseph Calleia and the three Ritz Brothers in *The Gorilla*

At the end, he is discovered bound and gagged in a hidden room. Eventually, he gets the opportunity to let out one of those hearty laughs that he does so well, as he finally explains the whole mystery of the gorilla's identity.

A decade into his Hollywood career, this was the first time that Atwill found himself largely wasted in yet another red herring role. Did he mind? Or was he happy just to pocket the $1,000 a week paycheck that Fox were paying him?

The Sun Never Sets (1939)

This is an entertaining stiff-upper-lip action yarn about British Empire exploits in the Gold Coast, with half the cast seeming to suffer malarial delirium at some point. Unfortunately, Rowland V. Lee's direction lacks any real spark, and much of the movie is routine. Lee, fresh from *Son of Frankenstein*, is re-united with some of the crew from that film (such as set designer Jack Otterson) as well as the cast, including Basil Rathbone and Lionel Atwill.

Atwill is Dr. Hugo Zurof, a monocle-wearing, goateed scientist who ostensibly studies ants in Africa, but in fact is a madman who wants to rule the world. He is mining rare minerals used to make weapons and instigating riots and terrorism all over the world, using a secret radio, hoping to cause global chaos so that he can step in and take over—ruling the world as if he were leader of a giant colony of ants. All very topical as WWII was imminent when this was released.

Zurof drives around Africa in an outrageous stretch-Winnebago, barking orders to his many underlings and African servants. He is very much a character in the mould of a James Bond villain, even if the script never quite gives him moments that would allow him to let rip. Even so, he has numerous substantial scenes.

One is a long sequence in his Winnebago in which he behaves with fake charm and politeness to district officer Douglas Walton, promising him that he won't stir up any trouble at his gold mines, but then shows his true colors as soon as Walton has left, barking orders at his lackeys and boasting of his discovery of molybdenum: "Every manufacturer of war materials in the world has to have molybdenum," he says with a clenched fist.

Douglas Fairbanks, Jr. and Lionel Atwill in *The Sun Never Sets*

Later he has an entertaining one-on-one scene with Rathbone, the pair seated in front of a cabinet displaying an ant colony. Dr. Zurof becomes more than a little excited as he describes how ant society works: "It's a government that exists, it's complete and it works ... perfectly."

"To me it's a horror," responds Rathbone.

Zurof continues, going into mad scientist mode: "It's the basis of all my success ... I study life here in its elemental

Dr. Hugo Zurof (Atwill) from *The Sun Never Sets*: "Liners on fire! Planes mysteriously exploding! War ships blown up! Until there is panic everywhere."

stages and what I find, I apply to the administration of my business. I'm afraid you won't find any of the ideals of British administration in that ant heap. This is an empire that knows its business and applies its laws ... rigidly." Realizing he may have given too much away about his intentions, he gives an enjoyably sinister Atwill stare, then composes himself, returning to a gentlemanly demeanor. It's a memorable bit of acting from Atwill.

The scene gets even better as Zurof gives a loaded warning to Rathbone about what might happen if he interferes in his dealings with the natives: "They may be unpleasant. They can be *very* unpleasant."

Rathbone departs, and the scene shifts into high gear. Zurof's underling Delafons (Theodore Von Eltz) approaches. "You see," says Delafons, "he tries to make you say too much." Zurof explodes, becoming crazier and crazier.

"I don't care what he suspects," he shouts, then expounds his insane plans. "Propaganda can only do so much. Sabotage will do the rest. Liners on fire ... planes mysteriously exploding ... warships blown up ... Until there is panic everywhere. Everyone will be blaming everyone else." He gets more and more agitated. "And then war! War!"

Delafons has to intervene to prevent his boss from becoming over-excited. "Dr. Zurof!" he pleads. Zurof realizes he has lost control and snaps back into his charming persona.

"Yes, you're right, Delafons. I mustn't get angry." He picks up some tweezers, pulls an ant out of a jar and starts to quote from the Bible. "Go to the ant, thou sluggard. Consider her ways and be wise." He chuckles and places his monocle on his right eye. "Delafons, did it ever occur to you that it only takes one generation to make a dictator? It could be anyone—a paper hanger, a fruit seller, a sign painter, perhaps ... perhaps, even a scientist." He stares with scarily chilling eyes at Delafons. "It all depends on the man ... and his purpose."

It's a classic bit of Atwill, made even more delightful by that deft touch when his underling has to snap him out of his insane reverie.

The monsoon arrives and Zurof, in pith helmet and overcoat, pays a nighttime visit to Fairbanks. He has come to find out how much the British officers know about his plans, but throughout this scene he again feigns gentlemanly politeness, with Fairbanks having no idea of Zurof's true nature. Hearing that Rathbone has gone up-country in the rain, he chuckles with false bonhomie: "I must say, you British carry your sense of duty too far."

In *The Sun Never Sets*, Atwill has one of his most memorable death scenes. He is sheltering in a bunker with his henchmen, believing himself safe from the bombs raining down on them from above. Eventually Fairbanks breaks into the bunker and is greeted by the macabre sight of all the men frozen immobile in their places. When he touches one of them, the body falls over, quite dead. The extreme concussion from the bombs has been so great that they have all been stunned to death! Zurof sits wide-eyed in a chair. It's a deliciously macabre touch, that even in death, the legendary Atwill stare lives on! The camera indulges in a close-up of his stony face,

Randolph (Fairbanks, Jr.) pretends to be drunk in order to infiltrate the underground lair of Zurof in *The Sun Never Sets*.

an ant running over his forehead. He wanted to rule the world and treat its inhabitants like ants ... but the ants outlived him. "Everything dead but the indestructible ant," muses Fairbanks.

Some studio hype about this film made it into a 1939 issue of Britain's *Picture Show* magazine:

> How would you like to sit absolutely still with your eyes wide open and have lots of ants crawling over your face? Well, Lionel Atwill didn't like it any better than you would, but he had to do just that for a scene in *The Sun Never Sets*. The scene was one in which Lionel Atwill had just been killed as a result of the bombing of his bomb proof radio station. He died with his eyes open. The concussion also broke the glass on a large ant case, releasing the ants. The producer wanted a close-up showing the ants crawling over Lionel Atwill's face. So the actor had to sit absolutely still, as if dead, while more than a score of large red ants swarmed over his face.

The swarm actually appears to have been just two ants—or perhaps the rest had all disappeared into Atwill's hair by the time the cameraman got his shot.

Mr. Moto Takes a Vacation (1939)

This, the last of the eight Mr. Moto films, is the sort of film that is entertaining if approached in the right mood. It's fast moving, full of exotic locations and has a distinct flavor of film noir about it; most scenes take place either at night or in the rain and are full of characters in dripping, wet-soaked overcoats. The narrow streets of old Chinatown look good—they may have been recycled from another production.

Atwill is third-billed and gives an enthusiastic performance as Professor Hildebrand, the curator of a museum that houses the crown of the Queen of Sheba. Although

not a major role, Hildebrand is a still a prominent character. What is good about the part is that Atwill is given a wonderful opportunity to relinquish his sinister persona and showcase his talent for light comedy. Professor Hildebrand is an excitable, blustering character, all of whose security devices go wrong at the worst moments.

He is first discovered in his office perusing a selection of neckties and is berated by Joseph Schildkraut for wasting time. "There's no harm in a man trying to look his best," offers Atwill. "It won't do any

Professor Hildebrand (Atwill), Mr. Moto (Peter Lorre) and Wong (Honorable Wu) in *Mr. Moto Takes a Vacation*

good in your case," suggests Schildkraut sarcastically.

Giving a grand speech to a large audience, the professor looks to his left and sees a uniformed security guard yawning, prompting a classic double take from the abashed and wide-eyed Atwill. He is full of fluster and bluster as he demonstrates the museum's security devices—only to find that none of them work. When an alarm finally does go off, he flails about like a startled chicken, his monocle flying around on its chord.

At the climax, Peter Lorre and Joseph Schildkraut fight it out in the museum, knocking into various exhibits. "My antiquities! My mummies!" squeals the horrified Atwill.

"My goodness!" cries out another character.

The Secret of Dr. Kildare (1939)

Lionel Atwill, third-billed after Lew Ayres and Lionel Barrymore, does little in this mildly entertaining episode in the Dr. Kildare series. He plays Paul Messenger, a multi-millionaire Wall Street businessman, who comes to the doctors because his daughter needs help. It's a straight role and very much a supporting one.

He looks very dapper in expensive suit and Homburg hat. He is in only a handful of

"We've always been close. . .why can't you tell me what's troubling you!"

Although he plays Helen Gilbert's kindly father, Atwill can't help appearing sinister in this U.S. lobby card, in *The Secret of Dr. Kildare.*

scenes, explaining his daughter's odd behavior to the two doctors and telling Ayres how he separated from his wife. But he never gets into his stride. With Atwill's reputation, one inevitably expects that it will be revealed that he has murdered his wife, and this is the cause of his daughter's problems. However, it all turns out to be much less sinister; the script never goes down this route nor does it ever try to make Atwill's character into a heavy. Atwill acts impeccably throughout but it is one of his more forgettable roles.

Balalaika (1939)

Atwill is very poorly served in this overlong (102 minutes) musical melodrama set in Russia at the start of the 20th century. He plays Professor Marakov, music teacher and father of Lydia (Ilona Massey), and he accompanies his daughter on the violin while she sings in a bar called the Balalaika. She dislikes the rowdy, drunken Cossacks who frequent her bar and so one of them (Nelson Eddy), who also happens to be a prince, has to wear a disguise as a lowly Russian student in order to win her love.

Marakov is a communist conspirator intent on the overthrow of the monarchy. Atwill looks splendid, with silvery hair and an eccentric bushy beard that is not only parted in the middle but also curls upwards at the ends. It is fun to see him pretending to know how to play the violin, such as when he accompanies Lydia as she sings a Dietrich-style nightclub number, and in a long musical scene in which Eddy sings a Russian song to all the conspirators to convince them that he is not a spy, but one of them.

But Marakov is never more than a background figure. He gets no more than 30 lines of dialogue in the entire film, none of them memorable. For once, Atwill is not the heavy, nor the deceived lover, nor the red herring—just a benign father figure.

Atwill only participates in one scene of any dramatic significance, but it is rather a good one. He and a fellow conspirator (Abner Biberman) attend an opera in which Lydia is performing. Their plan is to shoot General Karagin (C. Aubrey Smith) and his son the Prince (Eddy), who occupy a box on the other side of the auditorium. But at the crucial moment, with Marakov aiming his pistol, the General receives a note, bangs on the balcony rail of his box, brings the performance to a halt and announces that Germany has declared war on Russia. Marakov decides to call off the assassination attempt because, "I can't. Not now. Russia's going to need them more than she needs us." But his fellow conspirator grabs Marakov's pistol and fires several shots at the General. If only rest of the film could have been as highly dramatic.

After this, Marakov is not seen again. We hear that he has been arrested, but that is all. It's a very ignominious exit for such a prestigious actor.

Russian revolutionaries Lydia Marakova (Ilona Massey) and her father Marakov (Atwill) as they appear in *Balalaika*.

At the opera Marakov and a fellow revolutionary (Abner Biberman) intend to assassinate a Russian general, in *Balalaika*.

The film livens up in its final half hour, with a well-staged sequence in the trenches of WWI, and some fairly well done closing scenes in Paris, where all the nobility have fled after the communist revolution. All the characters are now reduced to serving in a restaurant called the Balalaika, dreaming of former glories. What a shame that director Reinhold Schunzel did not show more flair, because this film's memorable subject matter and setting could have made it a classic, whereas in fact it is all rather slow and forgettable.

Charlie Chan in Panama (1940)

This is an entertaining and brisk (67 minutes) entry in the series, with Sidney Toler making a very good Chan. The Panama Canal setting is novel and interesting, and there are a dozen suspects in a plot to blow it up. Effective black-and-white photography falls into the film noir style and amusing dialogue from Chan livens up the action.

Third-billed Lionel Atwill plays Cliveden Compton, an English author of crime novels (who is later revealed to be a secret service agent). It's a minor red herring role for Atwill and he has only four scenes. His role begins promisingly with some saucy dialogue with 50-something Mary Nash, whom Atwill directed on Broadway back in 1929. Dressed in tweed jacket, flat cap and smoking a pipe, Atwill looks every inch the English

Chan (Sidney Toler) examines a poisoned cigarette while three suspects—Lionel Atwill, Jack La Rue and Lionel Royce—look on, in *Charlie Chan in Panama*.

gentleman. Nash, who does some wonderful spinsterish acting, asks him if he is pulling her leg, and he takes the opportunity to flirt with her. When she takes up the chance to smoke her first-ever cigarette, Atwill seizes the moment: "Miss Finch, you're shedding inhibitions every moment. Congratulations!" But unfortunately this saucy angle is not developed further.

Later, dressed in dinner jacket and (of course) Panama hat, Atwill has a brief scene in an Egyptian's tobacco shop and another in which he sneaks into the hotel room of Jean Rogers (better known as Dale Arden in the *Flash Gordon* serials) and steals her passport.

Finally, a closet is opened and Atwill's corpse tumbles out. He has been shot. His corpse stares upwards with open eyes. Surely this is an occasion where we can sense that Atwill's contribution to the film went beyond just acting. He may have suggested to director Norman Foster that the scene would pack an extra punch if he were to repeat a memorable device from *The Sun Never Sets* and have his deceased character stare upwards with chillingly immobile eyes. It's always delicious to see that wonderful Atwill stare being used to good effect and it certainly makes for a memorably macabre final shot of the actor.

Johnny Apollo (1940)

An engaging crime movie that never quite delivers the drama that the plot deserves. Edward Arnold is a business-man who ends up in jail. His son Tyrone Power has a falling out with him and, as a result, ends up turning to crime, eventually being locked up in the same prison. Dorothy Lamour is the mobster's moll who supplies a couple of musical numbers. Lloyd Nolan is good in a Bog-art-like role.

Lionel Atwill and Tyrone Power in *Johnny Apollo*

Lionel Atwill is sixth-billed in a perfunctory role as Jim McLoughlin, Arnold's attorney. He features prominently during the first 22 minutes but is not seen thereafter. Looking smart in a business suit, he is with Arnold when he hears that the police are coming after him. He is also at Arnold's side in the courtroom and subsequently has a couple of scenes with Power, telling him there is nothing he can do to help his father, and as a result finds himself on the receiving end of Power's ire.

Atwill looks and sounds as impeccable as ever, but is never given much to do by the scriptwriter. What a shame he wasn't given the much more important role of the sleazy, drunken attorney, taken by Charles Grapewin. At least this film noir style frames Atwill in a couple of attractive shots, such as one in which the shadows of a venetian blind fall on him.

The Girl in 313 (1940)

This low-budget 20th Century Fox program-filler runs less than an hour and is another example of how Atwill, having signed a long contract with the studio, found himself being featured in films that were unworthy of him. If he had chosen instead to carry on freelancing, who knows what film roles might have come his way.

In *The Girl in 313*, he plays Henry Woodruff, owner of a high-class New York jewelry store that stages fancy catwalk-style parades to show off its range of products.

Atwill's eyes light up at the sight of the valuable jewel in *The Girl in 313*.

We soon learn, however, that all is not as it seems; Woodruff has a racket going whereby he arranges for pieces of his jewelry to be stolen so that he can claim the insurance. The plot becomes more complicated. Atwill has an accomplice in Kent Taylor, but is he really crooked or is he working for the police? And Florence Rice seems to be a jewel thief—but then again, maybe she too is really part of a police snare to trap Atwill.

Such plot intricacies are mildly engaging, but the direction never really whips up much tension. The director was Ricardo Cortez, better known as an actor and here making the last of seven films on which he served as director.

Atwill is never given a chance to get into his stride and do what he does best, but nevertheless he has a reasonable amount of screen time. He is a business-like villain, never a nasty or brutish one.

In his first scene, one of his catwalk models (Kay Aldridge) faints and then, in the confusion, has a $50,000 diamond necklace snatched from around her neck as she lies on the floor. A policeman (Jack Carson) wants everyone in the audience searched, but Atwill isn't keen: "These people are my guests. I can't have them embarrassed." It's a line of dialogue that seems to foreshadow a line delivered during his own real-life court case just a year down the line, when he tried to protect guests at one of his wild parties.

Most of his dialogue serves merely to progress the plot. Atwill suspects Rice of being an agent of the police, so he stages an incident to test her trustworthiness, deciding to cut and run when things get too hot. But he does appear in one or two brief scenes, which give him a chance to do something a little different.

In one, he takes Aldridge for a drink in a swanky nightclub. Wanting to be alone with Aldridge, he is annoyed when Rice and Taylor invite them to join their table, and he is even more irritated when his already-tipsy date starts ordering large amounts of Benedictine and brandy. Atwill gets the chance to do a bit of restrained light comedy as his facial gestures express annoyance and exasperation. He even does a triple take.

Kay Aldridge, Lionel Atwill, Kent Taylor and Joan Rice in *The Girl in 313*

Later, two policemen grill Taylor and Rice, but Atwill suddenly appears from the next room and thanks the policemen for their time. It turns out they aren't policemen at all: Atwill has set the whole thing up and takes great pleasure in introducing them as two small-time crooks and very bad actors. The ruse has been enacted to test whether Rice is really a crook or working for the police.

Another brief flash of the Atwill charisma occurs when he scrutinizes an elaborate piece of ruby jewelry. His eyes light up with just a little touch of mania as he exclaims, "Beautiful!" At film's end, he is deprived of a decent closing scene. We merely see his picture on a newspaper's front page with a headline that reads: "Police Round Up Jewel Ring."

The closing credits list his character as Russell Woodruff, even though throughout the film he has been referred to as Henry Woodruff. Was there a last minute re-write, perhaps to avoid offending a real-life Woodruff?

Charlie Chan's Murder Cruise (1940)

This becomes another entertaining episode in the series, with a plot that is so sneaky that most viewers will be unable to predict the identity of the killer. Charlie Chan (Sidney Toler) is always ready with a Chinese proverb to suit every situation, and he invokes some especially amusing ones in this episode. Much of the action takes place on a fog-enshrouded ocean liner, and the creepy murderer is a strangler who skulks through the shadows dressed in black cape and hat, sporting a grisly beard. He wouldn't look out of place in an early 1930s haunted house chiller. The various red herrings include Charles Middleton (Ming the Merciless in the *Flash Gordon* serials), Leo G. Carroll and Lionel Atwill.

Atwill, third-billed, is better served here than he was in *Charlie Chan in Panama*. It's a much more prominent role and—unusually—he gets to survive right up to the final scenes. He plays monocle-wearing, pipe-smoking Dr. Suderman, leader of a party of assorted tourists who are on a world cruise. Atwill emphasizes the character's Germanic origins by rolling the occasional 'r.'

Naturally, the script wants us to think that he is the killer. For example, when Chan asks Dr. Suderman to show him to the room where a murder victim is lying, Atwill aims one of his intense stares at the sleuth. And later, Dr. Suderman looks on with unusual concern as Chan examines a suitcase strap that has been used to murder a victim. It would have been extremely satisfying to see Atwill revealed as the caped strangler, but in fact it turns out to be two other characters, played by Don Beddoe and Leo G. Carroll.

One scene is unforgettable because it seems to have uncanny parallels with Atwill's notorious private life. It feels like we are catching a glimpse of one

Sidney Toler, Marjorie Weaver, Robert Lowery, Atwill and Victor Sen Young in *Charlie Chan's Murder Cruise*

Robert Lowery, Atwill, Cora Witherspoon, Charles Middleton, Clair Du Brey, Victor Sen Young and Sidney Toler in *Charlie Chan's Murder Cruise*

of the actor's so-called "wild orgies." Charles Middleton's Bible-bashing character warns us that, "Passengers on a long cruise are likely to grow lax in their moral conduct," and, sure enough, shortly afterwards, Atwill's Dr. Suderman decides to organize a party. As the party progresses, the guests, some clearly intoxicated, engage in a hobby horse race. They include two young women, and Atwill, sporting a jaunty fez-like party hat, gets more than a little excited as he shouts encouragement from the sidelines, watching them in their party dresses, mounted on wooden hobby horses and trying to push them across the floor.

"Come on, Curly Lion!" he calls out to one of the women, and then turns to Chan, and says, "That's a hot one!" It would not surprise me to learn that it was perhaps Atwill's idea to spice up the dialogue by adding this line.

It is once again uncanny to think, that in several of Atwill's film and stage appearances, moments exist that contain clear parallels to when he admitted lying in court. This film contains yet another such parallel. Although he knows a murder has taken place on board, Dr. Suderman decides to keep the fact from his party so as to avoid upsetting them. "I try to protect my clients from all unpleasantness," he says. It's almost as if he were using the line as a dress rehearsal for the moment, two years later, when his lawyer delivered his statement in court: "I lied like a gentleman to protect friends."

In another scene, Dr. Suderman invites Chan to be the judge at the hobby horse races, and he exits the scene with a long series of drawn-out chuckles. Laughing was an art at which Atwill excelled.

One brief but memorably macabre moment occurs as the passengers are all disembarking. A telegram boy arrives, shouting "Mr. Pendleton! Mr. Pendleton!"

"I'll take that," says Atwill.

"Are you Mr. Pendleton?" inquires the boy.

"There's Mr. Pendleton," responds Atwill grimly, pointing at a coffin that is being slid into a hearse.

Boom Town (1940)

Although Atwill's role in this film is very minor, it does nevertheless feature yet another of those uncanny coincidences which foreshadow events in his private life.

"That's a lie!" shouts Clark Gable, pointing an accusatory finger at Atwill, who is standing in a witness box in a courtroom. Is Lionel committing fictional perjury just a few months before he would do it for real in 1941? We will probably never know, because it seems this scene may have been cut short. Atwill never gets a chance to utter a single line of dialogue in this scene, and all we see is a shot of him leaving the witness box after Gable has accused him of lying.

The film runs a very long 114 minutes, so it may well be that an even longer version had to be cut down to make it a manageable length. It does seem unthinkable that the scriptwriter would go to all the trouble of maneuvering Atwill's character into the witness box yet not develop the scene. It seems even more unlikely when one recalls Atwill's powerhouse courtroom scene in *The Silent Witness* nine years earlier; here was an actor famous for one of the great

Atwill, Hedy Lamarr and Clark Gable in *Boom Town*

courtroom scenes of all time, and yet he is reduced to what must surely be filmdom's least memorable witness box appearance.

Boom Town is an engaging drama with strong performances by Spencer Tracy and Clark Gable as oil prospectors. They receive good support from Claudette Colbert as the girl caught in the middle. Hedy Lamarr adds some glamour, but her performance leaves much to be desired. Early scenes in a Midwest oil town, where all the streets are a foot deep in mud, are fun.

Exactly one hour into film, Atwill makes his first appearance. Big John McMasters (Gable) has struck oil, made plenty of money and is thinking of moving East to New York. He meets bowler-hatted New York businessman Harry Compton (Atwill), who tries to talk him out of it because he doesn't want the competition. A little later he is seen again, very briefly, at an oilman's convention. And in New York, Compton pops up again at a horse race, in high spirits when his horse wins. When McMasters' success threatens to put Compton out of business, he pulls a dirty trick and tips off the government about some of McMasters' less-than-legal practices, leading to his arrest. He is also seen in a brief series of cuts, his gloomy face part of a montage of shots that depicts the financial collapse of his company. His final appearance is the courtroom scene to which reference has already been made.

In none of these brief scenes does he get any lines of dialogue that are worth quoting here; nor does he have any impact on the plot. Fox loaned Atwill to MGM for this one, and although he was no doubt happy to keep working and earning, he must have known it was a waste of his talents. With its stellar cast, this film was hugely popular and seen by a vast audience, so it's a shame that it wasn't a more memorable showcase for him. He didn't even get a mention in the film's trailer.

The Great Profile (1940)

Early chapters in this book have several times bemoaned the fact that no filmic record survives of Atwill on the stage. But wait a minute—there is a means by which we can see him in action on the stage, in a way—in *The Great Profile*. Atwill plays an

Onstage Atwill and Mary Beth Hughes find themselves acting alongside a very drunk John Barrymore, in *The Great Profile.*

actor who is seen onstage during a rehearsal and then again later at the play's opening night. Unfortunately though, these glimpses of Atwill the stage actor don't give much of a hint of his former Broadway glories, because his contributions to these scenes are so brief.

In fact, this may be Atwill's least memorable film. John Barrymore lampoons his stage image outrageously, and it would have been marvelous to see Atwill doing the same, but he doesn't engage in the same wild hamming that Barrymore does. In truth, he never really does anything at all. He appears just three times in the film, with one of those appearances lasting but a few seconds.

His first scene takes place in a Chicago theater where a rehearsal is taking place. Barrymore, as alcoholic actor Evans Garrick, his wife Sylvia (Mary Beth Hughes) and goateed Dr. Bruce (Atwill) are the three players on the stage. When Garrick loses his temper about his costume and has a childish tantrum, Dr. Bruce merely turns his back on the situation and stands at the back of the stage while Garrick and Sylvia argue. What an insult to Atwill! Here we have a man who was once one of the greatest stage actors now required by the script merely to stand silently with his back to us.

His second scene is the play's opening night. After the intermission, Garrick enters the stage as drunk as a skunk. Sylvia and Dr. Bruce look horrified. Garrick throws off his overcoat revealing he is wearing only long johns underneath. Dr. Bruce steps forward and tries to cover him up. He then has a couple of inconsequential lines before making his exit.

Later he is glimpsed leaving the theater and bids good night to the stage door porter.

This is a shocking waste of Atwill's talents. If the film had been made after his court case, it would make sense that the studio might want him to keep a low profile, but this was released in 1940 before the scandal flared up. One senses that 20th Century Fox only gave him the part to keep him occupied, perhaps in response to complaints that they weren't keeping him busy enough.

John Barrymore makes a drunken stage entrance, crashing through a prop door to the horror of fellow actors Mary Beth Hughes and Atwill, in *The Great Profile.*

Lionel Atwill

It is possible that there was more to Atwill's role than we see here. Some sources state a running time of 87 minutes; one Internet source states 82 minutes. And yet the version commonly available only runs to 69 minutes. Are Atwill's best scenes missing?

Barrymore is terrific as a brain-addled has-been actor liable to go missing for days on booze-filled benders. He milks each line of dialogue for every bit of comic effect and ham that he can. His drunken stage performances are hysterical; in one of them he is in a wheelchair and accidentally rolls backwards off the front of the stage into the audience. He alone makes the film worth seeing.

Man Made Monster (1941)

Lionel Atwill gives one of his classic mad doctor performances in this hugely enjoyable chiller from Universal. The film has a simple story unpretentiously told, fast-paced, running just under an hour and features stylishly lit black-and-white camerawork. In other words, it's the perfect antidote to all the soulless, formulaic Hollywood blockbusters.

It never, however, gets close to the best of the 1930s chillers. The chief reason is that director George Waggner (who also directed *The Wolf Man* the same year) was only a mediocre talent, but it is also held back because in the 1940s all the studios toned down the horror content of their films, fearing another ban on the genre like that which had been imposed by Britain in 1936.

As Dr. Paul Rigas, Atwill conducts unorthodox experiments in which he subjects live animals to doses of electricity. Naturally, he's not satisfied with animal subjects and wants to experiment on a human being. Fortunately, along comes Dan McCormick (Lon Chaney), survivor of a crash in which a bus collided with an electricity pylon, killing all on board except him. Dr. Rigas decides it will be fun to pump McCormick so full of electricity that he turns into a glowing, brain-addled killing machine.

Director Waggner and cameraman Elwood Bredell knew that they had *Hollywood's maddest doctor* on the set and make the most of him, giving Atwill plenty of intense close-ups and lighting him eerily from below. Waggner, under a pseudonym, was also scriptwriter, and he makes sure that Atwill is given plenty of choice lines. In fact, Atwill gets to deliver what is without doubt the most depraved mad doctor speech of his career.

Atwill's first scene is memorable. Scientist Dr. John Lawrence (Samuel S. Hinds) walks into a shadowy laboratory where a figure in a white lab coat is hunched over some outlandish, sparking equipment, whose purpose is as yet unknown. An electric glow emanates from the equipment, constantly fading then growing brighter. H.J. Salter's background music—one of his better themes—neatly suggests that something *outré* is going on.

The hunched figure, wearing large, sinister goggles, stands up and shrugs as if his experiment has been a failure.

Dr. Paul Rigas (Atwill), Dynamo Dan McCormick (Lon Chaney, Jr.) and Dr. John Lawrence (Samuel S. Hinds) in *Man Made Monster*

"Paul, why don't you give this up?" asks Dr. Lawrence.

"It will work. I know it!" says Dr. Rigas, with creepy intensity.

"This theory of yours isn't science," says Lawrence, "it's black magic."

"I believe that electricity is life," responds Dr. Rigas. "That men can be motivated and controlled by electrical impulse, supplied by the radioactivities of the electron. That eventually a race of superior men can be developed, men whose only wants are electricity."

Rigas turns Dynamo Dan into a lumbering automaton in this U.S. lobby card from *Man Made Monster*.

"But man, you're challenging the forces of creation."

"The forces of creation! Bah!" exclaims Rigas, throwing up his hands in disgust. Rigas goes into more detail about his crazy, Nazi-like plans to create a breed of electrically charged super-slaves.

"Sometimes I think you're mad," says Dr. Lawrence.

"I am!" responds Rigas without a moment's hesitation, throwing off his goggles and giving the sort of wide-eyed smile that only a madman can give. It's one of the supreme mad doctor moments of Atwill's career.

"Today," he continues, "we hold a human heart in our hands and watch it beat! Who can tell what tomorrow's madness may be!"

Later, newspaper reporter Mark Adams (Frank Albertson) says of Dr. Rigas: "I don't like that guy … I'll bet he spent his childhood sticking pins in butterflies!"

In a long and well-staged sequence, Rigas straps Dan to his electro-thermostatic table beneath the glowing equipment and subjects him to a huge dose of electricity. The outcome: When Dan subsequently goes to pat a dog on the head, sparks fly from his hands onto the nose of the poor little pooch. An effective montage sequence follows, depicting further experiments in which Dan is dosed with ever-increasing amounts of electricity, intercut with shots of Rigas in his goggles manipulating the controls of his equipment. Rigas is so obsessed with his experiments that he even slips Dr. Lawrence a sedative to get him out of the way when he begins to suspect something is going on.

Rigas straps Dynamo Dan in for his final dose of electricity and unleashes another mad doctor speech: "This is our final experiment. If we're successful, we will have proven a theory, which will revolutionize the world! A theory that will silence completely those scoffers who babble of trivialities."

This is another well-staged *mad lab* sequence, and its result is that Dan now exudes a ghostly glow of electricity. Rigas puts him in a rubber suit to conserve his energy, gloating over his success: "I can give you life … or take it from you!"

Dr. Lawrence enters the lab and wants to know what is going on.

"You must be mad," he says to Rigas when he sees the glowing automaton that Dan has become.

Exclaims Rigas triumphantly: "Of course I am mad! I have conquered destiny! [He laughs madly.] Think of an army of such creatures! Doing the work of the world, fighting its battles. Look at him, the worker of the future, controlled by a superior intelligence! We must assemble all the great scientists and show them this creature!"

"I believe that electricity is life," rants Dr. Rigas in *Man Made Monster.*

Lawrence threatens to call the police, but Rigas refutes his allegation that he has effectively murdered McCormick.

"He'll live ... a beautiful existence! No pain, no sorrow!"

At Rigas' command, Dan strangles Lawrence.

Soon the police have charged Dan with murder and this gives rise to yet another of the many courtroom scenes that are sprinkled throughout Atwill's career—and, almost inevitably, there is an uncanny parallel with Atwill's real-life court case. In the witness box, Rigas claims that he was out of the room when the murder took place. In other words, he commits perjury—and just six months later, he would do it for real in front of a Los Angeles Grand Jury.

"Of course I'm mad," declares Dr. Rigas in *Man Made Monster.*

Atwill's best scene takes place when he discovers Anne Nagel snooping around in his shadowy laboratory in a flimsy white gown. The success of his experiments has turned him quite mad.

"May I help you?" he says with feigned politeness when he catches her red-handedly looking through his notes. In his mania, he tells her all about his experiments. Why shouldn't he? He is clearly intending to dispose of her.

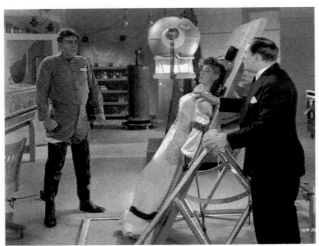

"Tonight," he gloats to her, "the whole world will be talking about Dan Mc-Cormick. Not just a handful of musty scientists, but the whole world!"

He takes an evil pleasure in admitting that he deliberately let Dan go to the electric chair. With an almost casual disdain, he admits that he was in control of Dan and ordered him to murder Lawrence.

"And they gave *him* a sanity test," says Nagel, appalled by Rigas' villainy.

"Yes," laughs Rigas, "ironical, isn't it?"

He then starts to back

"I've always found that the female of the species was more sensitive to electrical impulse," states Rigas to June (Anne Nagel) in *Man Made Monster*.

her up against his operating table. "You know, it's a curious fact," he continues, smiling with evil gusto the whole time, "but ever since my earliest experiments with rabbits and guinea pigs, I've always found that the female of the species was more sensitive to electrical impulse than was the male. It's fortunate that we met here!" He shoves her back onto the table. "Shall I show you how it was done?" he shouts, as he starts to strap her down.

It's the *exquisite villain* at his maddest, with Atwill delivering his lines superbly, his eyes ablaze with insanity. He acts with such intensity that he seems to believe every word he says. I believe that Atwill may have contributed to the dialogue in this speech. We may never be able to prove it, but Atwill's predilection for the risqué—indeed, the positively perverse—permeates every word of this exchange with Nagel. For me it is hard to imagine George Waggner coming up with dialogue that is so debauched.

Just in the nick of time, Dan, glowing with electrical energy, bursts in and saves the day. No longer under Rigas' control, Dan advances on him, forcing Rigas to take cover in an adjoining room. Unfortunately for Rigas, he grips the door handle at the same time as Dan grips the handle on his side. The result: Rigas gets fried.

This novel idea could have created one of Atwill's greatest death scenes. Unfortunately, the sequence must have been severely trimmed, making it far less powerful than it must have been as originally filmed. Perhaps Universal trimmed it, fearing it was so horrific it might cause another horror ban. Or perhaps the censor insisted on removing certain shots. Either way, all that remains is a very brief shot of Rigas standing rigidly. No shot exists of his hand touching the door, nor is a shot of his face as he gets electrocuted shown. Surely there must have been one originally? An even briefer shot follows in which he falls toward the camera. This latter shot is so brief, only half a second, that it suggests that the expression on Atwill's face was so ghastly that it was decided to snip it. Let's hope that one day someone will find the uncut version of this, because it must be a real powerhouse sequence.

Chaney gets a chance to act in the film's first half-hour, but once he becomes addicted to Atwill's electricity fixes, he is just a sluggish and slow-witted monster. John P. Fulton's special effects, which give Chaney an eerie glow, still look good today and must have been thrilling back in 1941 when nothing like it had been done before. The nighttime finale begins well, with Chaney picking

Dan interrupts Dr. Rigas' experiment on June, in *Man Made Monster*.

up Nagel in his arms and carrying her off through a forest. But the resolution is most disappointing, with Chaney getting snared on a barbed-wire fence, causing all the life-sustaining electricity to discharge from his body, killing him. Surely Waggner could have thought up something better than that?

The Mad Doctor of Market Street (1942)

This is a classic slice of Atwill at his B-picture, end-of-career best. The superb schlock title tells us we are in for a treat and, sure enough, Atwill is in just about every scene, knocking people out with chloroform, experimenting on resurrecting the dead and generally doing what mad doctors do best. The script gives him several energetic mad doctor speeches, and the camera frequently moves in for sinister close-ups, milking Atwill's persona for all its worth.

The first five minutes are excellent. The film opens with a stylish, rain-soaked shot of a cobbled street at night, with a sign that reads Market Street, lit up by flashes of lightning. A furtive, lone figure walks down some steps to a basement where he enters a shadowy apartment. Suddenly, from another room, Atwill emerges, eerily lit from below looking especially sinister in lab coat and beard. He is Dr. Ralph Benson, "Professor of Research," and soon we learn that he is conducting controversial experiments into suspended animation. His cash-strapped visitor is to be a well-paid guinea pig (played by Hardie Albright, who made a cuckold of Atwill in *The Song of Songs* back in 1933).

Dr. Benson, in best mad doctor fashion, can't resist showing off to his nervous patient. "You see, I've gone as far as I can in my scientific research among the lower animals," he says, indicating a monkey in a cage, "and my experiments in that field have met with complete success. But it is obvious that my findings will not be accepted by the medical world until they have first been demonstrated upon a … human being." The camera zooms in on Benson's smirking face as he utters those last two words.

As he continues describing his work, he gets increasingly excited, becoming almost Biblical in his choice of phrase: "Disease … the scourge of humanity … will be cast out!

Dr. Ralph Benson emerges, eerily lit, looking sinister in lab coat and beard, from *The Mad Doctor of Market Street.*

Human beings will be placed in a cataleptic state until a cure is affected. Then resuscitated and returned to normal life. Think of it, man! The span of human life will be prolonged indefinitely."

The patient gets onto a couch and then Hollywood's maddest doctor indulges in one of those irresistibly corny yet potent moments when he walks directly toward the camera lens, chloroform-soaked cloth in hand, a disquieting glint in his eye. The experiment is conducted, but it goes wrong and to Benson's dismay the patient dies. Just at that moment the police pull up in a car outside, and Dr. Benson decides that the best course of action is to flee out of a window at the back of his apartment. After this exciting beginning, the action cuts to an ocean liner at night. In the ballroom, a swanky dance is in progress and Dr. Benson looks on from the sidelines. He is now without his beard, smartly dressed in his best dinner jacket and bow tie, masquerading as Mr. Graham, an antiques dealer. A detective is on board trying to identify the murderer, but Graham engages him in some friendly conversation as they look out over a balcony rail—and then Graham hits him over the head and tips him overboard.

The action maintains its frenetic pace when the liner catches fire and everyone has to abandon ship. Graham gets into a lifeboat and finds himself washed up on a South Seas tropical island with fellow survivors, including Una Merkel, Nat Pendleton and Claire Dodd. Quite why the scriptwriters thought that setting a horror film on a tropical

island would be a good idea is a mystery. Possibly Universal made the film at the same time as *Pardon My Sarong* and the producers wanted to get their money's worth out of all the prop palm trees, feathered head-dresses and sarongs.

The survivors are captured by the natives who intend to throw them all on a fire. However, the chief's daughter has just died and Benson steps forward, claiming he can revive her. With a shot of adrenalin, he does just that, and cameraman Jerome

"You can't kill me, I tell you!" Atwill gets desperate at the climax of *The Mad Doctor of Market Street.*

Ash moves in for a couple of delicious extreme close-ups of Benson's face, an intensely maniacal glint in his eye. The girl revives and the natives revere Benson as a god. "You—God of Life! We—your slaves!" declares the native chief (played by Noble Johnson of *King Kong* fame).

From now on, Benson thoroughly enjoys his new position as island god. He is offered the chance of taking a young native girl as a wife but, in an exchange of dialogue that is seemingly at odds with the real-life Atwill, he rejects the offer, saying his research must come first. When he decides to experiment on a native girl, a poetic twist occurs to his usual tactic of approaching the camera with a chloroform-soaked rag—this time he does it with a chloroform-soaked tropical flower!

Atwill, Richard Davies, Nat Pendleton, Una Merkel and Claire Dodd in *The Mad Doctor of Market Street*

It's not long before he is pondering the prospect of marrying Claire Dodd, and to force her hand, he decides to put her boyfriend (Richard Davies) into suspended animation. So it's time for director Lewis to stage yet another chloroform shot, and this is the best of the three, with the grim-faced Benson advancing threateningly toward the viewer.

Dodd is on the receiving end of another of Benson's enjoyable mad doctor speeches: "You know, my dear, I shall be able to bring back to life a person who's been dead for three days or more. Just as the natives worship me, and call me the God of Life, so shall all the people of the Earth. Mark my words!"

However, Benson comes unstuck when a boy drowns and the natives give him until sunset to revive him, or they will strip him of his God-status. Benson knows that

The stare that made Atwill the maddest doctor of them all, in *The Mad Doctor of Market Street*.

he can't bring the boy back to life and he gets a terrific series of panic-stricken, sweaty-browed, extreme close-ups, as it dawns on him that he is going to be burnt alive. When the natives grab him to take him away, he shrieks, "You can't … you can't kill me, I tell you … I'm God of Life, remember? No, let me go! Let me go! You can't kill me! I'm God of Life! I'll bring him back!"

This thrilling moment is acted to perfection by Atwill and recalls that mesmerizing outburst in *The Silent Witness* way back at the start of his film career when he yelled desperately at the courtroom judge.

Mad Doctor of Market Street is never for a moment in the same class as the great horror films of the 1930s. Direction by Joseph H. Lewis (soon to become a B-director of renown) is routine and the plot is frequently daft. But as a vehicle for Lionel Atwill, the film is hugely enjoyable and essential viewing for his fans. The musical score is a treat. As well as Hans J. Salter's usual clunking horror riff, we are frequently treated to the haunting strains of Franz Waxman's music from *Bride of Frankenstein.*

To Be or Not to Be (1942)

This Ernst Lubitsch comedy is regarded as a classic in some circles, but for Lionel Atwill fans, it's yet another occasion where the actor is shamefully under-used. Carole Lombard and Jack Benny play a Polish husband-and-wife acting team who do their bit to resist the German occupation in war-torn Warsaw. All manner of comic situations arise, with Lombard pretending to be a spy and Benny masquerading as a doctor in league with the Nazis.

Atwill plays Rawitch, one of the actors in the troupe. The part had enormous potential, as the character is a dreadful ham given to overacting. The thought of seeing Atwill deliberately over-acting is a delicious one, but no scenes exist that developed this angle. Rawitch has so little screen time that very little is ever made of him.

Rawitch (Atwill) to Greenberg (Felix Bressart): "How dare you call me a ham," from *To Be or Not to Be*

On two brief occasions, we see Atwill dressed up onstage as King Claudius. In royal costume, he looks tremendous; over a long robe he wears a very regal, furred cape, and on his gray-haired head is a crown. But he is only ever seen in long shot, and his only purpose is to utter one line of Shakespeare ("O heavy burthen!") before leaving the stage to make way for Jack Benny to come on and deliver his, "To be or not to be" speech. Rawitch does get one droll moment in this outfit; he strides along one of the theater's corridors intoning "Mi, mi, mi, mi, mi" to prepare his voice before going onstage—and then walks into an overhead lamp, his crown clanking into it. How extraordinary, though, that Lubitsch has gone to all the trouble of having the costume department dress up the former Broadway legend so magnificently, and yet he doesn't bother to instruct cameraman Rudolph Mate to shoot a close image of him. Still, at least we see him in a stage role (of sorts) and can get a tiny inkling of what it might have been like to watch the Broadway Atwill.

Atwill's most memorable moment comes early in the film. A Jewish member of the troupe of actors turns to Atwill and says, "What you are, I wouldn't eat."

Lionel Atwill

"How dare you call me a ham," retorts Rawitch indignantly.

He is just a background figure in most of his scenes but is given the occasional chance to shine. "Well, you certainly fooled the English, didn't you?" he says with rather too much feigned *bonhomie* to Siletsky (Stanley Ridges), and then can't resist throwing in some poetry:

> The British Lion will drink his tea,
> From saucers made in Germany!

In *To Be or Not to Be* the actor Rawitch plays the part of King Claudius in Shakespeare's *Hamlet.*

He laughs heartily at his own good humor, until a colleague signals to him that he is overdoing things and, with a quick, "Heil Hitler," leaves the room.

He is provided with more substantial dialogue in another scene when he and the other actors are all masquerading as Nazi officers and march into the office of Sig Ruman, playing an actual Nazi officer. They are there to give Ruman a mock dressing-down, in order to whisk Jack Benny away to safety. Rawitch again gets carried away and has to be stopped in mid-speech by one of his colleagues.

The film had considerable poignancy at the time of its release, because Lombard had just been killed in an airplane crash.

Ghost of Frankenstein (1942)

In this fourth episode in Universal's *Frankenstein* series, Lionel Atwill plays one of his archetypal mad doctor roles. As Dr. Theodore Bohmer, he gets plenty of opportunities to don a white lab coat and play around with bizarre scientific apparatus. He even gets some choice mad doctor lines: "I must warn you," he says to Ygor (Bela Lugosi) just before removing his patient's brain, "this operation may not be successful. This may be the end of everything." And director Erle C. Kenton gives us a classic Atwill image as Bohmer, in surgeon's white gown, hat and mask, holds a cloth soaked in chloroform and slowly brings it gradually closer toward the camera.

Remarkably, in Atwill's very first scene, his dialogue appears to mirror the scandal that had so recently grabbed the headlines. Ludwig Frankenstein (Cedric Hardwicke) and Bohmer are dressed in surgeons' garb, and stand beside a patient on whom they have just operated. Frankenstein chooses to remind Bohmer of a past misdemeanor: "Medical science has advanced a great deal since you made your experiment, Dr. Bohmer. It's ... unfortunate that it had such tragic consequences."

In response, Bohmer looks hurt and snaps off one of his surgical gloves aggressively. "But you blazed a trail," continues Frankenstein. "It was you who pointed the way."

Bohmer seems to cheer up a bit in reaction to these complements, but as Frankenstein walks away, his true mood is revealed; in medium close-up an expression of bit-

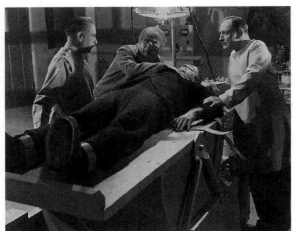

A gathering of grostesques in *Ghost of Frankenstein*: Dr. Frankenstein (Cedric Hardwicke), Ygor (Bela Lugosi), Dr. Bohmer (Atwill) and the Monster (Lon Chaney, Jr.)

terness crosses his face and he angrily throws aside the other surgical glove.

His assistant Dr. Kettering (Barton Yarborough) confers with him: "Why live always in the past, Dr. Bohmer? You've allowed that one mistake of yours to embitter your whole life."

"A mistake?" responds Bohmer, "No, no, no, no. Just a slight miscalculation, that's all." He leans on a piece of electrical equipment, a shadow falling across his face in classic film noir style. "In those days, I was the master and Frankenstein was just the pupil." He concludes his musing by repeating a line and loading it with all the significance he can muster: "But I made a slight miscalculation."

Logic tells us that the script and dialogue would have been written long before Atwill was cast in the role of Dr. Bohmer, and yet these lines seem to suggest that the actor is speaking to his fans and the public, acknowledging the lurid details that had so recently hit the headlines. There is no evidence that Atwill had any input into the script, yet can it be mere coincidence that these lines mirror events in his private life so closely? A look at the shooting script (as published by Magicimage in 1990) reveals that, surprisingly, Atwill's character originally had even more lines of dialogue that seem to refer deliberately to his recent court appearance. As originally planned, Dr. Bohmer's dialogue with Kettering continues:

> And what happened to me! I was discredited, disgraced … They took
> my license away from me … forbid me to practice.

The shooting script follows this with more dialogue that failed to make it into the completed film, with Dr. Bohmer describing himself as:

> … a dishonored and embittered man … I made a mistake … I was
> betrayed, dishonored.

Everyone on the Universal lot would have known of Atwill's high-profile court case, so is it going too far to imagine that scriptwriter W. Scott Darling wrote these lines with Atwill in mind for the role? Or is it perhaps possible that he and Atwill got together at some point during the scriptwriting process? All this is conjecture, of course, and the similarities may be accidental—but if so, it's an astonishing twist of fate that the script should be written in this way.

Penned after Atwill's first court appearance but before the subsequent one in which he was charged with perjury, Darling's dialogue even contains an uncanny prophecy of things to come. When Dr. Bohmer laments that he was forbidden to practice, neither Atwill not Darling could have known that in a few short months the actor would find himself forbidden from acting—by the Hays Office.

If all this is mere coincidence, then it is another of the many that run throughout Atwill's career. On the other hand, might this scene be another of those

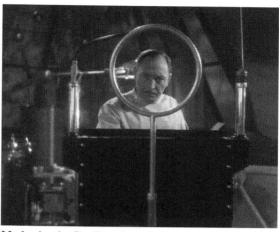

Mad scientist **Dr. Theodore Bohmer** at work in *Ghost of Frankenstein*

many occasions where Atwill contributed bits of business to his films, working closely with the director to reshape his lines? We will probably never know for sure what contribution, if any, Atwill made to the script. Since his career was now in decline and his role in this movie was a supporting one, one might not expect him to command sufficient clout in the film industry to influence the script. And yet it is impossible to watch these scenes without feeling that we are watching Atwill saying to the public, "Okay, we all know what happened, but I can handle it."

Ghost of Frankenstein is great fun from beginning to end. Thoughtful set design and camerawork make it look very classy. Atwill, Hardwicke and Bela Lugosi are all actors of great presence and lift the production. But the film is let down by Lon Chaney,

Bohmer can only stand idly by as the Monster demonstrates his power before his creator Dr. Frankenstein, in *Ghost of Frankenstein.*

Jr., who inexcusably fails to give the Monster any touches of character or pathos. Had his Monster shone in the way that Karloff's did, then this would be a film to cherish. The plot is deliciously crazy, with various characters all wanting different brains transplanted into the Monster's head. Frankenstein wants to transplant Kettering's brain, Ygor wants his own brain in there and the Monster wants to have the brain of a little girl he has befriended!

Evelyn Ankers is on the receiving end of some of the script's most enjoyably daft devices. In one priceless moment, she sees the faces of the Monster and Ygor staring in at her through a window. What's her means of dealing with the threat? She draws the curtains! And later, when the Monster creeps

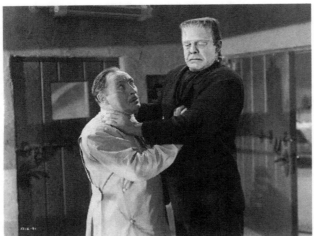

The Frankenstein Monster thinks that Bohmer has deliber- ately caused him to go blind, in *Ghost of Frankenstein*.

up behind her, Hardwicke calls out to her to run away. What does she do? She runs straight into the Monster's arms!

Atwill gets a fair amount of screen time, although he plays second fiddle to Hardwicke. He shows his nobler side in a good exchange between the two when Frankenstein asks for Bohmer's aid in dissecting the Monster, but Bohmer is horrified at the idea and refuses. But the muddled script later chooses to forget this noble streak and has Bohmer succumb readily to Ygor's tempting suggestions that he could redeem his tarnished reputation and become head of the medical profession.

"You weave a pretty fairy tale, crooked neck," responds Bohmer. Ygor suggests that they should team up, implant Ygor's brain into the Monster and then the pair of them can "rule the state, even the whole country!" Bohmer's eyes stare off into the distance as he considers the mad proposal.

There is a touching—and ironic—exchange between Frankenstein and Bohmer just after the brain transplant has been performed. Frankenstein thanks Bohmer sincerely for his expert assistance. Bohmer seems genuinely surprised by this show of gratitude: "That's very nice of you, sir," he says. The irony lies in Bohmer's deception of Frankenstein by substituting Ygor's brain for that of Kettering.

Atwill gets one of his more memorable death scenes. When the Monster, now with Ygor's brain, realizes that he has lost his sight, he turns on Bohmer, thinking the surgeon has deliberately tricked him. He throws him against the laboratory equipment, which throws up a shower of sparks, electrocuting him. It's a dramatic death shown in three effective shots angled from below. The third of these has Bohmer, open-mouthed and rigid, falling toward the camera—an action performed by Atwill himself, not a stunt double. It's a fitting end to "the maddest doctor of them all."

The Frankenstein Monster throws Dr. Bohmer against laboratory equipment, electrocuting him, at the conclusion of *Ghost of Frankenstein*.

The Strange Case of Dr. Rx (1942)

Posters promoting this film boasted a huge close-up of Lionel Atwill, eerily lit from below, sporting a sinister pair of thick-lensed spectacles. The aim was to make audiences think that he was going to be the villain in this detective whodunit. In fact, the film tries so hard to make us suspect he is the mysterious Dr. Rx that we soon realize it must be someone else. For example, when Patric Knowles gets abducted, his captor wears a hood that hides his face. It's an obvious device and eventually, of course, Atwill's character turns out to be just a red herring. As such, it's yet another instance of the actor's talents being shamefully under-utilized.

The film rolls along quite entertainingly, with Patric Knowles and Anne Gwynne playing a sophisticated couple who also does a bit of sleuthing. Comedy is supplied by Mantan Moreland as Knowles' valet, doing his wide-eyed routine very amusingly, and Shemp Howard (one of The Three Stooges) not so funny as a dumb cop. Bodies keep turning up with a note on them signed "Rx" and Knowles is determined to find the killer.

Most of Atwill's scenes are insultingly short. For example, 15 minutes into the film, he makes his first, very brief appearance in a courtroom scene. When the defendant suddenly collapses, Atwill rushes forward. "I'm a doctor," he says, and coming from Atwill, it's a remark that audiences cannot fail to enjoy.

He is glimpsed a couple of times driving a car and following characters around, but Atwill has no dialogue and audiences are by this time beginning to wonder if he is going to get any good scenes at all.

The plot seems to run out of steam about three-quarters of the way through and, as if the scriptwriter realized this, a sudden change of tone occurs. In fact, it's a total change of genre, and the film becomes a full-blown horror movie, with the abducted Knowles strapped down to an operating trolley, which a masked madman wheels through a laboratory full of sparking equipment … and housing a mean looking caged gorilla called Nbongo. The madman informs his victim that he is going to do a brain-swap operation, giving Knowles the gorilla's brain. Such a foul deed would be very much in Atwill's line, but the voice that does all the talking is clearly not Atwill's.

Only at the denouement does Atwill finally get some reasonable screen time.

Lionel Atwill as the sinister Dr. Fish in *The Strange Case of Dr. Rx*

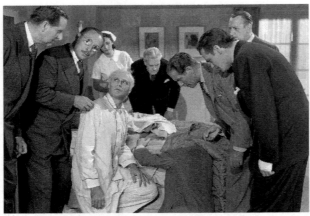

Knowles is recuperating in bed, his hair now turned pure white from the trauma. A policeman and various other characters are gathered round. Dr. Fish (Atwill) is brought in and right up until the last moment the script still tries to make us think he is the villain. But finally the real killer gives himself away (quite unnecessarily) and commits suicide. Knowles whips off his wig of white hair and they all live happily ever after.

Patric Knowles (in pajamas) has become a white-haired old man as a result of a terrifying experience, while Dr. Fish (second from left) looks on, from *The Strange Case of Dr. Rx.*

Dr. Fish now reveals that all along he has been working alongside Knowles on the case. The thick-lensed glasses are taken off—it seems he didn't actually need to wear them after all, and they were just part of a disguise (no, it's never explained why he should need a disguise).

He now becomes a jovial, avuncular fellow, puffing happily on his pipe, and he helps Knowles explain to the police how the murderer killed by means of a pen that could fire a poison dart, the effect of which was to leave the victim with the appearance of having been strangled. The plot seems quite crazy.

One character, talking about Atwill's character, asks Knowles, "Where did you catch this fish?" The feeble pun on his character's name causes much hilarity, and Atwill laughs extremely convincingly, even in a situation like this, when the joke isn't funny.

In all, Atwill probably gets a total of no more than two minutes screen time throughout the whole film. How the mighty had fallen.

The great Jack Otterson was art director, but nothing appears to equal his memorable work in *Son of Frankenstein*. The director was William Nigh, a routine talent who also helmed other low-budget horror films such as *The Ape* (1940, with Boris Karloff) and *Black Dragons* (1942, with Bela Lugosi).

The Spanish one-sheet poster featured a particularly striking image of Atwill.

Ray "Crash" Corrigan, who made a living playing gorillas and aliens in rubber suits, was Nbongo.

Pardon My Sarong (1942)

Today this seems like a fairly wretched Abbott and Costello vehicle, and yet incredibly it was the second-highest grossing film of 1942. I loved this comedy duo 30 years ago, but the duo has dated very badly, with Costello's screeching and squawking now serving only to annoy. And was Abbott's constantly abusive treatment of Costello ever that funny? About one in 20 of the gags are still amusing; that means audiences have to sit through a lot of routines which are plain dull.

Lionel Atwill (billed eighth in the opening credits and fifth in the closing credits) is Varnoff (never referred to as Dr. Varnoff, although some reviewers state this), a very forgettable villain who is after jewels on an uncharted tropical island. We don't encounter him until halfway through the film. He wears a dapper white suit and wide-brimmed hat. Atwill does his best to appear interested in the proceedings but must have been appalled by the low quality of script and dialogue.

In several perfunctory scenes, he is called on to converse with the natives, to speak over the radio to his henchmen and to arrange to have Costello sacrificed at the local temple. What must have been going through the actor's mind? He had just been through the toughest year of his life (so far) and now he was reduced to this role, making a mockery of his earlier achievements onstage and his classic screen performances opposite Marlene Dietrich and others. Was he bitter, or was he perhaps just glad to be still working in his *mellow* years, with the cash still rolling in?

In his opening scene, he disturbs Robert Paige and Virginia Bruce who have been snooping around in the overturned boat, which he uses as his office. To Bruce, he says, "The ancient treasure of this island fascinates me" and his stare lingers on her just a little longer than is necessary. Is it my imagination or does the actress look uncomfortable, perhaps thinking about the alleged wild activities of which Atwill had been accused?

In another scene, Paige uses Varnoff's radio to speak to his henchmen, and he does an impression of Atwill's voice—except that it sounds *nothing* like Atwill, just a generic English accent. Brave try, though.

In the less-than-funny closing scenes, Atwill is on board a motorboat engaged in a fistfight with Costello. At one point he is viciously twisting Costello's shoe, only to realize that Costello isn't in it. Handled better, it could have been a funny moment. Eventually he dives over board, and that is the last we see of him. Yet another instance of an Atwill villain not getting the closing scene he deserved.

The film is enlivened (but not much) by a few split-screen shots of a miniature temple on a hill. In

Varnoff (Atwill) and Algey Shaw (Bud Abbott) in *Pardon My Sarong*

one extremely eye-catching long shot of a cliff-face with a huge carved face at the top, Costello swings out on a vine from an opening in the cliff wall. If only there could have been more of this type of imaginative fantasy.

At the climax a long scene takes place in an elaborate temple set. This appears to have been converted from the memorable one used in earlier Universal productions *The Mummy's Hand* and *Green Hell*. There is also a great tap dancing routine performed by Tip, Tap and Toe, with one of the three dancers, Ray Winfield, doing some neat moves which prefigure Michael Jackson's sliding moonwalk, coming off as being more elaborate and far superior.

Varnoff is about to get his come-uppance in *Pardon My Sarong*.

Cairo (1942)

This MGM musical spy comedy is rarely seen—and for a good reason; script, dialogue and direction are all so mediocre that it is often a chore to watch. Robert Young and Jeanette MacDonald each think the other is a German spy, leading to a long series of less-than-inventive comic scenes. The script is full of knowing film references that come across as contrived rather than witty.

Sixth-billed Lionel Atwill is a monocle-wearing Nazi listed in the credits as "Teutonic Gentleman" and it is one of his most forgettable roles. He made the film after his first court appearance but before the second one, which nearly ended his career. It is another example of the legendary stage star appearing in a film that is less than worthy of him. Still, he was being paid $1,750 per week by 20th Century Fox, who loaned him to MGM for this effort, and the terms of his contract probably meant he wasn't in a position to turn it down. He could probably live with the scriptwriter's failure to come up with a name for the character.

He has only four short scenes in this 100-minute film.

In the first, he is sitting in a hidden room, puffing on a big cigar. (Was there ever a film in which Atwill didn't smoke?) The best thing about the scene is that Atwill has fun barking some vicious orders at fellow Nazi-sympathizer Mona Barrie, of whom he clearly disapproves. "My dear lady, tomorrow night will see the successful completion of your mission ... Now forget your feminine distaste for what you don't understand long enough to tell us what conceivable advantage was there in not killing the young man?"

When she suggests discussing it later, he snaps back, "We'll discuss it now."

When she begins to leave, he barks, "Sit down!"

She shows no interest in watching Eduardo Cianelli demonstrate how he can make a radio-controlled model plane fly into a block of steel and destroy it, but Atwill will not let her leave.

Lionel Atwill

"Sit down!" he snaps a second time, louder than before. She gives a speech about the glories of Nazism, and again says she is leaving.

"I said sit down!" barks Atwill this time with such a vicious stare that she complies. The demonstration is carried out and, when the plane hits the steel block and explodes, Atwill leaps out of his chair with delight, crying out, "Bravo, Ahmed!"

Ahmed Ben Hassan (Eduardo Ciannelli) demonstrates his deadly model airplane to Mrs. Morrison (Mona Barrie) and the Teutonic gentleman (Atwill), in *Cairo*.

Atwill is not seen again for about 40 minutes. Robert Young spies on the villains and Atwill gets a few unremarkable lines, which he speaks from inside a car, barely visible. Young is captured and driven to one of the great pyramids. Here Atwill, stylishly dressed in white summer suit and matching fedora, has his final scenes. He strikes a tuning fork on a wall, causing a gigantic brick to slide open and reveal a secret chamber.

"As long as I live," exclaims Atwill, hugely impressed, "high C will remain in my memory!"

Young says he has been a dope for not realizing earlier that they are all Nazis. "Anyone with half a brain could have seen you were a Nazi," he says to Barrie.

"How fortunate for us that you have such a limited supply," quips Atwill, bantering with villainous relish.

Atwill allows Young to escape and fly off in a plane—because it is the radio-controlled one that Atwill and his cronies are going to fly into a U.S. battleship. He makes a pretense of trying to shoot him as he flees, but he fires into the air and lets out one of his wonderfully earthy belly laughs. In the nick of time MacDonald and the police break into the hidden lair, and Young parachutes to safety.

It's all staged in a less-than-thrilling manner. Not only is Atwill deprived of a worthy death scene, he doesn't even get to say any final lines. He is simply frisked by the police and arrested.

Night Monster (1942)

As with *The Strange Case of Dr. Rx*, released earlier the same year by the same studio, Universal's posters promoting this film featured a large, eerie close-up of Atwill looking sinister. Once again, the aim was to lure audiences into theaters with expectations of seeing this great villain in action. And once again, one can't help thinking that those same audiences must have felt cheated by the fact that the actor is reduced to playing a very minor red herring with hardly any screen time. The same is true of Bela Lugosi,

The U.S. Window Card poster mistakenly suggested that its stars, Lionel Atwill and Bela Lugosi, would be the chief villains.

who was also awarded a sinister close-up on the posters but ended up playing a lowly butler.

What makes this state of affairs even more disappointing is that the script features two macabre characters that seem tailor-made for Atwill and Lugosi—and yet the parts were given to other actors. Ingston, the crippled central figure, would have been ideal for Atwill, who had famously played similar wheel-chair-bound, revenge-plotting characters in *Mystery of the Wax Museum* and *Beggars in Ermine*. The part of Agor Singh, an exotic Eastern mystic, would have suited Lugosi to the teeth. And yet the roles were given to Ralph Morgan and Nils Asther, respectively.

Atwill and Lugosi were top-billed, so what thought processes went on at Universal that ended up giving both their stars minor roles? Might we assume they deliberately did not give their two horror stars the bogeyman roles for fear that the plot's denouement would be too predictable? Or did some scriptwriter think he was being awfully clever by overturning audience expectations so fundamentally? If he did, then he was completely wrong, because if one imagines *Night Monster* with Atwill and Lugosi in the parts of Ingston and Agor Singh, then the film might have been something of a minor classic.

Even so, *Night Monster* is thoroughly enjoyable and, if audiences are in the right mood, they will enjoy every daft, creaky minute of it. Murders are happening at a spooky old house and the clichés and gimmicks are laid on thick and fast. There is a higher-than-usual collection of suspects and victims, including paraplegic Ralph Morgan, Eastern mystic Nils Asther, creepy butler Bela Lugosi, wisecracking chauffeur Leif Erickson and several others. Photography is classy; note for example a scene in the library in which flickering firelight illuminates the characters. A totally ludicrous sequence occurs in which Asther conjures up a kneeling skeleton. An unforgettably gruesome scene appears in which the bedcovers are pulled back from Morgan to reveal that he is not paralyzed at all. In fact he has no legs below his knees, and for good measure he detaches a prosthetic arm as well.

For Atwill fans this is a disappointment. It's probably one of the most forgettable roles of his entire career, even though he is second billed. He plays pompous Doctor King, one of three doctors who, we learn, operated unsuccessfully on Morgan and left him a hopeless cripple. We would expect Atwill to be a murder suspect, but in fact he's a murder victim and gets bumped off pretty quickly after arriving at the old house. He gets to throw some good exasperated glances at one of his colleagues, who has a habit of talking *ad nauseam* about his glandular experiments. And he demonstrates once again what a master he was at delivering a hearty laugh; this time it is in response to Morgan telling him his theory about how lost limbs can be re-grown. At least the exchange gives rise to one of his better lines of dialogue: "If I have been dragged down here merely to witness the cheap sideshow tricks of a charlatan, I beg to be excused." And he stomps angrily out of the room. This is 28 minutes into film, and he is not seen again. When his body is discovered, what a shame that his corpse is kept just out of frame, because a character says of it, "The horrible way his face is twisted. Those eyes ... !"

A gathering of suspects in *Night Monster*: **Frank Reicher, Leif Erickson, Ralph Morgan (in wheelchair), Francis Pierlot, Atwill, Nils Asther, Don Porter and Bela Lugosi**

Sherlock Holmes and the Secret Weapon (1942)

Atwill was badly served by many of his 1940s films, but on this occasion he was given a role into which he could really sink his teeth: Sherlock Holmes' archenemy Professor Moriarty. This film is one of the more entertaining entries in the detective series, partly because it strays luridly into mad doctor territory, boasting a marvelous scene that features some implied but nevertheless horrific blood-letting. How this managed to sneak past the normally squeamish censor is a mystery.

This film looks classy throughout, thanks to good camerawork by Les White and Jack Otterson's sets. The shadowy steps that lead up to Moriarty's dockside hideout are clearly the work of the same set designer who created the marvelous sets of *Son of Frankenstein*. The pace is brisk, the plot always catches interest and Basil Rathbone is excellent as Holmes.

Moriarty (whose name is carelessly misspelled "Moriarity" in the closing credits) is rarely seen in the film's first half—apart from a shadowy mugging in a passageway, when the attacker doesn't just strike his victim over the head, he follows it up with some enthusiastic strangling too. But once Moriarty has played his cards and revealed himself about midway through the film, he becomes a prominent figure, featuring in several memorable scenes, relishing some face-to-face encounters with Holmes and doing full justice to some full-blooded dialogue. In fact, he is center-stage throughout the last 12 minutes of the film, a thrilling final section that contains some of Atwill's best screen villainy. In one scene he even gets to play the mad doctor, donning a surgeon's white gown.

He wears ghastly prosthetic eyelids, and Holmes describes him to Kaaren Verne thus: "A large man, his eyes heavy-lidded, a thin film over the pupils ..." To which Verne replies: "His eyes—they were like a snake's."

Atwill's Moriarty openly admits that he enjoys villainy for its own sake and relishes the chance to pit his wits against Holmes. His scenes with Rathbone are delicious games of cat-and-mouse, with both parties thinking they have the upper hand until another twist is added to the mix.

For example, during their first encounter—in which Atwill gets a chilling extreme close-up—he is clearly delighted that they are face-to-face again. In fact, he is so

delighted that he lets out one of those delightful chuckles. "Just like old times, eh?" he quips, "the battle of wits, of superior intellects." Holmes mentions the missing scientist, giving Moriarty an opportunity to indulge himself: "Valuable as your doctor and his code are to my business, I think my main interest in this affair is the chance it gives me to battle with you again."

A delicious moment occurs when Moriarty pulls out a pistol and Holmes expresses disappointment that Moriarty is going to be so commonplace as to shoot him. "Come now, this is not Professor Moriarty, the master criminal I once knew. A dock rat could do as much."

The snake-eyed Professor Moriarty (Atwill) in *Sherlock Holmes and the Secret Weapon*

Moriarty enjoys the accusation, seeing it as a chance for him to go one better. "Did you think I was going to shoot you, Mr. Holmes. Oh ho … tsk, tsk, tsk … dear me, no. This is simply to prevent a troublesome scene." It's a memorable exchange of dialogue and ends with Moriarty having Holmes gagged and sealed in a wooden box that he plans to have taken out to sea and thrown overboard.

A brief torture scene occurs in which Moriarty tries to get information out of Dr. Tobel (William Post, Jr.). Moriarty and his henchmen hold him down and keep repeating, "What is the name of the fourth man?" Moriarty, standing at the foot of the bed, grabs the victim's legs, pulling them toward him. The victim screams in pain. Now, much as it is always a pleasure to see Atwill getting up to a bit of brutality, on this occasion it is not clear exactly what he is doing to the victim. Just grabbing his legs and pulling him to the foot of the bed seems less like a torture and more like a bedtime romp. Perhaps the original scene was more horrific but Universal was forced to tone it down?

Having captured Holmes a second time, Moriarty takes great pleasure in explaining to him, with utter confidence, that no chance of escape exists, no chance of any passer-by hearing him can occur and that Scotland Yard will never find their location. His confidence is such that he tells his hoods to let go of Holmes and lets him walk around the room freely. This scene and what follows is an example of the *exquisite villain* doing what he does best. Even though Rathbone probably gets most of the best lines, it is still one of the most memorable exchanges of dialogue in Atwill's screen career, and it is worth quoting some of it.

The two enemies sit down in armchairs, and converse as if they were old friends having a fireside chat.

"Now Holmes, what shall it be? The gas chamber, the cup of hemlock, or just a simple bullet through your brain?"

"You disappoint me, Professor."

"Indeed?"

"Yes," responds Holmes, calmly reaching for a cigarette and lighting it. "Somehow I always thought that in the end, you'd prove to be just an ordinary cutthroat."

"You know me better, Holmes."

"Gas … poison … bul-

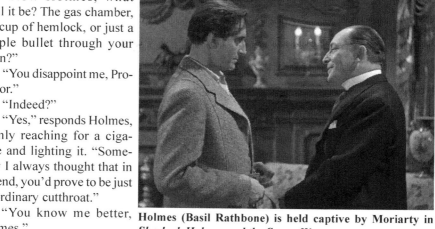

Holmes (Basil Rathbone) is held captive by Moriarty in *Sherlock Holmes and the Secret Weapon.*

lets," says Holmes, mocking these common devices. "I assure you, Professor, were our positions reversed, I should have something more colorful, more imaginative to offer."

"I am satisfied to be the winner," replies Moriarty. "I shall be alive …"

Holmes baits Moriarty further by declaring again that he would be the more imaginative executioner.

"And what, my good Mr. Holmes, could you have conceived that would have been much more colorful?"

Holmes then describes the process of draining five pints of blood from a man. "I should have you placed on an operating table, inject a needle into your veins and slowly draw off your life's blood."

"The needle to the last, eh, Holmes?" smiles Moriarty, sitting back in his armchair and relishing every moment. (This is a knowing reference to Conan Doyle's original stories that Holmes uses opiates.)

"The needle to the last, eh, Holmes?" quips Moriarty in *Sherlock Holmes and the Secret Weapon.*

"Slowly, drop by drop, the blood would be drawn from your body," continues Holmes. "You would be aware of every exquisite second to the very end. You would be watching yourself die scientifically, noting every reaction and in full possession of your faculties."

Moriarty's sadistic tendencies are aroused by this image. Although he stays externally calm, he taps his fingers on the arm of his chair in a way that hints at inner excitement. His eyebrows raise, and he smiles.

"Interesting," he says with huge understatement.

Then Moriarty seizes the upper hand: "You've played into my hands, Mr. Sherlock Holmes." He rises to his feet and reveals that he just happens to have "a fully equipped hospital" in the room next door.

This fine scene is followed (after a brief cut to Watson and Inspector Lestrade) by a sequence that finds Atwill now garbed in the mad doctor's white gown. This time Atwill gets all the good lines. Holmes is strapped to an operating table while Moriarty and two of his goons look down at him.

Moriarty grabs his captive Holmes' legs in the odd torture scene from *Sherlock Holmes and the Secret Weapon.*

"Drop by drop, Holmes," coos Moriarty ecstatically, "drop by drop." He sighs loudly. "In a way I'm almost sorry. You were a stimulating influence to me, but it was obvious to me that I should win in the end." He reaches down to his semi-conscious patient and almost lovingly lifts one of his eyelids, checking on his condition. "Closer to the end, Holmes, closer and closer!" How Moriarty enjoys every minute of his final victory over his archenemy.

"Each second a few more drops leave your desiccated body! You can feel them, can't you? You're perfectly conscious, aren't you, Holmes?" Atwill smiles insanely while speaking these three lines; this is Atwill at his perverted finest, hinting at unspeakable depths of sadistic depravity.

But Holmes isn't finished yet. "I shall be conscious long after you are dead, Moriarty."

"Hah!" responds Moriarty with a laugh. "Still the same old swaggering, conceited Sherlock Holmes!"

Needing to escape, Moriarty realizes there isn't time to drain the final drops of blood from Holmes and that he needs to finish things more quickly. He grabs a revolver. "You'll have to forgive the crudity my friend. This is only the *coup de grace*!"

Watson and Lestrade break in at the last moment. Moriarty is shot in the hand and director Roy William Neill allows him a delicious close-up. It's a fine example of how Atwill could exude sheer evil, despite doing very little with his face.

The U.S. insert poster

Lionel Atwill

It looks like the game is up for Moriarty, but he flees behind a sliding panel. Lestrade and Watson rush out to rescue Dr. Tobel. Moriarty re-emerges from the secret compartment, walks to another room and activates another secret door. He is about to step into it when Holmes emerges from it, gun in hand. Another brief battle of wits ensues, until Watson momentarily distracts Holmes, allowing Moriarty to knock the gun out of his hand. Moriarty makes a dash down the secret corridor—but in his haste he overlooks the fact that Holmes

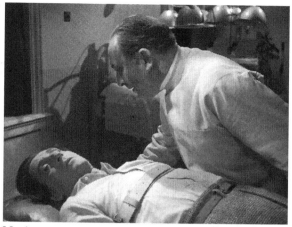

Moriarty tends to his "patient" Holmes with almost loving care, even as he drains the blood from his body, in *Sherlock Holmes and the Secret Weapon.*

has left a trap door open and he plunges 60 feet into a sewer below. The last that is heard of him is a long scream and a splash.

This is a thoroughly nasty end to a thoroughly nasty villain.

Junior G-Men of the Air (1942)

This 12-episode serial from Universal is a wretched affair. It stars some of the Dead End Kids and Little Tough Guys, and their wisecracking antics and sub-Three-Stooges slapping has dated badly. In fact I wonder if it could ever have been that funny. Each episode is filled with repetitive fistfights and shoot-outs, none of them filmed with any flare. Abundant stock footage of old airplanes appears frequently, which may appeal to a niche viewing audience.

Some quaint miniature work is employed in some episodes, and it is always a pleasure to see just how effects were achieved in the days long before computers. For example, a large miniature set is used for shots in which a plane lands and then drives straight into a secret hangar. Another eye-catching use of miniatures shows a bi-plane hitting the ground and tumbling over. One episode is enlivened by some ingenious miniature work showing a dam exploding and water flooding through it.

In this U.S. lobby card, the Baron and one of his underlings plot "Satanic Sabotage" in *Junior G-Men of the Air.*

The Baron (Atwill) is the evil leader of an organization called the Black Dragon, in *Junior G-Men of the Air.*

Lionel Atwill is third-billed as The Baron, leader of an organization called the Black Dragon, which aims to weaken America's military defenses in advance of an invasion by his country (presumably Japan, although it is never explicitly said). In one of the oddest make-ups of his career, he sports Asian prosthetic eyelids. His dark hair is slicked back, he wears spectacles—and, of course, he chain smokes.

This serial serves Atwill very poorly. In most episodes he appears only very briefly and, more often than not, sits at a desk in his office and dispenses a few orders to his henchmen. In one episode he doesn't appear at all. For the first three episodes, he never even gets up from behind the desk. What were the scriptwriters thinking?

In Episode 4, he actually stands up at his desk for the first time, and shortly afterwards, he is seen in a different room! Is there no end to the imagination of the writers? Even better, he is given a couple of grinning medium-close-ups. In this episode, his mad scientist persona starts to move up a gear, and he at last has a couple of colorful lines: "Thanks to science, we can destroy any airplane motor ever built!" And later: "When our work is done, American planes will fall from the sky ... helpless! ... destroyed!" Despite the poverty of the material, Atwill seems to be enjoying himself in these scenes.

The pace improves slightly in the last two episodes when the state guard is called in to attack the farm where the Baron and his army of Japanese are hiding. This is all great fun and includes an amusing shot in which a miniature army truck is blown 20 feet into the air. The final episode, to increase the tension, features the sight of a deadly farm tractor with a machine gun mounted on it.

As with most serials of the period, eager anticipation exists that the final episode will include a dramatic confrontation with the villain. The Baron has repeatedly treated one of his lackeys, played by Turhan Bey, very harshly, and hence exists the expectation that perhaps Bey will turn on him at the end. Unfortunately, this idea never occurred to the scriptwriters.

In the final episode, the junior G-men break into the Baron's secret office and find him slumped over his desk—presumably he has committed suicide. But in a clever twist, he suddenly leaps up, gun in hand: "Drop those guns, please." He then delivers the first half-decent lines of dialogue he has had in all 12 episodes: "Though I have failed, my countrymen elsewhere have succeeded. This morning they attacked Pearl

Harbor and Manila. Your Pacific fleet is destroyed, your army routed. The great ocean empire of the Pacific is ours!" But then he gets shot in the shoulder by a government agent and is carted off, still alive.

Surely the Baron deserved to have a proper death scene?

Frankenstein Meets the Wolf Man (1943)

In this lively horror film, Atwill makes the third of his five appearances in Universal's series of *Frankenstein* films. After his unforgettable Inspector Krogh in *Son of Frankenstein*, it was to become a downward spiral for the actor in a series of increasingly insignificant roles. It had continued with his spirited performance as Dr. Bohmer in *Ghost of Frankenstein*. Now, in *Frankenstein Meets the Wolf Man*, he has a lesser role as the jovial Mayor of Vasaria. It's very much a supporting role but at least he is given two or three good moments, and he is much more of a presence than he was the following year in *House of Frankenstein*, when the scriptwriters hardly used him at all.

His first scene takes place over halfway through the film. As ever, Atwill's attire is as impeccable as his diction, and he sports a dapper jacket and velvet waistcoat, smok-

Lionel Atwill, Ilona Massey, Patric Knowles, Maria Ouspenskaya and Dwight Frye in *Frankenstein Meets the Wolf Man.*

ing a huge meerschaum pipe. He is in his office conducting a meeting with Baroness Elsa Frankenstein, played by Ilona Massey (who four years earlier in *Balalaika* had played Atwill's daughter). She is seeking to sell the old castle and the Mayor has arranged for a potential buyer to be there too. Lawrence Talbot (Lon Chaney) enters the room.

When Talbot asks if he can speak to the Baroness alone, it gives Atwill a brief opportunity to exercise his flair for light comedy. Slightly abashed to be asked to leave his own office, and perhaps thinking of the impropriety of leaving the pair alone, he nevertheless agrees to the request—after giving the two of them several comic wide-eyed stares, drumming his fingers nervously on the table and muttering, "Why, er … certainly, certainly."

He re-enters the room later and, as he talks to the Baroness, some folk music strikes up outside. "It's the Festival of the New Wine," the Mayor tells her and invites the pair to stay in town for it.

The Festival gives rise to the only full-blown musical number in the Universal *Frankenstein* series, with one of the locals leading his fellow townsfolk in a rousing song. The musical routine has a nifty twist in that it ends when Talbot grabs the singer by the throat, scaring the life out of him and the rest of the crowd! Tempers are calmed and a few minutes later the Mayor arrives on the scene, now in more casual attire,

Atwill and Dwight Frye in *Frankenstein Meets the Wolf Man*

topped by a Tyrolean hat with a feather in it.

"Baroness," he asks, "will you give me the honor of the next dance? At our Festival of New Wine, gentlemen, it's a man's privilege to ask any lady for a dance."

What follows is a rare sight in the Atwill canon, two joyful shots in which he takes the Baroness in his arms, animatedly dances off into the crowd with her and the pair spin around four or five times. The smiles on both of their faces as they bounce around look to be quite genuine. Since Atwill and Massey were known to be friends in real life, one can imagine that they had a lot of fun rehearsing for this sequence. At the end of the dance, the Mayor politely kisses the Baroness' hand and they rejoin Talbot at his table.

In the same week that Atwill filmed the dancing scene, he was sentenced to five years probation for perjury and accused of holding wild orgies at his home. How marvelous that we get a little glimpse of this allegedly wild behavior here in *Frankenstein Meets the Wolf Man*. And what a true professional he was, to be able to put on a show of jollity even while his whole world was falling apart around him.

The Monster (Bela Lugosi) wanders into the town during the Festival and causes mayhem. Eventually, Talbot coaxes the Monster onto a horse-drawn coach and the pair rides off. Immediately afterwards, Atwill and various townspeople are seen walking into the local tavern, and a suggestion exists that some of Atwill's footage may have been cut. He is sweaty-browed, looks bedraggled and his face is smudged with dirt, suggesting he has been out searching for the Monster in the woods. Research has failed to establish any evidence of any planned or actual scenes depicting this search, so perhaps it must just be regarded as a quirk of the plot.

The townsfolk start to get angry and want the Baroness to be locked up, but the Mayor steps in. It's a chance for Atwill to demonstrate the bullish authoritarian tones that he did so well. "As long as I am Mayor of Vasaria," he says firmly, "justice shall be preserved. *I* shall decide what's to be done in this village."

Curt Siodmak's script develops Atwill's speech further.

"Haven't we tried before to get rid of the Monster by force?" he says to the crowd of townspeople. "We burned down the sanitarium, and yet we didn't destroy Frankenstein's fiendish creation. We must be more clever this time. Let's use our brains for once … There's no use in storming the ruins. We must pretend to be friends with the Monster."

"Yes," sneers the tavern keeper, "why not elect it Mayor of Vasaria!"

After much activity in Castle Frankenstein, which doesn't involve Atwill, another scene in the tavern occurs, and once again Siodmak gives Atwill a few decent lines.

The Mayor sits around a table with Dwight Frye, the tavern keeper (Rex Evans) and another man. The tavern keeper comes up with a plan that involves a dam that is situated in the hills above the castle.

"Blow up that dam," he says, "and they'll drown like rats—all of them!"

But the Mayor, on the side of justice and decency as ever, is having none of it. He stands up, leaves his drink unfinished and tosses a coin disapprovingly at the tavern keeper. "You're drunk, Vazec," he says. "That's why I don't take your word seriously. Otherwise I'd order you arrested for conspiring to endanger the lives of this community." And he storms out.

In a U.S. lobby card, Lionel Atwill, Ilona Massey and Patric Knowles (far left) confront the villagers from *Frankenstein Meets the Wolf Man.*

After this, wild excitement breaks out in the castle, with Patric Knowles' Dr. Mannering bringing the Monster back to full strength, a fight erupting between the Wolf Man and the Monster, and the dynamite blowing up the dam and flooding the castle. In some of the final shots, the Mayor looks on with other townsfolk as Vasaria is finally free of the curse of the castle.

The film always looks good, thanks to some outstanding sets (a creepy village graveyard, the cavernous office of a police station, etc.) and thoughtful camerawork. It further benefits from an enthusiastic performance from Lon Chaney, Jr. as Larry Talbot, the tortured Wolf Man. Maria Ouspenskaya is memorable as the Gypsy woman Maleva, and horror fans will enjoy seeing Dwight Frye in a small role as one of the angry villagers. The opening credits are fun, too, with the vapor from a vial of bubbling liquid transforming into the names of cast and crew. Regrettably, though, Roy William Neill was a merely competent director.

Captain America (1944)

Unlike Atwill's three other serials, this one actually seems to appreciate the qualities of its star villain and offers him several good scenes. In his other serials he is usually little more than a background menace, but in some episodes of *Captain America*, he is the star of the show, getting more screen time than any one else. Episode 11, for example, is entitled *The Dead Man Returns* and both title and subject matter sound like they belong in a 1940s horror film, with Atwill operating a perpetual life machine that can revive the dead. And Episode 14, accurately entitled *The Scarab Strikes*, features Atwill at his most brutal, giving an elderly man a thoroughly good thrashing with a leather whip!

In fact, Atwill seems to be enjoying himself in *Captain America*. And with good reason—it was his first film work since *Frankenstein Meets the Wolf Man* in late 1942,

and he must have been glad to be back in front of the cameras. He plays museum curator Dr. Maldore, who also happens to be the Scarab, the master criminal behind a recent spate of murders.

Captain America (Dick Purcell) is a fairly mundane superhero; his skills seem to be the ability to drive a car, ride a motorbike and engage in a fistfight. Gail (Lorna Gray) is not only a sweet-faced heroine, but she also shows herself to be no slouch when it comes to fighting villains; in one episode she takes a pistol out of her handbag and shoots one of the hoods dead.

The Scarab (Atwill) admires a stash of jewels with his two henchmen, Bruber (John Davidson, on left) and Matson (George J. Lewis), in *Captain America*

The script moves with purpose and pace throughout, with many episodes enlivened by featuring a different mechanical super-weapon. They include a giant vibration machine that can destroy buildings, an electronic fire bolt that looks like a converted movie projector (and can burn through steel and concrete) and a robot truck that has no driver and is controlled remotely by the Scarab.

The credits at the start of each episode include images of the prominent cast members, a caption telling us their name and the name of the character they play. In Atwill's case a memorable shot of him appears, backed in film noir style by the shadows thrown by his mad-scientist equipment. He unleashes one of his legendary stares, initially looking outraged, then sinister, as he places a monocle in one eye.

Episode 1 opens memorably with three murders, all accompanied by the sound of Atwill's offscreen voice. Each victim holds a small brooch in the shape of a beetle and appears to have slipped into a trance. "This is the voice of the Scarab," intones Atwill. "I command you to drive your car over the cliff." Or, even better, "You will walk to the window and step out … into eternity!" And lastly: "You are under the power of the Scarab, Jackson. Your weapon is in the right-hand draw of your desk. Use it!"

Soon afterwards, Atwill, playing archaeologist Dr. Cyril Maldore, has a strong scene with fellow scientist Professor Lyman (Frank Reicher, who years earlier had played the captain of the ship in *King Kong*). Maldore brazenly reveals to Reicher that he is the Scarab. The reason he can be so brazen is because he has just offered Reicher a cigar, the fumes of which are about to render the victim helpless and put him into a submissive trance.

What is the objective of this dastardly villain? He wants to get his hands on a giant *vibrator*. Clearly this did not have the connotations it has today, and the vibrator in question is a giant-sized contraption that can cause the destruction of buildings. But nowadays it is impossible to hear some of the dialogue and not laugh. In the aforementioned scene with Reicher, Maldore tells him that the Scarab wants to get his hands on the plans for his vibration machine.

Lionel Atwill

"How did you find out about my vibrator?" asks Lyman nervously.

"For the short time you have to live, your mind is completely under my control," Maldore informs the now-helpless Lyman. "I want to know more about the vibrator."

This episode ends in Lyman's laboratory, where his assistant Dr. Gregory (an uncredited role for the great Edward Van Sloan, legendary player from both *Dracula* and *Frankenstein*) gives a demonstration of the vibrator. Naturally, the bad

The three good images of Atwill in the Chapter 10 lobby card for *Captain America* include a shot (top middle) of him lighting a drugged cigar for Frank Reicher.

guys enter and turn the dials on the vibrator up to full power. "The vibrator!" Gregory cries out, "if it isn't shut down, the building will collapse!"

In Episode 2, Atwill plans to extract some information out of Lorna Gray. He greets her with an affable smile on the steps of the District Attorney's office and shakes her hand. What she doesn't realize is that on one finger he has a ring with a small needle that injects her with a trance-inducing drug.

"Your ring—it's sharp. It scratched me."

Dr. Maldore maintains his affable smile. "For a purpose," he tells her, with complete confidence in the effectiveness of his fiendish ring. He leads his now-helpless victim off to a discreet corner. "You are under a powerful hypnotic influence that forces you to obey me." In close-up he interrogates her and gives her orders.

This episode also includes some gruesome flourishes; a nasty death scene occurs when a character gets a pitchfork thrown into his back, and another character is almost flattened (deliberately) by a tractor.

Atwill is the star of the show in Episode 4, getting more screen time than anyone else. In a reading-of-the-will scene, various evil expressions cross his face when he feels he has been cheated of his just rewards. This episode's mechanical weapon is the robot truck, and at the climax, Atwill takes to the steering wheel and has a lot of fun trying to make Captain America fall from the truck's roof, and then he sends the truck crashing into a building, where it explodes.

Episode 5 has a delicious moment when the Scarab offers fake sympathy to one of his intended victims: "You've been through a terrible ordeal. Is there anything I can do to help?" The episode has a bonus: Lorna Gray is strapped beneath a giant guillotine!

In Episode 8, a Mayan blowpipe and a bomb on a plane are the weapons of choice. Atwill is found plotting in his museum headquarters, and the scriptwriter gives him an entertainingly sarcastic put-down of one of his cronies: "You should be proud of yourself. Captain America has made a fool of you on every job you attempt."

The U.S. three-sheet poster

Episode 10 continues the fun and strays into mad scientist territory, with one of Dr. Maldore's colleagues demonstrating a perpetual life device that can bring dead animals—and perhaps humans—back to life. Naturally the Scarab wants to get his hands on this device, and the moment gives Atwill some of his best dialogue so far. It seems like he is about to drop the refined, gentlemanly persona and, at last, become the crazy villain that we know he really is.

"If this device works," he says, staring off dreamily into space, "I must have it. I've always dreamed of an elixir that would give me power over death itself."

Later he attends the demonstration and asks the inventor the inevitable question: "Can the machine be used to restore human life?" After a dog is resuscitated, Atwill shakes the hand of the inventor and offers his congratulations—even though the audience is fully aware that he plans to steal the device.

A fun moment occurs later when Maldore lies on the floor and pretends to be out cold, but when Captain America isn't looking, he opens those steely eyes to let us know that he is listening to all that is being said.

Episode 11 (*The Dead Man Returns*) is outstanding. The Scarab's number one henchman Matson (George Lewis) has been killed, but the perpetual life machine is used to revive him. However, a million volts of electricity are required. Conveniently, the Scarab just happens to have a machine that will generate the necessary voltage, and it's a huge contraption that looks like something out of *Metropolis* and lights up with great showers of blinding sparks. Matson is wired up, given the required dose of electricity and then is injected with the serum that will revive him. Sure enough, a minute later his eyes open and he gets up out of the box in which he has been lying. It's like *Man Made Monster* all over again. Except that Atwill deliberately holds back, playing the refined gentleman instead of the raving madman.

Atwill is again the real star of this episode and has plenty of screen time. At the start of the episode, he dreams up his plot to revive Matson: "I'll make arrangements to recover the body, and when we do, I'll force Dr. Lyman to perform an experiment that will amaze even the District Attorney!" And he stares off into space, delighted by his own villainy as he polishes his monocle.

Later he takes great pleasure in showing off his electricity generator to the horrified Dr. Lyman: "This apparatus, Dr. Lyman, is capable of generating all the electricity you could *possibly* need!" The generator is started up, producing a fearful shower of sparks.

"If you refuse to revive Matson," says Atwill with relish, "your last moments will be spent in there, Dr. Lyman!" The dead patient is brought in, lying in a coffin-like box. Atwill delivers another rich line: "If Matson does not revive, Lyman, *your* body will be used in the next experiment!" Sure enough, Matson revives, stepping drowsily out of his coffin still dressed in the white garb from the morgue.

Episode 12 has a well-staged scene where the Scarab is in the D.A.'s office, still pretending to be an upstanding citizen, and he offers to try to identify a masked criminal. The criminal, trying to put the D.A. off the scent, says that Dr. Lyman was the Scarab. Atwill can't resist a bold repost: "That's preposterous ... You might just as well accuse *me* of being the Scarab."

Later Atwill gets a classic master-villain line. He instructs Matson to kill Captain America and one of his own henchmen. Matson says, "I'll drop them the minute they come through the door."

"Not quite so quickly," responds Atwill, tapping Matson with his walking cane. "Before they die, let them know that theirs is the fate of all who attempt to thwart the Scarab!" Great stuff.

The episode ends with a wild two-minute car chase featuring the rare sight of Atwill in the driver's seat of the lead car.

Episode 14 (*The Scarab Strikes*) is something special. Lionel Atwill rolls up his shirtsleeves, grabs a leather whip and gives an elderly man a thoroughly good thrashing! It's a totally unexpected moment—he has been so well mannered and urbane up to this point. But suddenly he reveals his full sadistic nature, relishing the moment. It's like a return to the glory days of *Captain Blood*, when he took a rod to Errol Flynn.

What a scene this is!

"You're very headstrong," quips the Scarab with villainous irony when the old man, who holds the secret of the location of some Mayan treasure, refuses to talk. "But there are ways of making you talk. Tie him up to that chandelier!"

The Scarab walks over to a fireplace whose mantelpiece is adorned with all manner of farming instruments, and he just happens to find a multi-tailed leather whip, which he caresses with a smile on his face. His careful preparation for the evil deed makes it clear that this is going to be a *serious* whipping. Calmly relishing the occasion, he slowly removes his hat and jacket. He starts to remove his gloves but then, glancing briefly at the whip, decides to keep one on—naturally he doesn't want to get any blisters from his ghastly work. One sleeve is rolled up as he looks with evil purpose at his intended victim. Then he enjoys toying with his victim, showing off his cat-o'-nine-tails. Next he adopts a solid pose, has a practice swing and then unleashes the first strike. The camera cuts to a shot of the victim reacting.

"There are ways of making you talk," threatens the Scarab in *Captain America*.

The scene cuts to the good guys for a minute, but when we cut back to the farmhouse, the thrashing is still going on; although the camera focuses on a phone ringing, the whip can be heard in the background striking the victim. It is clear that the punishment has been going on uninterrupted for a long time.

The camera pans left to show the Scarab delivering another violent blow.

"I'll talk," groans the victim.

"Cut him down!" says the Scarab with a satisfied smile. As he walks over to the telephone, he flexes his right arm a couple of times, loosening up the overworked muscles, thereby emphasizing that he has really been putting his back into his task.

The possibility exists that Atwill may have had some creative input into this scene. For one thing, he adds clever little bits of business, such as keeping on the one glove and the flexing of the over-worked right arm. But more than that, we can well imagine that

The Scarab enjoys showing his weapon of choice to his victim (John Hamilton), in *Captain America*.

Atwill had a discussion with the director along these lines: "I've been holding myself back for 13 episodes so far— isn't it time I were allowed to show what a truly black villain I really am?" Here was a chance for Atwill to recreate the legendary whipping scene from *Captain Blood*. One can imagine that directors Elmer Clifton and John English probably jumped on the suggestion, thinking: "Why not? What a great idea!" Of course all this is merely conjecture.

In a thrilling finale to this episode, Captain America is engaged in a fistfight in the farmhouse while the Scarab is flying in a light aircraft overhead dropping bombs on him! When he sees his third and final bomb hit the target, the Scarab gives a smile of maniacal glee. Atwill is the star of this episode, receiving far more screen time than Captain America.

After the thrills and spills of Episode 14, the final chapter is something of a disappointment. Even so, Atwill is prominent throughout and has some good dialogue once again. An opening caption card features a handsome medium-shot of Atwill looking very dapper, with his monocle in place, above the caption: "The Scarab ... bombs the warehouse where Captain America is attempting to rescue Hillman."

When Gail refuses to divulge some information, the Scarab says, "I have the means of making you tell me the truth!" He then takes great pleasure in calmly showing Gail the truth serum with which he will inject her. "Unfortunately for you," he adds with a wry smile, "the effects never wear off, and you will spend the rest of your life in an insane asylum ... a hopeless idiot!" He then approaches her, in best mad doctor style, with hypodermic needle in hand. Gail gives him false information, and a short while later the Scarab realizes that he has been duped. "So you lied to me. No one can do that to me and live!"

This chapter's deadly weapon is a mummifying gas. He shows Gail a shriveled mummy in a sarcophagus, then ties her up in a glass tank and tells her the same fate awaits her. "I'm afraid the District Attorney will hardly recognize Miss Richards when he finds her a withered mummy!"

The gas starts to fill the tank but of course Captain America arrives in the nick of time. A long fistfight erupts between Cap and the Scarab, with Atwill's stunt double (Duke Green) getting truly knocked

The Scarab and Matson seem intense and determined, and this is only from Chapter 1 of *Captain America*.

around. But the Scarab should have been on the receiving end of a much nastier punishment, considering all his earlier evil deeds. It would have been marvelous to see Lionel getting a dose of his own mummifying gas and slowly shriveling up before our very eyes. Instead, he is finally knocked out cold by Cap, followed by a closing scene in which we learn that he has gone to the electric chair. How odd that the scriptwriters didn't make him suffer more.

The Lady in the Death House (1944)

This is a pleasant 55-minute PRC potboiler with an entertaining twist. The state executioner (Douglas Fowley), whose job it is to pull the lever on electric chair victims, discovers that he must execute his own girlfriend. Fowley's character, as well as sending criminals to their death, also happens to be a research scientist who thinks he may have found a way of reviving corpses—including those that have been electrocuted. This suggests the film is going to develop an enjoyable mad-doctor horror angle, and with Lionel Atwill top-billed it seems a certainty that there will be some action involving madmen in white lab coats.

But the theme of corpse-revival is barely touched on—evidence, perhaps, of a clumsy script rewrite?

Unusually for this period in his career, Atwill, starring alongside Jean Parker, has a rare good-guy role. He plays pipe-smoking criminologist Charles Finch, who recalls one of his cases in flashback, wherein he is determined to save Parker from being wrongly sent to the chair. After the effect of the perjury court case on his career, Atwill must have been pleased to get this major non-horror role, even if it was a low-budget one. He is in almost every scene, although he has no standout sequences or particularly juicy dialogue. Yet he shines nevertheless.

Atwill's superb voice provides the highly charged narration for the dramatic opening scenes in jail, as Jean Parker walks slowly to the electric chair: "The last mile, the last, long walk to the death chamber, and … eternity. An eye for an eye, a life for a life. It is so written. The state, which cannot give life, demands a right to take life. Mary

Kirk walked those 39 steps unafraid, leaving behind a letter … a document of courage." And then the film cuts to Atwill holding that very letter, recounting the events to a group of listeners.

Atwill shows once again that he could do gentle comedy in an entertaining scene in a bar where Fowley wants to propose to Parker but is too nervous, and each word has to be prompted out of him by Atwill, who even does a

Criminologist Charles Finch (Atwill), Mary (Jean Parker) and Brad (Douglas Fowley) in *The Lady in the Death House*.

brief double-take at one point.

There are a couple of occasions when one can't help but wonder whether the scriptwriter was making oblique references to Atwill's recently publicized libidinous reputation. At one point one of his listeners infers that Atwill was attracted to a girl in one of his cases.

"How about the little blonde who met you in the Grotto tonight?"

"Suzy?" Atwill responds with a dismissive laugh.

But his accuser continues: "You're a wolf in criminologist's clothing."

In the film's closing shot, back in the Grotto bar, Atwill senses that he may need to go to the rescue of a pretty young girl, and a smile crosses his face that has a distinct hint of the lascivious about it.

As ever, Atwill's delivery is impeccable. Especially enjoyable is his line to Marcia Mae Jones, who feigns shock at Atwill's suggestion that one of her boyfriends may have a key to her back door: "If you will forget your indignation, perhaps I can save your sister from the electric chair!" A little later he says to Jones, "You lied to me several times. Who are you protecting?" and surely this line must have made Atwill recall his own perjury case.

At one point he fluffs his lines slightly when he says: "She tried to get some Mary … money for Mary," but it's so brief as to be almost unnoticed, and the budget probably didn't stretch to a re-take.

Lionel Atwill interrogates Marcia Mae Jones from *The Lady in the Death House*.

Lionel Atwill

The climax is a reasonably exciting race against time to save Parker from the chair, but director Steve Sekely doesn't have the skill to make it the classic sequence it could have been.

The screenplay was written by Harry Hoyt (director of 1925's *The Lost World*) and he provides one amusingly risqué exchange of dialogue (not involving Atwill). A girl is overheard at a bar saying, "So after all that, what could I do? I just had to accept the mink coat." There are also some great optical wipes that move the action from one scene to the next, some designed like the hands of a clock, others like the hand on a dial.

Secrets of Scotland Yard (1944)

For this Republic potboiler, Lionel Atwill found himself once again playing a wartime codebreaker, just as he had in *Rendezvous* (1935)—but this time it's the Second World War, *not* the First. He plays Waterlow, one of a team of British codebreakers working for Sir C. Aubrey Smith, and one of the team—but which one?—is a German spy. Waterlow, always puffing on his pipe, is a constant supporting presence throughout and, after Smith gets bumped off, becomes more prominent when he is promoted to fill the post.

Atwill played in numerous films where he was one of many suspects but usually turned out to be a harmless red herring. As a rule, the scripts made him appear sinister to encourage the audience to think he was the guilty party. In *Secrets of Scotland Yard*, however, he plays a perfectly inoffensive and unremarkable middle-aged chap with nothing sinister about him whatsoever—a sure sign that this is going to be one of those rare films where Atwill actually is the culprit.

His dialogue is consistently unremarkable throughout the film, except in his last scene when he finally reveals his true colors.

Usher (Edgar Barrier) and Waterlow are alone in a dimly lit room at night trying to crack a vital code. Usher writes the solution on a blackboard. Waterlow reaches into a drawer, pulls out a gun, leaps up and points the weapon at Usher.

"Rub it out, Usher," he commands.

"Of course," says Usher, the truth dawning on him. "It was you who killed John and Sir Christopher."

"Rub it out," barks Waterlow more emphatically.

"You're a great race, you Nazis, when you've got guns in your hands. Without them what have you? A Europe ... the world ... for yourselves."

A code-brreaking session shows Atwill, John Abbott, Stephanie Bachelor and an identified player in *Secrets of Scotland Yard.*

"That's a brave speech for a man's last speech," responds Atwill in best villainous fashion. "You're so right, so sure of yourselves, you English. The only man who is right is the man with a gun."

He goes on to reveal that his mother was German: "The only one I ever loved." It's his last line. A second later, Usher has shot him dead.

Not a great scene, but enjoyable nonetheless.

John Abbott and Martin Kosleck are among the sinister characters encountered on the way to the denouement. The director was George Blair, who does a competent job but never rises above the routine.

House of Frankenstein (1944)

The sixth entry in Universal's *Frankenstein* series saw a gathering of the studio's three big monsters: Dracula, the Wolf Man and the Frankenstein Monster. The result, for many fans of vintage horror, was a highly enjoyable if lightweight fantasy concoction. But for Lionel Atwill this may well represent the low point of his entire film career. No wonder that toward the end of his life he was bitter about the way Hollywood treated him. In *House of Frankenstein*, he probably gets no more than four minutes of screen time and only has nine lines of dialogue, none of them of any consequence.

His role as Inspector Arnz holds the promise of a reprise of the glories of Inspector Krogh in *Son of Frankenstein*, with potential dramatic confrontations with the film's

Inspector Arnz (Atwill) and the Burgomaster (Sig Ruman) in *House of Frankenstein*

monsters. But the encounters *never* happen. In fact after the episode with Dracula (John Carradine), which ends about half an hour into the film, Atwill is not seen again.

He is first encountered playing a jovial game of chess with the town's Burgomaster. Soon afterward he attends Professor Lampini's Chamber of Horrors, a traveling freak show. He wanders around the various caravans, but Edward T. Lowe's script only gives him one line of dialogue. It is unforgivable that, once Atwill had been cast in the role of Arnz, no one thought to beef up his role and add some extra dialogue. Lowe had previously written the scripts for two Atwill films, *The Vampire Bat* and *Sherlock Holmes and the Secret Weapon*, so he was certainly aware of Atwill's potential, and had he known Atwill was to be in the film, he might well have expanded the role. At the freak show, a joke is made about one of the exhibits (a woman locked in some medieval stocks) and it elicits a hearty laugh from Atwill—something that, as we have noted many times elsewhere, the actor could do so well. No dialogue, though.

After attending the show, Inspector Arnz walks along a foggy path, bidding farewell to his companions. That night, he is briefly seen in bed answering a phone call telling him that a man has been murdered. He gets no more dialogue. He rides on horseback (or at least a stunt double does) to the scene of the murder and looks alarmed when Peter Coe tells him that Anne Gwynne has been abducted and is being held captive in a horse-drawn carriage ridden by Dracula. Again, the scriptwriter

Lionel Atwill on horseback in *House of Frankenstein*

shamefully gives Atwill no dialogue at all. Even when, a few minutes later, he catches up with Dracula and watches him transform into a skeleton, Atwill just looks on, saying nothing. This is a disgraceful waste of such a fine actor.

Greg Mank tells us that Atwill was paid $1,750 for six days' work but, unless some scenes were removed, it is hard to see how it could have taken more than two days to film all of the actor's very brief appearances. If he was on the set for six days, then there must have been an awful lot of hanging around doing nothing.

Just imagine how magnificent Atwill would have been in the role of Dr. Niemann. Boris Karloff is excellent in the part, but I feel that Atwill would have been so much better, adding new dimensions of malice and insanity. But after the court case, Universal may have been reluctant to give him a prestigious starring role.

The classy sets and camerawork ensure that *House of Frankenstein* always looks good, but Erle C. Kenton's direction never rises above the routine, which is a great shame because, in the hands of a more talented director, this could have been something really special.

Raiders of Ghost City (1944)

This 13-episode Universal serial is Lionel Atwill's only foray into Western territory. It consists of an endlessly repetitive succession of shootouts, wild coach rides, horse chases and various other incomprehensible goings-on. Direction (by Ray Taylor and Lewis D. Collins) and script (by Morgan Cox and Luci Ward) leave a lot to be desired and it certainly is not half as much fun as *Captain America*, the serial which Atwill made just six months earlier.

Atwill plays Alex Morel, a Confederate bad guy, who dresses grandly in the Southern style, with cravat, fancy waistcoat and top hat. As the serial progresses, however, we learn that he is actually Erich Von Rugen, a Prussian (i.e., German) in America to steal gold so that his nation can buy Alaska. We learn that he has a hidden chamber beneath the Golden Eagle Saloon, from where he masterminds his mysterious organization.

In many of his scenes he is seated, which gives the impression that perhaps the actor wasn't well enough for more prolonged physical exertion. In fact, he looks very weary in some scenes, and those eyes that normally sparked with charisma look especially tired. The legendary Atwill cold stare is conspicuously absent—it's as if the stressful events of the last few years had taken their toll and snuffed it out. Worse, he is clearly unaware that any connection exists between his poor health and his chain smoking, since he puffs on fat cigars in most of his scenes. This was in an age when people believed that the only harm that could come from smoking was a persistent hack. Atwill was most likely blissfully ignorant of the cancer that had already started to eat away at his lungs.

But he has some moments of fine villainy. In Episode 1, he is on board a train and uncouples the rear carriage, sending it hurling backwards downhill. Very occasionally, the scriptwriter remembers to allow Atwill's character to develop a little, giving him a half-decent bit of dialogue. For example, he turns nasty toward one of his underlings, telling him, "Don't ask any more questions … not unless you want a hearse to call here for you."

Atwill has even gone to the trouble of learning some German and speaks a couple of sentences—including calling his cohort a *dummkopf*!

In Episode 5, it is announced that the Civil War has just ended with the Confederates surrendering, and Atwill has a brief scene at the bar that forces him to speak a line that must have caused him a lot of inner pain. "I figured you didn't believe in surrendering," states one of Atwill's henchmen, to which he replies, "A soldier should fall in battle." His son John had been killed by enemy action just three years earlier.

How must Atwill have felt making this serial? For one thing, his weekly paycheck of $1,250 was much less than the $2,000 he had often been accustomed to in the 1930s. He would have been aware that all his scenes were weak and his dialogue unremarkable. For example in Episode 10, he suffers an especially cruel indignity. At the shootout climax of this episode, the hero (Dennis Moore) grabs him around the neck and uses him as a shield against some gun-toting villains, then roughly pushes him aside … and he is forgotten about for the rest of the episode.

In the climax of Episode 11, one character is subjected to a nasty Indian torture device; each ankle is bound to a different tree which, when a rope is cut, will spring back and split him in two. It's the sort of nastiness that audiences would expect Atwill to be overseeing, but Atwill isn't involved in the sequence.

In serials, an expectation exists that in the final episode the villain will get his comeuppance in grand style. But regrettably, in *Raiders of Ghost City* this never happens. After a fight in the

Atwill and Virginia Christine as they appeared in *Raiders of Ghost City*, the formerly intense Atwill stare now extinguished by life's harsh blows.

Lionel Atwill

basement lair—using a double—Atwill gets shot accidentally by one of his own men and falls to the floor dead. "That's the last of Morel," says Dennis Moore, very anti-climactically. So poor old Lionel doesn't even get a memorable death scene.

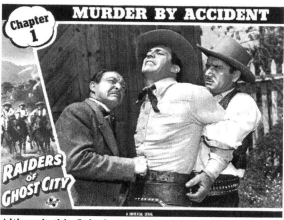

Despite the serial's shortcomings, Atwill was as ever pleased to be acting and keeping busy, something that is suggested by a remark made by his co-star Virginia Christine (in an interview with Greg Mank from *Hollywood's Maddest Doctors*):

Although this fight between Atwill and Dennis Moore looks exciting, it's a publicity still and does not actually occur in the serial.

> Lionel Atwill was a great ham, a poseur, and I mean that as a compliment. We got along very well—he was a delight.

Fog Island (1945)

This is a dreary film whose dreariness is made even worse by the dire musical soundtrack. The fact that the film only seems to exist in a dark print these days doesn't help either ... and almost every scene takes place at night in darkened rooms. This could have been a plus factor in the hands of a talented cinematographer, but Ira Morgan shows little flair.

The plot involves an embittered ex-con (George Zucco) who seeks revenge on all the people who put him in prison, and he invites them to spend a night at his isolated house on a fog-enshrouded island. One would think these characters would know better, but they are tempted by the thought that he might be hiding a stash of loot somewhere. Various uninteresting events occur—including a brief séance in which a table levitates—but nothing demonstrating any imagination.

The film has only two memorable moments. One is a great speech by Zucco, just after Lionel Atwill has stabbed him. His wide-eyed

Alex Ritchfield (Atwill) and a gathering of other potential murder victims from a lobby card in *Fog Island*.

The U.S. one-sheet poster shows that Atwill's movie character is not above stabbing people in the back.

rambling reveals he has gone quite mad, and he is delighted that, by becoming a murder victim, he has finally identified the man who murdered his wife.

The other memorable moment—and the film's key plot device—is the climax in which four characters (including Atwill) have been trapped in a cellar room that is slowly filling with water. They are soon up their necks in water and fight among themselves as they cling on to life. Atwill is the last to go under and is seen in a couple of memorable medium-shots looking quite terrified. He certainly earned his pay on this film, and must have spent a considerable time immersed in water. Atwill gets little opportunity to shine—he just does what the script requires of him, which isn't very much. For most of the film he looks smart in dinner jacket and bow tie, even when he is stabbing Zucco with a chisel blade (the actual strike seems to have been clumsily cut out) and dragging Zucco's body around the cellar. Later he commits another and even more dastardly murder when he stabs Jacqueline de Wit in the back.

In his first scene with Zucco, some of Atwill's dialogue has a painfully ironic slant. Atwill, out of breath after the steep climb up to Zucco's front door says: "The cigars may have cut my wind a bit but I still smoke 'em when I want 'em." Little could he have known that 18 months later he was going to die of lung cancer.

Over a fireside cigar, Zucco accuses Atwill of trying to get money out of him. Atwill spits back: "I advise you to be careful of your accusations, Leo." It's one of those classic Atwill lines, delivered with equal measures of polish and venom.

He stabs Zucco with the chisel. Zucco delivers a tremendous death speech. "You see now Alec, you're not as clever as you thought you were. You see now, don't you, that you've played right into my hands. You see now Alec … you've convicted yourself, Alec … you've sealed your own doom … You've signed your own death warrant ..." And then he slumps down dead. What gives this scene an extra edge is the manner in which Atwill looks on so calmly, puffing on his cigar as though he didn't have a care in the world.

Once again, Atwill proves himself a master at delivering a laugh. For example, he chuckles with evil smugness when he catches Jacqueline de Wit in the act of secretly opening a hidden compartment in a mantelpiece. And he laughs heartily when, having been held at gunpoint by Jerome Cowan, Veda Ann Borg reveals that the gun isn't loaded. Atwill carries it off successfully.

Crime Inc. (1945)

This low-budget PRC crime drama represents an all-time low in Lionel Atwill's film career. Back in 1945, *Picture Show* magazine was impressed:

> Gangster melodrama ... gains in suspense and thrills as it goes along ... Vigorously acted and directed.

But today it seems very limp. Lew Landers directs without enthusiasm and the script lurches from one gangland killing to the next, without much impetus. Fourth-billed Atwill plays Pat Coyle, a lawyer in cahoots with Crime Inc., a syndicate of organized criminals. He doesn't get a great deal of screen time.

We first encounter him arriving at a nightclub in his best dinner jacket and bow tie. Two ladies at a nearby table notice him. "That's Pat Coyle," says one, "the celebrated criminal lawyer." "Ooh—isn't he handsome!" coos her elderly lady companion, paying Atwill an unusual compliment.

Crime Inc. even hold respectable board meetings, and it is at one of these that Atwill, acting as chairman, is given his only chance to have any impact on the film, leading the proceedings with his customary authority.

In another scene in a police station, Atwill delivers his only decent lines in the whole film. He intercedes as the sergeant is about to book his henchman Leo Carrillo: "If you do, sergeant, I'll serve you with a writ so fast, your head'll swim." That is about as good as the dialogue gets in *Crime Inc.*

Lionel Atwill, Leo Carillo, Martha Tilton and Tom Neal in *Crime Inc.*

Later when he and his cohorts are all being arrested, he is told the charge is murder. In response, Atwill lets out one of his splendid chuckles and says, "Now I know it's a gag." But the smile disappears from his face as he is led away in handcuffs.

He thinks the police have no evidence on them, but in a novel courtroom denouement, an incriminating film of all the suspects is screened. The camera pans along the row of seated hoods and gives Atwill one last chance to demonstrate his acting skills. Whereas the other actors just stare at the screen, Atwill looks nervously right and left, milking the moment. It's only a minor gesture, but it shows that even at the very end of his career, Atwill was still coming up with interesting little touches and was determined to give a quality performance—at least as much as the script allows.

Atwill makes the best of a bad lot in *Crime Inc.*, but it's a significant comedown for such a fine actor to find himself wasted like this.

House of Dracula (1945)

Lionel Atwill is better served here than he was in *House of Frankenstein*, a film that practically ignored him. He still only has a supporting role, but at least he gets a fair amount of screen time. This is his fifth and final appearance in the Universal *Frankenstein* series—and each time he played a different character. Here he is Inspector Holtz, who tries to keep order in the town of Vasaria as various monsters create havoc, barking orders at the alarmed townsfolk to keep them calm.

His first scene establishes his character perfectly. Following a murder, a crowd of nervous townsfolk gather outside the police station. Inspector Holtz, smartly dressed in a policeman's uniform, peaked cap and leather jackboots, stomps out onto a raised platform at the top of a flight of steps. Then he dictates to the assembled masses.

"Go to your homes, all of you!" he commands them. "Go home. If I find the person who started a rumor we have a crazy man here, I'll lock him up!"

Holtz then proceeds to explain to Dr. Edlemann (Onslow Stevens) and his nurse Miliza (Martha O'Driscoll) that a man called Lawrence Talbot (Lon Chaney, Jr.) had earlier walked into the police station and demanded to be locked up in a cell. Edlemann reassures Talbot that it's not possible for a man to transform into an animal, and, right on cue, the rays of a full moon fall into the cell and Talbot turns into the Wolf Man right in front of them!

The onlookers all do their best to look horrified—although it must be said that, apart from a few wide-eyed stares, they all take this amazing sight surprisingly calmly.

After another murder, Atwill has a good little scene when he barges his way into the castle and demands to see Talbot, whom he suspects is the killer.

"Your man Siegfried's been murdered," he says to Edlemann, although looking accusingly at Talbot, "by the person who rode into the village with him tonight ... His throat was torn open as though by some enraged animal."

Edlemann asserts that Talbot could not be the murderer as he is recovering from delicate surgery.

But Holtz is not convinced and retorts, in Atwill's best bombastic style, "I respect

Inspector Holtz (Atwill) and Steimuhl (Skelton Knaggs) in *House of Dracula.*

your word, Doctor, but a murder has been committed. It is imperative that I search your premises immediately." These are the type of lines that Atwill, with his perfect diction, does so well.

This is the scene where sharp-eared film historian Greg Mank detected the background sound of out-of-shot Atwill letting out a cough. Sure enough, a sound that could well be a cough is heard—and is it Atwill? It very well could be. If it is Atwill, unable to hold back a cough, then it is poignant evidence of the bronchial cancer that was spreading in him while he was filming *House of Dracula.*

In town later, Holtz is called on to interrupt a gathering of locals, one of whom is Steinmuhl (Skelton Knaggs, giving a memorable portrayal of a village simpleton in the sniveling style of Dwight Frye). Steinmuhl is convinced that Edlemann is the murderer. But evidence is in short supply, and Holtz talks him out of it.

In this staged publicity shot, the Frankenstein Monster (Glenn Strange) attacks Inspector Holtz and an unidentified actor in *House of Dracula.*

"Good heavens," barks Holtz, "you're worse than a gossiping old woman." He tells Steinmuhl and the townspeople to go home.

In Atwill's final scene, Holtz once again bursts into the castle, only to find that Edlemann has now gone quite mad and has resurrected the Frankenstein Monster. When Holz tries to intervene, Edlemann throws him against some electrical equipment that starts sparking and electrocutes him quite rapidly. He falls to the floor (or rather his double does) presumably dead. It is a death scene very reminiscent of the one in *Ghost of Frankenstein,* although on this occasion it is filmed with much less inventiveness and is over in a mere few seconds. A familiar publicity photograph shows Holz and another policeman grappling with the Monster; the moment never appears in the film's final cut.

One important question inevitably arises. Why is it that Atwill, who very recently had portrayed mad doctors for Universal in *Mad Made Monster* and *Ghost of Frankenstein,* was not given the part of Edlemann? Was it because, after the court case, the studio was nervous of giving him a role that was too high profile? Or might it have been because the role required considerable levels of fitness—especially in a long scene in which Edlemann is pursued through the town and across the countryside—and that Atwill, even with the help of a double in some shots, was simply not up to the task? Or was it simply that the studio felt he was ideal for the part of the police inspector, having played similar roles before? Whatever the reason, it is tantalizing to imagine him in the far meatier role of Edlemann, who is given several good speeches in the best mad doctor vein.

The sets (by John B. Goodman and Martin Obzina) always maintain a classy Gothic elegance and the shadowy camerawork by George Robinson makes the most of them. Robinson even includes a couple of wonderful shots in which a carefully positioned light source causes the shadows of characters to be hugely exaggerated. Shots of the castle perched on the edge of the cliff, with waves crashing on the rocks below, feature an attractive matte painting. John Carradine as Dracula is dignified and clearly he has decided to rein himself in and dispense with any chewing of the scenery—a shame,

because he does ham so well. Lon Chaney, Jr. is good again as Lawrence Talbot, but has less to do than in the preceding film in the series. Jane Adams gives a very spirited performance as the pathetic hunchbacked female nurse who, although hoping to get her back straightened, instead ends up being thrown down a flight of stairs. Onslow Stevens as Edlemann acts enthusiastically, and seems to especially relish the scenes in which he becomes a sunken-eyed, smirking vampire. The script is full of enjoyably daft ideas from beginning to end. If only director Erle C. Kenton had been able to imbue it all with more style and ingenuity.

Genius at Work (1946)

This is the penultimate film that Lionel Atwill worked on, and it contains one of his most outrageous performances. Who would have expected, after seeing him play the impeccably dressed heavy in approximately 70 films, to see him in a scene where he shaves off that signature moustache, dons women's clothing and then struts around in high heels and a knee-length skirt? It's all part of the wild

A Universal publicity photo showing Atwill as Inspector Holtz from *House of Dracula.*

and unforgettable finale of *Genius at Work*, a low-budget film that, up until this point, is less than thrilling.

The stars of the film are comedy duo Wally Brown and Alan Carney, whose dialogue and comic routines are always stubbornly mediocre. They play two radio performers who get mixed up with the villainous activities of a master criminal known as the Cobra. Their sassy blonde scriptwriter, played by Anne Jeffreys, goes along for the ride. The only reason for watching the film today is to see Atwill playing the Cobra, assisted by his henchman Stone, played by Bela Lugosi. It was the seventh and final pairing of the duo.

The Cobra, described colorfully by one character as "this vicious human reptile," is a villain of the sophisticated school, often seen wearing a silk smoking jacket and puffing on cigarettes through

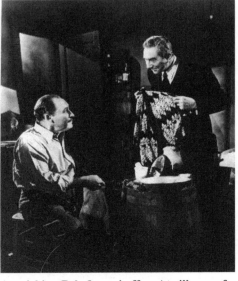

A smirking Bela Lugosi offers Atwill some female clothing in *Genius at Work.*

Lionel Atwill

a long, elegant holder. In his public guise he is Latimer Marsh, "the great criminologist." Atwill gets a lot of screen time as he and Lugosi get up to their nefarious activities, all of which are pretty second-rate and without much motivation. The weak plot consists of little more than a series of episodes in which Atwill and Lugosi try to prevent Brown, Carney and Jeffreys from revealing the identity of the Cobra.

The Cobra lives in a lavish mansion, one room of which has been stuffed to the rafters with every sinister prop that could be found in the RKO storerooms. These include

Wally Brown, Alan Carney, Atwill and Anne Jeffreys in *Genius at Work*.

a guillotine, an iron maiden and wax dummies of an executioner about to chop off a man's head with an axe. Atwill takes great pleasure in showing his guests around his "hobby" room and, given that we know about Atwill's interest in murder trials, it almost feels like we are being shown a room in his real-life home. (Intriguingly, the props in this room also include several of Willis O'Brien's stop-motion models from *King Kong* and *Son of Kong*, including a triceratops, a cave bear, a stegosaurus and a giant spider.)

The final 10 minutes must not be missed. The Cobra and Stone decide that they will pay a visit to the radio station so that they can bump off Brown and Carney. Sensibly they decide to arrive in disguise. Stone, equally sensibly, chooses a disguise made up of a false beard, glasses and a hat. The Cobra, on the other hand, decides that it is pantomime season and turns up in drag. Someone came up with an extra twist—he'll be an elderly lady in a wheelchair, who is pushed by her *husband* Lugosi!

Did scriptwriters Robert E. Kent and Monte Brice dream up the whole thing? The sequence is such a shift of gear from the rest of the film that it suggests another hand was involved. Once again, no evidence exists that Atwill had any creative input, but might that other hand have been his? And if so, might it have been Atwill's way of responding to rumors that he had a fondness for cross-dressing? These dubious rumors are mentioned in a 1996 biography (*Old Soldiers Never Die* by Geoffrey Perret) of

The Cobra (Atwill) traps Carney and Brown in *Genius at Work*.

Douglas MacArthur, former husband of Atwill's wife Louise, and it may be that it was MacArthur who started the rumors as a way of discrediting the man who had stolen his wife. Greg Mank (in *Hollywood's Maddest Doctors*) suggests the sequence may be "a sly jab at Atwill's old notoriety as a cross-dresser." Whatever the genesis of the sequence, Atwill certainly throws himself into the role wholeheartedly and appears to be enjoying playing up those lurid rumors. It's an episode to treasure, but we will probably never know whether or not Atwill contributed any bits of business to the action.

Seated in his wheelchair wearing a flowery hat and with a veil partly concealing his face, Atwill looks funny enough, but when he gets out of the chair and stomps around in high heels, he's hilarious. From his hiding place behind the grill of a ventilation duct, the Cobra fires some poison darts at the two radio presenters. But when they fail to drop down dead, the Cobra's state of mind becomes as disturbed as his dress sense. He takes out a pistol and aims it at them, despite Stone's protestations that the sound of gunshot will give away their hiding place. Fleeing from the police, he ducks into a room, gets out of his female clothing and climbs out of a window—even though he is on the 11th floor of a skyscraper.

Atwill is disguised as a little old lady, with Bela Lugosi and Alan Carney in *Genius at Work*.

What follows is a great little action sequence like something out of an old Harold Lloyd silent comedy, with the Cobra, Stone and the two comedians all inching their way along a ledge on the outside of the building, backed by rear projections of the street hundreds of feet below. Of course there are dizzying moments when someone nearly topples over the edge, only to be pulled back by his clothing at the last minute.

The sequence includes a delicious moment when one of the comedians nervously inches his way around a corner only to be confronted by a grim-faced Atwill coming the other way. Atwill's face is eerily lit from below by a spotlight, and his murderous expression, combined with the absence of his customary moustache, give the fleeting impression that we are looking once again at the face of Eric Gorman, the fiend from *Murders in the Zoo.* A few moments later, the Cobra gets a reasonably exciting death scene, shot by a policeman and then falling dramatically off the edge of the building (with the help of Atwill's stunt double).

Lost City of the Jungle (1946)

According to the old saying, one should go out with a bang, and Lionel Atwill certainly did that at the end of his very last film. His final scene in the 13-chapter serial *Lost City of the Jungle* is one befitting Hollywood's maddest doctor. At the controls of a plane, he is attempting to escape with his booty, a chest containing the rare mineral Meteorium 245. When he gets into an on-board fight with one of his henchmen, he fires a pistol and accidentally hits the treasure chest, which explodes in a huge fireball, taking the plane and its two occupants with it.

This serial is probably best known for the fact that Atwill became terminally ill during its production and that, as a result, many of his scenes were filmed using a double, George Sorel, shot from behind. Although true, this has given the misleading impression that not much can be seen of Atwill in the finished product. In fact, there are very few scenes that make use of Sorel, while Atwill gets considerable screen time—in fact more than he often got in some of his earlier feature films.

Lost City of the Jungle is the last time Atwill wore that trademark monocle and the last time he barked orders to villainous underlings—the finale to a once-great career. It's frequently badly directed, clumsily edited and full of stock footage (from *Lost Horizon* and elsewhere) and yet is great fun throughout. Plenty of accomplished miniature work (such as a plane flying low through a jungle, and an exotic temple which collapses in a man-made earthquake) appears, including even a few matte paintings, such as an eye-catching one of temples in a Himalayan town.

When we first meet Atwill, he wears a pair of pince-nez eyeglasses and also the bushiest beard of his career as Sir Eric Hazarius, "war-monger, manipulator of fascistic cartel, super-salesman of armaments." In all subsequent chapters, he has shaved off the beard and disguises himself as clean-shaven Geoffrey London, a snappily dressed archaeologist in a white Panama hat, white suit and spats. He is part of an expedition to a hidden Himalayan town in Pendrang, "an isolated jungle basin in the Himalayas," populated with every type of non-Caucasian extra that Universal could locate. The hero and heroine are Russell Hayden and Jane Adams (who was so effective as the sweet, hunchbacked assistant in *House of Dracula*), playing spies who try to expose Hazarius.

In Atwill's opening scene (in Chapter 1), he is the passenger in a car being followed by spy Russell Hayden. The fact that he puffs on a fat cigar suggests that even this late in his life, Atwill (and most other smokers in those days) was still unaware of any connection between his health and any harm that a lifetime of chain-smoking might do to it. The scene ends spectacularly when his car veers off a mountain road and plunges hundreds of feet, exploding in a ball of flames (done convincingly in miniature). But he turns up a few minutes later—or rather his double George Sorel does, because poor old Lionel was lying sick in bed at home. At first, the beard and dark glasses are a good enough disguise to fool audiences into thinking they are watching Atwill, but it clearly is not him, even though his voice is dubbed over Sorel's on two occasions in this scene. This gives rise to a question. Were these lines lifted from footage that Atwill had previously shot, or did Universal get the old trouper to speak a few lines from his sickbed? Atwill, for whom acting was in the blood, would have been only too happy to oblige.

In several chapters, Atwill has little to do apart from give orders to his various underlings from his basement lair. But in other chapters he really shines, especially in Chapters 7, 8, 12 and 13.

Lionel Atwill as Sir Eric Hazarias in *Lost City of the Jungle*

In Chapter 7, Hazarius, still operating under the identity of Geoffrey London, accosts Stanton (Hayden) on the steps of a Pendrang back street, and an exchange of wry dialogue ensues. "You know, Stanton, I have a feeling that you're going to leave here rather suddenly." Stanton accuses him of being Sir Eric Hazarius. "Confidentially … just between the two of us …" (He places his monocle in his eye with a theatrical flourish) "… I am really … Geoffrey London." He smirks conceitedly, pleased at his teasing joke. It's satisfying to see that, even this late in his career, Atwill still has some of his old sparkle.

John Gallaudet, Atwill and John Miljan in *Lost City of the Jungle*

In Chapter 8, Atwill is again given plenty of screen time, plus a couple of entertaining speeches. He pretends to be the good guy with Dr. Elmore (John Eldredge): "My only purpose is to benefit humanity. To help make the world a better place. To convince people by this action that I am not the apostle of disaster that they believe." But Elmore is having none of it and does not believe him. Revealing his true colors, Atwill places his monocle in his eye. "Now that we understand each other, let's get down to business. Now Dr. Elmore, I'm going take you where you'll be only too glad to do what I want."

Later in the same chapter, he trots up the stairs leading from his hidden basement, suggesting that although near to death, he was a trouper and carried on as best he could.

Stanton is trapped in a room in the dilapidated House of Beggars, and right at the end of this chapter, Atwill delivers an enjoyable, gloating speech as he talks to Stanton over a radio. "Even getting rid of you, Stanton, presents difficulties. I had hoped to use the House of Beggars to demonstrate to Dr. Elmore the futility of resisting me."

Chapter 12 is a lot of fun and again gives Atwill plenty to do. He is discovered in the jungle speaking

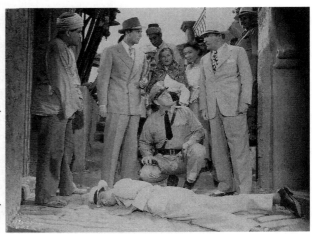

In *Lost City of the Jungle*, when a dead body appears, Lionel Atwill cannot be too far away.

Lionel Atwill

with two of his henchmen and then asking the tribesmen where he can find the Cave of the Eternal Sun, which he believes contains the prized Meteorium 245. He shows a cold disregard for local customs. When told that only the village elders can visit the Cave of the Eternal Sun, he says, "From now on, things are going to change." In a dastardly act, he shoots the village chief in the back. At the temple in the Cave, Hazarius meets an elder who guards it. Displaying an ancient tablet, Hazarius declares, "I am the Sun Messenger. I came to see the Eternal Sun, to learn if it is well cared for."

One of his henchmen foolishly looks in the chest that contains the Meteorium without first donning protective clothing (actually some moth-eaten old woolen robes). There is an almighty flash of light and a scream … and the poor chap gets completely disintegrated by a powerful radiation blast. The villainous Sir Eric orders his surviving henchman to bash the elder on the head, at which point the pair abscond with the chest. A car chase follows, with Sir Eric shooting out of the passenger window at Stanton and Tal Shan (Keye Luke).

Chapter 13, the final installment, is not as rip-roaring a final chapter as might be hoped, but at least Atwill again gets plenty of screen time, as well as the spectacular death scene already mentioned.

Appendix 1
The Top-Five and -Ten Lists

(Each Top Five/Ten is not in any particular order.)

Simple but stunning design for the one-sheet poster for *Doctor X*.

Top-Five Lionel Atwill Screen Performances:

1. Baron von Merzbach in *The Song of Songs*
2. Eric Gorman in *Murders in the Zoo*
3. Sir Austin Howard in *The Silent Witness*
4. Inspector Krogh in *Son of Frankenstein*
5. Dr. Paul Rigas in *Man Made Monster*

Top-Five Lionel Atwill Horror Film Performances:

1. Eric Gorman in *Murders in the Zoo*
2. Ivan Igor in *Mystery of the Wax Museum*
3. Inspector Krogh in *Son of Frankenstein*
4. Dr. Paul Rigas in *Man Made Monster*
5. Dr. Xavier in *Doctor X*

Top-Five Lionel Atwill Non-Horror Film Performances:

1. Baron von Merzbach in *The Song of Songs*
2. Sir Austin Howard in *The Silent Witness*
3. Professor Moriarty in *Sherlock Holmes and the Secret Weapon*
4. Colonel Bishop in *Captain Blood*
5. Dr. Hugo Zurof in *The Sun Never Sets*

Top-Five Scenes:

1. *Murders in the Zoo*—Making love to Kathleen Burke
2. *The Song of Songs*—The wedding night scene
3. *The Silent Witness*—Atwill in the witness box
4. *Mystery of the Wax Museum*—The unmasking scene
5. *Man Made Monster*—Confronting Anne Nagel at the climax

This U.S. title lobby card contains similar art to the top-ten rated 24-sheet poster

Top-Five Most Brutal and Sadistic Scenes:

1. *Captain America*—The whipping
2. *Murders in the Zoo*—Being beastly to Kathleen Burke
3. *Sherlock Holmes and the Secret Weapon*—Draining the blood from Holmes
4. *Captain Blood*—Taking a rod to Errol Flynn
5. *Secret of Madame Blanche*—Refusing to allow Irene Dunne to see her baby

Top-Five Speeches:

1. *The Vampire Bat*—The speech that begins: "Mad? Is one who has solved the secret of life to be considered mad?"
2. *The Silent Witness*—The witness box speech that ends: "I'll say anything you want! I did it! I did it! I did it! I did it! I did it! I did it!"
3. *Murders in The Zoo*—The "love" scene that includes the line, "I'm not going to kiss you! *You're* going to kiss *me*!"
4. *Mystery of the Wax Museum*—The immortality speech: "My child, why are you so pitifully afraid?"
5. *Man Made Monster*—The speech to Anne Nagel that includes the line: "I've always found that the female of the species was more sensitive to electrical impulse than was the male...."

The U.S. pressbook herald

In fact, there are so many good speeches in Atwill's film career, that I list two more that are worthy of special note:

6. *Lady of Secrets*—The telephone speech.
7. *The Sun Never Sets*—The mad scientist speech that ends: "And then war! War!"

Top-Five Make-ups:

Unlike other horror actors, Atwill usually acted without any elaborate make-ups, but there are some interesting exceptions.

1. *Mystery of the Wax Museum*—Blackened skin, patchy hair, a deformed nose, a bulbous upper lip, a mutilated chin ... truly horrible!
2. *Hound of the Baskerville*—Thick-lensed round glasses and bushy beard.
3. *Sherlock Holmes and the Secret Weapon*—Heavy *reptilian* eyelids.
4. *Junior G-Men of the Air*—He wears bizarre eye prosthetics to make him look Japanese, and he also sports dark, slicked-back hair and spectacles.
5. *Genius At Work*—Atwill dressed as a woman in knee-length skirt and high heels

Top-Five Death Scenes:

1. *The Man Who Reclaimed His Head*—After an intense struggle with Claude Rains, his head is hacked off with a sword and then stuffed into a bag.
2. *Ghost of Frankenstein*—Fried by some sparking laboratory equipment
3. *The Sun Never Sets*—After he is stunned rigid and open-eyed by overhead bombing, ants crawl over his forehead.
4. *Murders In the Zoo*—Strangled by a giant python
5. *Fog Island*—Drowned in a cold, lightless dungeon

Top-Five Bottom-of-the-Barrel, Least-Memorable Film Roles:

1. *The Great Profile*—Such a minor role, he barely registers
2. *House of Frankenstein*—Only nine lines of dialogue
3. *Boom Town*—He barely registers in a few very brief scenes.

4. *Strange Case of Dr. Rx*—No more than two minutes' screen time in total and he plays a red herring

5. *Night Monster*—He plays a very minor red herring with very little screen time.

Top-Ten Movie Posters:

Selected because they have especially good images of Atwill.

1. *Murders in the Zoo*—U.S. one-sheet; Terrifying artwork close-up of Atwill with an evil glint in his eye and a madman's grin

2. *Doctor X*—The U.S. one-sheet has great design with the three stars framed by a giant letter *X*.

3. *Mystery of the Wax Museum*—The 12-sheet has a fine Atwill profile and a memorably risqué tag line.

4. *The Vampire Bat*—The U.S. one-sheet has a striking image of Fay Wray, snared in the steely-eyed Atwill's grasp.

The U.S. one-sheet poster

5. *Man Made Monster*—The U.S. one-sheet has a creepy green color scheme and a memorable image of Atwill in mad scientist goggles.

6. *Man Who Reclaimed His Head*—The U.S. one-sheet has a stunning image of Atwill apparently strangling Claude Rains (even though in the film it is Rains who has the upper hand).

7. *Lady of Secrets*—The U.S. one-sheet features a suggestive image of a lurking Atwill voyeuristically watching Ruth Chatterton and Otto Kruger.

8. *The Wrong Road*—The U.S. one-sheet boasts an imposing eerie, blue image of Atwill.

9. *Son of Frankenstein*—The French *grande* poster has stunning artwork of a key image from the film's climax: Atwill's false arm has been ripped off.

10. *Strange Case of Dr. Rx*—The Spanish one-sheet has a marvelous green close-up of Atwill, with beams of light emanating from his eyes.

Appendix 2
Coincidences ... Or Are They?

"I don't believe destiny is controlled by a throw of dice," said Lionel Atwill in *The Devil Is a Woman*, "but it couldn't have been merely a succession of accidents."

A number of incidents in Atwill's stage and screen career seem to suggest that indeed there *was* some higher power throwing dice and controlling his life. All actors occasionally find themselves playing roles that have coincidental similarities with events in their real lives. But in Atwill's case, these coincidences seem to crop up with uncanny frequency. Am I reading too much into these instances ... or was Fate playing some cruel game with Atwill throughout his career? Were these perhaps not just coincidences, but warnings? Parallels exist with various incidents in Atwill's life, but the most common coincidence, which recurs again and again, has Atwill playing a character that commits perjury in a witness box. Was Fate trying to tell him something? Or was it simply that Atwill had lied successfully so many times in his films that he thought he would be able to get away with it in real life when the time came to give evidence in court?

What follows is a list of some of the more significant coincidences.

		Film, Stage or Radio Scene	Real Life Scene
1	THE FLAG LIEUTENANT (1908-09)	Atwill's character lies to protect the reputation of a friend on a battlefield. As a result, he finds himself accused of cowardice in action. Only at the last minute does the truth come out, and he is saved from a court martial and his honor is upheld.	Atwill said he lied in court to protect the reputation of friends. As a result, he found himself convicted of perjury. Only later was he allowed by a judge to change his pleas to "not guilty" and all charges were dismissed.
2	DEBURAU (1920)	Deburau is happily married with a son, but falls for a female admirer, causing his marriage to collapse. Subsequently he catches his lover red-handed with a new man. Deburau tries to revive his career by returning to the stage, hoping to recreate one of his former triumphs. Deburau is hissed from the stage and becomes a broken man.	Atwill was happily married with a son, but fell for a female admirer (Elsie Mackay), causing his marriage to collapse. Subsequently he caught Elsie red-handed with a new man. Atwill was metaphorically hissed from the stage when a court case destroyed his career. Atwill tried to revive his career in 1943 by returning to the Broadway stage and reviving one of his old plays.
3	THE COMEDIAN (1923)	In this play's last act, Atwill's wife leaves him and he tries in vain to win her back.	Less than 18 months later, Atwill's wife left him and he tried in vain to win her back.
4	THE SILENT WITNESS (1932)	Atwill's character commits perjury in a courtroom scene. He lies in order to protect his son from being found guilty of a crime.	Atwill committed perjury in a 1941 court case. He lied in order to protect some of his friends from being implicated.
5	MURDERS IN THE ZOO (1933)	He bursts in on the love nest apartment of his wife and her lover, hoping to catch them in flagrante. She is planning to flee to Paris.	In 1925, Atwill burst into the love nest apartment where his wife was with her lover. She was planning a trip to Europe.
6	THE SONG OF SONGS (1933)	Pistol in hand, he intends to shoot his unfaithful wife (Marlene Dietrich) but is talked out of it.	In 1925, revolver in hand, he intended to shoot his wife's lover but was talked out of it.
7	THE GREAT GARRICK (1937)	Atwill's character delivers a speech how actors are idols, but they should be fearful of the fact that public opinion can change fast and turn to ridicule.	Atwill, the former Broadway idol, became an object of ridicule after the very public humiliation of court case.

8	HIGH COMMAND (1937)	Cross-examined during a court-martial trial, Atwill's character appears to commit perjury.	Four years later, Atwill commits perjury for real in a courtroom.
9	HISTORY IS MADE AT NIGHT (radio show) (1940)	Atwill's character tells a courtroom: "I wish to tell the court and the jury that your whole case ... is built on perjured testimony. My story on the stand was a lie from start to finish."	A year later, Atwill committed perjury for real in a courtroom.
10	CHARLIE CHAN'S MURDER CRUISE (1940)	Atwill's character organizes a wild party where drunken young women cavort on wooden hobbyhorses.	Atwill was alleged to hold wild drunken parties in his home.
11	CHARLIE CHAN'S MURDER CRUISE (1940)	Atwill's character says, "I try to protect my clients from all unpleasantness."	Soon afterwards, Atwill had a statement of his read in court: "I lied like a gentleman to protect friends."
12	GIRL IN 313 (1940)	Adopting a mock-virtuous demeanor, Atwill's character says to the police, "These people are my guests. I can't have them embarrassed."	Atwill did and said much the same thing, and for the same reason, in a courtroom.
13	BOOM TOWN (1940)	In a courtroom scene, Clark Gable accuses Atwill's character of committing perjury.	A few months later, Atwill committed perjury in court.
14	MAN MADE MONSTER (1941)	In a courtroom scene, Atwill's character commits perjury, giving a false account of events.	Less than six months later, Atwill committed perjury in court, giving a false account of events at one of his parties.
15	GHOST OF FRANKENSTEIN (1942)	Atwill's character has lost his reputation and status as a result of some undisclosed past mistake, which has made him a bitter man.	Atwill had just survived the mistake of getting caught and landing in court. The case harmed his career and made him a bitter man.
16	FOG ISLAND (1945)	An out-of-breath Atwill quips that he has had to cut down his smoking.	Atwill died of lung cancer and pneumonia the following year.

Lionel Atwill

Acknowledgments

This story of one of Britain's finest, yet most unsung, actors has been compiled with assistance from many others who have helped in a variety of ways. This includes helping me to locate hard-to-find DVDs, doing invaluable proofreading, lending me visual material and providing me with screen captures. They include some of Britain's longest-serving horror film aficionados, including Tim O'Sullivan, Pete Vickers (thanks for the proofreading par excellence), Adrian James, Andy Muggridge, Andy Larkin and Tony Mechele. Many thanks to Greg Mank, author of the excellent *Hollywood's Maddest Doctors*, for so generously answering many of my questions and providing me with material.

Thanks also go to my publisher Midnight Marquee Press, Inc., Gary J. Svehla and Aurelia Susan Svehla, for their tireless efforts in putting the book together and for having the vision to appreciate the merits of a book on Lionel Atwill.

I would also like to thank the helpful members of staff at the various public institutions where I conducted so many hours of research. They include the British Library in St. Pancras, the British Newspaper Library in Colindale, the Theatre Archive of the Victoria and Albert Museum in Kensington, the Cinema Museum in Kennington, London and (via email) Jeremy Megraw at the Billy Rose Theatre Division of the New York Public Library.

My thanks also go to two people who have played a special role in this story, Lionel Atwill's son Tony and his great-niece Leslie Dale. It has been a pleasure to get to know them. They have graciously and willingly supplied me with information and visual material, and also answered endless questions.

"H" is for Horror! Neil Pettigrew poses with his rare British quad poster for the 1947 re-release of *Son of Frankenstein*. Just to the right of the film's title you can see a small letter "H." In the late 1940s, the squeamish British censor insisted that all horror films be given an "H" certificate and no one under 16 years of age was allowed into the cinema. (Photo by Mark Mawston.)

Author Biography

Neil Pettigrew has been a fan of vintage horror films since 1967. He has written articles for *Famous Monsters of Filmland, Cinefantastique, Midnight Marquee* and other magazines. He is author of *The Stop-Motion Filmography* (1999), which discusses the films of Ray Harryhausen, Willis O'Brien and others. He is currently at work on a book about his three great-great-aunts who were Victorian artists' models. He is a graduate of Leeds University with a Bachelor of Arts degree in English Literature. His greatest adventure was traveling around all 76 provinces of Thailand in search of old movie posters, an adventure which included retracing the footsteps of Merian Cooper and Ernest B. Schoedsack (makers of *King Kong*), who traveled through the region of Nan when making *Chang* in 1927. He is hoping to publish a book about Thai movie posters. One of Neil's other passions is campaigning to preserve that wonderful British institution, the pub. Neil has spoken on radio and television about the architectural and social importance of his country's rapidly disappearing public houses.

INDEX

If you enjoyed this book,
write for a free catalog of
Midnight Marquee Press titles
or visit our website at
http://www.midmar.com

Midnight Marquee Press, Inc.
9721 Britinay Lane
Baltimore, MD 21234
410-665-1198
mmarquee@aol.com

Made in the USA
Middletown, DE
28 December 2019